PENGUIN BOOKS

THE PENGUIN HISTORY OF NEW ZEALAND

Michael King is one of New Zealand's leading historians. Over three decades he has written or edited more than 30 books, most of them New Zealand history or biography. He has won a wide range of awards for this work, including the New Zealand Book Award for Non-fiction, the Wattie Book of the Year (twice) and the Montana Medal for Non-fiction.

He was a contributor to the prestigious *Oxford History of New Zealand* and has written for all five volumes of *The Dictionary of New Zealand Biography*.

Dr King has taught or held fellowships at seven universities in New Zealand and other countries, including Georgetown University in Washington DC, where he was Visiting Professor of New Zealand Studies. He is currently Senior Research Fellow at the University of Waikato

THE PENGUIN
HISTORY OF NEW ZEALAND

Michael King

PENGUIN BOOKS

PENGUIN BOOKS

Published by the Penguin Group
Penguin Books (NZ) Ltd, cnr Airborne and Rosedale Roads, Albany,
Auckland 1310, New Zealand
Penguin Books Ltd, 80 Strand, London, WC2R oRL, England
Penguin Group (USA) Inc., 375 Hudson Street, New York, NY 10014, United States
Penguin Books Australia Ltd, 250 Camberwell Road, Camberwell,
Victoria 3124, Australia
Penguin Books Canada Ltd, 10 Alcorn Avenue, Toronto,
Ontario, Canada M4V 3B2
Penguin Books (South Africa) (Pty) Ltd, 24 Sturdee Avenue, Rosebank,
Johannesburg 2196, South Africa
Penguin Books India (P) Ltd, 11, Community Centre, Panchsheel Park,
New Delhi 110 017, India
Penguin Books Ltd, Registered Offices: 80 Strand, London, WC2R oRL, England

First published by Penguin Books (NZ) Ltd, 2003

1 3 5 7 9 10 8 6 4 2

Copyright © Michael King, 2003

The right of Michael King to be identified as the author of this work in terms of
section 96 of the Copyright Act 1994 is hereby asserted.

Designed by Mary Egan
Typeset by Egan-Reid Ltd
Printed in Australia by McPherson's Printing Group

ISBN 0 14 301867 1

A catalogue record for this book is available
from the National Library of New Zealand.

www. penguin. co. nz

Contents

Unsettlement: *post-1950 AD*

Posthistory

For

Lewis King
Spiro Zavos
and
Peter Munz

Who fed and enlarged
an appetite for history

Always to islanders danger
Is what comes over the sea
ALLEN CURNOW

A nation is bound together not by the past, but by the *stories*
of the past that we tell one another in the present.
ERNEST RENAN

New Zealand's fertile plains were the last that Europeans
found before the Earth's supply revealed itself as finite. Our
relationship with them has been completely unsustainable
... [We] have exploited these islands' richest ecosystems
with all the violence that modern science and technology
could summon ... [We] must live with the rest of nature or
die with the rest of nature.
GEOFF PARK

Preface

New Zealand history sometimes seems extraordinarily compressed and close at hand. From the study in which I write, I look out on Maungaruawahine and Ruahiwihiwi, hilltop pa that still bear the imprint of the men and women of Ngati Hei, who fortified them. Over the range behind us is the sandbar where Roger Green discovered an East Polynesian pearl-shell lure, the only authenticated artefact that ancestors of the Maori brought with them from their island homelands in the Pacific. Up the inland end of our estuary is a wooden boom built in the days when kauri logs were floated down the valley for collection and transport to sawmills on the Waitemata.

Then there are the people. In my student days I knew Tom Seddon, born in 1884, who in childhood had enjoyed the company of his father's friend George Grey. So I had shaken the hand of someone who had shaken the hand of Sir George Grey, Governor of New Zealand at the time of the Northern Wars. And Grey had shaken the hand of Hone Heke. Much later I knew Whina Cooper, whose father, Heremia Te Wake, had been born two years before the signing of the Treaty of Waitangi. These proximities gave me the *feeling*, if not quite the reality, that I was but one generation removed from the most momentous events of nineteenth-century New Zealand history; and that made those events seem all the more vivid and close to my own lifetime. Writing this book has confirmed that feeling.

A few words are in order, perhaps, to say what *The Penguin History of New Zealand* is and is not.

It is *not* an encyclopaedia that attempts to tell the story of every district and hamlet and to name every famous New Zealander from All Blacks to the first European child born in Waipukurau. A compendium of those proportions is being assembled by the Ministry of Culture and Heritage for transmission alongside the ministry's online edition of *The Dictionary of New Zealand Biography*. It was not my intention to duplicate those ventures.

Instead, this volume provides an overview for understanding the unfolding of New Zealand history as a whole over the near-millennium that the country has been occupied by humankind. In particular it identifies the myths that have shaped New Zealand cultures and provided them with cohesion and coherence. It examines too what happens when those myths are challenged. It reveals how societies are conditioned not so much by events as by group memories of events. And it confirms that the basic needs driving human history are the search for secure places in which to live, eat, shelter, reproduce and practise cultural or spiritual values.

It is currently fashionable to speak of the 'histories' of a country, as if there are many *versions* of national history (which there are) and many ways of *approaching* such histories (which there are), and as if they were all of equal value and validity (which they are *not*). This book is unashamedly *a* history of New Zealand in the sense that its narrative has been conceived by and passed through the mind and sensibility of a single historian, and in the sense that it identifies some explanations – the hows and whys of history – as more plausible than others.

The text does, however, draw on a range of sources, Maori and Pakeha, male and female, privileged and unprivileged. And it draws on the work of fellow historians who have preceded me into the field and into print. The most important of those sources and colleagues are named with respect and gratitude in the acknowledgements.

One further point needs to be made. While I have relied often on the work of colleagues, this book is not written *for* other historians. Much of what I say and the manner in which I say it will be familiar terrain for professional peers. Instead, this volume is directed at curious and intelligent general readers, Maori and Pakeha, who are *not* historians. It focuses on things which such readers in the twenty-first century ought to know – and, perhaps, *need* to know – about the history of their country.

MICHAEL KING
Coromandel Peninsula

Prehistory

1

A Land Without People

In Queen Charlotte Sound on 17 January 1770, Joseph Banks, naturalist on James Cook's first expedition to the South Seas, caught a last vibration of primordial New Zealand – a land where bush grew to the water's edge and trees were filled from ground level to canopy with copious bird and insect life:

> This morn I was awakd by the singing of the birds ashore from whence we are distant not a quarter of a mile, the numbers of them were certainly very great who seemd to strain their throats with emulation... [Their] voices were certainly the most melodious wild musick I have ever heard, almost imitating small bells but with the most tuneable silver sound imaginable.

'For all its exuberance and beauty,' one of Banks's successors would write, '[that] dawn chorus was a mere echo of what could have been heard four hundred years before, for by 1770 around half of New Zealand's bird species were already extinct. Gone were the great booming calls of the moa (which we know about from their convoluted, bony tracheas), the screaming, mewing and cawing of a billion seabirds (which even in Banks's day were banished from the main islands), and the unknowable sounds of the native ducks, giant geese, and yard-high flightless rails, native crows and giant harriers.'

These creatures were gone, along with the flightless wrens and the giant eagles, because the first human inhabitants had carried with them to New Zealand rats and dogs, and the ability to hunt and to make fire. And further extinctions would be triggered by the very visit that allowed Banks to hear that still-impressive remnant of the dawn chorus. Norway rats infested Cook's barque *Endeavour* and found their way ashore wherever the ship attached itself to land by rope or gangplank. These cunning carnivores, loosed onto a bird population that had evolved without mammalian predators, would initiate another round of carnage that would take further virtuosos out of Banks's avian choir – piopio, kokako, saddleback and others. Thirty-two New Zealand bird species disappeared after the arrival of New Zealand's first human inhabitants; another nine would follow as a result of European animal introductions.

Had any events preceding human invasion been as catastrophic for the country's flora and fauna? Certainly natural disasters – earthquakes, volcanic eruptions, floods, the advance and retreat of ice ages, the rise and fall of parts of the country above and below the sea – all these had taken a toll over geological time and had a crucial bearing on what creatures survived and what characteristics evolved to make their survival more likely. In New Zealand the dinosaurs had perished 65 million years before, as they had elsewhere on the globe; but the sphenodons or tuataras who had been their contemporaries from Jurassic times persisted, in New Zealand but nowhere else, for reasons that remain obscure.

At least one environmental cataclysm affected New Zealand shortly before the beginning of human colonisation and may have had a bearing on some of the earliest bird extinctions. The Chinese chronicle *Hou Han Shu* recorded that, in the reign of the Emperor Ling Ti (168–189 AD), the sky was for many days 'as red as blood'. This reference is corroborated by a Roman document, the *Historia Augusta*, which reports that some time before the Deserters' War (186 AD) the sky was seen to 'burst into flame'. Another historian of the Roman era, Herodian, lists strange portents seen in the reign of the Emperor Commodus (180–192 AD): 'Stars remained visible by day, and others became elongated, seeming to hang in mid-air.'

Such celestial displays could be consistent with the after-effects of a massive volcanic eruption. The only eruption known to have occurred on such a scale at about that time is that of the Taupo rhyolitic vent. This explosion, possibly the most powerful and destructive anywhere on Earth in the past 5000 years, emerged from the crater now known as Lake Taupo in the centre of the North Island of New Zealand. It was almost ten times as powerful as the better-known Krakatoa eruption in 1883 and is likely to have sent tsunami radiating into the Pacific, over-running low-lying islands and reaching the mainlands of Asia and America.

If the essence of environmental history is, as some claim, the imprint of the natural world on human society, then the Taupo eruption could qualify as the first recorded event of the historical era in which New Zealand made an impact on the wider world.* There was, however, no contemporary knowledge of where the

---

* It is, of course, by no means certain that the phenomena observed in China and Italy were caused by the Taupo eruption. Scientists are not yet agreed on a date for its occurrence – although, oddly, they do know the month, March, because of berries preserved on trees toppled by the blast.

volcanic phenomena originated. Nor can we be sure that there were witnesses to the cataclysm in the land of its occurrence – no evidence of occupation, in other words, nor stories based on it.

One other piece of evidence relating to this period intrigues by its ambiguity. Carbon dating of the bones of kiore, the Polynesian rat, suggests that the creature may have become established in New Zealand as long as 2000 years ago. The contemporary decline of birds – the owlette-nightjar, for example, and one species of duck – appears to support the presence of rats at that time. Should these dates be confirmed and the supporting evidence verified, they would support an irrefutable argument in favour of an early Polynesian landing on the coast of New Zealand.

The only means of transport available to kiore was Polynesian vessels. The rats' presence in the country so far ahead of organised human settlement, for which there is as yet no evidence, suggests that a discovering canoe landed in both the North and South Islands around 2000 years ago and then headed back to Island Polynesia, or that the occupants of a canoe remained somewhere in New Zealand at that time but failed, because of low numbers, single gender or lack of adequate resources, to establish a continuing colonising population. A third possibility is that a small founding group abandoned the country or was wiped out because of some unexpected natural disaster, such as the catastrophic effects of the Taupo eruption.

The inescapable fact remains, however, that to date no direct evidence has been found of a human occupation of New Zealand – no hearth fires, no tools, no human remains or the remains of creatures butchered by humans – earlier than the thirteenth century AD. And it is in the latter period, when occupation and evidence coincide, making it possible to build narratives, that the human history of the country must begin. Everything that occurred before that – the formation of the land, the evolution of its plants and of its bird, animal and insect inhabitants – falls into the categories of prehistory or natural history. And, thanks to the sciences of geology, palaeontology and palaeobiology, it is possible to establish the sequence and chronology by which a fragment of the supercontinent of Gondwana became the islands of New Zealand, which humankind began to colonise around 800 years ago.

Maori, first human inhabitants of the country, had two mythological stories to account for its existence. In the first, Mother Earth was ripped from the embrace of the Sky Father:

> Ranginui was joined in amorous embrace to Papatuanuku. Within this clasp the world was in perpetual darkness and the nakedness of Papatuanuku was covered with vegetation that thrived in moisture. The sons of Rangi and Papa lamented the conditions in which they were forced to live between their parents. Eventually they resolved to act. Tumatauenga suggested that the parents be killed. Tanemahuta objected. It would be sufficient, he said, to prise them apart and let Ranginui stand above and Papatuanuku lie below.
>
> All but one son agreed and took turns at trying to effect the separation. None succeeded until Tanemahuta placed his shoulders against the earth and his feet on the sky. Slowly he straightened his body and the parents began to give way. When he had succeeded, the children of Ranginui and Papatuanuku knew light for the first time. And the children of Tanemahuta – the trees, birds and insects of the forest – were able to see and breathe. The earth remained a nurturing mother, but the sky became a stranger to them.
>
> The son who had objected to the separation, Tawhirimatea, was angered by the pain to which his parents had been subjected. He followed his father into the sky and from there begot his own

offspring: wind, rains and storms. These he unleashed on Papa-tuanuku and the children of Tane, disfiguring the land and uprooting trees and plants. Tanemahuta meanwhile went on to shape the first woman out of earth and to breathe life into her. Then he procreated with her and produced a line of men-like gods and god-like men.

This story, which Maori shared in broad outline with Poly-nesians in other parts of the Pacific, answered basic questions about how the earth and the elements came to be and the relationship of humankind to them. It was the starting-point of the genealogy that began with the void, led to Ranginui and Papatuanuku, continued through named ancestors and the lines of living believers and persisted through future descendants. It revealed that the gods – the elements – were born of the earth and the sky, and that humankind was born of the gods – a satisfactory metaphor for the source of life. It was one of a number of cultural strands that provided coherence and cohesion for pre-Pakeha Maori society and exhibited some of the textures of that society's imaginative life. It was comple-mented by another story, also derived from wider Polynesia, to account for the specific existence of the North Island of New Zealand:

Maui-tikitiki-a-Taranga wanted to go fishing with his older brothers, who refused to take him. So he hid under the bottom boards of the canoe and did not reveal himself until the vessel was far out to sea. The brothers were annoyed by this and wanted to return him to shore, but by this time the land was too far away. So they began to fish, and after a time they filled the canoe with their catch. Now Maui produced his own hook, the barb of which was made from a fragment of his grandmother's jawbone. The brothers refused him bait so Maui struck his nose and smeared the hook with his own blood. He lowered his line and almost immediately hooked a fish of great magnitude. The only way he could haul it up was by reciting a chant to make heavy weights light.

When the enormous fish reached the surface Maui left the canoe to find a priest who could make an offering to the gods and perform the appropriate ritual. He warned his siblings not to touch the fish until this was done. As soon as he was gone, however, the brothers leapt from the canoe and began to scale the fish and to hack bits off it. The fish raised its fins and writhed in agony. Then the sun rose and made the flesh solid underfoot, its surface rough and mountainous because of the brothers' mutilation. It remained that way and the name given to it was Te Ika-a-Maui, the fish of Maui.

Both these stories are apt analogies for the tectonic shifts which, 80 million years ago, prised loose from Gondwana the land that would become New Zealand. The climax of Maui's expedition is a poetic evocation of the upthrusting, down-thrusting, volcanism, glaciation and erosion which sculpted New Zealand's modern land forms. The whole process, from the formation of Gondwana until the human occupation of the country, took 680 million years, the age of its oldest rocks.

The rest of Gondwana eventually became the continents of Australia, Africa, South America and Antarctica, and the sub-continent of India, all of which would in due course undergo colonisation by mammals and hominids. The fragments that became New Zealand, however, lacked land mammals other than a few species of small bat. Those pieces of land made up an arc of primordial landscape, vegetation and creatures which largely disappeared elsewhere. This arc preserved Gondwana ferns and conifers. It carried at least two species of land dinosaur, theropods and hypsilophodonts, which, like all their kind, became extinct around 65 million years ago, and freshwater crocodiles that may have died out at about the same time. It also carried tuatara, a representative of the Rhynchocephalia order of 'beaked headed' reptiles which once inhabited Asia, Africa, Europe and North America but became extinct in those places more than 100 million years ago, along with ratite ancestors that evolved into the flightless kiwi and eleven species of moa, at least three kinds of primitive frog, and the forebears of weta insects and the worm-caterpillar peripatus.

All these latter creatures survived into the era of human settlement, together with other ancient species that crossed the ocean when the gap between what would become New Zealand and Australia was still narrow, as it was until around 60 million years ago – wattlebirds such as huia and kokako, ancestors of the New Zealand wrens, and bats.

What would ensure the uniqueness of New Zealand's landscape, flora and fauna was the fact that the country had been torn loose from Gondwana prior to the evolution of marsupials and other mammals. All its vegetation and animal life continued to evolve in the absence of such predators. And the places that mammals would take in the ecosystems of other countries – *all* other major land masses apart from Antarctica – would in New Zealand be filled by birds, insects and reptiles. Weta, giant crickets, grew into the largest insects on earth and hunted like mice. Some of the birds – giant geese and rails, species of duck, the kakapo parrot, some of the wrens – joined the ratites as non-flying ground-dwellers. The largest raptor ever known, *Harpagornis moorei* or Haast's eagle, weighed up to thirteen kilograms and developed a wing span of up to three metres; it preyed on giant moa, whose pelvic bones would be punctured by the eagle's enormous talons. Of the moa, one species, *Dinornis giganteus*, was the tallest bird that ever lived, exceeding ostrich in both size and weight; others resembled 'feathered forty-four gallon drums atop stumpy legs, their necks ending in absurdly tiny heads'. As ancestors of the Maori would discover, birds dominated this largely forested kingdom from coastal bush to inland ranges, and across grassy plain and alpine tussock.

The whole ecosystem, surrounded by 18,000 km of coastline that hosted fish, shellfish, seabirds and marine mammals, developed over a period of 82 million years into what one twentieth-century ecologist would call 'a larder of protein'. And that larder was much better stocked for the fact that there was no predator – no thylacine, no bear, no wolf, no large cats – to raid it, and, of course, no humans. Even as recently as 10,000 years ago humankind had spread to and over every habitable continent on Earth, including New Zealand's nearest neighbour, Australia. And this occupation and colonisation had major effects on the subsequent evolution of plants, animals and land forms. But not in New Zealand. In New Zealand, as an early geographer put it, 'a land without people waited for a people without land'.

Taken literally, such an expression is of course anthropomorphic and inherently ridiculous. The land itself has never 'waited' for anybody or anything; it simply is. And life goes on in all its complexity in whatever biosphere evolves, whether or not humanity is present. Indeed, if a land without people *could* make a choice, it would most likely opt for *continuing* absence if people were to become the instrument of predation on plants and animals, destruction of habitats and, in general, the shredding of ecosystems and pitching many of the creatures in them towards extinction. And yet the aphorism has a point. New Zealand *was* a long time – 680 million years – in the making; its human inhabitants arrived a mere split second ago in geological time. And those who did eventually find a home there did so because many of them had been uprooted and displaced from other parts of the globe.

If the country's geological, natural and human history were

represented by an hour on a clock face, then the land began to detach itself from Gondwana at one second past twelve, its dinosaurs were gone by twelve minutes past, its cargo of Gondwana birds was being supplemented by avian immigrants from Australia by a quarter past, volcanic eruptions and uplifts of land were laying the foundations of modern ecosystems by half past, and the ice age that would shape much of the surface landscape of 'modern' New Zealand had begun at less than two minutes to and ended at half a second to one. This tiny fraction of time is all that is left for the redistribution of flora and fauna into the configurations that humankind would encounter. And then humanity itself arrives, Maori *and* European, within the space of 300ths of a second to one o'clock.

What those human colonists would find was a land that was ancient but, because of earthquakes and volcanic activity, geologically unstable. It was also ecologically unstable because of shallow soils, high rainfall and the limited range of species locked into its ecosystems. The fact that these creatures had no inherited defences against human predation, or against predation by other species that humankind brought with them, made them especially vulnerable. In the case of Maori, those introduced species were rats and dogs (and, perhaps, pigs and fowl, which may not have survived initial settlement). In the case of Europeans, a far wider range of people, animals, plants and pathogens was carried to the country as part of the process of establishing 'neo-Europes' – landscapes altered to remind settlers of their lands of origin and to enable them to generate livelihoods from the kinds of extractive or agricultural activities with which they were familiar.

So drastic was the impact of European settlement that one geographer was moved to note that human-sponsored modification of landscapes which had taken place over twenty centuries in Europe and four in North America had occurred in New Zealand in only one century. And an environmental historian, Alfred Crosby, likened the process to 'giant viruses fastening to the sides of a gigantic bacterium and injecting into it their DNA, usurping its internal processes for their own purposes'.

Crosby's view implies philosophical and moral questions. Are human beings to be viewed as *part* of nature, and therefore as a legitimate element of any ecosystem to which they choose to attach themselves? Or are they, because of their inherent selfishness, hubristic sense of superiority and unrivalled capacity for manipulation, an inevitably alien and malevolent ingredient in ecosystems that have evolved in their absence? Or is it simply that humankind has failed thus far to exercise its intelligence and technologies to ensure that natural resources are used sustainably and other species not sacrificed unnecessarily to human greed?

This history offers no absolute verdict on such moral questions. They will still be there at the end, hanging unanswered over the story that follows. And that story will confirm that history occurs only because humankind has, for hundreds of thousands of years, sought congenial and secure places in which to live, eat, shelter, reproduce and build cultures. Those cultures have always been influenced most profoundly by human interactions with the environments in which they were located, and by competition among human groups for access to and use of the resources of those environments.

These realities point to some of the major themes of New Zealand history. Another set of themes arises from the mythologies that New Zealand societies – Maori and Pakeha – devised to explain and justify their presence in the country, and to give meaning and social cohesion to the lives of their peoples.

What distinguishes New Zealand's history from that of other human societies is that these themes have been played out in a more intensive manner, and at a more accelerated pace, than almost anywhere else on Earth. For this reason, their course and consequences have interest and relevance for human history as a whole.

Settlement

2

Seeds of Raiatea

Despite a plethora of amateur theories about Melanesian, South American, Egyptian, Phoenician and Celtic colonisation of New Zealand, there is not a shred of evidence that the first human settlers were anything other than Polynesian. Physiological, genetic, linguistic, mythological, artefactual and botanic evidence blends into a symphony of accord on this conclusion. The only points in doubt are precisely where these people launched their expeditions of colonisation, when and where they arrived, and how many of them founded the New Zealand Maori population.

The search by such late nineteenth- and early twentieth-century scholars as Edward Tregear and Stephenson Percy Smith for the origins of the Maori (were they Aryan? were they a lost tribe of Israel?) is now recognised as irrelevant. Maori people and culture as encountered by European navigators in the seventeenth and eighteenth centuries evolved in New Zealand. And the forebears of Maori, the Polynesians, developed their culture in the central South Pacific, most probably on the islands of Tonga, Samoa, Uvea and Futuna. Antecedents beyond that point are more speculative, though increasingly the subject of scholarly consensus.

That consensus now accepts that several hominoid species evolved simultaneously in Africa, diverging from other primates around five million years ago. Fossil remains have revealed that one of those species, *Homo erectus*, reached Asia and Indonesia, the latter in the form of Java Man, some 1.8 million years ago. But these human-like creatures travelled no further geographically, though they may have survived until as recently as 50,000 years ago.

Less than 100,000 years ago another group, *Homo sapiens*, the ancestors of modern humankind, also emerged from Africa. Genetic analysis shows that part of this migration travelled north and east, into central Asia, and then westward into Europe. Another branch took an easterly route along the edge of the Arabian peninsula, around the perimeter of India and eventually on to the coast of South-east Asia and the archipelagos of Malaysia, Indonesia, New Guinea, New Britain and the Solomon Islands.

The section of this population that remained on the edge of the western Pacific Ocean became the first ancestors of today's Melanesian people. The group who went south were the founding population of the Aboriginal and Torres Strait Islander people of Australia. Their movements were possible because the last ice age had shrunk sea levels and the Indonesian islands were attached to Eurasia in a geographic unit now called Sunda. And New Guinea, Australia and Tasmania were joined in a landmass now referred to as Sahul. The earliest migrants, therefore, both *Homo erectus* and *Homo sapiens*, had been able to travel largely on foot, requiring only short island-hopping voyages, probably by raft, to get from Sunda to Sahul.

By around 10,000 years ago the ice age was over and sea levels had risen, isolating the archipelagos of the Philippines, Indonesia and New Guinea, detaching Australia from New Guinea and Tasmania from the Australian mainland. Movements of populations through the region would then be possible only by people with well-developed maritime technology. And such a people emerged from the mainland of South-east Asia some 5000 to 6000 years ago and pushed out eastwards into the central Pacific, where no human beings had preceded them.

They are known from their language group as Austronesians. And the spread of that language shows that, astonishingly, some travelled as far west as Madagascar. Others went eastwards, along the Malaysian and Indonesian archipelagos, along the coast of New Guinea and the Bismarck Archipelago, first settled by Aboriginal colonists more than 30,000 years earlier, and eventually as far as Easter Island and the coast of South America.

These voyages, ranging around more than half the globe at a time when Europeans had not yet ventured beyond the Mediterranean or the coast of their continent, were analogous in daring and accomplishment to the later exploration of space. Indeed, the Pacific Ocean with its widely spaced islands dotted across a vast surface was a kind of terrestrial mirror for the galaxy, the Milky Way, which provided Polynesian sailors with stellar markers for celestial navigation. Peter Buck, the great Maori anthropologist, called his forebears 'Vikings of the Sunrise'. He would have done them, and Northern Europeans, greater honour had he referred to the Vikings as Polynesians.

Beyond cultural imperatives, what made the prodigious voyages of the Polynesians and their Austronesian ancestors possible was the introduction to South-east Asia of the sail and the invention of the outrigger to stabilise dug-out canoes on ocean voyages. While their predecessors had, for the most part, walked, the Austronesian-speakers entered the Pacific and the Indian Oceans as mariners with the technology, the curiosity and the courage to carry them where no human beings had preceded them.

By 4000 years ago one section of these people was making distinctly incised Lapita pottery on the islands of the Bismarck Archipelago. The subsequent spread of that pottery, to New Caledonia (whence came the name Lapita), Santa Cruz, Vanuatu, Fiji, and ultimately to Tonga and Samoa by some 3000 years ago, has enabled archaeologists to trace the 'footprints' of these ancestral Polynesians. On Tonga and Samoa, a region that has come to be known as West Polynesia, the migrants appear to have paused for the best part of a millennium, developing, refining and consolidating that set of cultural characteristics we now recognise as Polynesian. They included the form of Austronesian language ancestral to New Zealand Maori, a pantheon of named gods, systems of kinship and rank, pervasive concepts such as mana and tapu, and distinctive shapes for their stone adzes. These people had also brought with them animals and plants, some of them transported from as far away as the South-east Asian mainland: pigs, dogs, rats, fowls; and culti-vated plants such as taro, yam, gourds, bananas, breadfruit, pandanus, sugar cane and paper mulberry. They may also have carried with them the coconut palm.

Many of these things, the impedimenta of intellectual and material culture, would be carried forward in another migra-tion, this time into the islands of East Polynesia, almost 1000 years after the colonisation of central Polynesia. There the culture would be modified further, linguistically, conceptually and artefactually, into forms more directly related to those inherited by New Zealand Maori. And it would be the identical shape in New Zealand and East Polynesia of contemporary artefacts and ornaments in stone and bone (adzes, chisels, fishhooks, harpoon points, pendants), together with a shared mythology, that would make explicit the immediate ancestry of the Maori.

East Polynesians had one more taonga or cultural treasure which they would bring with them to New Zealand, and which would, ultimately, prove crucial to the survival of their people and the further development of their culture there: the kumara or sweet potato. In contrast to everything else that these migrant people had lugged from island to island, the kumara had not come from the west. It was a vegetable from Central or South America, originating probably in Peru. This uncomfortable fact is susceptible to one of only two possible explanations: either voyagers from South America carried the vegetable into Polynesia (which was the theory of the Norwegian adventurer Thor Heyerdahl); or Polynesians themselves sailed as far east as continental America and returned with the kumara to Island Polynesia. The latter theory is more likely. It is given additional weight by the fact that the coconut seems to have been taken from South-east Asia to Central America, where it was flourishing in the time of Columbus – and the most likely explanation is that it was carried across the Pacific to the Americas by Polynesians. Apart from the kumara, there is no other unequivocal evidence of South American influence in Polynesia, and no trace of South American genes among Polynesians; but there *is* evidence that, by the first millennium of the Christian era, Polynesians were making extraordinarily widespread return voyages throughout the Central and South Pacific.

For many years Western scholars argued about whether the Polynesian colonisation of the Pacific – a stupendous achievement when one confronts their starting-point and the area of ocean enclosed by the triangular boundaries of Hawai'i, New Zealand and Easter Island – was a consequence of deliberate or accidental voyaging. A careful study of available navigation techniques and computer simulations of voyages, allowing for prevailing winds, currents and weather systems, have led to the inescapable conclusion that Polynesian voyaging *was* wide-ranging and *was* deliberate. As they moved eastwards, navigators tacked and searched largely in upwind quadrants away from their points of departure, in directions from which they could most easily and most safely return downwind. This ensured three outcomes: that they had a means of getting home, whether or not they discovered new islands; that initial voyages were conventionally two-way; and that such voyages of discovery would precede voyages of deliberate colonisation, which would then make for a known and reported destination with appropriate navigational directions. This was the sequence and pattern of voyages that would have preceded the more difficult Polynesian discovery and colonisation of New Zealand.

As they sailed, navigators would search for signs of land beyond the visible horizon: the presence of birds feeding offshore or migrating (and, in the years preceding the introduction of the kiore, the numbers of sea-feeding birds would have been immensely larger than in modern times); cloud formations which attached themselves to as yet unseen atolls; changes in the patterns of ocean currents and swells. These signs in combination created what have been called 'island screens', which greatly enlarged the navigator's potential target areas. Stars at night and the direction of the sun and ocean swells by day enabled navigators to maintain a running fix on their position and to repeat voyages or to pass on sailing directions to subsequent travellers.

This combination of techniques permitted the discovery and

settlement of the islands of West and East Polynesia, and took its practitioners as far east as Easter Island and South America. With such possibilities exhausted, subsequent exploration would have been attempted 'across' the wind, which permitted the discovery of the Hawai'ian Islands to the north and, across and downwind, the difficult but by no means impossible 3000 km journey south-west to New Zealand.

Why were such voyages made at all? What drove Polynesian travellers eastwards, then north and southwards, other than the techniques which made such movement possible? We can only speculate. Some pressures would have been environmental: overcrowding, shortages of gardening space, depletion of lagoon resources. Other oral traditions speak of disagreements and warfare among kin, of sons who failed to inherit land or status, even of cannibalism, propelling island settlers into the role of their forebears, that of island migrants. But such circumstances were occasions for leaving home rather than causes.

James Belich identified what he called an 'ethos of expansion' which assured Polynesians that 'new lands had always been found in the past, and therefore would be in the future. Failed migrations told no tales.' One can take this concept further. There was clearly something spiritually significant about the movement eastwards. Early burials in Polynesian islands had corpses trussed into a sitting position and facing east. And a proverb carried from Island Polynesia to New Zealand may also express part of the reality of that ethos: 'E kore koe e ngaro, i ruia mai i Raiatea.' (I shall not perish, but as a seed sent forth from Raiatea I shall flourish.)

There may have been a phase in Polynesian culture in which the urge to discover new lands was strong, even irresistible; as was, perhaps, the belief in personal and corporate invincibility, strengthened by proven navigation techniques and the development of large, fast and safe outrigger or double canoes under sail. In addition, there was confidence in the interventionary attention of protective deities – Polynesian tradition is replete with stories of individuals and crews saved from disaster by one or other of the gods – and in the power of priests to mediate between such deities and humankind. When the navigator Ru was travelling from Raiatea to Aitutaki, for example, his canoe sailed into a whirlpool which began to suck the vessel and its crew into the depths of the ocean. They were saved by a sacred invocation to Tangaroa:

> Tangaroa i te titi
> Tangaroa i te tata
> Whakawateangia te kare o te moana
> Whakawateangia nga kapua o te rangi
> Kia tae au ki te whenua
> I tumanakohia e au

As Belich observed, 'magic, prayer and technical skill packaged each other'.

Evidence from the New Zealand region alone indicates just how confidently and how extensively widespread voyages may have been made. Ivory fishhooks and chert on Enderby Island in the sub-Antarctic Auckland Islands reveal that the Polynesians were there, at the very least visiting, around 1350 AD. Similar carbon dates and fragments of Mayor Island obsidian link sites in the Kermadecs and Norfolk Island to New Zealand at about the same time. And adzes from the original colonisation of Pitcairn Island show an extraordinarily close affinity to those found in contemporary New Zealand sites.

At some point in the past millennium, however, possibly around the fourteenth or fifteenth century AD, the era of widespread Polynesian voyaging ceased. This may have occurred because of the change in climate that produced colder, windier weather and rougher seas, or, possibly, because of a change in cultural priorities. And this literal and metaphorical alteration in direction left colonists on the margins of their cultural and geographical triangle, especially in New Zealand and Easter Island, isolated from other Polynesians. It may also have led to the abandonment of earlier settlements on Pitcairn, Henderson, Norfolk and the Line islands – which were viable only in an era of regular contact with other food and population sources. By this time, however, the great voyages of exploration had been accomplished, and the Polynesians had become the most widely dispersed people on the planet.

3

The Great New Zealand Myth

If popular mythology is to be believed, the discoverer of New Zealand was a Polynesian voyager named Kupe. Oddly, this myth was Pakeha in origin rather than Maori. Maori came to embrace it solely as a result of its widespread publication and dissemination in New Zealand primary schools between the 1910s and the 1970s.

One version of the narrative sequence that David Simmons characterised as 'the Great New Zealand Myth' went like this:

950 AD: the Polynesian navigator Kupe discovers New Zealand.

Between 950 and 1150 AD: Moriori people arrive in New Zealand.

1150 AD: the voyages of Toi and Whatonga lead to first Maori settlement.

1350 AD: the 'Great Fleet' of seven canoes arrives in New Zealand from Island Polynesia.

After the fleet came, fighting ensued between Maori and Moriori. Some Moriori were killed, some intermarried with Maori, and the remnants escaped to the Chatham Islands.

The Kupe part of this sequence was told as follows in the Department of Education's *School Journal* in February 1916.

Kupe ... lived on the island of Tahiti, though his father was a Rarotongan. His ... canoe was named Matahorua, and, in addition to the crew, it carried Kupe's wife and daughters. The Matahorua was accompanied by another canoe, the Tawirirangi, commanded by a chief named Ngahue.

For many days there was no sight of land to gladden their hearts. Weary and worn out by the long voyage, and faced with starvation, they eagerly scanned the unbroken horizon. At last Kupe's wife, after gazing fixedly over the sea, exclaimed, 'He ao! He ao!' (A cloud! A cloud!), and pointed to a distant white cloud such as sailors often see enshrouding the land. Cheered by the hope that shone in his wife's eyes, Kupe seized the steering-paddle and directed the prow of his canoe towards it. As he drew nearer it rose higher and higher. Able to read the signs of the sea as they could read the faces of their children, the voyagers now felt almost certain that they had reached their goal. 'Aotea! Aotea!' (The white cloud! The white cloud!) they shouted as they strained at the paddles, forgetful of all their weariness ... Then beneath the fleecy whiteness appeared a dark streak of bush-clad hill and valley, and they knew that before them lay the land they had seen in their dreams, and for which they had braved tempests and faced even death itself.

It was as 'Aotea' that New Zealand became known those long centuries ago. Kupe called the ... North Island 'Aotearoa' – the Long White Cloud; and today Europeans who love to keep alive the old names will call New Zealand Aotearoa.

It is not difficult to see why the story was embraced with enthusiasm by those very Europeans directly appealed to in the

School Journal story. It was an inspirational account of the discovery of New Zealand. It gave names, Kupe and Ngahue, to Polynesian navigators who would otherwise be nameless. In its full elaboration through a series of adventures around the New Zealand coast involving moa, greenstone and a fight with a giant octopus, the saga gifts New Zealand a founding myth every bit as majestic as the stories that Pakeha settlers carried with them from Europe (Jason and the Argonauts, the labours of Hercules). Its telling was part of a process that fitted Maori tradition into the cultural patterns of late nineteenth- and early twentieth-century Pakeha New Zealand, which was looking for stories of resonance and nobility to make the human occupation of the country seem more deeply rooted and worthy of pride than it might by virtue of its (at that time) rather thin European heritage.

All that is understandable and excusable. And, one might add, that same account became a source of pride for Maori and an antidote to the concurrent and widespread view that Tasman and Cook 'discovered' New Zealand. As myth, then, the Kupe story worked well and had much to commend it.

The problem that late twentieth-century scholars had with it, Maori and Pakeha, is that, as told here and as compiled by its progenitor, amateur ethnologist Stephenson Percy Smith, the story had no sound basis in Maori tradition. About half the tribes in New Zealand have Kupe stories, but they are by no means congruent and can, in fact, be divided quite distinctly into east and west coast versions. In areas where he *does* figure, Kupe is a contemporary of the ancestors of the major canoes and located about twenty-one generations ago or in the fourteenth century AD. The Kupe of authentic mythology was not always associated with the name Aotearoa, and in more than one version of the story Aotearoa was given as the name of his canoe.

The Smith version of the Kupe story and its dissemination in the *School Journal* and other literature, and the title of the first widely read general history of New Zealand, William Pember Reeves's *The Long White Cloud* (1898), all popularised and entrenched the notion that the Maori name for New Zealand had been and still was Aotearoa. After decades of repetition, Maori themselves came to believe that this was so. And, because shared mythology is ultimately more pervasive and more powerful than history, it became so.

In fact, in the pre-European era, Maori had no name for the country as a whole. Polynesian ancestors came from motu or islands, and it was to islands that they gave names. The North Island was known to them principally as Te Ika a Maui, the Fish of Maui, in recognition of the widely accepted belief that the land had been fished from the depths of the ocean by Maui-tikitiki-a-Taranga. A smaller number of tribes knew the island as Aotea (though this was also the name given to Great Barrier Island) and as Aotearoa, most commonly translated, as in the Kupe story, as Land of the Long White Cloud, but perhaps more properly rendered as Land of the Long Clear Day or the Long White World. The second Maori King, Tawhiao, from Tainui, called his Kingitanga bank Te Peeke o Aotearoa, thus favouring Aotearoa as his preferred name for the North Island.

The South Island was known variously as Te Waka-a-Aoraki, the canoe of Aoraki (the ancestor frozen in stone and ice as the highest peak in the Southern Alps), and as Te Wahi Pounamu (the place of greenstone) and Te Wai Pounamu. Stewart Island to the south was Rakiura.

In the Maori world all these names would persist in simultaneous usage until around the middle of the nineteenth century. From that time, some Maori and Maori publications began to favour Nu Tirani and its variants, transliterations of the words New Zealand and conveniently applying to all the islands that would make up the modern nation state of New Zealand (the Treaty of Waitangi of 1840 and its 1835 predecessor, A Declaration of the Independence of New Zealand, used these forms). Apart from Tawhiao's bank, operating in Waikato in the 1880s and 1890s, few Maori opted for Aotearoa. In the early years of the twentieth century, however, with the growing circulation and popularity of Stephenson Percy Smith's version of the Kupe story, Maori use of the term Aotearoa to refer to New Zealand as a whole increased, especially in oral culture. By the twenty-first century it was entrenched as the Maori name for New Zealand, though many South Island Maori, favouring Te Wai Pounamu as the name for their own island, recognised Aotearoa as a name for the North Island only.

The conclusion that a historian might draw from the foregoing is that it is highly likely that there *was* a Maori ancestor called Kupe who sailed to New Zealand from Island Polynesia. But he certainly did not travel at the early date specified in the Smith story. It is also unlikely that he was the 'discoverer' of the country, but the number of placenames associated with him – particularly in the Hokianga, Mercury Bay and Cook Strait regions – make it probable that he was one of the earliest ancestors of the Maori to leave descendants and therefore memories in those parts of the country. And, finally, New Zealand was certainly not known to Maori as Aotearoa in the pre-European times. Just as certainly, it *is* called that now by most Maori of the modern era.

The story of Toi and Whatonga, also compiled by Stephenson Percy Smith, concerns a Tahitian chief and his daughter's husband who, in the middle of the twelfth century AD, became separated at sea by a storm and then set out to look for each other. Toi, the chief, ended up living in Whakatane among the

Moriori people who had landed in New Zealand after Kupe's voyage. Whatonga found him there. The eventual settlement of these two men with their entourages in the Bay of Plenty was described by the purveyors of the myth as the first permanent habitation of New Zealand by 'Maori' colonists.

An examination of Smith's sources in the twentieth century revealed that the story was not derived from Maori traditions. The Toi who lived in the Bay of Plenty did so in the thirteenth to fifteenth centuries, according to local genealogies. Another Toi, from Arawa tradition, was contemporaneous with the Arawa canoe. There is no Maori story from any source that tells the Toi–Whatonga story in the Smith sequence, or which places Toi in the twelfth century.

After Kupe, however, the second leg of the Great New Zealand Myth was the epic journey of the Great Fleet. Here is the *School Journal* version read and taught over decades to hundreds of thousands of New Zealand children in primary schools, and used as a basis for similar stories in a wide range of secondary literature.

> We shall now tell of the Coming of the Fleet ... About five hundred years ago, in the fourteenth century, a number of vessels set sail [from Island Polynesia] for New Zealand, their crews wearied by the fierce intertribal wars in which they had been constantly engaged, and glad to seek a more peaceful home in the fair land of Aotearoa, whose beauties had been so often described by voyagers who had visited it. The canoes in which they migrated, seven in number, were the Horouta, Takitimu, Arawa, Aotea, Tainui, Mataatua and Mamari ... Some of the canoes were specially built for the voyage. Giant trees were felled and were shaped and hollowed out by skilled and noted chiefs [with] adzes made of greenstone taken from New Zealand by Ngahue ... All the vessels set out about the same time, the Takitimu being last to leave ...

After recounting the voyages of the individual canoes and the many setbacks and adventures that befell their crews, the narrative concludes:

> Of the further movements of these immigrants it would be tiresome to tell ... [Sufficient] to say that they mingled with the Maoris already here, and founded the great Maori race that occupied both the North Island and the South Island when the white man came. After the arrival of the fleet, canoe voyages between New Zealand and Polynesia became rare ...
>
> We have now seen how the islands of New Zealand were discovered and peopled by a race which ... spread over the islands of the South Seas. Trimming their lateen sails to the trade-winds, they explored the vast Pacific in primitive outriggers and cumbrous double canoes – probably the most daring and adventurous navigators the world has ever seen. Obeying the call of adventure, and following the lure of Hine-Moana, the Ocean Maid, they laid down countless sea roads, and boldly faced the tempestuous open sea when few European sailors ventured to lose sight of land.

As with earlier stories, this account too had been compiled by Stephenson Percy Smith, supposedly from Maori informants. It was another saga redolent of derring-do, which Pakeha New Zealanders were quick to embrace and add to the founding mythology of the nation as a whole. Maori too would have felt uplifted by the story's themes and accomplishments and the fact that they were descended from such enterprising and courageous people. Inasmuch as it showed groups of Maori from different places and backgrounds acting together for the common good, the Great Fleet would also become a metaphor for kotahitanga (the fundamental unity of Maori origins and aspirations over and above tribal divisions). So taken were the first two generations of Maori educated to this tale that tribal leaders – Apirana Ngata, Te Puea Herangi, Maharaia Winiata – organised a series of hui in 1950 to celebrate the 600th anniversary of the arrival of the Great Fleet, which by this time had grown to nine canoes.

Alas and again, as in the case of Kupe's deeds, the Great Fleet story proved to be without verifiable Maori foundations. David Simmons's extensive research of nineteenth-century sources found that the fleet as a concept occurred only rarely in Maori tradition. One Ngati Kahungunu tradition spoke of six trees being cut simultaneously for five canoes, and some Tainui and Arawa stories spoke of those canoes setting out together. But the remainder of the canoe traditions were of individual voyages, albeit sometimes linked to a knowledge of others, and Percy Smith had come up with his date of 1350 AD by simply averaging out a great number of unrelated genealogical lines, from Mataatua, which was said to have arrived fourteen generations before 1900, to Aotea, which was calculated to have landed 26 generations before that date.

As for the Moriori people who, according to Smith and his colleague Elsdon Best, had come to New Zealand between Kupe and the Great Fleet and greeted Toi and Whatonga, the basis for their existence turned out to be even shakier. Moriori, according to (again) the *School Journal*,

> were a race inferior to the stalwart Maoris, and ... were of Melanesian, not Polynesian origin ... No one knows whence they came, nor why they came ... They were ocean waifs occupying three canoes that had been carried away by a storm from some island to the westward ... As time rolled on they increased in numbers, until they occupied many parts of the island ... They were slight in build, and had dark skins, upstanding or bushy hair, flat noses, and upturned nostrils. They had a habit of looking sideways out of the corners of their eyes, and were an indolent

and chilly folk [who] afterwards settled the Chatham Isles ... In their new home they became peace-loving, timorous and lazy [and] as hopelessly isolated as Robinson Crusoe on his island.

Precisely who the Moriori of the Chatham Islands were and where they came from is dealt with in the following chapter. Suffice it to say now that almost everything said about them here – that they were Melanesian, that they preceded the ancestors of the Maori, that they were driven off the mainland to the Chatham Islands, that they were 'timorous and lazy' – is demonstrably wrong. But for hundreds of thousands of New Zealand children, the version of Moriori history carried in the *School Journal* and other publications which drew from that source, reinforced over 60-odd years by primary school teachers, was the one that lodged in the national imagination.

The Great New Zealand Myth, synthesised in the early years of the twentieth century, was demolished in the last decades of the same century. The principal points of demolition were that the country had been settled far earlier than the fourteenth century date given for the Great Fleet migration (c. 800 AD became a consensus among prehistorians in the 1970s), that there had been no 'Moriori' settlement from Melanesia, and that there had been no 'Great Fleet' in 1350 AD.

By the early twenty-first century, however, the pendulum of scholarly hypothesis was swinging back to a point closer to the Great New Zealand Myth. While the bulk of the New Zealand Maori founding population had clearly come from East Polynesia, there was some evidence of early contact with Fiji and West Polynesia. While the Great Fleet concept remained suspect, it became increasingly clear that a significant number of migration canoes had set out from an East Polynesian 'inter-action sphere' at about the same time. And that time, while probably not around 1350 AD, may have been within 100 years of that date – and considerably later than the dates which the first professional archaeologists in New Zealand had initially proposed.

So the Great New Zealand Myth was, if not rehabilitated, at least credited with a renewed degree of plausibility. The story of the Polynesian settlement of New Zealand assembled with the tools of modern scholarship, however, is more complex than the Percy Smith narratives, more difficult, and infinitely more interesting.

4

Landfall

All verifiable evidence – from archaeology, genetic analysis, carbon dating, burnt pollen remains and disposition of volcanic ash showers – points to New Zealand having been first settled in the thirteenth century AD, during the era of widespread Polynesian ocean voyaging. This probability is confirmed by the discovery of Mayor Island obsidian on Raoul Island in the Kermadec group, halfway between New Zealand and tropical Polynesia, which can have been left there only in the course of return journeys to one or more Pacific islands. The genetic diversity of Kermadec kiore is further confirmation that those islands were a staging-point for multiple voyages from both directions.*

---

* The suggestion that kiore were in New Zealand earlier than the thirteenth century AD (see Chapter 1) is merely evidence of a possible Polynesian *landing* on the New Zealand coast; coinciding evidence of *settlement* is conspicuously absent. Other problems too about the early dates for kiore bones (such as the fact that they appear to precede even the human settlement of East Polynesia) have yet to be resolved.

It seems most likely that, matching the pattern elsewhere, New Zealand was located during a voyage of discovery and settled as a result of subsequent and deliberate voyages of colonisation by several, possibly many, canoes. Geneticists and demographers have calculated that a population of 100 to 200 founding settlers, including at least 50 women, was needed for the Maori population to reach its estimated size of 100,000 by the eighteenth century. Analysis of kiore mitochondrial DNA suggests that there were multiple colonisations by the rat in New Zealand – meaning many introductions, which in turn indicates a number of canoe settlements. The likely sequence of discovery and then settlement is also suggested by elements common to Maori tribal traditions, almost all of which speak of primary discoverers preceding the canoe voyages of organised colonisation. The question of whether those named figures were responsible for the discoveries themselves, however, is complicated by the fact that, like Maui's, some of their names appear in Island Polynesian traditions in similar roles.

Thanks to the well-preserved evidence of material culture – stone adzes, bone fishhooks and harpoon points – there is no doubt that the major source of Polynesian immigration to New Zealand was the islands of East Polynesia. Precisely which islands may never be known for certain. The distribution of tools and materials uncovered by archaeologists reveals that, at the time of the settlement of New Zealand, those islands – the Society, Marquesas, Astral and Cook groups – were part of what anthropologists call a 'regional interaction sphere', meaning that contact among them was extensive and frequent. It is likely too that emigrants heading for New Zealand set out within a short space of time from more than one of those island homes. Such a scenario is confirmed by the fact that New Zealand kiore display genetic markers that link them to both the

Society Islands and the Cooks, though not to the Marquesas.

More than one scholar has suggested that pervasive differences between the pronunciation of North and South Island Maori, retained even as successive North Island tribes migrated to the south, may be another indication of different sources of migration from different islands. This diffusionist theory, however, overlooks the possibility of just such variations developing over time and with a degree of isolation within what might have been, originally, a more homogeneous migrant group. More marked variations in dialect developed on the Chatham Islands after they were settled from New Zealand in the fourteenth or fifteenth century.

There is a single piece of evidence at variance with the hypothesis that New Zealand was settled from East Polynesia. Part of the DNA record of New Zealand kiore indicates a link with the rats of Fiji and West Polynesia. This suggests to Lisa Matisoo-Smith, who undertook the analysis, that 'rats may have been introduced to New Zealand from a more westerly location before the successful human settlement from central east Polynesia'. No evidence of West Polynesian culture has yet been found in the archaeological record, which supports the view that this contact may have been fleeting and not part of the organised settlement of the country.

Nominating a date for the initial settlement of New Zealand is rather more problematic. A revision of carbon dates for the earliest New Zealand sites thus far investigated by archaeologists reveals none earlier than the thirteenth century AD. And one such site, at Tairua on the eastern side of the Coromandel Peninsula, dated to the late thirteenth or early fourteenth century, also contained the single unequivocally Island Polynesian artefact found in New Zealand in an archaeological context: a pearl-shell fish lure. Identical lures had been picked up previously from eroded middens in the same coastal region. While the latter have been detached from a datable habitation site, their presence increases the likelihood that the eastern Coromandel was one of the sites of first settlement and that the first people there either came from tropical Polynesia themselves or were closely associated with or descended from those who did.

The Kaharoa eruption, which originated from Mount Tarawera and cast ash over 30,000 square kilometres of the North Island, has been reliably dated at 1314 AD, plus or minus 12 years. And the first fossil pollen associated with significant deforestation as a result of fire in the North Island has been found at the same level and just below Kaharoa ash – indicating that the fires occurred just before and at the same time as the eruption. Other fossil pollen remains increase in the fourteenth and fifteenth centuries and coincide with the destruction of large areas of forest on the eastern coast of both the North and South Islands, particularly in Hawke's Bay and Canterbury. Given a human presence, and with it a greater likelihood of both accidental fires and fires lit to provide easier access to game such as moa, and given the sharp decline in the numbers of moa and other flightless birds over the same period, it is reasonable to associate these fires with human agents. It is also reasonable to date from these fires the first major human-sponsored modifications of the New Zealand landscape, and with them major modifications to flora and fauna.

A thirteenth-century date for the initial settlement of New Zealand is later than those given previously for the beginning of the Maori era of settlement – 800 AD is cited most frequently in the previous literature. But the earlier carbon dates on which this conclusion was based turned out to be verifiably wrong, and a decision to trace such settlement from the 1200s is more soundly based on the range of evidence currently verifiable. It is still an informed guess, however, and there is always a possibility that new evidence will provoke a further twist of the kaleidoscope that will move the settlement pattern towards different configurations.

Where in New Zealand were the first landings made? The inevitable absence of concrete archaeological evidence for such an event – original habitation sites were probably at river mouths or in sand dunes and likely to have eroded or been built over in the era of European colonisation – makes the question impossible to answer confidently. The discovery of the pearl-shell lures on the eastern Coromandel establishes a connection with these early colonists, but not necessarily their place of arrival. Maori canoe traditions may have some relevance here, although the purpose of such traditions was to establish connections with specific places, resources and people, not to recount a disinterested history, and some of them may have referred to internal migrations within New Zealand, not to the journey from a former island home.

Descendants of at least four traditional canoe groups – those of Tainui, Mataatua, Horouta and Nukutere – name the eastern Bay of Plenty as their place of first landfall (and some go further, naming Whangaparaoa on the cusp of the East Cape as the place their ancestors first stepped ashore). And the unplanned arrival at the same part of the coast of one of the late twentieth-century canoes accomplishing a repeat voyage from the Society Islands increases the possibility that ancestors too may have first come ashore there. Other canoe traditions (three) tell of fetching up on the eastern side of North Cape, and (two) off the northern Coromandel Peninsula. All are consistent with possibilities allowed by wind and tide, and with modern computer simulations. The fact that at least some of the crops that the colonists brought with them survived the voyage and initial settlement suggests that colonisation from at least some canoes occurred in the warm upper half of the eastern North Island.

Clusters of earliest known habitation sites – the north-east of the North Island from Houhora to the Coromandel Peninsula, both sides of Cook Strait, and the south-east of the South Island – provide another basis for speculation. Archaeologists such as Jack Golson and historians such as Belich have suggested that these might represent 'resource islands', regions where early settlers chose to hunt, garden and gain access to mineral resources, for as few as three separate canoe groups which arrived in the country at more or less the same time. Such an explanation would solve the problem of how a group of colonists managed to spread so rapidly and apparently simultaneously from one end of the country to the other. One could then speculate that, as the early abundant resources of large birds and seals were exhausted, these three groups later joined forces and reproduced, only to divaricate subsequently into the dozens of groupings of the tribal era as populations grew and previously co-operative exploitation of remaining resources became instead increasingly competitive.

Against that possibility, closer analysis of artefacts (fishhooks, for example) has shown subtle differences in the material culture of the Houhora and Coromandel settlers. The growing consensus among prehistorians is that there are likely to have been considerably more than three foundation groups, that these groups would have explored the *whole* of the country rapidly to locate its mineral and food resources (in addition to the Auckland Islands in the south, people had visited Jackson Bay in South Westland by the early fourteenth century); and that they probably arrived within a short time of one another.

Discussion of such possibilities will never amount to more than a juggling of hypotheses. But some certainties remain. The first New Zealanders *were* East Polynesian immigrants. They began organised settlement of the country around 800 years ago. Their descendants were the New Zealand Maori encountered and described by Europeans in the seventeenth and eighteenth centuries. And a much larger group of descendants still identifies as Maori, celebrates its identity and nurtures its confidence with Polynesian cultural memories, some of which date back to that time of arrival: 'For I shall not perish, but as a seed sent forth from Raiatea I shall flourish.' In the thirteenth century, such messages served to prepare a people for a journey of migration; in the twenty-first century, they fortify the descendants of those same people for the journey of life.

Far as it was from tropical Polynesia, New Zealand did not represent the terminus of 5000 years of Austronesian/Polynesian migration. There were still further journeys to be launched. Mention has been made of a way station on Raoul Island in the Kermadecs established from New Zealand, and of the extraordinarily close similarity of adzes found on Pitcairn Island to those found contemporaneously in New Zealand. There is also evidence that a short-lived Polynesian attempt to settle Norfolk Island may have originated from New Zealand.

But the major voyage still to be made after East Polynesians reached New Zealand was on to the Chatham Islands, some 800 km east of the South Island. Some time in the fourteenth or fifteenth century, possibly after no more than a century's occupation of the mainland, a group of New Zealand Polynesians transferred themselves by canoe to this cluster of isolated low-lying islands directly in the path of the Roaring Forties. Here again analysis of kiore DNA is helpful. The tightly clustered nature of the genetic data suggests a single settlement of people at one time, and provides proof that the source of migration was New Zealand. By the time that New Zealand Maori and the indigenous settlers of the Chathams came into contact with one another again in the early nineteenth century, thanks to European vessels, neither people had any surviving knowledge of the other nor of their common origins in East Polynesia and on the New Zealand mainland. As a result of this encounter, the Chatham Islanders began to refer to themselves as Moriori, their dialectal version of the word Maori (from 'tangata maori': ordinary people).

The Chathams culture had by this time diverged from that of Maori in several important respects. The islanders had a 'level' society, with no distinction between aristocrats and commoners; they had developed their own version of the Polynesian language; they had no horticulture, because the climate would not allow the root vegetables Polynesians carried with them to grow there; and, perhaps most significant, they had discarded warfare as a means of settling group disputes and substituted the practice of dual hand-to-hand combat, which would cease as soon as one party drew blood. Their material culture lacked the elaborations of so-called classic Maori culture, in particular intricate carving and a wide range of tools and ornaments; but was, in its pared-down simplicity, adequate to meet the needs of Chatham Islands' inhabitants.

Of the fact that Moriori *were* Polynesian and shared ancestry with Maori there was – or should have been – no doubt. Their language was Polynesian and, despite differences in pronunciation, shared many words with Maori and no other languages. They appeared Polynesian in their stature and features and their skulls revealed the classic Polynesian 'rocker' jawbone. Not only were their tools of the same East Polynesian style and variation as those of early Maori, but some of those found on Pitt Island would turn out to be made from New Zealand materials (obsidian and argillite).

Despite this overwhelming volume and weight of testimony, some late nineteenth- and early twentieth-century scholars convinced themselves and a gullible New Zealand public that Moriori were *not* Polynesian. Professor J. H. Scott of the Otago University Medical School reported that skeletal evidence showed that Moriori resulted from an interbreeding of Polynesian and Melanesian antecedents and that the Melanesian element was stronger because the 'cranial capacity is somewhat less'. A group of German scientists published a paper proposing that Moriori most closely resembled the 'extinct' Aboriginal people of Tasmania. John Macmillan Brown, a professor of classics and English and a dabbler in ethnology and history, dismissed the idea that Moriori had any Polynesian ancestry at all.

The most coherent statements about the relationship of Moriori to Maori – and, as it turned out, the most erroneous – came from the amateur ethnologists who were the founding members of the Polynesian Society: Stephenson Percy Smith and Elsdon Best. Smith proposed in his second volume of *The Lore of the Whare-Wananga* (1915) that Moriori were an 'inferior' and 'dark-skinned' people who occupied New Zealand prior to Maori, and that they were subsequently partly absorbed and partly driven out by the more intelligent and more enterprising later-comers, who had arrived in New Zealand as part of a 'fleet' migration from Island Polynesia. Best, in a 1916 article in the *Transactions of the New Zealand Institute* that revealed collaboration with Smith, filled in further details. He claimed that Moriori were 'a people much inferior to the Maori in appearance and general culture [with] thick projecting lips ... bushy frizzy hair, dark skin and flat nose[s] ... with upturned nostrils. Their eyes were curiously restless, and they had a habit of glancing sideways without turning their head.'

This saga with its lurid allegations of Moriori physical and mental 'inferiority' was assembled from contaminated and unrelated fragments of so-called Maori tradition. It had no basis in history or ethnology. Yet it was, as noted previously, published in the Department of Education's *School Journal* and distributed to every primary school classroom in the country. This action, supported by subsequent publications which repeated the story, coloured public perception of the indigenous Chatham Islanders for the next three generations.

Condemned by a late twentieth-century ethnologist as a 'virulent myth', the construct was a consequence of social Darwinist ideas current at the time of its invention. It explained the plight and demoralisation of Moriori in the nineteenth century as evidence that they were an 'inferior' people unable to adapt either to the neolithic world in which they had previously lived or to the 'modern' age of European colonisation. If they were, *ipso facto*, inferior to Maori – who had flourished in their pre-European society and showed signs of being able to negotiate the effects of colonisation, even to assert themselves in the face of it – then the explanation must lie in Melanesian ancestry. This conclusion followed because it was believed that Melanesian skin colouring (the basis for the origin of that designation), hair texture and physical features all indicated a lower order of human evolution than that displayed by the more 'Aryan-looking' Maori.

Further, the very notion that Maori had displaced and colonised a more primitive people was both evidence of *their* superiority and an implicit justification for what Europeans, representatives of a still higher order of civilisation, had done to Maori in turn ('in colonising you and your country we did no more than that which you had already done to Moriori'). All the pleasing and convenient resonances of the Moriori myth ensured that it enjoyed a popular currency among Pakeha New Zealanders, and among many Maori, long after it had been disproved by the Dunedin ethnologist Henry Skinner in the 1920s.

After the 'virulent myth' had been further demolished in more public arenas by a television programme in 1980 and a professionally written history of Moriori published in 1989, another story, equally erroneous and equally innocent of evidential connections, arose phoenix-like from the ashes to take its place in the public mind. This new myth, seized on uncritically by the popular press, generated more reverberations that a new generation of New Zealanders in turn would find comforting. It was yet another variation on the notion that the ancestors of the Maori had not been the discoverers and first inhabitants of New Zealand.

This time it was alleged that the honour and distinction of first landfall and footfall had gone to a group known as Waitaha (or, more grandly, 'the Nation of Waitaha'). The ancestors of these people had allegedly sailed into the Pacific not simply from Asia, but also from Africa and South America. In a kind of cultural version of the geologists' Gondwana scenario, proponents of Waitaha said that the ancestral groups had brought with them concepts and technologies apparent in the earlier human histories of all those continents. The eventual discoverers of New Zealand had sailed there from Easter Island more than 2000 years before Polynesians arrived. They were a peacable people, in harmony with the land and the sea. Their secret history, 'hidden ... in the trees and in the stones' and withheld from Pakeha scholars for 200 years, would be published in 1995 as *Song of Waitaha: the Histories of a Nation*.

The Waitaha myth presented a range of difficulties for historians and prehistorians. There was not a skerrick of evidence – linguistic, artefactual, genetic; no datable carbon or pollen remains; nothing – that the story had any basis in fact. Which would make Waitaha the first people on Earth to live in a country for several millennia and leave no trace of their occupation. This lack of evidence, the story's proponents would claim, was because Waitaha stone structures had been mistaken for natural formations or Maori artefacts, and because their history had been kept 'secret' from both Maori and Pakeha scholars. And, to confuse the picture further, elements of the story *did* have a basis in Maori tradition: there had been tribes in both the North and South Islands who used the name Waitaha.

In the South Island, some of those genuinely descended from the Maori Waitaha people and the tribes which had subsumed them, Ngati Mamoe and Ngai Tahu, embraced with enthusiasm a scenario which made them far more than one Maori tribe among many: a pre-Polynesian civilisation which could be said to have prior rights over Maori. Some Maori from other regions who saw similar political and ideological advantage in the Waitaha myth also abandoned their previous and authentic tribal affiliations to become, instead, descendants of and spokespeople for the Nation of Waitaha.

For Pakeha supporters, and they outnumbered Maori, the story had multiple appeal. It carried on the popular Victorian notion of cultural diffusion, which held that any cultural innovation displayed by a 'primitive' people, such as the moai statues on Easter Island, had to have come from a more 'highly civilised' people elsewhere. It incorporated the neo-Darwinist conviction that the representatives of 'higher civilisations' were pale-skinned, as some of the ancestors of Waitaha were said to be. It supported New Age beliefs about the desirability of living in a sacramental relationship with the natural environment, the energies of stones and crystals, and abilities to derive information from 'cosmic consiousness', ley-lines and the 'earth's harmonics'. And it completely undercut contemporary Maori resource claims against the Crown by arguing that Maori were not in fact descended from the first inhabitants of New Zealand, unless they also found and acknowledged Waitaha ancestry. In this last instance, the Waitaha myth became a neat substitution for that of Moriori: 'Maori did to Waitaha what Pakeha did to Maori; therefore Maori have no legal or moral high ground from which to argue for compensation for the effects of colonisation.'

Not a single scholar, Maori or Pakeha, accepted the validity of the Waitaha Nation scenario, and standard histories of New Zealand failed to dignify it even with a mention. But that in no way diminished its popular appeal. Media interest in freakish stories ensured that the public appetite for such stories was sustained. And to the myth of the 'secretness' of Waitaha traditions could be added the allegation that reputable scholars sought to 'suppress' the Waitaha story because it conflicted with paradigms on which their careers and employment depended. And so, for the initiates, the myth of the Nation of Waitaha was sustained by a self-reinforcing circle of argument and delusion, of misperception and misrepresentation, that permitted no admission of evidence or common sense from outside the circle.

5

First Colonisation

The land that the ancestors of the Maori settled was unlike any they had encountered in their remembered island past. To begin with it was enormous – 1600 km from the northern tip of Maui's Fish to the base of Aoraki's Canoe, with 18,000 km of coastline. The landscapes ranged from coastal beach and broadleaf coastal forest to estuarine swamps, enormous inland plains, podocarp-covered hills, sub-alpine ranges and mountains capped with snow – to which the formerly tropical Polynesians, having never seen such a substance previously, gave the name huka or foam. There were thermal regions and at least six active, or soon-to-be-active, volcanoes. Compared with the dimensions of Polynesia's basalt islands and coral atolls, the resources of this new country – its minerals, its forests and the big-game food provided by giant birds and seals – would have seemed vast and inexhaustible. Even the days themselves were longer in summer and therefore fuller than in equatorial regions.

Second, New Zealand's temperatures and climates varied

beyond Polynesian knowledge and expectation: sub-tropical in the north, temperate in the central region and cold beyond anything they could have imagined in the south. This factor would influence which of the crops they brought with them could grow, and where, and which they would have to discard. Climate would also determine what garments they would need to wear in different parts of the country, what natural materials they would choose to make them, what technical skills they would have to invent in order to make use of such new materials, and what kinds of houses they would need to build for shelter and warmth.

It was the adaptation to the new environment of the concepts and practices they brought with them, and the new skills and practices they developed to meet unfamiliar environmental challenges, that transformed East Polynesian island culture into that of New Zealand Maori. And that transformation occurred over at least three identifiable stages, which historians have termed colonial, transitional and tribal.

The Maori colonial era began the moment East Polynesian migrants stepped ashore and continued through the first phase of settlement and adjustment. It is the period formerly referred to as 'Archaic Maori' or, in Roger Duff's famous phrase, 'the Moa Hunter period of Maori culture'. Duff, fresh from the excitement and revelations of his excavations on the Wairau Bar at the head of the South Island, was right to highlight the role of moa in the economy and material culture of early settlers in that part of the country. But his phrase suggests an overly simplistic understanding of what was happening to early Maori in that era throughout New Zealand.

Archaeological investigation of the earliest habitation sites shows that moa *were* a major source of protein – and in some cases the major source – for settlers in some parts of the country, especially the east coast of the South Island (estimates of the number of birds killed, or at least cut up, at the mouth of the Waitaki River range from 29,000 to 90,000; and further south, at the Shag River mouth, at least 6000 moa were slaughtered over a relatively short period of occupation). Given the size of the largest birds, the enormous amount of meat they carried (drumsticks alone the size of a leg of beef) and the relative ease with which, having no ingrained fear of ground-based predators, they would have been caught in coastal shrubland and on inland plains, the reliance of many colonial Maori on this food source is no surprise. Even the smaller 'bush moa' had a body mass comparable with that of turkeys. The Wairau Bar excavations also revealed that early Maori used moa eggshells the size of rugby balls as water carriers, and moa bone for the manufacture of fishhooks, harpoon heads and ornaments.

Other factors too were important to the economy, material culture and lifestyle of early Maori, however. The 'resource islands' which made up what may have been the regions of first settlement – the east coast of the Far North and Coromandel Peninsula, Cook Strait, and the south-east coast of the South Island – also provided access to seals, to minerals for tool-making and, in all but the southernmost sites, suitable areas for the cultivation of some of the plants the colonists had brought with them: kumara, yam, taro, ti, gourd and paper mulberry (of the eight possible root crops and eleven tree crops cultivated in tropical Polynesia, only six would grow in New Zealand).

So moa were a significant source of protein, of bones for ornament and fishhook manufacture, and, possibly, of feathers for use in cloaks. But other large birds were slaughtered – the flightless goose, an enormous rail now known as the adzebill, swans and pelicans, all of them, like the moa, exploited to the point of extinction after little more than 100 years. The fur seal, sealion and elephant seal were also killed and eaten in such large quantities that, after just over a century, their formerly crowded rookeries were deserted everywhere but in Foveaux Strait and Fiordland. Other sea mammals such as dolphin and pilot whales were also taken by harpooning. And in each resource area heavy use was made of local minerals for the manufacture of flake knives and adzes – obsidian from Mayor Island, basalt from Coromandel, greywacke from the Hauraki Gulf, argillite and serpentine from the Nelson region, and chert and silcrete from Otago. Further, the movement of some of these materials, especially Mayor Island obsidian, shows that settlers in the three or four principal regions of early settlement were in communication with one another and either traded or exchanged goods or made minerals available to one another by allowing freedom of movement throughout the country as a whole.

While the main emphasis for the first century or so of settlement was on locating resources, hunting, and to a lesser extent on foraging for shellfish and fish, it is a mistake to portray these early peoples, as some writers have done, solely as hunter-gatherers. The fact that six of the plants they brought from tropical Polynesia survived shows that from the outset, at least in the more northerly settlements, attention was given to planting, nurturing and harvesting them. They were cultivated throughout the period of Maori colonial settlement so as to be available to play a more important role in post-colonial Maori life, when the big game was gone. Continued gardening, in other words, constituted a dietary insurance policy.

The disposition of early settlement sites, and their size and character, point to an important conclusion. The lifestyle of these people was, if not quite nomadic, certainly mobile. They would occupy a home base, probably the place where gardening and tool-making took place, and a constellation of 'stations' for activities appropriate to certain times of the year – hunting moa or seals, foraging for seafood, collecting minerals. It is probable that whole communities took part in these activities as they moved from place to place and that there was less specialisation than in the later and more stationary tribal era.

Louise Furey has described one base settlement in Northland occupied in the early fourteenth century.

> In total, 3200 objects are known from Houhora. These include adzes, ornaments, fishing gear, bone harpoon points, bone needles, tattoo chisels, bone chisels and awls, and manufacturing tools such as stone drillpoints, hammerstones, sandstone files and scrapers. These ... show that there was a full range of activities taking place at Houhora. The people were engaged in everyday activities to procure food, to manufacture ... objects in wood, stone and bone, and ... participating in other activities encompassing the social dimension, for example competitive sports such as dart throwing, or tattooing ...
>
> Snapper was the dominant [food] species ... followed by seals. But in terms of calorific value seals exceeded all other species. The moa were probably caught some distance away from the village and brought back as dismembered carcasses ... Seals were brought back to the site whole if pups and lighter juveniles, but adults are only represented by bones which were attached to large muscles ... Dolphins were hunted using small bone harpoons. The meat was cut up and cooked in an umu, mandibles used to make fishhooks and teeth drilled and strung as necklaces ... [The] significant lack of vertebrae for the number of fish represented ... evidence of fish drying in the summer and of storage for later use ... [There is also] evidence of preserving birds. These people in the early fourteenth century were already following a seasonal round of food procuring, preservation and storage which persisted for hundreds of years.

Significantly, skeletal remains from early settlement sites show the inhabitants to have been well nourished and healthy, even though they seldom lived beyond their late 30s. Historians have speculated that one consequence of this health, itself a result largely of the high-protein diet available to the first generations of settlers, would have been a high rate of fertility. Skeletal remains again reveal that women may have borne as many as four or five children, and this would have led to a rapid population increase – and therefore to additional pressure on food resources in the first two or three generations of settlement.

As a determinant of culture and lifestyle, the Maori colonial period appears to have lasted between 100 and 150 years. After that relatively short period, the big game was all but exhausted. The northern seal rookeries were deserted, in part because hunters had killed mothers and pups along with adult males. Moa became extinct because of the profligate manner in which this resource too was exploited (a process the Australian ecological historian Tim Flannery would refer to as 'future-eating'). With the moa had disappeared a range of other birds, mostly flightless, some of them humanly hunted to extinction, others pursued and killed at the egg, fledgling or adult stage by the rats and dogs which the East Polynesians had brought with them. Most mainland sources of shearwaters and petrels, which nested in burrows, would also have disappeared from a combination of intensive hunting and rat and dog predation.

Another factor which accelerated the extinctions was destruction of habitat. Pollen and charcoal cores in swamps reveal that for whatever reason a series of major fires occurred in the fourteenth and fifteenth centuries, destroying forests especially in Hawke's Bay and down the east coast of the South Island, but also in inland areas of the North Island and on parts of the Northland and Coromandel peninsulas. The period of the fires coincided with the spectacular decline in the numbers of moa and other large, hunted birds. It is possible that fires began as an effort to clear open living spaces and, later, to drive surviving moa and other ground birds out of their places of hiding. Once started, many fires may have flared out of control. Another theory is that they represent an effort to encourage the growth of bracken fern, which in the Maori tribal era became an important food source. There may be some truth in this, but it is scarcely adequate to explain the full extent of deforestation. The hypothesis that links this with a more desperate and reckless phase of hunting is more plausible.

Who were the people of this era? That is a difficult, if not impossible, question to answer historically. Maori whakapapa offer names without remains – that is, stories without evidence – while archaeology offers remains without names – evidence without stories.

Maori oral tradition has much to say about the voyages of respective canoes to New Zealand, but little about how people lived in the period of initial settlement. The exception is the large number of stories about ancestors naming geographical features – important markers in tribal tradition that validated occupation and mana whenua, the right of the descendants of discoverers to hold authority over such places. The very absence of other kinds of stories, of how people became established in a strange land, has led to speculation that some canoe traditions may refer to internal migration within New Zealand rather than voyages from Island Polynesia. The point of oral tradition, however, was that it recorded what people needed to know to understand and justify present circumstances, not 'domestic' detail about how people lived and worked in an earlier era. In most parts of the country, even knowledge of the moa itself, that considerable contributor to the health and well-being of colonial Maori, had dropped out of remembered tradition by the time of European settlement. With moa gone, there was no reason to recall them down succeeding generations.

Roger Duff's description of the boulder bank separating the estuary of the Wairau River from the sea in the north of the South Island is, however, sufficient to conjure up some of the activities of early Maori who lived there. In some ways these are similar to and in others different from their contemporaries in Houhora. This site was almost certainly a seasonally occupied hunting camp rather than a village home-base.

> [The] boulder bank would prove the most suitable site for their fishing and fowling economy, and the northern tip of it the obvious spot to settle on. Here the river mouth gave access to the sea, for fish and trading expeditions, while along the sea beach accumulated the large quantities of firewood necessary in a treeless spot. The whitebait and kahawai ran seasonally into the river and lagoon; herrings, eels and flounders formed a more permanent population; and banks of edible shellfish thrived at the entrance ...
>
> In addition the extinct swan flourished in this favourable estuary ... as well as great numbers of [duck] ... Finally ... the site was well placed for hunting the large numbers of moas whose bones are spread today over the 15 to 20 acres of the main occupation site ... [Perhaps] they were rounded up in the Wairau plain or driven down from the Vernon hills, and in either case herded round the base of the Mataora lagoon and then driven along the trap of the boulder bank to the *cul de sac* provided by its northern end ... [Another] possibility is that these birds were hunted some distance inland and brought by canoe or raft down the Wairau River to the camp site. Of the methods of taking the swan and other water-fowl we may be reasonably sure ... [Advantage] would be taken of the annual moult when the birds were unable to fly, and could be rounded up ...
>
> [The] first signs of Moa-hunter occupation occur on the inner slope of the main ridge ... which occupies a halfway line between

the sea beach and the lagoon. The signs here are most obvious and include a line of pits or ovens, surrounded by masses of midden refuse ... [It] would appear to have been the main cooking area of the settlement and situated for convenience some three chains from the main habitation site. This latter hut area ... carries extensive though not obtrusive signs of long continued occupation. The most important burial area ... occurred on the outer fringes of it ... Bones of moas, dogs, seals, birds, fish etc. are found evenly distributed everywhere, but [moa] eggshell is more common in the hut area.

Helen Leach and Philip Houghton have reconstructed a more specific account of the living circumstances of a 35- to 40-year-old woman whose remains were excavated in Palliser Bay on the northern side of Cook Strait. This community, perhaps transitional rather than early colonial, was one that did not rely on moa for protein or raw materials.

In life she stood 162.6 cm tall ... , was fairly robust and right-handed. She had given birth to between two and four children. By the time of her death she was suffering from quite severe wear [and abscessing] on her teeth ... Evidence of arthritis in the spine may be linked to the deterioration in health that accompanied these infections. Her diet (or the sand that blew into her food) was clearly very abrasive.

[The] small community in which she lived occupied a group of sleeping huts and cooking sheds on the north bank of the ponded mouth of the Makotukutuku River ... Although seasonal trips were made to catch birds such as tuis and parakeets and to gather berries from the forested valleys of the Aorangi mountains ... , the coastal village was permanently occupied because of proximity to its gardens and seafood resources. The gardens were located on the old raised beach ridges and swales just behind the village. Their shallow stony soils which had formed under coastal scrub had been cleared by fire ... Of the tropical crops introduced by her ancestors, this woman grew mainly the kumara and gourd, best suited to the harsher climate and light soils of the area. In autumn the kumara harvest was carefully stored within enclosed pits close to the cooking sheds.

When not occupied by gardening, she gathered seafood from the intertidal platform, especially paua, topshells, limpets, and crayfish. Some of the fish eaten at the village were caught inshore using circular hooks of bone and shell, but when sea conditions were suitable the men caught fish such as barracouta and kahawai by trolling lures behind canoes. Rats and eels were trapped close to the village and domestic dogs were killed to supplement the meat of sea mammals such as dolphins and seals.

During the summer months, food gathering included items for preservation. The long hours of daylight were fully occupied with the splitting of eels and other oily fish for drying, and the weaving of kete for storage ... [Her] heavy work-load in summer and autumn would have slackened in winter and she was fortunate to have fresh water and firewood close at hand throughout the year. Her death, in her fourth decade, would not have been unexpected since few adults survived long, given their physically demanding life-style. She was buried in the vicinity of several family members and a pet dog ...

In the fourteenth and fifteenth centuries, with the demise of big game, early Maori were required to make major adjustments in their culture and lifestyle in order to survive. They did so by extending and intensifying their remaining sources of food production and foraging.

Gardening would have become increasingly important; in all but the lower half of the South Island, it may eventually have been responsible for up to half the total food requirement. Foraging too would have remained a large part of the routine of daily life: of food sources that had had some significance previously, especially salt and freshwater fish and shellfish, and of the raw foods of the forest (hearts of nikau palm and cabbage tree, berries and drupes when seasonally available, especially the kernel of the karaka berry). It may have been around this time that 'wild' plants such as karaka, cabbage tree and bracken fern began to be semi-cultivated. And birds which had been ignored in the era of big-game hunting would now become an important food source: weka, pigeon, kiwi, tui and others. The flighted bush birds would always be difficult to catch, however, and would never be taken in large numbers because Maori lacked adequate projectile weapons. Spears were difficult to use in thick forest, and snaring became the preferred option. It is probable that the experience and the penalties of pursuing larger game to extinction would have led to the development of more sustainable practices in the hunting of remaining birds of the forest and sea.

The period of the fourteenth and fifteenth centuries has been termed transitional for two other reasons. One is a gradual alteration in art forms, from the unequivocally East Polynesian shapes and motifs of the earliest settlers towards those that came to be associated with classic Maori culture; these alterations were especially noticeable in wood carving and items of personal ornamentation such as hei tiki. This period was also the phase in which Maori groups became less nomadic, more settled in defined territories, and began to form those larger associations based partly on kin and partly on areas of occupation that would be the major social characteristic of the tribal era.

Several factors contributed to the concentration of activities on more restricted areas of occupation. First, the demise of big game and the growth of population gave communities less incentive and opportunity to roam over large areas of the country. A diminution in the use of the original ocean-going canoes and their eventual obsolescence might have been another factor in this lifestyle change. Second, the very concentration on the more efficient exploitation of other food sources, especially gardening, required communities to become more 'sedentary' and more disciplined in the focus of their activities. Third, the practice that developed of preserving kumara tubers in storage pits (a process that had been unnecessary in a tropical climate) meant that communities had to remain with those pits, particularly in an era of larger population when competition for resources meant that less well-provisioned neighbours might be tempted to raid your larder. This last factor more than any other gave impetus to the rise and spread, from north to south, of fortified hilltops which came to be known as pa. They probably originated from a need to protect kumara tubers; but they persisted and became more important when population growth, competition for all resources, the pursuit of mana or authority for one's own group, and a generally more martial culture meant that communities increasingly had to protect themselves from immediate neighbours or from marauding enemies from further afield.

It was a combination of all these factors – but especially the growth of population and increased competition for resources which that growth brought – that favoured the growth of tribal organisation and culture through the fifteenth and sixteenth centuries. This development was not consistent throughout the country. In the south of the South Island, for example, because of smaller populations and less competition for resources, people remained more nomadic for longer and may eventually have become tribal largely because of absorption by peoples who had migrated from the North Island, where they had already developed the characteristics and patterns of tribal culture. Even in the north, however, the archaeological record shows that some groups would retain something closer to a hunter-gatherer culture at the same time as near-neighbours were becoming more settled and more tribally organised. The record also suggests that those who retained some of the features of Maori colonial life longer than other groups eventually fell victim to the larger-scale organisation of purpose and resources which tribal culture allowed. In other words, in the North Island and top of the South Island, in order to retain congenial places in which to live and proximity to food and mineral resources, there would have been strong incentives to become part of larger groupings of people and to develop tribal structures. This in turn created a concomitant ability to call upon larger and more organised groups for such co-ordinated activities as gardening and net fishing, and fighting in attack or defence.

Through the transitional to tribal phases of New Zealand Maori culture another development also occurred. Whatever their reasons for emigrating, the first settlers, the colonists, would have been intensely conscious of the cultural and physical landscapes they were leaving behind in Island Polynesia. It is probable, too, that they would have had to abandon kinsfolk, whose absence would have been mourned. They would have continued to tell the accumulated stories of those places to themselves, and to children and grandchildren, all with a view to – as had become customary in Polynesian cultures – keeping alive the names and deeds of recent ancestors.

As generation followed generation in the new land, however, and as the more recent experience of a migratory voyage and the measures needed to ensure survival in what was initially an unfamiliar environment generated another cycle of sagas for oral tradition, awareness of and concern for the places of origin would have diminished. Those places would have receded to the status of a kind of Arthurian world which was eventually little more than a hazy background to the history and experience steadily and vividly accumulating on Te Ika a Maui or Te Waka a Aoraki. They would never be entirely forgotten or unacknowledged; they would continue to be recalled in such ritual phrases as 'Hawaiiki-nui, Hawaiiki-roa, Hawaiiki-pamamao' (Hawaiiki being the traditional word for homeland). But they would ebb further away from remembered human experience and into the realm of mythology.

At the same time many of the placenames and stories which had been carried from the homelands were localised and transplanted. New Zealand acquired its quota of Hikurangis, Maunganuis and Motutapus and other names familiar through-out Polynesia. The existence of Ranginui and Papatuanuku and the doings of Tane Mahuta and Tangaroa and their siblings came to be seen as referents to the sky and soil and sea and fauna of New Zealand. Maui-tikitiki-a-Taranga became a local cultural hero in addition to being a Polynesia-wide one, and natural features in the landscape, including the North Island itself, came to be attributed to his doings.

In other words, over succeeding generations the cultural focus shifted steadily away from cultures of origin to a singular awareness of and commitment to the adopted homeland. At the same time new technologies and practices were tried for meeting new environmental challenges: different kinds of dwelling and clothing to keep warm, different ways of growing, gathering, preserving and storing food. New forms of carving and ornamentation reflected both different working mediums and shifting perceptions of cultural and spiritual realities. A new mineral such as pounamu (greenstone) allowed the develop-ment of more elaborate carving, and the fine fibres of New Zealand flax the weaving of more comfortable and more beautiful garments.

What all this added up to was the process by which an imported culture, that of East Polynesians, left to develop in isolation, became an indigenous one: Te Ao Maori. And that new culture would focus fully on the islands of New Zealand and its human, animal and botanic inhabitants. It would offer those human inhabitants a comprehensible place in the cosmos and a prospect of physical and spiritual security – or at least as much of those things as could be expected in a world where life was, if not invariably nasty, then sometimes brutish and short.

6

Te Ao Maori

While the development had begun sporadically and proceeded at different rates in different parts of the country, the emergence of classic or tribal Maori society by the sixteenth century was close to being a nationwide phenomenon. (The major exception was the lower half of the South Island, where many Maori still lived largely nomadic lives and where an inability to grow kumara and a low population density had resulted in a near-absence of fortified pa.) While Maori life and customs would continue to change in response to new human and environmental challenges, the configurations of the tribal era could be seen as the accomplishment of successful colonisation of the country.

Like colonisers elsewhere, the East Polynesian ancestors and their immediate descendants had learned, by trial and error and committing some major mistakes, to turn New Zealand's natural and environmental conditions to human advantage (how many people perished, one wonders, in the search for a safe way to prepare the otherwise poisonous kernel of the karaka berry for human consumption?). They learned too to attain bodily comfort and physical shelter in a range of climates and temperatures, and psychical and spiritual security by localising the presence of deities and the application of propitiatory ritual. They thus managed to survive as a viable population and, as we have seen, to convert an imported culture into a tangata whenua or indigenous one with recognisable antecedents in East Polynesia but now connected inextricably to the roots and soil of New Zealand.

What were some of the characteristics of this culture?

First, and perhaps most important, individuals found a place in it, and hence in the whole cosmography of Maori thought, through whakapapa or relationship. But they were not conscious of being Maori, nor would the word 'Maori' (meaning 'ordinary') have been used in this way. New Zealand Polynesians, long separated from other races and cultures, had no words for race or culture, not even to describe their own. Identity and worth were found in family and tribal connectedness, not in membership of a race or a people, nor in individual qualities or achievements. Membership of a tribe was based on descent from a founding ancestor or, in some cases, a foundational canoe. Lines of descent formed the basis for tribal membership and association, just as they provided the major paradigm by which Maori defined the spiritual and natural worlds and their connection to them.

Identity was linked to both ancestry *and* place and was expressed through proverbs and waiata (songs) and patere (assertive chants) associated with one's people and their rohe or tribal territory. Tuhoe people living at Maungapohatu in the Urewera, for example, would, in place of a surname, recite their whakapapa back to Huti, progenitor of the hapu Tamakaimoana. At the same time they would declare the tribally identifying proverb, 'Tuhoe moumou kai, moumou taonga, moumou tangata ki te Po' (Tuhoe extravagant with food, with precious things, and with human life).

Individuals from outside could marry into a tribe and become part of the network of kinship privileges and obligations. Indeed, such marriages knitted together alliances which often served as a basis for neighbourly or inter-tribal co-operation, or for settling what had previously been mutually damaging disputes. But it was only the *descendants* of such a marriage who could be considered to have full membership of the tribe and the ability to pass such membership on to their descendants in turn.

Several words were and are used to denote tribe. One is iwi (whose meaning is also 'people' or 'bones', both stressing intimate relationship and connectedness); another is hapu (which also means 'pregnant'). In general usage, hapu came to refer to the smaller, more intimately related unit of tribe, and hence is sometimes translated as sub-tribe. And iwi referred more often to a wider unit, to which many hapu were related but among whose people they did not necessarily live. In the region south of Auckland, for example, Waikato would come to be identified as an iwi that took its name from the river that formed the valley in the centre of its rohe, whereas its many component tribes, such as Ngati Mahuta, Ngati Tipa, Ngati Whawhakia, who sometimes co-operated in common causes and sometimes fought one another, would be called hapu. Over them all, iwi and hapu, was the federal waka designation, which indicated that they were all descended from the crew of the Tainui canoe.

The reality of Maori life was scarcely ever as schematised or as 'tidy' as this model suggests, however. Individuals detached from their natural parents as a result of births from unsanctioned unions, bereavement, feuds or adoption might move between or among hapu and iwi. New hapu might form and find territory of their own as the existing group became too numerous for the home locality, or as individual rangatira quarrelled with relations and led their immediate followers to places where there was relative safety or less stress on food and material resources. Sometimes such migrations led nascent hapu to districts well away from those of the tribe's previous habitation. A section of Ngapuhi in the far north of the country, for example, traced their descent from Mataatua tribes in the central Bay of Plenty.

There *was* social differentiation, and this may have become stronger over the time that Maori were isolated from their Polynesian kin, with whom they shared the notion that humankind could be divided into aristocrats (rangatira) and commoners (tutua). Rangatira had more mana – more 'ancestral efficacy' and the authority that accompanied it – than did commoners. That mana was to a large extent inherited and, if those who possessed it led socially responsible lives or accomplished memorable deeds, it was enlarged. The qualities of mana and tapu (personal 'sacredness' or 'untouchability') were regarded as manifest more intensely in those rangatira who possessed the status of ariki or paramount aristocrats. Such leaders, bound by all the spiritual complications that surrounded intensified tapu, most often 'presided' as focal points for community identity and loyalty rather than actively leading their people in war or peace. Their words would be influential in determining tribal strategies, however, for they were seen as potential intermediaries between deities and humankind and between ancestors and descendants.

These categories too were flexible rather than immutable. All commoners had rangatira links somewhere in their ancestry, and these could be activated by outstanding achievement in the arts of war or peace. Some members of rangatira families lost their status as a result of disregarding community responsibilities or severe social offending – mana was as easily diminished as it was aggregated. Defeated and captured rangatira became slaves, but they could regain their former status if they succeeded in escaping from their captors or eventually obtaining an honourable release. On the other hand, some who lost mana became so dispirited that they declined physically and psychically and died.

Another way that rangatira or tutua could enlarge their mana was by becoming tohunga or experts in activities of a physical, artistic or spiritual nature. The word itself meant 'chosen'. Those who became tohunga did so not simply voluntarily, but because they displayed aptitudes at an early age which indicated to their elders that they had been chosen by deities to perform particular functions (perhaps fishing, carving, tattooing or genealogical recitation). The promising candidates were then, of course, chosen again by mentors who ensured that latent talent was enhanced by specific knowledge and training.

The country as a whole was divided into a notional network of rohe over which particular iwi and hapu held mana whenua or authority over the land and its resources. Such rohe were most often delineated by geographical features such as mountains, rivers and valleys, or by botanical markers such as forests or individually identified trees. Authority was established and consolidated by length of occupation, active exploitation of resources, and/or conquest of previous occupants. Those who did not belong to a particular district as a result of tribal membership or occupation needed permission to enter territory that was not their own and to make use of its food or mineral deposits. Failure to seek and obtain such authorisation within a context of reciprocity could provide a pretext for punishment of an individual or for inter-group warfare.

For all the differences of status within Te Ao Maori – between ariki and rangatira, between rangatira and commoner, between tohunga and those who were not so chosen, between slaves and everybody else, between tangata whenua (people of a particular place) and tau iwi (people from elsewhere), between men and women, adults and children – for all these differences, pre-European Maori society was relatively homogeneous. Despite tribalism and a strong sense of regional identity, the basic concepts and values of the culture were recognised and accepted from one end of the country to the other. The very language spoken was, despite regional and dialectal variations, the same everywhere. A person from Muriwhenua in the far north could, if necessary, make himself or herself understandable to people from Murihiku in the far south.

The twin dynamics driving this society were those that had contributed most to the formation of the tribal pattern: competition for resources and the pursuit of mana. When people lived in kinship-based communities with an ample sufficiency of resources to support life, then there was every prospect that life would be settled and secure – unless a competing neighbouring group coveted those resources or believed that they had a contestable right to gain access to them; or unless some members of the home group had diminished, or appeared to diminish, the mana of their neighbours. In either situation, violence might ensue as the party which viewed itself as wronged took combative action to correct an imbalance or to drive competitors off disputed territory.

The recognised mechanism for regulating such behaviour was the concept of utu – often translated into English as 'revenge', but more properly meaning 'reciprocity' or 'balanced exchange'. Utu determined that relations among individuals, and between families, communities and tribes, were governed by mutual obligation and an implicit keeping of social accounts: a favour bestowed, which increased the mana of the donor, required an eventual favour in return from the recipient; and an insult by one, real or imagined, also activated an obligation to respond in kind.

In many respects, and in many places, 'positive utu' ensured social stability, particularly within the community or hapu: favours given led to favours returned; koha or gifts offered, to koha received; gifts of resources in which one group was rich, such as basalt or muttonbirds, to an acceptance of other resources within the gift of neighbours in which one was not rich. In this manifestation, utu laid the basis for co-operative and trading relationships. Where the equation embraced negatives, however – the unauthorised use of a section of forest for hunting, the passing of an insult, the rape of a female relation – then the response might be a martial one, depending on the wounded party's view of damage to mana. As Angela Ballara has noted, warfare was a 'learned, culturally determined [response] to offences against the rules of Maori society.' In such circumstances utu was not an option – it was an obligation.

Because it was intimately connected with the quality of day-to-day life, and to all-important matters of individual and group mana, this process of social accounting engaged considerable attention in Maori communities. When the balance of generosity or power was in your favour, your own mana and that of your people was enlarged; when you were considered in debit to your neighbours, and *knew* that you were so considered, your mana was diminished. Living and planning for living was not simply a matter of ensuring that individuals and groups had access to sufficient food to physically nourish community life; it was also a matter of levelling any perceived imbalance of utu in your favour. Sometimes this required war with neighbours or more distant adversaries, and if you were successful in combat then you rectified what you had regarded as an imbalance. If your neighbours shared your view of the circumstances that led to conflict, you may also have rectified matters in their eyes too. If they did not, then the outcome of the most recent engagement became yet another wrong to be righted at some time in the future, possibly years or even generations distant (when Ngapuhi tribes came to possess muskets ahead of other Maori in the early nineteenth century, they set about settling scores that were in some instances many decades old).

So long as Maori possessed only hand-to-hand weapons and lacked large quantities of portable food, warfare was probably not endemic. It usually took place in the summer months, and often resulted in the deaths of no more than a handful of combatants (there were exceptions, such as the prolonged campaign of the Marutuahu federation of Tainui tribes for mana whenua over parts of the Coromandel Peninsula, and the Hingakaka or 'fall of parrots' battle between Waikato–Maniapoto and the west coast tribes of Tainui in the 1800s, in which thousands of men are said to have fought). Nor were all Maori forever at war with all other Maori. When James Cook encountered New Zealanders for the first time in the eighteenth century, he observed that some of them, at Anaura Bay on the East Coast of the North Island, for example, lived in 'profound peace', without fortifications of any kind; at other places, such as the eastern Bay of Plenty, he found the population clustered in fortified pa apparently in a state of constant readiness for war.

The need for such 'readiness', which could be a symptom of a current 'active' dispute or, in the case of Cook's observations, a reaction to his presence, was unlikely to be continuous. The very existence of fortified pa was often a sign that those who lived near such complexes sought to discourage attack and wanted to make conflict *less* likely, not more so. In other words, there were times when tribes were at war – and almost every tribe that survived into the post-European era had traditions about past combat. But there were also periods, often lengthy, when communities lived without war, cultivating their gardens, foraging for seafood or bird meat, trading with their neighbours, making stone and bone artefacts, building or renovating houses and canoes.

These communities ranged from single extended families, to a handful of households, to quite large hapu groups of up to and over 500 people. Usually they were based close to water and food resources and to cultivations. Sometimes communities continued to move seasonally among hunting, foraging and gardening stations as they had in the Maori colonial era. Horeta Te Taniwha, who met James Cook in Mercury Bay in 1769, for example, was there because his relations came over the range each year from Coromandel Harbour to garden on the more favourable soils and sites on the eastern side of the peninsula.

While, as we have seen, warfare may not have been endemic, it was normal and prudent in the North Island for kainga or 'living' sites to be close to fortified hilltop pa sites to which communities could retreat in the event of combat or threat of combat. Many of these pa were elaborately constructed, with ditches, banks and palisades and an interior stronghold, and they often proved impregnable to sieges, which in any case rarely lasted long because of the shortage of easily portable and preserved food to support an invading party. Such man-made, or 'man-modified', defences were among the features of Maori life that evolved in a more extensive and more complex manner in New Zealand than elsewhere in Polynesia. Moreover, the intelligence, strategic sense and versatility they exemplified had consequences for Maori relations with European colonisers in the nineteenth century.

At times when warfare was absent, Maori life was organised predominantly around food growing, foraging, tool-making, and maintenance of dwellings, canoes and pa sites. Cultivation was carried out communally, with men most often responsible for clearing land and digging, and women for planting and weeding. Foraging too – fishing, shellfish gathering, birding and harvesting fern root (a primary source of starch, especially in southern areas where kumara could not be grown) – was most often performed communally and seasonally. The seasons were determined either by supply, as certain plants, birds and fish were available only at particular times of the year, or by the need to conserve supplies (Maori learned, after the disappearance of big-game birds and seals, to harvest remaining resources sustainably). When certain items became scarce, they were likely to have a rahui or prohibition placed on them by the priestly tohunga until the resource was replenished.

Such tohunga, or 'chosen ones', held high status as mediators between deities and humankind, and as the people who knew the incantations to propitiate the forces of nature, invoke protection, heal, and, in some instances, bring misfortune on others by the use of makutu or black magic. Other tohunga were able to achieve mana as specialists of other kinds. Carvers, for example, were greatly admired and valued. The skill of their work on wood – door lintels, house gables, canoe prows – increased the mana of the whole community and also enhanced protection by representing or further propitiating gods. This art form too, created entirely with stone tools until the late eighteenth century, reached heights of intricacy and delicacy seldom seen elsewhere in the Pacific. The ability to work stone and bone was also prized, for the production of essential tools such as adzes and fishhooks, and for the quality of ornaments such as pendants and hei tiki. New Zealand pounamu (jade or greenstone) was especially valued for the production of fine chisels and as a material for personal ornaments. Like Polynesians elsewhere, Maori had no access to metals prior to the eighteenth century.

Tattooing was another form of personal decoration that developed and became more elaborate with the passage of time. Men were marked, or more accurately incised, primarily on the face and buttocks, women largely on the face and breasts. Only in the Marquesas Islands did this practice achieve comparable intricacy, with patterns apparent in both positive and negative aspects. The Maori practice of the art was eventually distinguished by the use of a straight blade in preference to the serrated chisels which have been excavated from early Maori sites. The serrated blades injected pigment into the skin; the straight ones introduced the pigment but also left a grooved scar that was more like carving in appearance than it was like tattooing in other parts of the world. This was yet another instance of tribal Maori culture differing from both its culture of origin and Maori colonial usage.

Spiritual tohunga, carvers, canoe-builders and tattooists were, almost without exception, men. Women were believed to noa or contaminate the tapu that surrounded these activities. Gender distinctions were apparent also in the practice of another craft. Only women prepared flax for weaving – gathering leaves of the plant, stripping out the fibres, softening and colouring them – and wove it. While early Maori had brought paper mulberry with them to New Zealand, and it was still being cultivated in Mercury Bay when James Cook was there in 1769, the inadequacy of bark clothing in New Zealand conditions made the working of flax – and the making of garments worn as rapaki or kilts and as cloaks, and mats used to cover the floors of dwellings – of enormous importance to the culture, and the skills of women expert in the craft were highly valued.

On the whole, social *mores* gave greater weight to men's roles than to women's. In most places, leadership was based on male rather than female primogeniture. Both sexes could inherit rangatira status, mana and tapu from male *and* female antecedents, and among some tribes, such as those on the East Coast of the North Island, women were visible among the front ranks as tribal and community leaders and spokespersons. Exceptional women took such roles in other rohe, such as those of Ngapuhi and Tainui. Early European observers noted some mistreatment of Maori wives by husbands, but that may not have been a common social feature (and the wives concerned may have been taken from the ranks of slaves). Children were generally well treated and indeed indulged by their own relations. Outside this context, though, little more mercy was shown to women and children than to adult men in times of inter-group conflict. As Maori oral tradition recorded, and ancient burials have confirmed, elderly people, women and children, along with defeated male warriors, were periodic subjects for torture, killing and cannibalism.

One burial site confirming such practices was found in a rock cleft at Palliser Bay on the southern Wairarapa coast. The cleft held the remains of four small children and a man.

He was about 50 years old, regarded highly enough to have food especially prepared for him over the ten years since he lost his teeth ... [Lines] in his bones show that he suffered famine for thirteen successive years in his childhood, but he survived to become a strong and active adult – a worker and a warrior. His arm bones were fractured three times, presumably by enemy weapons. The fact that he survived these fights may suggest that the enemies suffered even more.

But one day . . . the old warrior's foes caught up with him. They seem to have raided his village while the fit adults were out fishing or foraging, and he was at home taking care of his grandchildren. A nine-month-old baby buried with him shows no evidence of illness; a two-year-old shows marks of violence; and we can guess that the four- and five-year-olds in the graves complete the list of victims. Their kin may have returned just too late to attempt a rescue. The two-year-old was mortally wounded, not killed outright, and might have survived long enough to die in its parents' arms. The burials were hidden, perhaps from fear that the enemy might return and desecrate them. This tale is no less tragic or human for being told in bones.

In contexts such as this, life for Maori in the highly competitive tribal era was sometimes brutish. And it was also, by modern standards – but not by those of the time – short. The average life span was probably no more than 30, and skeletal remains reveal that, nationwide, few men or women lived beyond their late 30s. To be in one's 40s was to acquire kaumatua (literally 'no father') or elder status. To reach 50 was exceptional. Such remains also reveal that quite a significant number of people suffered from malnutrition for parts of their lives, and that from their late 20s most would have been suffering from arthritis, and from infected gums and loss of teeth resulting from the staple diet of fern root and the residual sand in shellfish. The healthy-looking 'elderly' men James Cook commented on favourably in Queen Charlotte Sound in 1770 were probably only in their 40s.

Despite such harsh realities, and despite tribal competitiveness, regional identities and periodic warfare, trading among Maori as an extension of the reciprocity principle was highly developed. By the fifteenth century South Island Maori exported greenstone to other parts of the country or facilitated access to it by emissaries of North Island tribes. Bay of Plenty settlers continued to oversee the distribution of Mayor Island's fine-grained obsidian. Nelson and D'Urville Island residents quarried and distributed argillite. Food that was readily available in some districts but not in others, such as pigeon or titi (muttonbird), was preserved in fat in gourds or kelp bags and bartered. Maori were prepared to travel long distances for minerals and food. And, although ocean-going craft had disappeared from New Zealand by the eighteenth century, canoes were used extensively for river, lake or coastal transport in the course of trade.

That trade, as shown by the distribution of pounamu, basalt, obsidian and other minerals, extended the length of both major islands. And, by the seventeenth century, Maori had settled habitable parts of the country from Te Hiku-o-te-Ika, the Tail of Maui's Fish in the north of the country, to Rakiura in the far south.

Northern tribes, descended from various origin canoes, sometimes came together as the Aupouri or (further south) Ngapuhi federations to undertake joint enterprises or celebrate their inter-connectedness. At other times constituent parts of both federations might be at war. South of their rohe but still north of Auckland, Ngati Whatua were dominant. The tribes of Tainui waka held mana whenua from the east coast to the west immediately south of Auckland. Their southern boundaries pushed close to Ngati Tuwharetoa in the central North Island and to other tribes of the Te Arawa federation to the east of Ngati Tuwharetoa. Mataatua waka descendants such as Ngati Awa and Tuhoe were the major peoples in the central Bay of Plenty and inland from that coast. Out to the far west of the island the Taranaki tribes sometimes federated under the name and protection of their mountain, which was still occasionally erupting into the eighteenth century. Ngati Porou and the related iwi Ngati Kahungunu were major tribes down the East Coast of the North Island. Ngati Tara and Ngati Ira held mana whenua on the northern side of Cook Strait, which they knew as Raukawa Moana.

In the South Island, Rangitane were dominant to the immediate south of Cook Strait, and Taranaki people would migrate to the north-western corner. But the island as a whole, south of Kaikoura, was the rohe of Ngai Tahu, who migrated there from the North Island and fought and intermarried their way south in the seventeenth century, eventually absorbing their predecessors Ngati Mamoe and Waitaha. On the West Coast, the section of the tribe who came to be recognised as the guardians of the pounamu were known as Poutini Ngai Tahu.

According to their own traditions, some of the North Island tribes, such as Te Arawa and Tainui, had occupied their respective rohe from the time that the ancestral canoes had deposited founding populations. Other groups, however, had obtained and secured their territories through migration and fighting. The Marutuahu federation of tribes on the Coromandel Peninsula, for example, who were of Tainui origin, had had to fight their way into the region in the sixteenth century in the face of strong opposition from older tangata whenua groups, Ngati Hei and Ngati Huarere. Ngati Huarere were virtually destroyed as an independent iwi by this martial holocaust. Their experience was not untypical of tribes who suffered heavy defeats and who were eventually absorbed by their victors – and so, having no one to tell their stories, disappeared from Maori oral tradition and therefore from history.

In total, the occupants of the physical domains of Te Ika a Maui and Te Wai Pounamu and the spiritual and cultural domain of Te Ao Maori probably numbered around 100,000 to 110,000 by the eighteenth century AD.* The competitiveness of the culture meant that there was a constant need to remain alert against possible attack, and hence the retention of fortified pa near most centres of population. But, 400 or 500 years distant from the era of widespread ocean voyaging, New Zealand Maori were now insulated by distance from Island Polynesia and from envoys from Europe who were beginning to intrude on the central Pacific domain. They were, in effect, the last major human community on Earth untouched and unaffected by the wider world.

Apart from the times of sporadic inter-tribal conflict, when existence was threatened by violence, enslavement or death, life would have been as culturally rich and as physically pleasant as anywhere else on Earth in comparably neolithic times. But the balances and certitudes developed over at least five centuries of occupation of New Zealand would be tested in the seventeenth century and seriously challenged in the eighteenth. Then at last Europeans would succeed in perforating the membrane of distance and introducing Maori to the rest of their species – and to all the cultural, technological and pathogenic impedimenta carried by humankind as a whole.

----

* 100,000 was James Cook's estimate of the Maori population in 1769–70; it is also the estimate of modern demographer Ian Pool, who believes that, if this figure is not correct, it would be slightly on the high side. Extrapolating from other data, however, including the effects of the musket wars from 1818 to 1839, a slightly higher figure, 110,000, seems more likely.

7

Distance Perforated

Had Maori known of the existence of the rest of the terrestrial world in the seventeenth century, they might have found it strange – indeed, unbelievable – that their isolation was about to be ended by citizens of small countries located on the opposite side of the globe.

What about the neighbouring Polynesians with their former traditions of widespread ocean voyaging? What about the ancient culture of China, which as recently as the fifteenth century had possessed an enormous navy? What of the Tamils, the Moguls, the great civilisations of the Middle East, all of them older and geographically closer to the South Pacific than Europe? Why was it Europeans who were extending and attempting to take control of the known world?

To all of which, of course, there is no easy answer. Most West European nations in the seventeenth and eighteenth centuries were gripped by an ethos of expansion every bit as powerful as that which propelled Polynesians out into and around the Pacific in earlier centuries. But with that ethos, in the case of Europe, came a post-Renaissance explosion of learning in philosophy and science, an evolving maritime and military technology that allowed the export and movement of weaponry superior to that in other parts of the world, a sense of God-given racial and cultural superiority over other peoples, and an immunity to the diseases they carried, which had the power to lay waste peoples whose long isolation from the Eurasian continent meant that they lacked such immunity.

To this volatile and powerful combination, reduced by one historian to the phrase 'guns, germs and steel', Maori would eventually prove to be as vulnerable as the peoples of North and South and Central America, the continent of Australia and the rest of the Pacific. Fortunately for Maori, and thanks only to the relative isolation of New Zealand and the vicissitudes of history, the full force of Europe's colonising ethos did not arrive in one vast ocean swell. Instead it was ripples of the waves from other centres of military, commercial and scientific activity that lapped New Zealand's shore. And that, initially, was a phenom-enon with which Maori could cope.

The first ripple, and with it the first opportunity to open a datable, chronological history of New Zealand, was an eddy of the commercial aspirations of the Dutch East India Company in the string of large islands north of Australia then known as the East Indies. On 13 December 1642 Abel Janszoon Tasman, commander of a two-ship company expedition, sailed over the western rim of the sea that would eventually bear his name. '[Towards] noon,' he wrote, 'saw a large land, uplifted high ... southeast from us about 15 miles, made our course ... direct for [it].' What he saw was the mountainous west coast of the South Island off a promontory now known as Perpendicular Point, a little north of Punakaiki.

Tasman and his 110 sailors and soldiers were 121 days out of the port of Batavia (Jakarta in post-colonial Indonesia). They had sailed west to Mauritius, then east towards the continent of Australia, then known to Europeans only by parts of its northern and western coasts. Their instructions were to find the Unknown Southern Continent ('Terra Australis Incognita') which cartographers and geographers believed filled the southern centre of the Pacific Ocean to balance landmasses in the northern hemisphere. But Tasman's primary responsibility was not cartographical. It was to seek opportunities for trade in gold and silver, spices and fabrics. And if the expedition discovered precious metals and minerals, Tasman was to represent himself 'not to be too eager for [them] in order to keep the wild savages unaware of the value of the same'.

Heading east from Mauritius, Tasman's vessels had managed to miss entirely the southern mainland of Australia, but did brush the south and eastern coast of the island which the expedition called Van Diemen's Land, after the governor-general of Batavia, but which would later be called Tasmania. There the crew found signs of human habitation but failed to see the 'wild savages', who appear to have concealed themselves. In any case, the Dutchmen had been warned by their East India Company masters that 'no barbarous people are to be trusted [so] you must always be well armed and carefully on guard ...'

Eight days sailing from Van Diemen's land they then beheld the cloud-covered alpine spine of the island known to its inhabitants as Te Wai Pounamu. There too no 'wild savages' took to the water to greet them and, indeed, the coastline before them was harbourless and dangerous to ships under sail. The two vessels, Tasman's flagship *Heemskerck* and an armed transport, the *Zeehaen*, then tacked north. Four days later, about two kilometres off Whanganui Inlet, Tasman 'saw in various places smoke rise where fire was made by the inhabitants'. This was the earliest indication that the expedition had been sighted by Maori, who were about to become, for the first time, characters in narratives other than their own stories.

The following day, 18 December 1642, the ships rounded the massive sickle of Farewell Spit and anchored in the bay Maori knew as Taitapu. We have no record of what the people there, Ngati Tumatakokiri, made of the spectacle of the three-masted vessels and their billowing sails. What they saw would have been as unfamiliar to them as extraterrestrials approaching in spaceships, and possibly as frightening. Up to this time they had had no reason to suspect that there were people in the world who looked different, or who thought and behaved differently, from themselves. According to their own stories, they were humankind, and all of humankind. Who, then, were these strangers?

For what followed, we have only the accounts of the Dutch witnesses. Ngati Tumatakokiri, themselves originally invaders from the north, were attacked by waves of descending North Island tribes in the eighteenth and early nineteenth centuries and annihilated as an iwi. They left no descendants to transmit coherent versions of the first encounter between New Zealand Maori and European people whose beliefs and technologies had propelled them halfway around the globe to discover, explore, assert and lay claim.

The Dutch journals make the cause and course of what happened clear enough, however. In the thickening dusk of 18 December, two double-hulled canoes packed with Maori put out from shore to inspect the ships. '[They began] to call out to us in a gruff hollow voice but we could not in the least understand any of it; [they] blew also many times on an instrument which

gave sound like the moors trumpets ... [We] had one of our
sailors ... blow back to them in answer ... those of the Zeehaen
[did] likewise.'

Given what we know about similar encounters in the
following century, it is likely that the locals were asserting
their identity and mana and raising their own morale by
challenging the visitors to fight. The Maori convention was to
take the offensive in an uncertain situation so as to encourage
themselves and discourage an adversary, and thus make their
own survival more likely. It was by this time a long-established
code of behaviour that would have been comprehensible to
other Maori.

It was not comprehensible to Tasman's men, however, who
failed to recognise that a highly specific protocol had been set
in motion. Dutch trumpeters from both vessels had returned
the Maori calls made from pukaea, long wooden trumpets –
imagining, perhaps, that this would establish a basis for
congenial mutuality. In the Maori view, however, all that
happened was that a challenge to fight had been issued and
accepted. The outcome was inevitable but, as far as the Dutchmen were concerned, wholly unexpected.

> On 19th in the morning early a vessel of this people having in it
> 13 men approached our ships ... [They] were, as far as we could
> see, of ordinary height but rough in voice and bones, their colour
> between brown and yellow, had black hair [topknots] right on
> top of the crown of the head ... upon which stood a large thick
> white feather ... [Their] clothing was (so it appeared) some mats,
> others cottons [probably beaten bark] ...

When the *Zeehaen*'s cockboat was being rowed from the
Heemskerck back to its mother ship, another canoe also
containing thirteen Maori rammed it. '[They] dashed over the

same violently ... on which violence 3 of the Zeehaen's people were killed and the fourth through the heavy blow was mortally injured ... After this ... detestable affair we ... diligently fired our muskets and guns ... but we did not hit them ...'

The body of one dead crewman was taken ashore by Maori, possibly to be cooked and eaten, a ritual means of absorbing the mana of a vanquished foe ('the first of many European imports consumed in New Zealand was a dead Dutchman', James Belich would write). Tasman's instructions were specific about not engaging in warfare with local peoples, so he ordered his vessels to depart ('we could not expect to make here any friendship with these people').

As the crews raised anchors and sails, however, eleven more canoes, 'swarming with people', pushed off from shore and came at them with speed. The locals clearly thought that they had gained the upper hand and were keen to deliver the *coup de grâce*. When the first canoe got close to the *Zeehaen* the Dutch crew began to fire at it and felled a man standing in the bow. At which point the Maori flotilla dropped back and allowed the European vessels to depart without further pursuit.

Sailing away, Tasman called the place Murderers' Bay. Two hundred years later British settlers renamed it Golden Bay – not after the beaches on the southern shoreline replete with golden sand, but after an accidental discovery of gold in the area, the very metal Tasman had been instructed to give priority to finding.

The Tasman expedition's merchant and artist, Isaac Gilsemans, drew a sketch of the mortal encounter which, as an engraving, would eventually enter world literature as the first published representation of New Zealand Maori. To the modern eye, there is nothing especially Polynesian about the appearance of the men who fill the canoes (no women were sighted).

This is not surprising. Gilsemans may not have been sufficiently close to the locals to recognise individual or detailed features (the faces, for example, are without tattoo). Other illustrations from the same voyage indicate that most of Gilsemans's human figures tended towards the generic rather than the specific. What is clear is that some of the canoes, lashed together, were double-hulled for greater capacity and stability, at least one had a triangular sail, and the men, some bearded, some not, had their hair pulled upwards in topknots. Most were naked above some kind of loin covering. One man standing, perhaps the person of authority who had been shot, wore some kind of cloak from the shoulders.

Out of Murderers' Bay, the Dutchmen failed to confirm the existence of the passage of water between the country's principal islands, whose presence was suggested by a powerful flow of water. They sailed up the desert-like west coast of the North Island, sighting nowhere safe enough to risk a landing. There *were* harbours, including two major ones, the Manukau and the Kaipara. But Tasman was too far out to sea to recognise the entrances. Much of his map of this coast was reconstructed from sightings north and south of the features marked. Because of cloud cover, they missed Mount Taranaki, but did see Karioi south of Raglan. Gilsemans's coastal profile drawings which accompanied the ship's journal show that the crews did sight the opening of Kawhia Harbour, but failed to investigate it as a potential entrance to sheltered waters. They did see Maori again, 30 to 35 of them on the ridge of Great King Island off the northern tip of the North Island. The reported gigantic size of these figures may have resulted from the use of early Dutch telescopes, which were insufficiently refined to give an undistorted view. Again crew members were unable to land, partly because of surf and currents and partly, perhaps, because the now-gigantic inhabitants, throwing stones and shouting at the Dutchmen, had become demonised in their European imaginations.

And so they abandoned the country on 6 January 1643 without having once set foot on it. Tasman took his expedition north and 'discovered' some of the islands in the Tonga group and others in the northern sector of Fiji. He eventually returned to Batavia via the northern coast of New Guinea. Having failed to step ashore on New Zealand, Tasman had no reason to suppose that it was the cornucopia of spices, precious metals and cloths that his principals in the Dutch East India Company had been seeking. Because of the supposed absence of exploitable and tradable resources, and the apparently intransigent character of the inhabitants, New Zealand would be left to its isolation by the envoys of Europe for more than a century – though Tasman's map of the country's west coast, bearing, as one historian put it, some resemblance to a ragged question mark, would now appear on charts of the world. Its location there would tantalise navigators of the future and leave open the possibility that Terra Australis Incognita spread further east and inland from the littoral the Dutchman had traced.

Tasman called the new country Staten Land, because he speculated that it might be the western extremity of the Staten Land off the south-west coast of South America named by his countryman Jacob Le Maire in 1616. When late in 1643 this was perceived to be impossible – the South American location having been identified by Hendrik Brouwer as an island – an anonymous cartographer in the Dutch East India Company renamed Tasman's line of coast 'Nieuw Zeeland' or, in Latin, 'Zelandia Nova'. This was clearly intended as a matching name for 'Hollandia Nova', by which the western coast of Australia was at that time known (Holland and Zeeland being neighbouring Dutch maritime provinces).* It was over the name Zelandia Nova that the newly recognised country appeared on European charts of the Pacific Ocean and the known world from the middle of the seventeenth century. By the late eighteenth century, this scratch of coastline would be identified variously as New Zeeland, New Zeland and, eventually, New Zealand.

With Tasman's departure, the inhabitants of Zelandia Nova had no further recorded contact with Europeans for another 126 years, sufficient time for the Dutchmen's visit to recede into the mythology of Ngati Tumatakokiri and to leave no impression at all on the oral traditions of other tribes. And since Ngati Tumatakokiri eventually disappeared without recording their recollections and understanding of what they saw in Taitapu in December 1642, those insights were lost to history for ever.

Nor was Tasman himself much better recalled three and a half centuries later by Pakeha New Zealanders or the descendants of his fellow countrymen, though they at least had narratives based on his journal by which to remember him. They also had, in the land he discovered for Europe, mountains, a glacier and one national park named after him. But only three of the placenames he bestowed survive on the map of modern New Zealand; and the few discreet memorials commemorating his offshore movements there appear to be in the 'wrong' places. Even a statue raised to his memory by the Dutch community in

---

* The eventual conversion of the Dutch name into English should have been 'New Sealand'. The spelling incorrectly adopted misled some commentators into supposing an historical connection with Denmark, whose principal island has also assumed the form Zealand in English. In 1990 a Maori activist, Titewhai Harawira, went to the Netherlands to ask the Dutch authorities to reclaim the name New Zealand in order to facilitate the country's reversion to a Maori name. She was unsuccessful. In any case, there was no unanimity among Maori as to what that name should be.

New Zealand in 2000 had been recycled from an earlier exhibition in Barcelona.

Like James Cook, the navigator who eventually followed him into that same corner of the south-west Pacific, Tasman was largely unprivileged and worked his way up the ranks from common sailor by virtue of what he learned at sea. Unlike Cook, however, the Dutchman was never perceived as a hero or a role model for other mariners. The best that can be said of and for him, perhaps, is the verdict of John Beaglehole, the great historian of the European exploration of the Pacific and citizen of the country Tasman discovered for the wider world.

> Greatness is a relative term, and one would not wish to bestow it upon Tasman unmodified. He was not a great leader; he has left no legend. Of his character indeed we know but little ... rough probably, well salted from the southern sprays, eyes set in a skin seamed with intent gazing, with a voice that had borrowed more from the tempest than from converse with the polite ... probably he was respected more than loved by his subordinates. But respect he must have, the respect due to at least first-rate professional competence.

8

The Arrival of Europe

Like a meteorite which appears, flares and disappears, Abel Tasman's short encounter with New Zealand and its inhabitants in the summer of 1642–43 left no lasting imprint. For the Maori of Golden Bay and the Three Kings Islands, Tasman's ships and men constituted a brief exotic vision of unrecognisable people and incomprehensible technologies that were, literally, visible one day and gone the next.

More than 126 years later, however, there was an umbilically linked sequel. In Tahiti in July 1769, Lieutenant James Cook of the British Royal Navy completed his observation of the transit of the planet Venus across the face of the sun. He then opened secret Admiralty instructions to sail south until he either discovered Terra Australis Incognita or else 'fall in with the Eastern side of the Land discover'd by Tasman and now called New Zeland'. Cook carried out these instructions. And his rediscovery of New Zealand was an encounter of a very different order from Tasman's.

In a six-month-long circumnavigation of the country in the barque *Endeavour*, a converted North Sea collier, James Cook met with Maori on dozens of occasions, on board ship and in their settlements ashore. He even sailed 20 km up the Waihou River at the head of the Hauraki Gulf and into the interior of the country. Thanks to the presence of the Tahitian ariki Tupaia, who had boarded the *Endeavour* at Raiatea and learned sufficient English to communicate with the ship's master and crew, Cook was also able to communicate with the New Zealanders and thus allow a transfer of information in both directions across the same cultural divide that Tasman, with disastrous consequences, had been unable to bridge. As Anne Salmond has noted, 'not only did the Europeans have extensive opportunities to observe Maori life in different parts of the country, Maori people of various tribes had the first opportunity to examine Europeans at close quarters – to trade with them, to fight with them, to become infected with European diseases and to work out strategies for dealing with [them]'.

The first New Zealanders compelled to devise such strategies were Rongowhakaata people of the East Coast of the North Island. Some of them, when they saw the *Endeavour* in Poverty Bay on 8 October 1769, believed it to be a floating island; others suspected it was a giant bird. Both phenomena, floating islands and birds, featured in their mythology and such identifications fitted what they saw into the cosmography with which they were familiar. Like the Ngati Tumatakokiri people of Golden Bay, however, Poverty Bay Maori paid a price for confronting the unknown visitors. When a Maori party approached the *Endeavour*'s pinnace ashore on the bank of the Turanganui River and ceremonially challenged the crew, a sailor judged their intention to be hostile and shot one man dead. The following day another local was killed for snatching a sword from an Englishman and brandishing it menacingly.

Cook, son of a humble farm labourer and a plain Yorkshire-man of modest learning but considerable humanity, regretted these casualties, neither of which he had ordered. He was carrying instructions from the Earl of Morton, President of the Royal Society, which had described native populations of the places he might visit as 'human creatures, the work of the same omnipotent Author, equally under his care with the most polished European ... No European nation has the right to occupy any part of their country ... without their voluntary consent.' After only a fortnight off the New Zealand coast, Cook's naturalist Joseph Banks noted that a canoe-load of potential aggressors had dropped astern after the Englishmen had fired over their heads: 'not I believe at all frightened,' Banks said, 'but content with having shewd their courage by twice insulting us. We now begin to know these people and are much less afraid ...' Unlike Tasman, Banks and Cook recognised that bravado was an inherent element in Maori competitiveness and capacity for survival. After such exchanges, assured of both their own courage and their own safety, New Zealanders were often willing to accept offers of friendship and to settle down to bartering, a process close to the Maori custom of reciprocity and recognised in most parts of the country that the Englishmen visited.

Cook's circumnavigation and mapping of New Zealand – 'precise, comprehensive and consistent', in the later words of one Cook scholar – represented an expert feat of seamanship and cartography. He determined the proportions and shape of the country with considerable accuracy, mistaking only Banks Peninsula for an island and Stewart Island for a possible penin-sula. In this manner, alongside his immediately subsequent mapping of the east coast of Australia, Cook largely disposed of the myth of Terra Australis Incognita and established that

Tasman's single line of cartographic scrawl was in fact an indication of the two principal islands of New Zealand. He recognised the relationship of Maori culture to that of the Tahitians, and deduced rightly that the two peoples must share a source of origin.

With Banks and the ship's artists, Cook began the process of documenting the language and material culture of Maori in the eighteenth century. The corpus of knowledge which he and his men assembled on all his visits to New Zealand would be a boon to scientists, historians and anthropologists for the next 200 years. Cook's sober but positive reports on the resources of the country, especially its timber and flax, its seals in the southwest and the quantity of whales in the surrounding seas, led directly to a quickening of British interest in New Zealand and to the establishment of extractive industries there in the late eighteenth and nineteenth centuries.

In the course of his three voyages and four visits to the country (two in 1773–74), Cook spent a total of 328 days off or on the coast of New Zealand. For Maori, the consequences were far-reaching, although they did not immediately change the cultural pattern or the quality of day-to-day Maori life. The bartering introduced Maori to metals, especially in the form of nails, which were immediately sought after for their efficacy and long life in the form of chisels, gouges and fishhooks. Sexual encounters brought the unpleasant phenomenon of venereal disease to communities where Cook's crews stayed for longer periods, particularly in Queen Charlotte Sound. The Englishmen left vegetables, especially potatoes and turnips, which would become major items in the Maori diet and economy (just 20 years after Cook's visit to the Hauraki district, English ships' crews found an abundance of potato cultivations from Tapu south to Hikutaia). They introduced Maori to European firepower in the form of cannons and muskets, though Cook did not leave firearms in the country. And, thanks to the presence of Society Islands Polynesians – Tupaia on the first voyage, Hitihiti on the second and Mai (or Omai, as he was called) on the third – Cook's visits communicated to Maori the fact that a world wider than their own existed over the horizon, and that it was made up of other Polynesians as well as races, cultures and technologies that differed from their own.

Cook's relations with Maori were, on the whole, as cordial and mutually respectful as he could make them. On the first two voyages, in particular, he had been determined to act as an 'enlightened' leader. There *were* misunderstandings, and there were further shootings; and in 1773 ten crew members of the *Adventure*, the vessel accompanying Cook's ship *Resolution*, were killed and eaten at Grass Cove on Arapawa Island in Queen Charlotte Sound. When Cook learned of the episode and returned to the Sound on his third voyage, he did not respond punitively, believing that the cannibalised men may themselves have acted provocatively. He was told by Maori who took part in the killing that one of the sailors concerned had taken an adze from a would-be barterer, but offered nothing in return. The owner of the adze had then seized some food from the sailor, who retaliated. Thus was generated what became a mortal fight. It was typical of Cook that he took the trouble to find out what actually happened and, when he had done so, to act with restraint. Moreover, for the most part, he acted with moderation and with common sense in the course of all four visits to New Zealand. But he failed to do so in Hawai'i in 1779 in the circumstances that led to his death in Kealakekua Bay.

Cook was also responsible for transporting Maori, for the first time in probably 400 years, from New Zealand back to Island Polynesia. Te Weherua was a genial young man who attached himself to the navigator in Queen Charlotte Sound during Cook's final expedition. He insisted that he wanted to travel to Huahine with Omai, the Society Islander whom Tobias Furneaux had taken to London in 1774 and whom Cook was taking home again in 1777. After much pleading Cook agreed to the proposition, and Te Weherua and an even younger relation, Koa, travelled on the *Resolution* to the Cook Islands, Tonga, and eventually to the Society group. There, according to William Bligh, the two New Zealanders remained with Omai until about 1780, when their protector died. They too then died, apparently from grief. It would be another two decades – into the sealing and whaling era – before any Maori had opportunities to make comparable voyages.

In the twentieth century, some Maori, Polynesians and others would succumb to the 'fatal impact' view of history, which held that all European contact with Polynesians in the eighteenth century had been an almost unmitigated disaster for the peoples of the Pacific. According to this perspective, Cook was an icon of imperial history who carried with him the ideas that would eventually subvert those of indigenous cultures and colonise them, the technologies that would make indigenous tools and weapons redundant, and, even more disastrously, the pathogens that would eventually kill hundreds of thousands of people who had no immunity to them. 'His voyages epitomise the European conquest of nature, fixing the location of coastlines by the use of instruments and mathematical calculation, classifying and collecting plants, animals, insects and people.'

Most Maori who came into contact with Cook during his visits, however, particularly in Mercury Bay, the Bay of Islands and Queen Charlotte Sound, appeared to respect and admire him. While he was not given the ceremonial status of ariki in New Zealand, as he was in Tahiti and Hawai'i, Maori none the less recognised in him qualities that they regarded as rangatira or aristocratic. One and a half centuries after his voyages to New Zealand, the great Maori anthropologist Te Rangi Hiroa (Sir Peter Buck) would speak of him to another Maori leader as 'to tatau tipuna, ko Kapene Kuki' (our ancestor, Captain Cook). Horeta Te Taniwha of Ngati Whanaunga, who was a small boy when the *Endeavour* was in Mercury Bay in November 1769, reportedly told Lieutenant-Governor Robert Henry Wynyard in 1852:

> There was one supreme man in that ship. We knew that he was the lord of the whole by his perfect gentlemanly and noble demeanour. He seldom spoke, but some of the [crew] spoke much. But this man did not utter many words: all that he did was to handle our mats and hold our mere, spears, and wahaika, and touch the hair of our heads. He was a very good man, and came to us – the children – and patted our cheeks, and gently touched our heads.

Cook's view of Maori, in turn, was that they were 'of a Brave, Noble, Open and benevolent disposition . . .' Like his crew, Anne Salmond notes, Cook was affected by his encounters with Maori, 'surprised [by their] sexuality, infuriated by their attitudes to property, and shocked by . . . cannibalism'. But he was never in any doubt that they, like the Europeans they confronted, befriended and even wept over, were fully human – on each side there was 'savagery and kindness, generosity and greed, intelligent curiosity and stupidity'.

Unlike Tasman, Cook became and remained a hero in both the land of his birth and in at least two of the countries whose coasts he had charted, Australia and New Zealand. In the latter, more of his placenames were retained than those of any other European navigator or surveyor, and to those would be added the attachment of his own name to the country's highest peak (known to Maori as Aoraki), to the strait separating the North Island from the South, and to hundreds of other minor geographical features, communities, suburbs, streets, schools and hotels. Banknotes and consumer products too would bear his likeness.

All this was in part a recognition of his exceptional seamanship and cartographical skills (his charts remained in use well into the nineteenth century and in some instances into the twentieth), and of the fact that the scope of his voyages – from Europe to New Zealand and back, from Antarctic to Arctic, literally 'farther than any man has been before me' – were as worthy of marvel and celebration as the travels of Odysseus or the journeys of Polynesian star navigators. But even more, perhaps, the gestures of naming were an acknowledgement of the honest and humane way that Cook had, on the whole, dealt with indigenous peoples, and of his essential humanity. Posterity would also value the fact that he was a plain man, systematic and thorough, a 'genius of the matter of fact'. The greatest compliment his biographer John Beaglehole could pay him was that Cook 'saw and [by his own lights] reported truly', an understatement that would have been characteristic and worthy of the man himself.

One unexpected theme to emerge from New Zealand history of the eighteenth and nineteenth centuries was the close proximity of French colonial initiatives in the South Pacific to those of the British. In 1769, Cook's first expedition was followed closely by that of a French explorer. Jean de Surville sighted the North Island only two months after Cook's men and passed within 80 km of the *Endeavour* in the course of a storm and poor visibility off the country's north-east coast. De Surville remained two weeks in Doubtless Bay, where he was welcomed by local Maori, who were almost certainly better prepared for the visit by what they knew of Cook's recent contact with neighbouring people in the Bay of Islands. After his chaplain, a Dominican Catholic named Paul-Antoine Léonard de Villefeix, had conducted the first Christian service in New Zealand waters on Christmas Day 1769, de Surville left the country and took with him a Te Patupo chief named Ranginui, in retaliation for a Maori theft. Ranginui's death from scurvy off the coast of South America almost three months later prevented his becoming the first New Zealand Maori to visit a country other than his own and, possibly, becoming the first of his people to convert to Christianity.

The next European navigator to visit New Zealand, Marc-Joseph Marion du Fresne, was also French and brought two vessels around the Northland coast in April 1772. He put men ashore at Spirit's Bay and Tom Bowling Bay, and then proceeded to the Bay of Islands, where he and 26 of his crew were killed by Maori in June, apparently as a result of breaching tapu. In retaliation, and in the process of repelling further attacks, the surviving crew members levelled a village and killed between 200 and 300 local Maori. Julien Crozet, who led the punitive expedition, was moved to comment that 'there is amongst all the animals of creation none more ferocious and dangerous for human beings than the primitive and savage man ...' This outcome, like the burning of the vessel *Boyd* in Whangaroa Harbour in 1809 in retaliation for the mistreatment of a Maori crew member, emphasised the considerable potential for cross-cultural misunderstanding between Maori and European, and that the violent consequences of such misunderstanding could be catastrophic for both parties (as many as 70 Europeans may have been killed in the *Boyd* incident).

Other scientific or exploratory visits to New Zealand in the eighteenth century were brief and involved little or no contact with Maori: George Vancouver, who had been one of Cook's junior officers, was in Dusky Sound with two ships in 1791 en route for the north-west coast of America; Alessandro Malaspina took a Spanish expedition into Doubtful Sound in February 1793; and, the following month, the Frenchman Antoine Raymond Joseph Bruni d'Entrecasteaux paid an equally brief visit to Northland as part of a voyage in search of the missing navigator La Pérouse.

Vancouver's 1791 expedition had an unforeseen consequence: the discovery of the Chatham Islands, which would eventually become part of the fledgling state of New Zealand in 1842. Vancouver in the *Discovery* was accompanied by the brig *Chatham* commanded by Lieutenant William Broughton. As the two vessels headed away from New Zealand towards a rendezvous in Tahiti, they became separated by a severe storm. The *Chatham* was blown further east than its designated course, and early on the morning of 29 November 1791 the crew sighted the north-west corner of Chatham Island.

Broughton ordered the ship to sail eastwards along the island's northern coast while he mapped and named its features. By late morning they were off the small harbour known as Kaingaroa, and Broughton decided to go ashore with eight men in the ship's cutter. There, on that northern Chathams beach, they met a group of Moriori men and attempted to barter cloth and beads for Moriori tools and ornaments. A misunderstanding ensued and, when Moriori appeared to become threatening, Broughton's men fired muskets and killed a local man, Tamakaroro. Broughton and his men returned to the safety of their ship and sailed on to Tahiti, and thence to the north-west coast of America, where they secured the right of British merchants to harvest sea-otter furs.

What is most interesting about their encounter with

Chatham Islanders, perhaps, is that the Moriori view of what had occurred was a live part of the island's oral history when Europeans settled there in the nineteenth century. The people who had met Broughton and his men were members of the Wheteina or north-eastern Moriori tribe, and they had named Broughton Manu Katau (right-handed bird) and referred to him and his companions as 'people of the sun' on account of their light skins. Like Maori on mainland New Zealand, they interpreted what they saw in terms of their known experience and mythology. They believed, for example, that the rigging of the *Chatham* was fish nets. When they saw sailors smoking they said, 'See the fire of Mahuika proceeding from their throats.' They likened the sound of muskets to the cracking of whips made from bull kelp.

Moriori were a peaceful people who had, generations earlier, outlawed warfare. They believed that it was they, not the visitors, who had been responsible for the violence. At a subsequent council of all Moriori on Chatham Island, it was agreed that future visitors would be greeted with an emblem of peace. And when the next European vessel arrived a decade later, a sealer out of Port Jackson in New South Wales, Moriori, according to one of their chroniclers, 'laid down their spears and clubs ... and placed one end of a grass plant in the hands of the captain'. The man who performed this ceremony also 'made him a speech of welcome [and] threw over him his own cloak...' This became the standard Chathams welcome for visitors until 1835, when two Maori tribes took terrible advantage of the custom and colonised and enslaved the islanders.

All these early encounters between Maori and Europeans, and between Europeans and Moriori, contained the seeds for future patterns of racial and cultural relations in New Zealand in the nineteenth and twentieth centuries. In most respects, other than in technological development and knowledge of the wider world, Maori were more than a match for Europeans. They were lively and curious and the competitive dynamic of Maori tribal society, induced and sustained by the constant pursuit of mana, personal and corporate, made them versatile and adaptable and potentially strong allies, particularly when they managed to incorporate Europeans into their networks of mutual obligation.

But Maori would also be seen, as they were in the eyes of the surviving members of Marion du Fresne's expedition, as inconsistent, unreliable, even treacherous. This was because their vivacity and versatility were matched by a set of preoc-cupations – especially those involving mana, tapu and utu – that were different from those held by Europeans. Maori would take up many of the gifts which Western culture and technology had to offer (initially, metal for tools and European clothing; later, agricultural implements, a wider range of fruit and vegetables, literacy, and even Christianity). They would experiment with these things and turn them to Maori purposes, meeting Polynesian standards of relevance, often with results which were, for Europeans, surprising. If these tools and concepts did not meet Maori expectations, they were discarded; if they did, they would be used in distinctively Maori ways, to strengthen Maori values and institutions. Not for nothing would a well-known twentieth-century New Zealand poem about New Zealand history repeat the refrain, 'it was something different, something/ nobody [meaning no Europeans] counted on'.

Oddly, some of the most negative episodes in the course of these early cross-cultural encounters may have worked to New Zealand's long-term advantage. The deaths of Europeans on Tasman's, Marion du Fresne's and Cook's voyages were among the factors that led the British Government to establish its new penal colony in New South Wales in 1788 in preference to New Zealand. Australian Aboriginal people were assumed to be less martial than Maori, less organised and vigorous, and therefore easier to control in the operation of a colonial enterprise. This decision protected Maori from a concerted attempt at foreign colonisation of New Zealand for a further 50 years and gave them time to better adjust to the implications – the advantages and the disadvantages – of what would initially be a small European presence in their country. And *their* country it was to remain, unequivocally, until February 1840.

9

Maori Engage the World

Europe moved even closer to New Zealand with the establishment of the British penal colony at Port Jackson in 1788, and the satellite convict settlements on Norfolk Island (from 1789) and at Hobart (1803). But it was not simply the physical proximity of Europeans in those places that brought them into contact with the Maori world: it was very basic European needs in Europe. 'Wars in Europe created a demand for timber and flax,' Anne Salmond has noted, 'while European cities and machines required sea-mammal oil for lubrication and lighting.' She might have added the need for gentlemen in London to wear seal-fur hats. New Zealand just happened to be, at least initially, a rich source of all these commodities.

The consequences of both the new proximity of Europeans and the opportunities they brought for commercial activities were foreshadowed in the British Government's instructions to New South Wales Governor Arthur Phillip in 1788: that he take immediate steps to procure New Zealand timber and flax, both of which were essential commodities for a naval power and whose potential in New Zealand had been commended with such enthusiasm by James Cook and Joseph Banks. And yet there were, initially, brakes on such developments. The British East India Company had been granted a Crown monopoly on all trade in the Indian and western Pacific Oceans, and only the Royal Navy was exempt from this arrangement. The number of naval vessels at Phillip's disposal was limited, and it would take some years for independent entrepreneurs to establish themselves in the Australian colonies and to recruit labour from the small number of free workers available and the slowly growing pool of former convicts who had either earned their tickets of leave or managed to escape from servitude. The latter would eventually prove invaluable for such activities as sealing, because they wanted opportunities to work away from Hobart or Port Jackson (soon to be known as Sydney), where they might be recognised and apprehended.

As the eighteenth century merged into the nineteenth, Sydney and Hobart became major bases for sealing, whaling and trading throughout the wider region – either as home ports for Australian-based enterprises or for provisioning vessels from Britain, the United States and France. Having these bases in their own colonies hosting Royal Navy ships gave the British a strategic advantage over the Americans and French, both of whom were sporadically at war with Britain up to 1815, and at the same time intent on increasing their influence in the south-west Pacific.

The first Europeans actually to live in New Zealand were seamen who jumped ship from vessels out of Sydney in order to escape from despotic captains, leaky ships or lives which had been characterised up to that point by crime or misfortune (most appear to have been undischarged convicts on the run).

These individuals, who came to be known as Pakeha Maori, joined Maori communities in the Hauraki district, the Bay of Islands and Murihiku, and soon after in other parts of the country, took Maori wives, begat Maori offspring, lived according to Maori customary law and within the kinship network of mutual obligations. In some cases they took Maori moko or tattoo. Maori insulated them from the circumstances they wanted to turn their backs on. They gave Maori the benefit of whatever expertise they had in the arts of horticulture or animal husbandry, and they were available to act as mediators and interpreters when Maori communities were confronted with would-be traders, explorers or missionaries.

Few of the names of the earliest Pakeha Maori are remembered now, though some of them have contemporary Maori descendants. A handful of the next generation of their kind, Jacky Marmon and Frederick Maning in the Hokianga, John Rutherford in the Bay of Islands, Barnet Burns on the east coast of the North Island, ensured that they would be known to posterity by writing about their experiences (Rutherford with perhaps more fiction than veracity). Of the original Pakeha Maori, Thomas Taylor was one of four crew members who ran away from the Sydney-based vessel *Hunter* in the course of a timber-gathering expedition up the Waihou River in 1798. When he next saw Europeans, Taylor reported with some pride that he had taken a Maori partner and, thanks to his close association with the Ngati Paoa chief Te Haupa, he had accompanied Hauraki war parties inland in the intervening three years.

Two other known and early named Pakeha Maori were James Cavanagh, a convict who escaped from his ship near the Cavalli Islands in 1804, and George Bruce, another convict who absconded from the *Lady Nelson* in the Bay of Islands in 1806 and who became a 'brutal and unfaithful husband' to Atahoe, daughter of the Ngapuhi chief Te Pahi. There was at least one woman Pakeha Maori in the Bay of Islands at the same time, convict mutineer Charlotte Badger; and a Tahitian named Jem lived among the Aupouri people north of the Bay of Islands from about 1810.

It was seals in the south rather than timber in the north, however, that generated the first European commercial operation to New Zealand in the early 1790s. That too was driven by commercial considerations beyond New Zealand: in this case the willingness of the Chinese in Canton and Macau to accept sealskins in payment for the tea to which the English had become so addicted. James Cook had reported on the abundance of the New Zealand fur seal (*Arctocephalus forsteri*, named after one of the naturalists on his second voyage) on the south-west coast of the South Island. On the basis of that intelligence, the first Australian-based gang of sealers was dropped off in Dusky Sound by the vessel *Britannia* in 1792, a mere two decades after Cook's visit. They built the first European-style house in New Zealand before being collected the following year with 4500 seal skins. Other gangs followed in the same area in 1793, 1795, 1801 and 1803, and dozens more on that coast and into Foveaux Strait and around Stewart Island between 1803 and 1810.*

The conditions to which the sealers were subjected were harsh. They would be dumped on often inhospitable coastlines with minimal supplies and left to fend for themselves for months at a time. It was expected that, in addition to killing and flensing seals and treating the skins, they would live off the land and shoot what game they could (the options being limited largely

---

* The reason for the brief gap in visits to New Zealand between the late 1790s and the early 1800s was the discovery of the Bass Strait seal colonies in 1797.

to seals and birds). Sometimes they were sufficiently long in one place to grow vegetables, but usually on exposed sites with poor soil. Sometimes they overlapped with South Island Maori who were also on foraging expeditions. After 1810 there were violent clashes in which people on both sides were killed, the worst of them at the so-called 'Murdering Beach' near Otago Harbour in 1814 and 1817.

Indirectly, sealing was responsible for the establishment of the first European community in New Zealand, albeit a transitory one. That first gang in Dusky Sound, fearing that they had been forgotten, began to build a vessel to transport themselves back to Sydney. They were collected in 1793, however, and left the half-built ship on blocks. In 1795 another vessel arrived in the sound, the *Endeavour* (not to be confused with Cook's barque of the same name). Its master intended to finish the half-built boat and catch seals to finance the voyage. In the event *Endeavour* sank in Facile Harbour, thus becoming New Zealand's first known shipwreck, and 244 people were stranded in Dusky Sound, an astonishing 46 of them convict stowaways, and at least two, Elizabeth Bason and Anne Grey, women. They were forced to live off the land, or more accurately the sea, in a far from hospitable environment. Most of the group got away the following year, by which time the uncompleted ship had been made seaworthy and *Endeavour's* longboat converted into a second vessel. The remaining 35 half-starved survivors were not rescued until May 1797.

The peak time for successful sealing on the New Zealand coast was the first decade of the nineteenth century. The vessel *Favorite* took over 80,000 skins from Foveaux Strait in 1805. But 'so ruthlessly and thoughtlessly' was this slaughter accomplished that within a very few years there were no more large cargoes of skins to be taken from the former mainland rookeries.

As one historian has noted, each operator reasoned that, if he did not take every animal he found, the next gang would. The sealers' attention then turned to the Chathams and the sub-Antarctic islands, where the carnage continued – 8000 skins were taken from the Bounty Islands in 1807, and 250,000 from the Antipodes between 1806 and 1810. 'Such was the rush to these new bonanzas', wrote Rhys Richards, 'that several marooned gangs got left behind and forgotten': one on the Snares for seven years, another on Solander Island in Foveaux Strait for four and a half. This was exactly the circumstance in which Alexander Selkirk was abandoned for four years on one of the Juan Fernandez group of islands, giving Daniel Defoe his inspiration for *Robinson Crusoe*.

By this phase of the industry Maori too, mainly from Northland and Murihiku, were being recruited for sealing expeditions and taking their place alongside Englishmen, Irishmen, Scots, Australian Aborigines, Tahitians and Portuguese, and thus learning and carrying back to their own communities first- and second-hand information about a world beyond New Zealand. A sealing vessel aptly named *Commerce* was operating around Chatham Island in 1807 with a Moriori on board named Hororeka, who had already spent time living in the Bay of Islands and was able to act as an interpreter among Europeans, Maori and Moriori. And it was a Maori member of the abandoned Snares gang who eventually reported its privations and rescue.

From the early 1800s sealers began to defect to Ngai Tahu communities in the south of the country, some remaining there to raise pigs and grow vegetables to sell or barter to ocean whalers and other ships that were beginning to visit the ports of Foveaux Strait and Fiordland more often. One of the first was Thomas Fink, who settled near Bluff with a Maori wife in about 1805. Another was James Caddell, who in 1810 married Tokitoki, niece of the Ngai Tahu chief Honekai, and lived at Oue near the present town of Invercargill. Maori were again involved in a brief revival of sealing between 1822 and 1829, because the shortage of seals worldwide had raised the price of skins to a level where the industry seemed viable again. The English-born John Boultbee joined a Fiordland gang during this late resurgence and subsequently wrote a graphic account of the vicissitudes such men had to endure: both the good times – 'a blazing fire, flapjacks, pork and a singsong' – and the bad, as when the gang was attacked by Maori pirates from Banks Peninsula and had to fight literally for their lives.

There were insufficient animals left to sustain the revival, however. On the Chatham Islands alone, the numbers had dropped from around 20,000 to 'very few', and the first perma-nent European settlers there were disillusioned sealers who jumped ship in the late 1820s and early 1830s. Another group, who wrecked their brig, the *Glory*, on Pitt Island in 1827, managed to sail a longboat back to the Bay of Islands, a journey of 1300 km – one of the great survival stories of the sealing era in New Zealand waters. By the 1830s, however, the industry on the Chathams had all but collapsed, a victim of 'reckless efficiency'.

At the very time that sealing was undergoing its second decline, another industry based on the exploitation of marine mammals was growing locally and would eventually have a more enduring and far-reaching impact on New Zealand and its inhabitants. This was whaling. Initially it was primarily in pursuit of sperm whales and was carried out from ocean-going vessels, which needed ports near the whaling grounds to the north, south and east of New Zealand.

Like sealing, ocean whaling, which at first involved British vessels and later French and American ones, began to affect New

Zealand in the 1790s. Unlike sealing, it peaked in the 1830s. It was to service this enlarging 'fleet' that the settlement of Kororareka developed in the Bay of Islands, making the bay the first major arena for prolonged and intensive Maori–Pakeha interaction. In 1830, for example, as many as 30 ships were at anchor in the port, with crews totalling 1000 men, of whom as many as 300 could be ashore at any one time. The presence of these sailors, and the need for ships to replenish their supplies, led to Maori growing vegetables and pigs for sale and offering prostitution, and to an ever-enlarging number of riff-raff Europeans on shore providing alcohol and tavern entertainment. It also led to a growing amount of disorderly conduct, with no police force or indeed any system of law and order to protect life and property. Such circumstances led to Kororareka becoming known, with perhaps only slight exaggeration, as the 'Hell-hole of the Pacific'. Charles Darwin, visiting the Bay of Islands in the *Beagle*, in 1835, described its English residents as 'the very refuse of society'. French navigator Dumont d'Urville reported similar conditions in Port Otago in 1840, 'the Maori much degraded, the men undermined by alcohol purchased by coercing their wives and daughters into large-scale, very visible prostitution'.

There was another phase of the same industry, shore whaling, which involved harvesting mainly the southern right whale. Shore-based stations were established for this purpose from the late 1820s on the east coast of both main islands, around Cook and Foveaux Straits, and on the Chathams. They too reached their peak of activity in the 1830s, but had a much more marked effect on Maori communities than ocean whaling. The stations were mostly established close to Maori villages, or in some instances Maori moved settlements to be closer to them. Local Maori men worked alongside Pakeha, hunting whales in season and in the off-season growing vegetable crops for these small colonies and for trading. Maori women lived with or married European shore whalers, an association that founded some of the most prominent Maori families of the future – the Braggs, Solomons, Barretts, Loves, Keenans, McClutchies, Halberts, Manuels, and many others.

The impact of shore whaling was also more widespread than that of ocean whaling and of sealing. It had a considerable impact on Maori life on the East Coast of the North Island, in Taranaki, on both sides of Cook Strait and Kapiti and Mana islands, and on the south-east of the South Island. Communities there were introduced to European clothing, European technology in the form of tools, new varieties of domestic plants and animals, clinker-built boats, European-style housing and the English language – and, of course, to intermarriage.

Having said that, it needs to be stressed that the values and protocols of such communities remained largely Maori, that most descendants of mixed marriages identified as Maori, and that the whaling-based communities could not have been there at all if the local Maori chiefs and tribes had not permitted their presence. They were part of a gradually growing symbiotic relationship between Maori and Pakeha. Pakeha investors and workers gained access to raw materials for an industry that was highly profitable for the owners; Maori gained access to paid labour and to those aspects of European technology and culture that it suited them to have – and, on the whole, they did so without compromising their Maori cultural identity.

The very first shore stations were established in the late 1820s by Jacky Guard, a former convict and sealer, at Te Awaiti ('Tar'white', as it came to be called) in Tory Channel in the Marlborough Sounds, and by Bunn and Co of Sydney in Preservation Inlet in Fiordland. Guard later shifted his operation to Kakapo Bay, Port Underwood. His son John, born to Guard's Australian wife Betty in 1831, is believed to be the first Pakeha child born in the South Island (though he had, of course, been preceded by children born of Maori–Pakeha unions). When members of the Guard family became hostages to Ngati Ruanui after a shipwreck on the Taranaki coast in 1834, the soldiers from Sydney who rescued them were the first British troops to engage in armed conflict with Maori.

Other shore whalers, such as Johnny Jones of Waikouaiti and Edward Weller of Otakou, became immensely wealthy through the 1830s and lived on to participate in the organised European colonisation of the country (though Weller chose to move to New South Wales when he was unable to get confirmation of his vast land purchases after British annexation). Dicky Barrett, after an adventurous introduction to life in New Zealand as a trader and whaler, which included fighting alongside his wife's Ati Awa relations in their battles with Waikato Maori, was briefly the popular host of Barrett's Hotel in Wellington. But he lost this business as a result of overreaching himself on his whaling operations. Philip Tapsell, a Dane who had originally come to New Zealand as an ocean whaler, eventually prospered as a trader based at Maketu in the Bay of Plenty and fathered one of the most influential and high-achieving Arawa dynasties. Weller, Barrett and Tapsell, and other whalers like the half-Aboriginal Thomas Chaseland, all had Maori wives and families. But they were not Pakeha Maori in the sense that they did not become or attempt to become culturally Maori, even if their children did.

Tapsell, like so many other European traders who arrived in New Zealand in the 1820s, became heavily involved in harvesting timber and flax. Most such operations were initially organised and financed from Sydney. James Cook had reported on what he judged to be the value of New Zealand timber for spars and ships' hulls, particularly as a consequence of his journey inland up the Waihou River. As noted earlier, ships from the British East India Company had begun taking wood for spars and masts from the Hauraki district in the 1790s (at least five shiploads of timber were taken from the banks of the Waihou River between 1794 and 1801). But these early cargoes were of kahikatea, which rotted in water and did not find favour with ship-builders.

The timber industry did not burgeon in New Zealand until the 1820s, after expeditions to the Coromandel Peninsula by British naval ships seeking suitable wood for topmasts and spars that had formerly been available from North American and Baltic forests. Kauri, with perfectly straight, branchless trunks extending 30 metres or more, were ideal for the purpose, and flexible and enduring. These successful visits generated the systematic exploitation of kauri, which would continue unfettered for another century until the resource was almost entirely destroyed. Harvesting such timber, at first in Northland and on the Coromandel coast, also involved whole Maori communities in the cutting, shaping and removal of logs. And it brought traders to the country who eventually became leading New Zealand citizens in the era of organised European settlement, such as Thomas Poynton and Thomas McDonnell in the Hokianga and James Clendon in the Bay of Islands.

Similar synergies developed around the harvesting of flax, which was in demand in the maritime industry for the manufacture of ropes, canvas sails, nets and sacks. An early attempt to exploit Maori expertise in the preparation and working of flax occurred in 1793, when Lieutenant-Governor Philip King had two Northland Maori, Tuki Tahua and Ngahuruhuru, kidnapped and taken to Norfolk Island to train convicts in these skills. The experiment failed, however, because neither man knew anything about preparing flax, which, as products of their own culture, they considered was women's work.

Sporadic cargoes were shipped out from the Hokianga and the Bay of Islands in succeeding decades, particularly once Maori realised that offering flax for barter was the easiest and most assured way of acquiring muskets. But, despite the early instructions given to Governor Arthur Phillip in 1788, it was not until the early 1820s that the Government of New South Wales made concerted efforts to develop the New Zealand flax trade. Those efforts were eventually fruitful and led to a boom in the industry between the mid-1820s and early 1830s, when flax exports reached a peak. The plant was harvested all around the New Zealand coast, but particularly successful stations were established in Foveaux Strait, the Hokianga, the Bay of Islands, Kawhia and the two harbours to the north of it, Aotea and Whaingaroa, the Bay of Plenty (under Tapsell's direction) and the East Coast of the North Island.

In Kawhia from 1828, John Rodolphus Kent had married Tiria, daughter of the powerful Ngati Mahuta chief and later first Maori King, Te Wherowhero. He enlarged his flax trade to include cargoes of spars, pork and potatoes, which he ferried across the Tasman to Sydney. He would return with such merchandise as muskets, gunpowder and liquor. Kent later transferred the flax operation to Ngaruawahia, where he made good use of the Waipa and Waikato Rivers to bring large quantities of the harvested plant out of the interior of the Waikato valley and down to the Manukau Harbour for transport to Australia. This operation, in which he successfully directed a large Tainui labour force, was an anticipation of post-1840 projects which would see Waikato Maori become exporters of crops and goods to Australia and California.

William Webster, an American trader, operated a similar business from Whanganui Island at the mouth of Coromandel Harbour. Like Kent, he married the daughter of the most influential local chief, the same Horeta Te Taniwha of Ngati Whanaunga who had seen James Cook in 1769. Like Kent too, he used his Maori kinship associations to encourage Maori communities to grow fruit and vegetable produce and pigs for export, and to harvest timber and flax. He extended his operations to Great Barrier Island and, when the European settlement of Auckland was established in 1840, Webster's growers and workers supplied much of the town's early produce and firewood, the only source of fuel until Huntly coal became available in the 1850s. By late 1840, however, he had taken out more loans than he could service – as part of a plan to begin exporting to Britain and the United States – and much of his extensive land claims were not validated after annexation. He returned to the United States in some bitterness in 1847.

Commercial activity in New Zealand's frontier era between 1792 and 1840 thus highlighted a number of realities that had relevance for the country's immediate and long-term future.

One was that, given direction and encouragement by Pakeha with the necessary expertise and associations, Maori turned out to be capable and competitive entrepreneurs who could grow produce and harvest commodities such as flax and timber on a large scale. In this context, the co-operative structure of internal tribal organisation and the system of mutual obligation implied by the custom of utu were distinct assets, as was inter-tribal competitiveness.

Second, there would always be some commercial and industrial activities – which in the early days included sealing and whaling – that could gain traction in New Zealand only with investment from overseas. Third, in an unregulated and untaxed era, some entrepreneurs stood to make enormous profits. Fourth, opportunities for prosperity in a country of New Zealand's size would always depend to some extent on the state of markets with larger populations in other parts of the world. And, finally, it would become apparent from the unrestricted 'quarrying' of extractive resources – initially seals and whales, later timber – that unsustainable use of resources eventually annihilated the resource, a variation on the 'future-eating' phenomenon that had wiped out the country's big game and destroyed forests in the early years of Maori settlement. New Zealanders were destined to repeat this pattern of behaviour many times over before necessary lessons were learned.

Apart from the potential for rich pickings by those who were European, well organised, hard working and lucky, however, little of this was apparent at the time. And the very absence of any kind of government bureaucracy that allowed profits to go untaxed also ensured an absence of planning or co-ordination in the development of the country's resources. For some Maori, though, other forces were at work to encourage them to encounter and then reflect on the significance and potential value to them of a world beyond their own shores.

In addition to coastal contact with Europeans via harvesting and trading, there was another source of interaction between Maori and Pakeha in which Maori did, literally, discover the rest of the world. Having come themselves from a highly maritime culture, even though they had long since ceased to make ocean voyages by canoe, Maori turned out to be excellent crew members on European ships. They began to join ships' companies in the 1790s, not long after Tuki and Ngahuruhuru's voyage to Sydney and Norfolk Island at Lieutenant-Governor King's behest in 1793. By the first decade of the nineteenth century Maori were visiting Sydney regularly, and from the following decade travelling on vessels around the Pacific – Herman Melville's tattooed harpooner Queequeg in *Moby Dick* was in all probability based on a Maori crew member whom the author had met on the whaling ship *Lucy Ann* – and on to North America and England (at least two Maori, Matara and Ruatara, had visited London before 1810).

Successive governors of New South Wales encouraged Maori visits to the Australian colonies and had chiefs from Northland, such as Te Pahi, Ruatara and Matara, to stay with them, sometimes for long periods. One reason was that, by the early nineteenth century, governors had begun to understand the reciprocal nature of Maori society and felt that, if rangatira were made welcome in Sydney, Maori would in turn feel obliged to welcome Europeans, especially traders and missionaries, back home in New Zealand. And, by and large, that was what transpired, at least in the far north of the country. Another reason was that governors felt that extending their hospitality to chiefs was a way of introducing Maori to the values and refinements of civilisation and that, because of the hierarchical nature of Maori communities, if the chiefs were civilised, then the qualities of 'civilised behaviour' would trickle down to the rest of Maori society. This, by and large, did *not* happen – or at least not in the way that the governors expected it would.

The fact was that, despite the visits of European ships, despite the small number of Europeans choosing to remain onshore and live with Maori, despite the introduction of welcomed new commodities such as metal and domestic animals and plants, for many Maori the on-again, off-again nature of European presence was little more than 'a travelling sideshow, a diversion from intertribal exchanges'. And for Maori who lived in the interior of the country and only *heard* about Maori–Pakeha interaction, those encounters would have had something of an unreal or mythical character, not unlike some of their traditions of patupaiarehe or fairy people. Other emissaries brought by Europeans changed Maori life more potently than the presence of Europeans themselves: these were muskets, disease and new ideas about spirituality.

10

God and Guns

One reason that many Maori were, after an initial phase of curiosity, all but oblivious to the growing frequency of European contact with New Zealand is that they were preoccupied with a more fundamental issue: their survival and the survival of their families and hapu. Some Pakeha-introduced commodities such as metals and tools had made the business of day-to-day subsistence less onerous, but the introduction of the flintlock musket into the intricately woven fabric of Maori tribal society was both an advantage and – for some – a disaster.

Maori acquisition of muskets began as a spin-off from early trade with Sydney-based merchants for flax and timber. A flood of cheaply produced European weapons in the early nineteenth century made them, on the merchants' side, a favourite choice for goods to barter. For their part, Maori initially sought guns for hunting. Lacking projectile weapons – no bow and arrows, no slingshot, no boomerang – Maori had never found it easy to kill birds for food, particularly the smaller surviving forest birds, with traditional weaponry. And some sought guns simply for the mana of ownership, particularly when it was known that neighbouring rangatira had them.

Being still a martial people, however, it was not long before Maori began to use muskets in inter-tribal fighting. The first occasion appears to have been the defeat of a Ngapuhi war party by Ngati Whatua at Moremonui near Maunganui, between the Hokianga and Kaipara harbours, in 1807. In this instance, it was Ngapuhi who were equipped with muskets. But Ngati Whatua ambushed them and attacked with traditional weapons before Ngapuhi had sufficient opportunity to load or reload.

From that time, however, because of the nature of Maori kinship links, the custom of utu and the intense interest in how war was waged, the phenomenon of musket warfare spread. At first that spread was slow, but after 1820 it developed the momentum of an arms race. Those who did not have guns realised that they needed them to make their survival in warfare more likely. Those who did have them understood that they needed *more* of them to retain an advantage over their adversaries.

The experience of Ngati Korokoro was probably typical. Not long after the Moremonui action, 300 of them attacked Kai Tutae,* like themselves a hapu of Te Rarawa ki Hokianga. The defenders numbered only 30 but, thanks to their flax-trading activities, had muskets.

The 300 came bravely on, and seeing the insignificant band opposed to them, proposed to surround them and capture the lot. The Kai Tutae reserved their fire, but as the enemy advanced

---

* The name means 'eaters of excrement'. It originated in an assertive chant in which members of the tribe warned their adversaries that when they defeated them they would eat every morsel of the dead, 'including their tutae'. Ritual cannibalism was known as whangai hau – destroying the mana of the victim and thus leaving their kinsfolk without ancestral protection.

to within distance a gun was fired and the first of the attackers fell; and then one by one four others fell, and presently they fell in numbers, until a panic set in, and Ngati Korokoro fled to their boat. As they crowded into her they offered an easy mark and there was great slaughter ...

Such inter-hapu skirmishes in the north of the country aside, the real horror of the musket wars began with large-scale Ngapuhi raids out of their own territory from the early 1820s. Every tribe against whom Ngapuhi had a real or imagined historical grievance became the target of a musket-era version of blitzkrieg; and, in many instances, the attackers had firearms while their opponents did not.

The carnage was considerable, and tribal balances of power were rapidly overturned in Ngapuhi's favour. As one symptom of this, while these warriors and rangatira from the far north had no ambition to remain in the areas they subdued, they took back home with them a considerable collection of looted taonga (treasures and heirlooms) and slaves. As tribes to the south stepped up their own acquisition of weapons by organising intensive harvesting of flax and growing pigs and potatoes, they too – Ngati Whatua, Ngati Paoa, Ngati Raukawa, Ngati Maru, Ngati Tuwharetoa, Tuhoe – began to launch sudden raids of their own, though not, with the exception of Ngati Whatua, in the direction of Ngapuhi. With each of these actions, often justified by grievances that went back generations, they created grounds for further warfare on the part of those who survived attacks or who were absent from battles in which their relations were killed.

The fiercest fighting, historians estimate, took place between 1822 and 1836, and the level of violence peaked in 1832 and 1833. The whole country was affected, north to south, apart from the mountainous interior of what would come to be called the King

Country and the remote bays and valleys of Fiordland. While, as Angela Ballara has argued, the musket wars may have been a continuation of Maori political and social interaction from the late eighteenth century, they were carried on with more efficient weapons. And they took a heavier toll *because* of those weapons. Indeed, if any chapter in New Zealand history has earned the label 'holocaust', it is this one. In some actions – Hongi Hika's Ngapuhi against Ngati Paoa on the Auckland isthmus, for example, or against Te Arawa on Mokoia Island on Lake Rotorua – many hundreds of men, women and children were killed, and many more enslaved. Some small tribes were all but wiped out, with only one or two families surviving the fighting and its aftermath of executions.

Some of these actions involved considerable cruelty. In the wake of battles, for example, the captured killers of warriors might be turned over to the widows of the men they had slain, as happened to Tamaiharanui of Ngai Tahu. The resulting deaths were prolonged and painful. At Waitangi Beach on Chatham Island, the Ngati Wai hapu of Ngati Mutunga laid Moriori women staked to the ground alongside one another and left them to die slowly. Instances of gratuitous cruelty were certainly not universal. Maori probably had the same percentage of sadists and psychopaths as any other society. The fortunate victims were those who died quickly, even if they were then chosen for the ritual cannibal feasting that was believed to absorb the mana of the defeated. To outside witnesses, such as missionaries, these actions were profoundly shocking. To most of the Maori combatants, they were simply the tikanga or customs associated with fighting. Whether you won or lost, you knew what your expected role or fate would be. And you knew the truth of the whakatauki or proverbs that enshrined the values pertaining to war: 'Kia mate ururoa, kei mate wheke' (it is better to fight and die like a shark than an octopus), for example. But there are recorded instances of captives committing suicide or killing their loved ones rather than allowing themselves to be subjected to the customs associated with victory.

Several tribes were displaced by fighting, and such movements always had consequences for other peoples. The tribes of the Coromandel Peninsula, for example, virtually deserted their traditional rohe and moved inland, where room had to be found for them among their Tainui relations. The population of the Auckland isthmus was depleted, leaving a vacuum into which Ngati Whatua would spread from the north. Ngati Toa and Ngati Raukawa were pushed out of Waikato and made their way down the west coast of the North Island, fighting and defeating other tribes such as Ngati Apa, Muaupoko and Rangitane as they did so. Various Taranaki tribes joined them in actions against peoples in the far south of the North Island, such as Ngati Ira, who virtually disappeared at this time. Ngati Mutunga and Ngati Tama, having settled around Wellington and the top of the South Island in alliance with Ngati Toa, fell out with their allies and hijacked a ship to take them to the Chatham Islands in 1835. There they killed around 10 per cent of the Moriori population, which had stood at around 1600, and enslaved the survivors.

Those who wanted or needed to fight, for attack or anticipated defence, had to be involved for long periods in harvesting flax or producing pigs and potatoes. In 1814 in the Bay of Islands, the price for one musket was 150 baskets of potatoes and eight pigs. In 1822 it was 70 'buckets' of potatoes and two pigs. In some instances by the late 1820s, Maori used the smoked heads of slain enemies to trade for further muskets. In the case of Ngapuhi, much of the agricultural labour was undertaken by slaves. By the early 1830s, too, some slaves were being tattooed and killed specifically for the trade in smoked heads – a trade which the then Governor of New South Wales, Ralph Darling, attempted, with some success, to ban by law in 1831.

Once they had become accustomed to the need to rotate areas for planting, widespread production of the introduced potato also gave Maori more nutritious and more easily preserved and portable food than they had had previously (by the time of European arrival in New Zealand, Maori kumara were little larger than human fingers). This factor alone meant that taua or war parties could spend longer away from the home supply-base than in the pre-European era (2000 men carrying 1000 muskets at the height of Hongi Hika's campaigns in the early 1820s), though many Maori were reluctant to carry cooked food in canoes, because this would destroy protective tapu. They could also now lay indefinite siege to defensive pa formerly regarded as impregnable. The effect of all these factors was to increase the number of people killed in fighting and the after-math of fighting.

Hongi Hika of Ngapuhi is the fighting chief best remembered from this era. Hongi had been one of the survivors of the Ngapuhi defeat by Ngati Whatua at Moremonui in 1807 and replaced Pokaia, who died there, as war leader of his people. Despite the fact that muskets had not won the day for Ngapuhi on that occasion, Hongi recognised their potential value in attack and defence provided warriors were trained and drilled and chose battle locations and tactics that allowed such weapons to be put to best use. In the succeeding years Hongi organised the tribes that recognised his mana to grow the kinds of crops that could be used to barter for muskets and to do so on a larger scale than those whom he regarded as potential enemies. When the missionary Thomas Kendall met Hongi in 1814, he already had ten muskets of his own, one of which he had stocked and mounted himself ('the performance does him much credit, since he had no man to instruct him', Kendall said of the manner in which Hongi handled his weapons).

After spectacular military successes in 1818 and 1819, Hongi visited England and Sydney, initially in the company of Kendall. In England he helped Kendall and Professor Samuel Lee of Cambridge University compile *A grammar and vocabulary of the language of New Zealand*, the first such book and the one which laid the orthographic foundations of written Maori. Hongi also met King George IV and was sent home with a suit of armour which he subsequently wore into battle, the spectacle of which increased the terror of his opponents and led to the rumour that he was invincible under fire. He arrived back in the Bay of Islands with up to 500 additional muskets and his subsequent southern war campaigns took a heavier toll on opponents.

Like Maui-tikitiki-a-Taranga, Hongi came to be known and respected for his tactical cunning. At Te Totara pa in the Hauraki district in 1821, Hongi's representative sued for peace and asked for tatou pounamu (conciliatory gifts) in return for Ngapuhi's departure. Late that night, while the Hauraki people were celebrating their deliverance, Hongi and his taua returned to attack under cover of darkness and killed some 60 people still within the pa.

However much he terrified his enemies and would-be enemies, Hongi at home was far more than simply a man of war. Missionary families under his protection at Waimate, like those at Kerikeri, knew him as a 'mild, gentle and courteous man'. Samuel Marsden described him as 'a very fine character ... uncommonly mild in his manners and very polite'. Hongi personally supervised the planting of crops and participated in fishing expeditions. And yet his death, when it eventually occurred in 1828, was a vindication of the Biblical verse about those who live by the sword. While he was fighting his way into

Whangaroa in an attempt to settle back on his father's people's lands his chest was pierced by the ball of a musket, the weapon whose use he had done so much to popularise. He died a year later from the infection of the wound.

Other men who acquired reputations as great fighting leaders over this period included Te Morenga, Pomare, Tamati Waka Nene and Patuone of Ngapuhi; Te Wherowhero of Waikato and Te Waharoa of Ngati Haua; Te Heuheu Tukino of Ngati Tuwharetoa; Te Rauparaha, Te Rangihaeata and Te Pehi Kupe of Ngati Toa; and Tuhawaiiki and Taiaroa of Ngai Tahu.

Te Rauparaha, credited with composing what would become the most famous of all haka, *Ka Mate, Ka Mate*, was driven out of Waikato by a confederation led by Te Wherowhero. As he fought his way down the west coast of the North Island at the head of his people, he was the cause of almost as much disruption and panic as Hongi. He battled and defeated such tribes as Ngati Apa, Muaupoko, Rangitane and Ngati Ira as he led his people to Cook Strait, where they made their headquarters on Kapiti Island (soon to be the location of several important shore whaling stations). Then he and Ngati Toa waged campaigns against Ngai Tahu in the South Island, winning notable and (for the home people) costly victories at Kaikoura, Kaiapoi and Onawe, among other places. Distracted from their own internecine wars, Ngai Tahu recovered their balance and pushed Ngati Toa back to Cloudy Bay at the head of the island, having defeated a combined Ngati Toa–Ngati Tama taua deep in Murihiku territory near Mataura. Unlike Hongi, Te Rauparaha, known to his whaling friends as 'the old sarpent', and his nephew Te Rangihaeata, lived on to become formidable players in the manoeuvres that accompanied organised European settlement.

The last of the tribal musket wars may have been the clashes between Te Ati Awa and Ngati Raukawa in 1839, and between

Ngati Tama and Ngati Mutunga on Chatham Island in 1840, though armed war parties were still moving round parts of the North Island in the mid-1840s. Over a period of 30 years these actions had been responsible for the deaths of at least 20,000 Maori, and possibly many more. Even this figure would make these wars the most costly of any in which New Zealanders previously or subsequently took part. They ceased eventually in part because a balance of terror was achieved once all the surviving tribes were well stocked with muskets, and in part because land sales to Europeans had the effect of 'freezing' tribal rohe and making future conquest and migration impossible. Another factor was the influence of Christianity and its message of peace, which had begun to spread among Maori outwards from the Bay of Islands and the Hokianga in the 1830s.

Maori had always been a highly spiritual people. They recognised atua or spiritual powers in nature: in Tane Mahuta's offerings of food and shelter from the forests, in Tangaroa's gifts of fish and shellfish from the sea, even in the cleansing storms and winds of Tawhirimatea. There were also atua who resided in and protected particular geographical features and places.

Nothing was taken from the domain of these atua without respect, propitiation and expressions of gratitude. Maori religious beliefs – about atua, tupua, mana, tapu, noa and mauri – harmonised the workings of mind and body and spiritual realities with physical ones. The whole of existence was bound up in a unified vision in which each aspect of life was related to every other. These beliefs and the practices and rituals associated with them affected human behaviour from Te Rerenga Wairua in the north to Rakiura in the south.

All of which meant that Maori – so-called heathen – were far more receptive to consideration and discussion of religious issues, once bilingualism made such discussions possible, than were, say, the secularised humanists of the European Enlightenment and their successors. Maori believed already in atua; it did not require a large movement of faith to accept belief in a single God, Te Atua (indeed, there is evidence for a supreme deity, Io, in some Maori cosmologies). Maori already believed that tikanga or codes of behaviour regulated the workings of communities; it was not such a big transition to consider an alternative code, even if it did outlaw such aspects of tikanga Maori as eating human flesh or keeping slaves.

The major points of Christian belief that would contrast with tikanga Maori were the notions that natural man was a fallen creature needing to be redeemed by Christ's suffering and death; and that every human life – whether of rangatira, commoner or slave – was of equal value in the eyes of Te Atua and those who acknowledged Him.

Christian evangelising in New Zealand began in 1814. While the first Christian service in New Zealand had been the mass celebrated by Jean de Surville's Dominican chaplain in Doubtless Bay in 1769, the Frenchmen were not there to convert Maori. In any case, their lack of an interpreter meant that they would have been unable to make themselves understood had they tried to do so. The first Christian mission to New Zealand, and specifically to Maori, was launched by Samuel Marsden on behalf of the Church of England's Church Missionary Society (CMS) in 1814. And it came about largely because of the number of Maori visiting Sydney in the early years of the nineteenth century.

Marsden, a bluff Yorkshireman with 'heavy shoulders and the face of a petulant ox', was both chaplain to the New South Wales penal settlement and a magistrate. He was severe in dealing with convicts who reoffended and became known as 'the flogging parson'. But he went out of his way to meet and greet Maori in Sydney, and often had them to stay in his house and work on his extensive farm at Parramatta. He had even, in 1809, rescued the Maori sailor Ruatara, who was stranded in London, and taken him back with him to Sydney. It was this association in particular that led Marsden to set up the first CMS mission at Rangihoua in the Bay of Islands in 1814, on land that he would buy from Ruatara. Marsden conducted his first service in New Zealand on Christmas Day 1814. Preaching to a largely Maori congregation, he took his text from St Luke's Gospel, 'Behold I bring you tidings of great joy ...' In the New Year of 1815, Marsden visited Waimate and Omapere and thus made 'the first significant journey of inland exploration by a European ... and set a pattern for the missionary explorers who followed'.

Marsden left three lay workers at Rangihoua: Thomas Kendall, a schoolmaster, justice of the peace and self-appointed leader of the station; William Hall, a carpenter; and John King, a shoemaker and ropemaker. Marsden instructed them to institute a 'civilisation first' policy – that is, to instruct Maori in horticulture, agriculture and trade, in European manners and morals, and then seek to make them Christian. These three men and their families were unable to work together harmoniously, however, and all were eventually dismissed for various offences, including trading muskets with Maori, drunkenness and, in Kendall's case, adultery. At one point, in the course of his mission, Kendall confessed that the 'sublimity' of Maori ideas had 'almost completely turned me from a Christian to a Heathen ...' This was not the purpose for which Marsden and the CMS had placed him there.

The Revd John Gare Butler arrived in the Bay of Islands in 1819 as the mission's first resident clergyman and superintendent. He opened a second station at Kerikeri in the company of lay workers James and Charlotte Kemp. The house they built there was to survive as the oldest European residence in the country, and Kemp's stone store alongside it, completed in 1836, as the oldest commercial building. The Rangihoua site was abandoned. Despite the infusion of new blood, by 1822 the mission had still achieved not one conversion.* No real progress was made until Butler, like his earlier colleagues, was dismissed, for drunkenness, and the Revd Henry Williams, a former naval officer, assumed leadership of the operation from Paihia in 1823.

Williams overturned the 'civilisation first' policy and took steps to ensure that all new missionaries, including his brother William, became proficient in the Maori language so that they could preach in it as soon as possible (indeed, William's proficiency soon exceeded his older brother's and he went on to compile what would become the country's definitive Maori dictionary). Henry also prohibited further missionary involvement in the musket trade and took steps to reduce the mission's dependence on Maori for supplies – by encouraging farming and acquiring a schooner. Soon his mana among Maori was such that he was intervening successfully to prevent disagreements between Maori turning into outright warfare.

In the late 1820s Bay of Islands Maori at last began to offer themselves for baptism, and the number of conversions rose rapidly through the following decade. By 1842 there were over 3000 Christian Maori in the region, and others further afield as a result of Henry Williams's and Marsden's periodic trips to other parts of the country and the opening of stations at

---

* This astonishing record was, however, well exceeded by the German Moravian missioner in the Chatham Islands, Johann Gottfried Engst, who laboured in the field for 68 years without a conversion.

Kaitaia, Waimate, Maraetai, Kauaeranga, Puriri, Matamata, Mangapopuri, Rotorua, Otaki and Waikanae. Te Atua, the God of the Bible, was on the move. From the 1830s too the momentum had been increased by the activity of Maori evangelists, many of them former slaves who had been converted in Ngapuhi territory and then allowed to return home when their masters also embraced the new faith and rejected slavery as an institution. One of these, Piripi Taumata-a-kura, brought Christianity to his own Ngati Porou people in 1836.

Why was progress made at this time and not before? The answers are complex. Initially Maori were, as early accounts of their beliefs show, content and secure in their traditional view of the world and their place in it, and in the efficacy of their own atua. In the early days of the CMS missions, Bay of Islands people were happy to select from the so-called civilising influences on offer. Rawiri Taiwhanga, referred to as 'the first and the brightest jewel in the missionary crown of achievement', became a wonderfully versatile and successful horticulturist prior to his conversion, and later the country's first commercial dairy farmer. And yet, in the course of a decade spent in acquiring these skills, he and others initially retained and remained secure in their own cosmography. The erratic and petty behaviour of the original CMS workers at Rangihoua was never an example to inspire emulation, though Thomas Kendall acquired some mana through his friendship with Hongi Hika and his efforts to learn and write down the Maori language and spiritual beliefs.

By the late 1820s other influences were at work. The example of principled living set by the extended Williams family and the Kemps at Kerikeri did win Maori admiration, though Henry Williams was rather severe in his views on even rather innocent Maori customary practices. The literacy offered by the mission's schools at Kerikeri and Paihia was embraced with enthusiasm by a growing number of Maori adults and children, especially after the mission printer William Colenso began producing scripture in Maori – starting with some of Paul's epistles and moving on to William Williams's translation of the New Testament – from 1835. The loss of Maori lives in the musket wars and the vulnerability to European diseases exhibited by, in particular, Maori in the Bay of Islands, where European whalers were calling more and more often through the 1830s, may also have been a factor undermining the confidence Maori had formerly had in their own atua and karakia (prayers or chants). For a combination of reasons, therefore, the high degree of spiritual energy which Maori had always shown, and their deep interest in religious questions and practice, came to be relocated in the practice of Christianity. Karakia Maori were increasingly replaced by karakia mihinare, although the point should be made that this often occurred *without* Maori relinquishing a belief in their own gods. In this sense, perhaps, Maori did not so much convert *to* Christianity as convert Christianity, like so much else that Pakeha had brought, to their own purposes.

The Anglicans no longer had the field to themselves by this time. Wesleyans had arrived in 1822 and, with help from the CMS workers, William White, Nathaniel Turner and John Hobbs established a mission station at Whangaroa the following year. Their instructions were to 'propose the Gospel in its simplest and most explicit truths', and to refrain from owning land personally or trading with local Maori. They had a difficult time in this locality. According to one Maori historian, the Wesleyans 'taught domesticity, agriculture and ... prudery with little success, and Christianity with less ...' In 1827 their mission was sacked by Maori in the course of Hongi Hika's battles to fight his way back into Whangaroa. Turner and Hobbs abandoned the station and eventually set up a new one at Mangunu on the southern shore of the Hokianga Harbour, which was later relocated to Waima. In this district they made better progress. Throughout the 1830s the Wesleyans worked their way down the west coast of the North Island through regions that the Anglicans had not yet evangelised. They set up new stations in Tangiteroria on the northern Wairoa River, and in Raglan and Kawhia; they eventually established their largest Maori following among Tainui Maori of the Waikato.

Whereas the Wesleyans and Anglicans co-operated in the early years of their mission (the Turners and the Hobbses stayed with the Kemps at Kerikeri after the destruction of the Whangaroa station, for example), Protestants and Catholics did not. The Catholic missionaries, who arrived in the northern Hokianga from France in 1838, were the last of the major denominations to reach New Zealand (barring Presbyterians, whose presence had to await the Scottish colonisation of Otago and Southland from 1848). As Papists and as citizens of a country so recently and for so long at war with Britain, they were not welcomed by either of their predecessors. Nathaniel Turner told his southern Hokianga Maori congregation that Bishop Jean-Baptiste Pompallier and his Marist workers represented 'the Great Whore of Babylon', and sent them across the harbour to sack the first Catholic station on Thomas Poynton's property at Totara Point. Te Rarawa Maori protected the new arrivals. Even William Williams, in other circumstances an equable man, described Pompallier as a 'shrewd clever active man who ... hesitates not in the use of any means, whether lying or the employment of profligate Europeans in order to accomplish his purpose'.

Part of this prejudice was generated by the fact that many of the 40 to 50 Pakeha Catholics already living in the Hokianga in the 1830s, and some of their co-religionists in the Bay of Islands, were rough Irishmen 'given to drink and fornication'. They were the kind of Pakeha who, in the eyes of the Protestant mission-aries, set a bad example to Maori. Most of them, however, like Jacky Marmon and Thomas Cassidy, eventually had their unions with Maori women formalised and worked their way towards respectability.

Pompallier and his slowly growing band of priests and brothers set to work initially with as much enthusiasm as had their Protestant counterparts. They achieved notable successes in the northern Hokianga, where the respected timber mer-chant Poynton had already laid Catholic foundations among his Maori neighbours, and in the Bay of Islands, where Pompallier relocated his headquarters in 1839. From these bases they worked their way south and established further stations in the Bay of Plenty, the central North Island and the south-east coast of the South Island. By 1841 Pompallier reported that he had set up twelve stations throughout the country and baptised some 1000 Maori. This was fewer than his CMS rivals, but con-siderably more than the Wesleyans. Many of these 'converts' dropped away, however, especially during the Northern War in the mid-1840s.

As missionaries, the French had an advantage over their Protestant counterparts: they were celibate; they did not have wives and families to support; they could roam large areas of the country without having to worry about how families were faring in their absence; they appeared to refrain from sexual activity with Maori rather more successfully than their brethren (and Wesleyan William White and Anglicans William Yate and William Colenso were three more who would succumb to what their colleagues regarded as sins of the flesh). Before long, however, the Catholic clergy were complaining bitterly to Jean-Claude Colin, their religious superior in France, that Pompallier was withholding from them the financial resources that would have allowed them to feed, clothe and transport themselves with a minimal degree of comfort.

Pompallier himself, however, enjoyed certain personal advantages over his critics both inside and outside the Catholic fold. He was 36 years old when he arrived in New Zealand, handsome, intelligent and eloquent (thanks to Poynton's tuition he was preaching in Maori three months after his arrival). He was also the first bishop of any denomination to set foot in New Zealand* and was an especially 'commanding figure in long purple soutane and sash, episcopal ring and great tassled hat'. Unlike most Europeans in New Zealand at this time, and certainly unlike some of his more Calvinist-inclined rivals, Pompallier *looked* like the Maori idea of a rangatira Pakeha – like the kind of person Hongi Hika and other fortunates had reported seeing at the courts of monarchs. It was as a result of this striking impact that Maori would soon characterise Maori Catholics as Pikopo (from the Latin *episcopus* for 'bishop') to distinguish them from Mihinare (from 'missionary') for Protestant Maori.

With all the discussion of religion and religious concepts generated by competitive evangelising – and some Maori were *intensely* interested in talking of such matters, as the French clergy reported exhaustedly – it was scarcely surprising that the first syncretic religion composed of Maori and Judaeo-Christian ingredients emerged in the Bay of Islands and the Hokianga in the 1830s. This was the movement known as Papahurihia. There would be many more such examples in the course of the nineteenth century. The followers of such movements, made familiar with Christian scripture, identified strongly with the

---

* His Anglican counterpart, George Augustus Selwyn, every bit a sartorial competitor, would not arrive in the country until 1842.

Israelites of the Old Testament as a disinherited but Chosen People promised deliverance and fulfilment by God. They represented a belief by Maori in the existence of Te Atua, the God of the Bible. But that belief did not, in Maori eyes, preclude belief in the pantheon of Maori gods. Syncretic or 'Maori religions' represented a specifically Maori path to God and a rejection of the missionary assumption that European civilisation ought to *accompany* conversion, even if it was no longer necessary to precede it.

Papahurihia was so named after its founder, a Ngapuhi matakite (seer) and tohunga. Judith Binney, who has studied his beliefs more closely than any other scholar, writes that Papahurihia's identification of Maori with the Jewish people, and the use of the Biblical serpent as his channel, became important beliefs for his followers. As 'Jews', those followers were not Christian. '[They] were the chosen of God ... [He] hated the Protestant missionaries; they were said to be murderers, causing many deaths by means of witchcraft.' For some reason he was less judgemental about the activities of Catholic missionaries after their later arrival.

Papahurihia's impact was intensified by his skill as a ventriloquist who could conjure up 'spirit voices' from various directions, some of them making what was described as a 'whistling sighing' sound. He changed his own name to Te Atua Wera – the fiery god – and retained a following until his death in 1875, even though he had converted to Christianity 20 years earlier. In the southern Hokianga he still has adherents in the twenty-first century.

Earlier writers have suggested that one major reason for Maori to embrace Christianity in the 1830s, and to be attracted to syncretic religions such as Papahurihia, was the confusion and anxiety that arose from deaths caused by epidemics. Maori had no immunity to Pakeha-introduced diseases, the argument goes, and the prayers and rituals of their ancient religion had no beneficial or palliative effects on these illnesses; therefore they turned to new religions in an effort to mitigate their effects and protect individuals still living.

If there is any truth to this scenario, it probably applies only to the Bay of Islands and the Hokianga, where Pakeha contact with Maori was reasonably continuous over the two decades preceding the Treaty of Waitangi in 1840, and where European ships came and went from foreign ports with some regularity. The vast majority of Maori in other parts of the country, however – especially those living in interior regions such as Waikato, the King Country, Urewera, inland Hawke's Bay and Wairarapa, and those in the South Island north of the area around Foveaux Strait – had only indirect contact with Pakeha up to 1840. There is no evidence that periodic epidemics of 'rewharewha' – most probably influenza – reported in the Bay of Islands and Mercury Bay affected Maori outside those areas. Similarly, outbreaks of whooping cough in the Bay of Islands in the 1820s and 1830s and influenza in Foveaux Strait some time between 1817 and 1820 almost certainly spread no further than those places.

Demographer Ian Pool writes:

[The] Maori population was dispersed and had a low density. European contact was mainly restricted to ports and other coastal areas ... Thus care should be taken not to extrapolate from the experience of Northland ... nor to assume that the reported outbreak of any disease was nationwide. The necessary preconditions for the rapid transmission of disease throughout the entire population just did not exist in New Zealand prior to the Treaty of Waitangi [which would] open the way for the rapid influx of Pakeha population and thus inadvertently ... set up the mechanisms for the widespread exposure of Maori to imported diseases ... New Zealand before 1840 would have experienced therefore rather different conditions from some of the small islands of the Pacific ...

As Pool notes, this situation would change after 1840. Before then, however, it is likely that the combined effects of the musket wars, some infertility as a result of venereal disease, and localised epidemics reduced the Maori population from its 1769 level of 100,000–110,000 to around 70,000. For Maori, the real population plunge – and crisis – would occur from around the middle of the nineteenth century.

11

A Treaty

The establishment of the New South Wales penal colony in 1788 had given many Maori an opportunity to engage gradually and largely on their own terms with a minimal and, in the case of visiting traders or missionaries, sporadic European presence. As a result, prior to 1840, they were at no point overwhelmed by this presence as were, say, the Aboriginal people of Tasmania and parts of south-east Australia.

Everything that unfolded in New Zealand over the following 50 years – the trade, the sealing and whaling, the missionary activity, the number of Maori who visited Sydney and Hobart and eventually London – brought New Zealand into a progressively closer relationship with Europeans and, in particular, Europeans from Britain. And the only authorities outside New Zealand who revealed themselves to be genuinely interested in the welfare of Maori, and in particular how well Maori were faring in their interaction with Europeans, were successive governors of New South Wales, not to mention Colonial Office officials, leaders of the Anglican and Wesleyan mission societies and members of the Aborigines Protection Society – all the latter based in London. A consequence of all this was that, throughout the 1830s, New Zealand was pulled steadily towards a perma-nent and constitutional relationship with Britain.

The first formal step acknowledging that this process was in motion was the appointment in 1832 of the New South Wales viticulturist James Busby as the first British Resident in New Zealand: in effect, the representative of British law and order and diplomatic interests in the country. He arrived in the Bay of Islands to assume these responsibilities in May 1833 and was greeted by a missionary-organised Maori welcome at Paihia, a seven-gun salute and a hakari or feast. Busby himself added to the sense of occasion by distributing gifts of blankets and tobacco to the 22 chiefs in attendance. Nothing quite like this had happened in the Bay of Islands before and Busby took the opportunity to create an impression that his appointment was akin to a diplomatic posting and that he was the personal representative of the authority of 'the King'.

Several factors had led to his commission, which was initiated by the British Government but administered, parsimo-niously, from New South Wales. One was the need to protect New Zealand's trade with the Australian colonies (the value of New Zealand exports to New South Wales and Tasmania was around £20,000 by the early 1830s). There was also the need to protect the lives and interests of the growing number of British subjects living in New Zealand, including the families of the CMS and Wesleyan missionaries. And there was the fact that northern Maori had twice sent letters to the King of England asking for British protection: once when an armed French vessel visited the Bay of Islands in 1831 (though it turned out to be innocent of aggressive intention), and again in response to the participation of British seamen in Ngati Toa's kidnapping of the Ngai Tahu chief Tamaiharanui the previous year (Maori in the north feared that southern tribes might use the same tactics to punish Ngapuhi for their raids in the musket wars).

Busby's instructions from Governor Richard Bourke of New South Wales specified that he was to protect 'well disposed' settlers and traders, guard against the exploitation of Maori by Europeans and outrages committed against them, and recapture escaped convicts. He was given no means of enforcing his authority, however, and eventually came to be referred to as the 'Man o' War without guns'. He was also instructed to encourage Maori towards a more settled form of government, and in this limited respect, at least in his own mind, he did make some progress.

In March 1834 Busby organised a meeting of northern chiefs outside his house in Waitangi to choose a national flag, so that New Zealand-built and -owned ships could be properly registered and freely enter other ports. If his own despatches are to be believed, this task was carried out in a dignified and constitutional manner. An independent eyewitness account, however, by the visiting Austrian naturalist Baron von Hugel – sent abroad to recover from the defection of his fiancée to Prince Clemens von Metternich – made it clear that the ceremony was little short of a farce.

The assembled chiefs were not given a comprehensible account of why they were there and expressed much puzzlement that King William of England, who was kind enough to invite them to select a flag for New Zealand ships, was sufficiently unkind as to threaten to punish mariners who did not display such a flag. Then, asked to choose from one of three flags on offer, the chiefs politely proceeded to vote for all three. It took the intervention of one of the Williams family's Maori servants to compel each chief to opt for only one flag, write down the preferences as votes, then announce a result. One flag, an ensign that became known as the 'Flag of the Independent Tribes of New Zealand', was left flying and the alternatives hauled down. A naval officer called for a 'triple hurrah' while the frigate *Alligator* fired off a 21-gun salute. Europeans present were then invited to sit down for an elegant lunch, while the assembled chiefs were given a cauldron of cold porridge, which they were obliged to eat with their fingers.

A second and equally contrived ceremony took place again at Waitangi in October 1835. This time, in exchange for a second cauldron of porridge, Busby persuaded the same chiefs and some additional ones to sign 'A Declaration of the Independence of New Zealand' by a 'Confederation of United Tribes'. This document, into which Maori had had no input, was designed specifically to thwart the French adventurer Charles de Thierry, who planned to establish an independent state in the Hokianga. It proclaimed, in English and Maori:

> We, the hereditary chiefs and heads of the tribes of the Northern parts of New Zealand ... declare the Independence of our country, which is hereby constituted ... an Independent State, under the designation of The United Tribes of New Zealand.
>
> All sovereign power and authority within the territories of the United Tribes of New Zealand is hereby declared to reside entirely and exclusively in the hereditary chiefs and heads of tribes ... who also declare that they will not permit any legislative authority separate from themselves ... nor any function of government to be exercised within the said territories, unless by persons appointed by them, and acting under the authority of laws regularly enacted by them in Congress assembled.

The document also thanked King William for acknowledging the Maori flag, and asked him to continue to act as the 'Matua' or parent of their infant state. It was signed initially by 34 chiefs, and subsequently by a further 18.

The Governor of New South Wales, who was by this time growing tired of what he regarded as James Busby's whining requests for naval ships, policemen and other resources he was unable or unwilling to supply, called the declaration 'a paper pellet fired off at Baron de Thierry', who had already declared himself 'king' of Nuku Hiva Island in the Marquesas group. When de Thierry eventually arrived in New Zealand in 1837, it was to discover that his previous purchase of land in the Hokianga from Thomas Kendall was not recognised and that local Maori had no enthusiasm for accepting him as their monarch. Instead, he ended his days as a music teacher in Auckland.

The declaration of independence had no constitutional status and an official in the Foreign Office in London referred to it as 'silly and unauthorised'. It also had no reality, since there was in fact no national indigenous power structure within New Zealand at that time, tribal authority – or rangatiratanga, as it would come to be called after Henry Williams invented the word in February 1840 – being far more akin to a collection of 'nations'. Indeed, some of the 'United Tribes' were at war with one another within a year of signing the document. Nevertheless, the declaration became a foundation for the assertion of indigenous rights, and it *was* another step in the direction of a formal constitutional relationship with Great Britain.

In the years that followed, alarmist reports from Busby alleging the 'accumulating evils of permanent anarchy' and 'depopulation' as a result of tribal wars arrived at the Colonial Office in London at the same time as petitions from Sydney and New Zealand traders – all asking the British Government to intervene more strongly in New Zealand affairs to ensure safety and stability in the interests of British subjects and of Maori. There was also at this time in London disquiet that a private firm, the New Zealand Company – brainchild of the heiress-abductor and former convict Edward Gibbon Wakefield – was about to implement a plan for the formal colonisation of the country and set up some form of government of its own.

As a consequence of these concurrent concerns, the British Government, on the advice of its officials in the Colonial Office, decided to act. A naval officer in fragile health who had previously been to New Zealand, William Hobson, was despatched from London in August 1839 with instructions to take the constitutional steps necessary to establish a British colony. He was told to negotiate a voluntary transfer of sovereignty from Maori to the British Crown, so that there might be no doubt under international law about the validity of the annexation that would follow. In Sydney, Hobson was sworn in as Lieutenant-Governor of New South Wales, because the new colony would initially be a dependency of the Australian one. Hobson also recruited a handful of men to make up the nucleus of a civil service, almost all of whom would turn out to be ill-equipped for and ill-suited to the tasks allotted to them. He then sailed on to New Zealand, arriving in the Bay of Islands on 29 January 1840 to initiate what would come to be seen as the most important chapter in the country's history.

Waitangi, the name of the estuarine river that emerges below the site of James Busby's house into the western side of the Bay of Islands, means 'waters of lamentation'. It would turn out to be an appropriate label to attach to the Treaty signed in its vicinity in February 1840. While that Treaty was in part a product of the most benevolent instincts of British humanitarianism, and those who signed it on 6 February had the highest possible hopes for benign outcomes, the document would turn out to be the most contentious and problematic ingredient in New Zealand's national life.

The decision to annex New Zealand, and the instructions drawn up for the man who would become its first Governor, were deeply influenced by the evangelical religious beliefs of Colonial Office officials such as James Stephen (Colonial Under-Secretary) and Lord Glenelg (Colonial Secretary). These men were part of the same movement which had agitated for and brought about an end to slavery in the British Empire. Their concern for the welfare of Maori was genuine and profound. As time passed, however, and those same officials learned of the New Zealand Company's private-enterprise plan to colonise parts of New Zealand, the emphasis changed. By 1839, as Claudia Orange has noted, the Colonial Office was no longer contemplating its original plan, a Maori New Zealand in which European settlers had somehow to be accommodated, but instead 'a settler New Zealand in which a place had to be kept for Maori'. Inevitably, Maori interests would suffer as a consequence of being moved down the priority list.

While Lord Normanby, Secretary of State for the Colonies, insisted that Hobson was to negotiate a willing transfer of sovereignty from Maori to the Crown, problems would arise from the manner and speed with which the would-be Governor drafted the Treaty to accomplish this transfer. Hobson was given no draft document prepared by lawyers or Colonial Office functionaries. Instead, he had to cobble together his own treaty, with the help of his secretary, James Freeman, and British Resident James Busby, neither of whom was a lawyer. That done, Hobson recognised that a treaty in English alone could scarcely be understood, agreed to or even debated by Maori, so he had the missionary Henry Williams and his son Edward hastily translate the English version into Maori. All this occurred over four days, with the Maori version being prepared overnight on 4 February.

On 5 February copies of the Treaty in both languages were put before a gathering of northern chiefs inside an enormous marquee on the lawn in front of Busby's house. Present were hundreds of Maori, Hobson's entourage of officials and English and French missionaries, along with a solid phalanx of local Pakeha residents who were not allowed either to debate the text or to sign the document, except as witnesses, because it concerned only Maori relations with the British Crown. Hobson read the Treaty aloud in English, Henry Williams in Maori, and discussion between the proposers and the intended signatories followed. Because of his facility in Maori and because the other CMS missionaries supported both the Treaty and its constitutional consequences, it was inevitable that Williams spoke most often in defence of the document when asked by Maori about the meanings and implications of its clauses.

In English, the preamble announced that Queen Victoria regarded the 'Native Chiefs and Tribes of New Zealand' with favour and was 'anxious to protect their just Rights and Property and to secure to them the enjoyment of Peace and Good Order ...' Because of this, and because of the continuing influx of British immigrants into the country, the Queen wished to 'appoint a functionary properly authorized to treat with the Aborigines of New Zealand [rendered in Maori as 'nga Tangata maori o Nu Tirani'] for the recognition of Her Majesty's Sovereign authority over ... those islands ...' The establishment of such authority would lead to 'a settled form of Civil Government with a view to avert the evil consequences which must result from the absence of the necessary Laws and Institutions alike to the native population and to Her subjects ...' To bring all this about, the 'confederated and independent

Chiefs of New Zealand' – a deliberate echo of Busby's earlier declaration of independence – were invited to 'concur with three Articles and Conditions'.

The first article, and the key one for securing what was to follow, declared that the 'Chiefs of the Confederation of the United Tribes of New Zealand', and those who had not become members of the confederation, 'cede to Her Majesty the Queen of England absolutely and without reservation all the rights and powers of Sovereignty ... over their respective Territories ...'

Under the second article in English, which in time would become the most contentious, the Queen guaranteed to the chiefs and tribes and their families 'the full exclusive and undisturbed possession of their Lands and Estates Forests Fisheries and other properties ... so long as it is their wish and desire to retain the same in their possession'. At the same time the chiefs would give exclusive rights to the sale of land to the Queen and her representatives.

In the third article, the Queen extended to the 'Natives of New Zealand Her royal protection and imparts to them all the Rights and Privileges of British Subjects'. A final clause noted that the chiefs, 'having been made fully to understand the Provisions of the foregoing Treaty', accepted the spirit and the meaning of the document and would attach their signatures or marks to it.

There was much in this document alone that would have been difficult to convey to members of a culture which did not share the same concepts, vocabulary and political and legal structures – especially the notion of sovereignty. These difficulties were compounded by the fact that the Maori translation of the Treaty, the one most Maori would be addressing and debating and (if they thought they were in accord with it) signing, did not correspond to the English version in several key respects.

In the first place, the word used for sovereignty – that which the chiefs were asked to give away to the Queen of England – was rendered as 'kawanatanga'. Kawanatanga was an abstraction from the word kawana, itself a transliteration of 'governor', and hence meant literally 'governorship'. In the Declaration of the Independence of New Zealand, however, the word used for sovereignty had been 'mana', in the sense of 'authority over'. Future critics of the Treaty would thus be able to argue that the chiefs believed that they were retaining sovereignty, 'mana', and giving away only the right to 'governorship' of the country as a whole.

This impression would have been reinforced by the Maori wording of article two, which assured them that they retained 'te tino rangatiratanga o ratou wenua kainga me o ratou taonga katoa' – meaning 'the unqualified exercise of their chieftainship over their lands, villages and all their treasures'. This was rather more than the same article offered in English: 'full exclusive and undisturbed possession of their Lands and Estates Forests Fisheries and other properties . . .' Indeed, in future years, Maori debate would focus on the implications of the words 'tino rangatiratanga', which some would claim was an even more accurate rendition of 'sovereignty' than mana; they would further argue that, in guaranteeing Maori 'tino rangatiratanga', the Treaty was in fact guaranteeing Maori the right to continue to manage and govern their own affairs without interference by a civil or military authority.

Further confusion would arise over the term in article two 'ratou taonga katoa'. In the English version this supposedly corresponded to 'other properties' which Maori would be allowed to retain, but in fact the expression came to have far wider meaning: 'all their treasures'. It would be used in the future to argue Maori rights to material and cultural resources that were in no way envisaged by the English version or by those who proposed it.

None of these confusions was adequately identified or addressed in the discussion that took place in the marquee on 5 February. On the contrary, missionary explanations of the terms and concepts, particularly those given by Henry Williams, fudged precise meanings and potential contradictions and emphasised instead the protective and benevolent intentions of the document as it would affect Maori. 'I told them ... it was an act of love towards them on the part of [Queen Victoria],' Williams recalled. Clearly Hobson and his party, and apparently all the missionaries apart from the CMS printer William Colenso and the French Catholic Bishop Jean-Baptiste Pompallier, wanted the chiefs to sign as soon as possible and with a minimum of fuss. Most of the missionaries clearly believed that the Treaty was in *their* interests, and they almost certainly believed that it was also in the best interests of Maori, possibly 'the only way that the Maori could be saved from physical or spiritual extinction at the hands of the agents of vice', as one historian put it.

As might have been expected, different chiefs put forward a variety of reasons for supporting or opposing the signing of the document. At first the voices of opposition predominated. 'What do we want of a governor?' asked Rewa of the Ngai Tawake hapu of Ngapuhi. 'We are not whites nor foreigners. We are the governor – we the chiefs of this land of our ancestors ... Return! Governor, I, Rewa, say to you, go back.' Rewa was supported by Kawiti of Ngati Hine. 'What do you want here? ... We do not want to be tied up and trodden down. We are free. Let the missionaries remain, but as for you, return to your own country.'

If Hobson was becoming increasingly concerned about the tenor of the debate, he need not have been. It was a convention of whaikorero (Maori discussion) that all arguments, positive and negative, should be put. And about the real weaknesses in the Treaty, its ambiguities and contradictions, nothing was said. Many of them would become apparent only from a comparison of the Maori and English versions, and Maori were examining and discussing the Maori text only.

Eventually Tamati Waka Nene of Ngati Hao, a Wesleyan convert who had been protecting European traders in the Hokianga, began to steer discussion in another direction. '[Y]ou say [that] the Governor should return home?' he asked rhetorically. 'Had you spoken like that when the traders and grog-sellers came – had you turned them away – then you could well say to the Governor, "Go back", and it would have been right ... but now, as things are, no ... Governor! Do not go away from us; remain for us – a father, a judge, a peacemaker. You must not allow us to become slaves. You must preserve our customs and never permit land to be taken from us.' There has been some discussion among Maori and Pakeha scholars about whether Waka Nene had reached these conclusions of his own volition or whether he was parroting the views of his Wesleyan mentors. But such considerations have no relevance. Those *were* his views on the day. And he carried sufficient mana among his own people as a former fighting chief and more recently as a peacemaker for his arguments to be taken seriously.

As it happened, however, no clear consensus was reached among the chiefs in the course of a five-hour discussion on 5 February. And Maori preferred a consensus if at all possible. They therefore continued their deliberations late into the night on the river flat below Busby's house and lawn. The following morning 45 of them were ready to sign, either with their names or, as had become customary in such circumstances for those who were not literate, with part of their facial moko patterns.

Hobson and his officials were summoned hurriedly to allow this to happen lest official dilatoriness provoke a change of Maori mind (the many paintings and tableaux which show Hobson in full naval uniform serenely accepting Maori signatures is inaccurate; on the morning of 6 February he was wearing civilian clothes).

Shortly before the signing took place, however, Hobson was intercepted by Bishop Pompallier, who was worried that the embryonic state of New Zealand might adopt and entrench the British tradition of an 'established' church, and that that church would be the Church of England. He asked Hobson that Maori be told 'that all who should join the Catholic religion should have the protection of the British government'. Hobson agreed to this proposal with what Henry Williams called 'much blandness of expression'. To Williams's further annoyance, the Lieutenant-Governor (as he was until New Zealand became a full Crown Colony in 1841) asked Williams himself to convey this assurance in Maori to the reassembled chiefs.

To take the emphasis off protection for Catholics, Williams drafted a statement which said: 'The Governor wishes you to understand that all the Maories [sic] who shall join the Church of England, who shall join the Wesleyans, who shall join the Pikopo or Church of Rome, and those who retain their Maori practices, shall have the protection of the British Government.' Over 130 years later, some analysts would claim that this promise represented a 'fourth article' of the Treaty, and that it carried the same constitutional force as the first three. This, of course, is not correct. It was a promise that carried moral weight, and indeed it was carried out. But it had no legal or constitutional significance. The assumption that it might be used to enforce state protection and encouragement of Maori religious practices – 'ritenga maori', in Williams's translation – is misplaced.

The first Maori to sign the Treaty, with his own name, was Hone Heke Pokai, a Bay of Islands CMS convert who was a protégé, although not always a compliant one, of Henry Williams. Among those who followed were, as might have been expected, Tamati Waka Nene and his older brother and tuakana, Patuone. What might have been more of a surprise to Hobson was that the document was also signed by those who had spoken against it – although in the case of Kawiti, the traditional belief is that he did so because his people pressed him to sign (while his mark is with the 6 February signatures, it was added in the second week of May 1840). Subsequent signings with local chiefs took place at Waimate North and the Hokianga in February, and later in nearly 50 other locations in the North and South Islands. Hobson proclaimed British sovereignty over the whole country on 21 May 1840, before the signings were complete, making New Zealand a dependency of New South Wales, and a year later New Zealand's own charter came into effect, making the country a separate colony of Great Britain.

While all these steps met internationally recognised constitutional procedures, there were loose ends that would constitute grounds for debate over the following 160 years: the fact that Hobson's proclamation of sovereignty preceded the collection of Treaty signatures; the fact that some chiefs of large tribes declined to sign the document or were not asked to; the fact that more than one version of the Treaty was in circulation and subsequently signed; the fact that there were inherent contradictions between even the 'official' English and Maori versions; the fact that some Maori, with missionary encouragement, regarded the Treaty as being in the nature of a 'sacred covenant', in the Biblical sense, between themselves and Queen Victoria.

Almost 150 years later, when New Zealand governments tried to give judicial and moral effect to the document, they would seek to do so by defining yet another version, the 'spirit' or 'intent' of the Treaty. This was a clear admission that the document itself, in all its manifestations and *because* of all its manifestations, was neither a firm foundation for the construction of a state nor a blueprint for relations between governments and an indigenous people.

In 1840, however, the document served its original purpose. It enabled William Hobson, as the representative of the British Crown, to proclaim British sovereignty over the country and bring it into that family of nations known as the British Empire. Whether the Treaty meant *more* than this at the time is debatable. Hobson would have been utterly unable to govern the country, with a mere £4000, 39 officials and eleven 'alcoholic' New South Wales police troopers, had Maori not given their consent. At any time Maori could withdraw their consent, as they did on various occasions in the 1840s and 1860s, and the civil and military authorities were unable to establish or fully regain control of those parts of the country where 'rebellions' had occurred.

In 1840, however, the Treaty appeared to offer Maori certain guarantees, and many Maori had formed their own view of what those guarantees were and pronounced them acceptable. This degree of assent enabled Hobson to declare British sovereignty over the country and to set about the business of 'governing', at first from Kororareka in the Bay of Islands and subsequently, from February 1841, from Auckland, which Hobson named after Lord Auckland, one of his patrons in the Royal Navy. Now a full governor, appointed by the Crown in Britain and taking instructions from the British Secretary of State for the Colonies, he operated with the local assistance of two councils.

The Executive Council was made up of his three senior officials: Colonial Secretary Willoughby Shortland, Colonial Treasurer George Cooper and Attorney-General Francis Fisher. The first two of these men were notable for their incompetence and cupidity, and the third for his ill-health. Hobson had no substantial assistance from his officials until William Swainson replaced Fisher and William Martin became the country's first Chief Justice late in 1841. The second governing body, the Legislative Council, was composed of members of the Executive Council with the addition of three justices of the peace (one of whom was replaced by Martin after his arrival).

Hobson had also to appoint a Land Claims Commissioner to confirm or invalidate all land sales made before the assumption of British sovereignty, and a Protector of Aborigines, a position given to the respected former missionary George Clarke. The latter role prefigured the later Department of Native Affairs, but its integrity was compromised by the fact that Clarke was also to act as government land purchase officer. As a consequence, he came to be regarded with equal suspicion by European settlers and by Maori. Funds for government were initially to be raised by way of the Crown pre-emption clause in the Treaty of Waitangi: Maori could sell only to the agent of the Crown, and the Crown would on-sell to European settlers at a profit. It was an arrangement that suited only the Crown, and was abolished in 1844 by Hobson's successor.

Despite immediate difficulties, some of them caused by the intractability and ineptitude of Hobson's first officials, and some of them by the Governor's continuing ill-health after a stroke in March 1840, the British colonisation of New Zealand was able to proceed without any major initial breakdowns in adminis-tration or law and order. And it proceeded with all of the accoutrements implied by the term colonisation: transfer of people from one side of the globe to the other, exploitation of the country's material resources for the benefit of both settlers and distant investors. In the words of a later Maori High Court Judge, Eddie Durie, tangata whenua, the people of the land, would now be joined by 'tangata tiriti', the people whose presence was authorised by the Treaty of Waitangi. And the face of New Zealand life would from that time on be a Janus one, representing at least two cultures and two heritages, very often looking in two different directions.

12

Tangata Tiriti

While most Europeans in the first half of the nineteenth century referred to the native inhabitants of New Zealand as 'New Zealanders', the Maori text of the Treaty of Waitangi used the expression 'tangata maori' – ordinary people – to denote them. This indicates how Maori were referring to themselves by that time – and, indeed, recorded evidence of that expression goes back as far as 1801, to the journal of the ship *Royal Admiral* in the Firth of Thames. By the 1830s the word Maori on its own was in widespread use among Maori. And by 1860 Renata Tamakihikurangi of Ngati Kahungunu would go so far as to say to the European settlers of Hawke's Bay: 'Just as you are all English ... so we (Natives) are all one: Maori is my name.' In official usage, however, the word 'Native' was employed to describe the cabinet minister and government department responsible for Maori matters, and the Land Court until 1946.

The Treaty also employed the term 'pakeha' to refer to Queen Victoria's non-Maori subjects in New Zealand. Use of this word in Maori to denote Europeans was current in the Bay of Islands by at least 1814, when the missionary William Hall reported that he had been referred to at Te Puna pa as a 'rungateeda pakehaa' (rangatira pakeha: a European gentleman). There is no evidence in this or any other instance in early literature that the term was derogatory. It was simply a necessary descriptive word to distinguish European from Maori, and it probably came from the pre-European word pakepakeha, denoting mythical light-skinned beings. It may not have been universally popular in Maori from the beginning of Maori–Pakeha contact – some early references note the term tangata tipua and, in the far south, tangata pora to describe Europeans. But use of the word Pakeha was widespread among Maori by the 1830s.

The main reason for its spread, of course, was the growth of the settler population and the increase in the proportion of Maori who would have direct contact with Europeans. The number of Pakeha living in New Zealand in 1830 had been just over 300. Most of these settlers had come from Australia, some of them ex-convicts seeking to escape their penal pasts and some traders working for Australian-based timber and flax operations. A smaller percentage included those who had jumped ship from vessels originating in Britain, the United States and France. The population of missionaries and their families came largely from England (the Anglicans and Wesleyans) or from France (the Catholics). The total number of Pakeha settlers in 1840 was a little over 2000. By 1858 they would outnumber Maori by approximately 3000: 59,000 to 56,000. And by 1881 there would be around 500,000 of them. What caused this massive removal of population from one side of the world to the other?

In global terms, of course, the development of the new state of New Zealand in the second half of the nineteenth century was a subplot in the diaspora of Europeans that sent as many as

50 million people from the Old World to the New over a period of 200 years. These were the settlers who created neo-Europes in North America, Australia and southern Africa, taking with them the flora, fauna, agricultural and horticultural practices and architecture that enabled them to transform whole landscapes into a likeness of the places they had left behind. The forces which scattered them have been categorised by James Belich into those which 'pushed' and those which 'pulled'.

The 'push' or dynamic of ejection included such factors as European overpopulation, poverty, hunger, an inability to break out of class systems, and religious controversy or outright persecution. Scots who came to Otago and Southland from 1848, for example, were propelled largely by an urge to escape economic depression and its effects, and by the excoriating split between the Church of Scotland and Free Church Presbyterians. Thousands of Irish departures at about the same time were prompted by the devastating potato famines. The attraction lay in the promise of prosperity and healthier environments, prospects for social advancement without the hurdles of a class system and, for investors, opportunities to enlarge capital.

Much of the initial settlement of New Zealand in the 1840s was the result of private-enterprise immigration company schemes. The British Colonial Office had been persuaded to accelerate its plans for the annexation of New Zealand, and William Hobson to proclaim sovereignty before the Treaty of Waitangi had finished its perambulations, because of two of these private schemes.

One was French in origin, and resulted in the establishment of the Nanto-Bordelaise colony at Akaroa in August 1840. Had Hobson not already acted three months earlier, this settlement might have resulted in part or the whole of the South Island being annexed by France. As things transpired, however, organised French colonisation was confined to this small community (only 53 settlers in all) on Banks Peninsula, although individual Frenchmen and their families had found their way to such ports as the Bay of Islands and Tauranga. Because the inhabitants of Akaroa were nominally almost entirely Catholic, Bishop Pompallier established the first European station of his mission there in 1840, and for a short time it was a pleasant place for his culture-starved priests, and for the bishop himself, to renew their association with French cuisine, conversation and literature. Eventually, however, Pompallier closed the station as a mark of disgust at the religious apathy of the Akaroa colonists.

A far more substantial scheme was the New Zealand Company settlement of Wellington, also established in 1840, on the shores of Port Nicholson. This was the brainchild of the mercurial Edward Gibbon Wakefield. Wakefield had been imprisoned for three years as a result of abducting the schoolgirl heiress Ellen Turner in 1826, and while he was incarcerated he formulated his famous theories for what he called 'systematic colonisation'. The principal aim of this scheme, David Hamer has written, was to provide 'a balance between capital and labour. [Wakefield] believed that to succeed a colony had to attract capitalists and that the way to do this was to ensure that labour would be available to work on, and add value to, the property in which they had invested . . . [Land] should be sold at a price beyond the means of labourers, but their migration . . . could be encouraged by the expectation of one day buying land with their savings.'

Although the New Zealand Company was set up by well-heeled investors to apply these concepts to its New Zealand settlements, Wakefield himself was obliged to play a behind-the-scenes role because of the notoriety generated by the Ellen Turner episode. In that role he argued and charmed into co-operation an influential group of aristocrats and politicians, including the Earl of Durham, John George Lambton, Baron Petre, Sir William Molesworth, the brothers John and William Hutt, and others whose names would eventually grace New Zealand streets and towns. Two of the company's principal agents in New Zealand, however, would be Edward's brothers William and Arthur Wakefield, in Wellington and Nelson respectively. Edward himself would not set foot in the country until 1853, whereupon he began a brief and disappointing political career.

The Wakefields' plans for New Zealand sought to establish a 'Better Britain' or a 'Britain of the South' in which English class distinctions were preserved but where industrious artisans and farmers could more easily work their way towards prosperity and respectability. Company prospectuses and allied advertising told many lies about the nature of the new country (describing Wellington, for example, as a place of undulating plains suitable for the cultivation of grapevines, olives and wheat); by the time the truth was revealed, colonists had arrived and were unlikely to turn around at once and depart. And they were arriving in billowing numbers: Wellington had 2500 European settlers by 1841, and 4000 by 1843.

Wanganui was founded as Petre, after one of the New Zealand Company's aristocratic directors, to provide additional land for the overflow of Wellington settlers and to supply the mother settlement with pigs, pork and potatoes. Nelson and New Plymouth were founded as further New Zealand Company settlements in 1841. All three would have serious difficulties with local Maori as a result of questionable land purchases.

Two further ventures, the establishment of Dunedin as a Scottish Free Church settlement in 1848 and Christchurch as a Canterbury Association (Church of England) settlement in 1850, were based on New Zealand Company models and hence can be seen as offspring or beneficiaries of its major enterprises, which formally ceased when the company surrendered its charter to the Crown in 1850. Auckland alone of the main centres was established (in 1840) and grew without organised immigration. Its prosperity was ensured by its location on an isthmus between two navigable harbours and by Hobson's decision to relocate the country's capital there from the Bay of Islands.

While the New Zealand Company settlements contributed only about 15,500 settlers to New Zealand's founding population, they were disproportionately influential on account of being there first and establishing the ethos of their cities, three of which, with Auckland, would become and remain the 'main centres' and provide the foundation for the system of provincial government introduced in 1853. Christchurch, for example, would remain visibly English in character and appearance, and in the manners of its citizenry, for its first 100 years. And Dunedin, with its street names drawn from Edinburgh, its public buildings in stone and brick, and its scattering of Queen Anne towers, was still unmistakeably Scottish more than 150 years after its foundation.

No clear information is available on exactly what percentages of early immigrants were engaged in which occupations. But, as Jeanine Graham has noted, the New Zealand Company sought to attract 'respectful hard-working rural labourers and cultured men of capital' as its two categories of first choice. The Canterbury settlement, closer to land immediately available for agriculture and horticulture, wanted 'industrious immigrants of the labouring class' and small farmers, while the Marlborough Province, soon after its establishment in 1860, sought 'ordinary farm labourers, carpenters, and mechanics, navvies, bush hands, shepherds, miners and domestic female servants'. Shepherds were especially welcome if they brought their own dogs. Most female immigrants who were not wives or daughters came as domestic servants. In terms of national wealth, in the pastoral era of the 1850s and 1860s the colony's basic economic unit was 'an efficiently managed sheep-run of 10,000 acres or more'. Such stations, predominantly in Hawke's Bay, Wairarapa, Canterbury and North Otago, 'formed a settled community of about a score: family, shepherds and station hands'.

I. R. Cooper in *The New Zealand Settlers' Guide* assured readers in 1857 that:

> Those who arrive in the colony without capital will, if they enjoy good health, are sober and economical in their personal expenses, and are able and willing to work at any one trade, as farm servants, boatmen, shepherds, or house servants, soon realize a sufficient capital to invest in land, cattle or sheep, and thus to render themselves and their children independent.

Certainly a degree of adaptability and what might be regarded as upward social mobility is apparent in many individual families. The Olsons, for example, who came to Wellington in the 1850s as shoemakers, ran a hotel in Lyttelton in the 1860s and then settled in Taranaki as landowners and farmed in the 1880s. And it was the opportunity to make such adjustments that drew many colonists out from the United Kingdom, where such mobility was more difficult to accomplish, for economic and social reasons. Benjamin Shadbolt, transported in 1846 from Oxfordshire to Tasmania for burglary, won his ticket of leave in 1853, migrated to New Zealand in 1859 with sufficient capital to become, within a short period, a sawmiller, farmer, shopkeeper and publican on Banks Peninsula. By the time he died in 1862 at the early age of 57, he was a respected horse breeder and local body politician. His immediate descendants suppressed, or were never told about, the convict chapter of his life, which had enabled him to break out of rural poverty in England.

Like the Olsons and Shadbolt, the largest number of immigrants in the first 50 years of European settlement of New Zealand – close to 50 per cent – would come from England and Wales (the two countries are not distinguishable because early statistics lumped them together: evidence suggests strongly that the number of Welsh was considerably lower than that of English). Scots would make up the second biggest group, some 24 per cent, in contrast to Britain itself, where they made up only 10 per cent of the total population. Then came the Irish, whose numbers reached a peak of about 19 per cent in the wake of the New Zealand gold rushes of the 1860s. Of the minority groups, the largest were Germans, who settled in particular around Nelson. Scandinavians, Poles, French and Italians made up most of the rest. Chinese immigrants too arrived to take advantage of the gold rushes but were settled almost exclusively at first in Otago and Westland.

Despite these minor cultural variegations, New Zealand acquired a distinctly 'British' character as the nineteenth century advanced. Indeed, as commentators never tired of pointing out, the country became in some respects 'more British' than Britain itself, especially in expressing loyalty to the Crown and its willingness to take part in imperial wars. As Belich has argued, the British abroad tended to drop their narrower ethnic identities to form a new 'Us' while confronting a shared 'Them', who in New Zealand were Maori and Catholic Irish. 'Like the racial identities to which it was closely related, [Britishness] was a cloak you put on when you went out.'

There was certainly far more mixing of ethnic and religious ingredients on the colonial frontier than there was at 'Home'. Dr John Shaw in *A Gallop to the Antipodes* described his continual surprise at the manner in which people were living in New Zealand in the 1850s, apparently without many of the prejudices or preconceptions common to British people in Britain. He was also favourably impressed by the success of the 'mixed-race' communities around shore whaling stations. He describes, for example, visiting John and Kurupa Davis – he an African-American whaler, she a former Moriori slave – near the Guards' station at Port Underwood. Their cottage was identical to others in such settlements.

The roof, like that of a barn, was visible from the interior, from the rafters of which hung sickles, baskets, heads of Indian corn, bacon, knives, shears and a razor. The sleeping apartment was separated by a wall which terminated halfway between the roof and the floor. On top ... dangled several clothes belonging to the lady of the establishment ... [There] were no chairs, a long form being the only substitute ... The floor consisted of terra firma covered with logs of wood, teapots, wooden casks, kettles and a nail-box. There was an imitation cupboard, placed at the top of which were some preserves ... Lower down was a plate rack scantily furnished, beneath which ... were hoes [and] hatchets ... Across the chimney extended a spar on which were suspended pot-hooks and damp clothes waiting to be dried. The animals comprised of four cats, a few goats, numerous ducks and geese, cocks and hens ...

[In] came the husband, who most cordially shook me with his hand, as black as coal, with a face of the same complexion ... [We had] a good repast ... of wild pig as usual, with some capital potatoes, finishing with a pipe ... [I was] in the company of two individuals whose blood contained the savageism of three distinct races, in a miserable little cottage ... [But] the attention and hospitality that I received from these poor people made me solemnly feel the truth and beauty of the Scriptural declaration that God has made of one blood all the nations of the earth.

Thomas Cholmondeley, writing in 1854, was more taken by what seemed, by comparison with Britain, a spirit of ecumenism.

> What then is the religious condition of the ordinary colonist? He finds himself struggling in a new country, not as he struggled in the old – in the midst of a town or village community trained and minded like himself. No; English, Irish, Welsh and Scottish are flung together ... They compare thoughts, ways, actions and words; they discuss systems; exchange customs; sift, weigh and balance their arguments and positions one with another. From an old church catechism, down to some new method of planting potatoes, nothing escapes.

Even that most divisive element within British communities at Home and abroad – the Protestant–Catholic split – was observed less in New Zealand than in Britain itself. A Catholic aristocrat, Charles Clifford, became first Speaker of the New Zealand Parliament in 1854. Another Catholic, Frederick Weld, became Premier in 1864. An English member of the Religious Tract Society who visited New Zealand in 1880 was alarmed by the extent of Catholic–Protestant interaction he found. 'One can't help feeling that the spirit of tolerance is somewhat carried to excess when one finds Protestants patronizing the Roman Catholic bazaar. One admires their love more than their wisdom, their heart more than their head.' This early ecumenism worked to the benefit of such charitable aid workers as the French-Catholic nun Suzanne Aubert, and set a healthy precedent for the colony – a sense in which it could indeed be viewed as a 'Better Britain'. But it would be infected by a virus of anti-Irish and consequent anti-Catholic feeling in the early decades of the twentieth century.

The rate of immigration increased considerably after the 1840s. In the 1850s it was fuelled by provincial government schemes to entice new settlers in order to expand economic activity and to increase the political influence of the regions. In the 1860s the discovery of gold, first in Otago and then on the West Coast of the South Island and finally on the Coromandel Peninsula in the north, increased the population influx in those areas substantially. In the same decade military settlers were brought in from both Australia and Britain to defend colonists against perceived Maori challenges to British sovereignty and to settler safety. And, finally, central government campaigns in the 1870s and 1880s, devised by the entrepreneurial Premier Julius Vogel, attracted immigrants at a rate that swamped all previous experience and campaigns.

The net result was that, between 1831 and 1881, the Pakeha population of New Zealand had increased by 50,000 per cent. Of the 400,000 immigrants who came to the country, 300,000 remained there, while the number of births over the same period accounted for another 250,000 people. The character of New Zealand was changed for ever. Those who had to relinquish ground, literally and metaphorically, for this influx of 'foreign' people were the first New Zealanders, the indigenous Maori. And, in relinquishing ground, they would lose it.

13

Tangata Whenua Respond

Most Maori had welcomed European settlers when they first encountered them. Because of tribal competitiveness, rangatira saw Pakeha as a means of consolidating local power: they would be a potential source of muskets, trade goods and useful advice, intermediaries in negotiations with other Pakeha, and enlarge the mana of the sponsoring chief, kainga and hapu. Many chiefs spoke with pride of 'their' Pakeha. As John Owens has pointed out, the achievements of the pre-1840 era of Maori–Pakeha co-operation – in economic development, race relations and social controls – had been considerable. It is likely that Maori who signed the Treaty of Waitangi expected these conditions to continue, 'with emphasis on the small-scale community and the pressures of unwritten custom rather than the controls and legislation of [a] central government. Divisions, based ... on race, class and sect would have had little meaning.'

The large-scale immigration beginning in the 1840s brought a shift in perspective, however. The Ati Awa chief Te Wharepouri told William Wakefield, brother of Edward Gibbon, that he had participated in the sale of land to the New Zealand Company expecting about ten Pakeha to settle around Port Nicholson, one for each pa. When he saw the more than 1000 settlers who stepped off the company's first fleet of immigrant ships, he had panicked. The spectacle would have seemed like an invasion of extraterrestrials. It was beyond anything that Wharepouri had imagined.

Previous European settlement had taken place on Maori terms, with Maori in control of the process. Slowly, in the 1840s, Maori close to European coastal settlements began to realise the extent to which their identity and customs might be swallowed up by this mighty tide of strangers. Maori oratory of those years began to employ proverbs about the power of salt-water to contaminate freshwater (a nice metaphor, this, because Pakeha flesh was reputed to taste more salty than Maori), and the propensity of the kahawai for devouring the mullet.

It was from this time too that Maori began to display an increasing vulnerability to European-introduced diseases such as influenza and measles. As each new boatload of immigrants arrived, there was the possibility that they carried with them pathogens from the most recent strains of diseases prevalent in Britain or Europe. As Ian Pool notes, Maori were still 'only building up their basic immune stocks. From every [modern] perspective their living conditions were appalling: over-crowded, damp, unhygienic dwellings; and limited access to food resources [if] their land had been ... alienated through purchases ... This should have been a period of calm and partnership, in which Maori would be protected by the Crown from the loss of all their resources, from social evils and from exploitation ... [Instead it] resulted ... in a more rapid decline in Maori numbers than had occurred prior to the Treaty ...

Maori almost failed to survive [the next] half century ...'

Further, there was considerable dissatisfaction among Maori over the ways in which major land dealings were being conducted by some of the agents of colonisation, such as the Wakefield brothers. The first New Zealand Company land purchases in Wellington were carried out through the whaler Dicky Barrett, whose 'pidgin Maori' may not have been up to the task. Maori land was, of course, owned communally. On some occasions only one faction of the owners, whose claims might have been doubtful, were dealt with; others, less malleable, were bypassed. Sometimes the quantities of goods passed over in exchange were subsequently found to be inadequate. In the case of government agents, promises to set aside native reserves, even schools or hospitals in some areas, were not kept.

The most fertile seed for conflict in all this was mutual misunderstanding over what constituted land ownership. For European buyers it was a signed deed. For Maori it was a variety of factors, including inherited rights, rights obtained by conquest, and rights of occupation and use. Maori sometimes refused to recognise the validity of sales to Europeans which had been conducted with other Maori who were not authorised to act on behalf of the hapu or tribe as a whole, which were the result of trickery, or which had not resulted in subsequent occupation and settlement.

Almost all the mistakes that could have been made *were* made by the New Zealand Company land-purchasing agents in Wellington, Nelson and Wanganui. The Land Claims Commissioner appointed to investigate these purchases, William Spain, ruled that the company had to pay compensation to the Maori owners who had been inadequately remunerated at the time the land was sold. Spain was assisted by George Clarke junior, the Governor's Sub-Protector of Aborigines, who was especially critical of the way in which the company had carried out those dealings and submitted that it ought to pay an additional £1500 for the Wellington purchases, a demand that William Wakefield ignored. Wellington Maori did not want additional remuneration. Their argument* was that large parts of the land claimed by the company had never in fact been sold.

It was a fraudulent land deal which lay behind the first armed clash between Maori and Pakeha after the signing of the Treaty of Waitangi, and the only one ever to take place in the South Island. The major player, again, was the New Zealand Company. Captain Arthur Wakefield held a false deed to land in the Wairau Valley on the southern side of Cook Strait (he had bought it from the widow of a whaler who claimed in turn to have bought the land from Te Rauparaha of Ngati Toa). When a group of Nelson settlers, including Wakefield, attempted to clear Maori off the land in June 1843, fighting broke out and 30 Europeans were killed, along with about half a dozen Maori. The dead included Arthur Wakefield, who was executed by the Ngati Toa chief Te Rangihaeata in return for the death of his wife Te Rongo, who was also Te Rauparaha's daughter.

The Governor, Robert FitzRoy, who had succeeded Hobson after the latter died of a stroke in September 1842, held that the greater blame for the 'massacre', as the Nelson settlers called it, lay with the settlers themselves, because the land in question belonged to Ngati Toa. The anger and contempt of Wellington colonists at this verdict turned to fear when Te Rauparaha and his nephew Te Rangihaeata moved back to the northern side of Cook Strait to build and occupy a new pa at Plimmerton. Over the next three years these chiefs and their supporters were drawn into land disputes in the adjacent Hutt Valley.

---

* Upheld by the Waitangi Tribunal in 2003.

Te Rangihaeata took the view that the sale of the Hutt Valley by Te Ati Awa to the New Zealand Company was invalid because Ati Awa had settled the district under the mana of their allies Ngati Toa, and Ngati Toa had not been consulted about the sale nor paid anything from the proceeds. There were other complications too. Ngati Rangatahi from Whanganui and Ngati Tama had also been given cultivation rights there by Ngati Toa in recompense for their contributions to earlier wars, but they also had been paid nothing to vacate the district. Te Rangihaeata encouraged these tribes to resist Pakeha incursions into the Hutt Valley, even after he had been paid his long-delayed compensation for the sale. There were armed clashes at Taita and Boulcott's farm in 1846, supported by Rangihaeata's forces.

Ngati Toa built a new pa at Pauatahanui on the Porirua estuary, and the new Governor, Captain George Grey (soon to be knighted), moved troops into the area and built a naval fort at the mouth of the harbour. He arrested Te Rauparaha at Taupo Pa at Plimmerton, and then moved troops in to attack Rangihaeata's position. Before they arrived, Rangihaeata had moved his forces up the Horokiri Valley and there, at what is now called Battle Hill, in August 1846 they stopped the advance of the government troops, with casualties on both sides. Rangihaeata was eventually allowed to retreat to the Horowhenua district, where he was left unmolested and died during a measles epidemic nine years later. Te Rauparaha, meanwhile, had been held by Grey without charge for 10 months and then returned to his people at Otaki, where it became apparent that, because of his arrest, his mana and therefore his influence had waned. Like Te Rangihaeata, he began to attend church services but declined to convert to Christianity. He died in 1849 and was buried first near the Anglican church Rangiatea, and then on Kapiti Island, his old stronghold.

While tension had been mounting in Wellington in 1844, more serious and extensive conflict had broken out in the far north. Hone Heke of Ngapuhi, the first chief to sign the Treaty of Waitangi, had become disenchanted with the effects of European colonisation. He lamented the shift of the capital from Kororareka to Auckland, which had reduced the importance of the Bay of Islands, removed many of its former economic benefits and, in conjunction with the introduction of customs duties and shipping levies, contributed to a depression. Heke was further incensed by a government ban on the felling of kauri trees and by the hanging of Maketu, son of the Ngapuhi chief Ruhi, for the murder of a European family. To Heke, it seemed that the rangatiratanga promised to the chiefs in the Treaty had been usurped, and he decided to strike at British authority.

On 8 July 1844, Te Haratua, Heke's second-in-command, cut down the flagstaff at Kororareka. This had originally been a gift to the district from Heke, for the purpose of flying a Maori flag. Instead, it had been used by British forces to fly the Union Jack. Worried about the implications of this gesture, Governor FitzRoy requested additional troops from New South Wales but took no other immediate action. On 10 January the following year Heke cut down the replacement flagpole, and another on 19 January. FitzRoy then offered a reward for Heke's capture and established a military presence in Kororareka. Meanwhile Heke gained the support of his fellow Treaty-signatory Kawiti of Ngati Hine and together they attacked Kororareka on 10 March 1845. After one day's fighting – 600 Maori against 250 armed defenders – the Maori forces withdrew, leaving 20 Europeans dead and having lost somewhat more of their own fighters. In their wake a powder magazine exploded and set fire to much of the town. Maori and Pakeha joined in subsequent looting.

Two wars were waged in the months that followed, sometimes separately and sometimes simultaneously. Tamati Waka Nene and most Hokianga Ngapuhi chiefs attacked Heke and his allies in a revival of earlier tribal conflict. Then these kupapa or 'friendly' Maori (meaning friendly to the Crown) joined the imperial forces for joint action on Heke's and Kawiti's defended positions. The end came ten months later when Lieutenant-Colonel Henry Despard's troops breached Kawiti's pa at Ruapekapeka on a Sunday, after it had been deserted by the defenders.

James Belich, in his major revisionist analysis of the New Zealand Wars, argues that – in every sense that mattered – Heke and Kawiti won the Northern War. They were never defeated in any of its set-piece battles against imperial troops at Puketutu, Ohaeawai and Ruapekapeka (although Hokianga Ngapuhi succeeded in taking Heke's pa at Te Ahuahu). Few of their men were killed (about 60, to the imperial forces' 300). And Maori had succeeded in tying up the British forces in exactly the way they had sought to: 'By building new pa in isolated locations, the Maori were able to channel military operations into economically unimportant areas. A British force attacking a new pa could not simultaneously attack Maori base areas.'

When Grey succeeded FitzRoy as Governor, Heke sent him a similar message to those he had addressed to his predecessor: 'God made this country for us. It cannot be sliced ... Do you return to your own country, which was made by God for you. God made this land for us; it is not for any stranger or foreign nation to meddle with this sacred country.' Grey regarded this as provocative rather than conciliatory, and pressed on with plans to attack Ruapekapeka – though Heke, by then seriously injured, took no part in that battle.

Afterwards, Kawiti and Heke each made their peace with Grey. And Grey declined to seek retribution or confiscation, an implied recognition, perhaps, that neither chief had been defeated and that imperial forces would have found it difficult to maintain hostilities. Two years later Heke and Grey met at the Waimate North mission house and Heke handed over his greenstone mere to the Governor: 'not so much as a mark of respect and an emblem of peace,' Freda Kawharu has written, 'but as a token of acceptance of Grey's right to be in New Zealand and of Heke's expectation that the Queen's representative would honour the treaty. Symbolically, in Heke's eyes, by accepting the gift Grey was also accepting the responsibility of trusteeship.'

Two years later Heke was dead from tuberculosis, and Kawiti, who was older, survived him by only four years. He too left a message about his expectations for the future of his country and the role of the Treaty of Waitangi as a mediating influence between Maori and Pakeha. Wait, he told his people, 'until the sandfly nips the pages of the book [the Treaty]; then you will rise and oppose'. His descendants took this as an injunction to act when the promises of the Treaty were not kept.

The Northern War had several important consequences. It was followed by thirteen years of peace nationally, apart from some small-scale tribal skirmishes. Imperial troops developed a far higher regard for Maori skills in warfare than they had held previously. In particular, admiration was expressed for the ingenuity of the fortifications at Ohaeawai and Ruapekapeka. In the space of around 30 years Maori had developed their pa from strongholds designed to withstand physical attack with hand-to-hand weapons to those designed to withstand attack by muskets, then cannon, and finally to enable virtual trench warfare. Major Mould of the Royal Engineers made detailed reports on the Maori rifle pits and trenches. The effect of those reports was seen in the use of trench warfare in the Crimea in 1853, and, of course, even more so in World War I, where the machine-gun made underground defences a necessity.

The decade that followed the Northern War was, on the surface, one of peaceful interaction between Maori and Europeans. The modes of interaction, of course, differed in different parts of the country. Some Maori, such as Tuhoe in the Urewera and Ngati Maniapoto in what was soon to be called the King Country, saw virtually no Europeans apart from itinerant missionaries and traders. There is evidence, though, that these tribes and others were beginning to be affected by a high rate of viral and bacterial diseases and that this factor, along with decreasing rates of fertility, was contributing to a further fall in the national Maori population.

The Waikato and Hauraki tribes, at first under missionary direction, were expanding crop production and supplying virtually the whole of Auckland's flour and vegetable requirements. Some Tainui tribes began to export produce to Australia at this time, out of the ports of Auckland and Kawhia. Chatham Islands Maori too, helped by the fact that no one had, as yet, compelled them to release their Moriori slaves, were exporting potatoes to the United States (one vessel alone in 1850 bought 225 tonnes of potatoes for California, paid for in calico and printed fabrics). Missionaries were expressing the hope that, provided Maori eventually developed immunity to European diseases, the race had a bright future as an entrepreneurial people who could both support themselves agriculturally and earn a surplus to the benefit of cultural and community activities.

Some hapu were selling land willingly to government agents, especially in Taranaki and Hawke's Bay, to cater for the still-climbing numbers of European immigrants. Others by the 1850s were declining to do so, and going so far as to form land leagues actively opposed to further sales. The latter were experiencing and voicing many of the misgivings about Maori survival first expressed in the 1840s. By 1860 the European population in New Zealand surpassed that of Maori for the first time, and it seemed to some leaders that the very survival of Maori people and their culture might be under threat. These feelings, combined with crises associated with land sales, would make the 1860s the most volatile decade in the young nation's history.

Consolidation

14

New Settlers Take Control

British colonists established a foothold in the Crown Colony of New Zealand in the 1840s and, if they did not succeed in actually 'defeating' Maori who rebelled, they had at least kept the rebels at bay and secured the immediate zones of Pakeha settlement. By and large the new settlers were safe because most Maori who had an opinion on the issue consented to Pakeha being where they were, on small sections of the country's coastal fringe. One reason they consented was that they did not yet see the Pakeha presence as something that would substantially change the way Maori lived or behaved. In the next two decades, however, the demographic, economic and political impact of the new colonists would transform the country in ways that the tangata whenua could never have foreseen. That transformation occurred at several levels simultaneously.

One was in the exploration and renaming of many parts of the land. As Maori had done before them, Pakeha colonists set out to make the unknown known and to discover for themselves

the country's physical resources. They imposed a high proportion of new placenames, derived mainly from British places or
people, on parts of the country where they established ascendancy and in places apparently devoid of Maori occupation
(among the latter, mountains, lakes and rivers were especially
favoured targets). So Tamaki-makau-rau became Auckland, Te
Upoko-o-te-Ika became Port Nicholson and Wellington, Otakou
became Dunedin (the Gaelic name for Edinburgh), and so on.
All the major rivers in Canterbury were given English names,
though in time they reverted to their Maori ones. In some
instances the new names were translated back into Maori for
Maori use – Akarana for Auckland, Poneke for Port Nicholson,
Niu Terani for New Zealand itself.

The exploration and surveying of the land was another way
in which, by being made known to Pakeha and subject to
cadastral surveys and triangulation, fixing locations by instrumental and mathematical calculation – concepts and practices
unknown to Maori – the country was being appropriated at yet
another level. This appropriation was symbolic in some regions
and actual in others, where ownership of specific places changed
hands. Most of the coastline was surveyed by the naval vessels
Acheron and *Pandora* between 1848 and 1855, with particular
attention paid to actual or potential ports. Major investigations
on land were undertaken by such figures as William Colenso
(interior of the North Island, 1841–42), Edward Shortland
(Otago to Banks Peninsula, 1844), Thomas Brunner and Charles
Heaphy (West Coast of the South Island, 1846), Colenso again
(Hawke's Bay and inland North Island, 1843–47), Nathanael
Chalmers (Central Otago, 1853), Ferdinand Hochstetter (geographical surveys in the Auckland province and Nelson region,
1859). All the country traversed by these men – it was always
men at this time – was well known to Maori, and many of them

succeeded and survived only because they had Maori guides. But the journeys were made so that topographical features could be placed on otherwise blank provincial government maps, so that authorities might have some notion of which regions were suitable for farming, forestry or mineral exploitation, and so that subsequent travellers could find their way back to the geographical features described. In 1875 the central government agreed to undertake a triangulated survey of the country as a whole, and John Turnbull Thomson, who had done pioneering survey work for the Otago provincial administration, became the country's first surveyor-general; for the four years he held the position, he performed his duties with competence and distinction.

At the same time as European knowledge of the country was expanding and settlers were building houses, halls and churches on land claimed from forests, they were also practising intense colonisation of the flora and fauna. This was partly the process of creating a 'neo-Europe' – a world that looked and felt more like the one from whence they had come – partly the business of establishing animals, pasture and grains that could be husbanded to provide food and income, both national and individual, and partly an attempt to enlarge the opportunities for recreational hunting and fishing. East Polynesian colonists had introduced kiore, kuri (dog) and half a dozen plant species. Ship rats had been hurtling ashore from the time of Cook's voyages and the great navigator himself had left behind pigs and goats and some species of vegetable. Sealers and whalers had brought with them dogs and cats, more pigs, and more fruit and vegetables.

The predation of kiore on reptiles and on nesting and ground birds, of kuri on flightless birds, and of Maori themselves on forest and bird life – all these had taken an ecological toll on primordial New Zealand. But it was minor compared with the environmental effects of European colonisation. The great botanist Thomas Kirk estimated that the new plants introduced to New Zealand by Europeans prior to 1840 numbered a few dozen only. By 1870 there were almost 300, and by the 1930s over 1000, of which two-thirds had arrived between 1851 and 1900.

Birds, animals and fish were imported by local acclimatisation societies so that, according to one of them, 'the sportsman and lover of nature might then enjoy the same sports and studies that make the remembrance of their former homes so dear, the country rendered more enjoyable, our tables better supplied...' The Auckland society alone brought in more than 30 varieties in its first year. Nationally, in the 1860s, introduced species included salmon, rainbow trout, Californian quail, *Pinus radiata* and macrocarpa from the United States; starlings, blackbirds, sparrows, gorse, foxgloves, rabbits and red deer from Britain; black swans, possums, green frogs and eucalypts from Australia. Sheep and cattle were being introduced from the 1830s, and wool was to become the country's major export in the nineteenth century.

Collectively, these introductions had a traumatic impact. In the words of one historian, they not only transformed the appearance of the landscape, but also 'changed ecologies, and reduced, drastically, the range and ... population of many indigenous species'. Some of the species reduced or lost died because of destruction of habitat, some because they could not co-exist with introduced animals, and others because they succumbed to diseases introduced with exotic creatures. Initially poor judgements were compounded when further species were brought in to limit the disastrously prolific spread of others. Thus farmer-ecologist Herbert Guthrie-Smith described the liberation of weasels, ferrets and stoats in an effort to control rabbits as trying to 'correct a blunder by a crime'.

Among the New Zealand birds that disappeared in the nineteenth century were the piopio, native quail and Stephens Island wren. The latter, the only known example of a perching bird which lost its power of flight, was once common all over the country. Kiore wiped it out on the New Zealand mainland and on other offshore islands. It hung on on Stephens Island until 1894, when the Government built a lighthouse there and installed a lighthouse keeper. The keeper brought a cat, and almost every day the cat brought a wren to the keeper's door. In little more than a year the entire species was exterminated by this one cat. Other birds, such as the emblematically distinctive huia and the laughing owl, followed soon after. And a much larger clutch – takahe, kakapo, kokako, stitchbird, black robin and others – became endangered and were brought back from the brink of extinction only via a large expenditure of ingenuity and public funds. The upokororo or grayling, the country's most popular edible freshwater fish, also disappeared.

The largest sheep-runs in the country were established on the South Island golden tussock grasslands, which were often ploughed or burnt over and sowed with English grasses. In the North Island, forest had to be cleared and burnt and grass sown to make room and feed for sheep. In the country's early years as a Crown colony, sheep were by far the most favoured animal for farming: wool was easily transported and exported; meat could not yet be refrigerated; and the grass intake of one cow would feed eight to ten sheep. By 1858 the country had 1.5 million of them, at a time when the human population was just over 115,000. The sheep population had risen to 13.1 million by 1878, whereas over the same period cattle numbers were up from a mere 1400 to 5800.

As far as mineral resources were concerned, every region of New Zealand hoped to find gold and coal, the one seen as the basis for genuine prosperity, the other as an essential fuel that would reduce the wasteful burning of wood. It was in an effort to discover both minerals that the Austrian geologist Hochstetter had been enticed away from his Austrian imperial scientific expedition on board the naval frigate *Novara* in 1858–59. He wrote a favourable report on the Huntly coalfields, which would be mined systematically from the 1860s, and the books he wrote on wider New Zealand geology laid the foundation for serious study of the subject. Gold had been found near the township of Coromandel as early as 1852, but it was not discovered in easily accessible form and quantity until the strikes that opened up the Otago goldfields in 1861, and subsequently those on the West Coast in the mid-1860s and in the Hauraki district towards the end of the decade.

At the same time as the land and its resources were beginning to be explored and exploited by the new colonists, so was the country's system of government. In the Crown colony period, 1841–53, New Zealand was governed by three successive Governors – Hobson, FitzRoy and Grey – and their Executive Councils. As noted previously, the councils were made up of the Governor himself, the Colonial Secretary, the Attorney-General and the Colonial Treasurer, in that order of seniority. In addition there was a wider Legislative Council consisting of the Executive Council members plus three justices of the peace appointed by the Governor.

This constitutional arrangement was unpopular with European colonists, especially those in the New Zealand Company settlements of Wellington and Nelson, who were dissatisfied with many of the Governors' and Executive Council decisions, particularly those involving relations with Maori, and who sought popular representation in government and ultimately self-government. In an effort to appease this demand, the

Secretary of State for the Colonies, Earl Grey, despatched an extraordinarily complex constitution for George Grey (no relation) to introduce in 1846. The country was to be divided into two provinces: New Ulster (the North Island north of the Patea River) and New Munster (everywhere south of this line, including Wellington and the whole of the South Island). No explanation was given as to why the names of Irish provinces were being applied to a country on the other side of the world, though the north and south dispositions of the regions coincided. Each province was to have a Lieutenant-Governor, an appointed Legislative Council, and a House of Representatives elected by mayors, aldermen and councils of the province's townships. A General Assembly for the colony as a whole was to consist of the Governor-in-Chief (in the first instance Grey), a Legislative Council appointed by the Governor-in-Chief, and a House of Representatives elected by the provincial Houses of Representatives.

Grey assumed the new office of Governor-in-Chief on 1 January 1848, shortly after he had been knighted. But he declined to enact the new constitution in full on the ground that it would 'give to a minority made up of one race power over a majority made up of another'. He believed – and he told the British Government – that Maori would not agree to such an injustice. And, of course, there had been no suggestion of Maori representation at any of the new layers of government and administration. As a consequence of Grey's reservations, the Secretary of State was persuaded to suspend for five years those parts of the new constitution which allowed for election to provincial and general assemblies. Grey meanwhile would govern on 'as a despot', in Keith Sinclair's words, with appointed councils only for each province and no elected or part-elected national parliament. This decision drew rancorous comment from the settlers who, already less than satisfied with the modest degree of self-government offered, then had to endure it being whipped away from them.

For all the criticism levelled at Grey at this time and subsequently, the term of his first governorship was highly successful and represents the zenith of his long career in public life in New Zealand – which was to include being Governor twice and then Premier in the late 1870s, making him one of only two New Zealanders to hold both offices.* Was he, though, as his admirers submitted, 'Good Governor Grey'? Or was he a patronising and racist autocrat, as others have claimed?

George Grey became Governor of New Zealand for the first time in 1845 at the age of 33. He had already enjoyed an extraordinary career for one so young. Brought up by his mother – his father had died in the Napoleonic Wars eight days before George was born – he had run away from his English boarding school but studied with distinction at the Royal Military College at Sandhurst. He served in the British Army in Ireland for six years and was shocked by the poverty and the powerlessness of the Irish people. One conclusion he drew from that experience was that new lands should be opened up to allow opportunities for the poor of the Old World to better themselves.

From 1837 to 1839 Grey led two expeditions of exploration in Western Australia, neither of which discovered any places or resources of significance. They were, however, adventurous. On the first he was speared by an Aborigine, whom he shot; on the second he was shipwrecked. In 1839, still in Western Australia, he was appointed resident magistrate at King George Sound and that same year married Eliza Spencer, daughter of his predecessor there. Grey's contact with Aborigines gave him a

---

* The other, a century later, was Keith Holyoake.

lifelong interest in indigenous cultures and a paper he wrote for the Secretary of State for the Colonies on racial amalgamation was partly responsible for his being appointed Governor of South Australia in 1840, when he was still in his 20s. He was sufficiently successful in this role to earn his first term in New Zealand, where the initial challenge was to bring to an end the war in the north which had ignited during the term of his ineffectual predecessor, Robert FitzRoy.

Having accomplished this, though with some doubt over the question of who 'won', Grey set about the administration of wider Maori matters with considerable skill and a strong sense of justice. He went to some lengths to ensure that the terms of the Treaty of Waitangi were observed by the Crown and he constantly assured Maori that their land rights would be respected. With his Chief Land Purchase Commissioner Donald McLean, Grey evolved a system of hui for the discussion of land sales to the Crown – a procedure that recognised the communal nature of tribal ownership and gave all interested parties in the negotiations an opportunity to participate.* Land bought in this manner was then on-sold to settlers at a profit to the Crown, the major method by which Grey generated government revenue. In this period some 30 million acres of land was acquired from South Island Maori, in circumstances which would be challenged by Ngai Tahu in subsequent years, and three million in the North Island.

Grey also appointed resident magistrates in Maori areas to apply the law of the land with the help of Maori assessors. He

---

* There is some evidence that McLean, another controversial figure in New Zealand history, also made secret deals with some Maori chiefs. It is not clear whether this would have been done with Grey's approval. McLean would move even closer to the forefront of New Zealand public life as Minister of Native Affairs in a succession of ministries from 1869 to 1876.

subsidised mission schools and some Maori agricultural schemes (with money to construct flour mills, for example) and built several hospitals specifically for Maori patients. And he learned the Maori language and persuaded Maori authorities to commit their legends and traditions to writing, some of which he subsequently published (for example, *Ko nga moteatea me nga hakirara o nga Maori* in 1853, and *Ko nga mahi nga a nga tupuna Maori* in 1854). His collected papers, which eventually found their way to the Auckland Public Library, would turn out to be the largest single repository of Maori-language manuscripts in the world. Grey's understanding of Maori custom in the course of his first governorship enabled him to achieve successes that would have eluded other governors or politicians. William Pember Reeves tells of an occasion when a chief refused to allow the building of a road through his territory; Grey's response was to send the gift of a carriage to the chief's sister, after which, because of the law of utu or reciprocity, authorisation was forthcoming.

But he was no Apollonian hero or plaster saint. He had faults. One was his tendency to exaggerate the beneficial effects of his policies in his communications with London. Another was the inclination to blame problems on others, especially his predecessors. Grey had an autocratic temperament. And when, despite his own infidelities, he suspected his wife of forming an attachment with another man, he refused to speak to her for 36 years. On the whole, however, his first term as Governor of New Zealand was well executed. The high point may well have been the acceptance by the British Government in 1852 of his new draft constitution for New Zealand, which came into effect the following year, just after he had left the country.

This new blueprint for governance provided for elected provincial councils, each presided over by a superintendent, for Auckland, Taranaki, Wellington, Nelson, Canterbury and

Otago. Later legislation allowed Hawke's Bay to separate from Wellington (1858), Marlborough from Nelson (1859), Southland from Otago (1861), and Westland from Canterbury (1873). Over and above the provincial governments there was to be a bicameral Parliament consisting of an elected House of Representatives of 24 to 42 members, and an appointed Legislative Council of not fewer than ten. National legislation, having passed the two Houses, would be signed off by an Executive Council consisting of the Governor and – eventually – a ministry chosen by the House of Representatives. The leading minister would in due course be known as the Premier, and later, from 1902, as Prime Minister.

To be eligible to elect members to both the provincial councils and the House of Representatives, voters had to be male owners of property valued at £50 a year or leasehold valued at £10. Elections for the House of Representatives were initially to be held every five years, and the House would initially have 37 members elected by 5849 voters, around 100 of them Maori.* The Governor would for the immediate future retain responsibility for native affairs, and foreign policy would be controlled by the Government of Great Britain.

This constitution in effect brought 'The Crown' to New Zealand and laid the foundation for the manner in which the country was to be governed for the next 150 years. There would be changes: the franchise would be extended to all Maori men in 1867 and to all women in 1893. The ballot would be secret after 1870. The property qualification would be abolished in 1879 and plural voting in 1889; there would be variations in the number of seats in the House of Representatives, and in the

* By contrast, the country would have 2.6 million voters in 2003, 196,000 of them on the Maori roll.

frequency of elections (standardised at triennial after 1879); and
the Legislative Council would be abolished in 1950. But the
House of Representatives would persist, and those able to
command majority support in it would select ministries and
govern the country; and the elected leader of those majorities
would be the Premier and later Prime Minister. The powers
of the Governor, and after 1917 Governor-General, would be
steadily reduced until, by the latter part of the twentieth century,
they could and would act solely on the advice of their ministers.
They would continue to chair the cabinet on the occasions when
it acted as the Executive Council to sign parliamentary Acts
into law.

At the very outset, the provincial councils proved more able
than the national House of Representatives at finding workable
coalitions of interests and personalities. But both systems
became locked into a battle for supremacy that would last for
20 years. One reason affairs were initially so chaotic in the
House of Representatives was that the membership was a
mixture of strong personalities and varied regional interests.
Another was that most of the personalities involved had had
little experience of acting politically for the common good. A
third was the considerable anger that the members would at
first have no representation on the Executive Council, the body
that would make governmental and legislative decisions for
the colony as a whole. At the very first meeting of the House in
May 1854, Edward Gibbon Wakefield, who had arrived in
New Zealand for the first time a little over a year earlier and
been elected MP for the Hutt,* moved that the House of

---

* In the same election, Wakefield's volatile son, Edward Jerningham
Wakefield, was elected member for the Christchurch country seat. Neither

(Continued)

Representatives be given responsible as well as representative government immediately – that is, control over appointments to and the decisions of the Executive Council. It was passed by 29 votes to one.

The country's Administrator, Robert Wynyard, filling in between Grey's departure and the arrival of the new Governor, Thomas Gore Browne, put three members of the House 'unofficially' on the Executive Council: James Edward Fitzgerald, the Canterbury Provincial Superintendent, and Henry Sewell and Frederick Weld, both future Premiers. After seven weeks, when it had become apparent that these first three 'ministers' had no powers, they resigned. When Gore Browne arrived in 1855, however, he announced that he *was* authorised to introduce responsible government and a new election for the House of Representatives was held before the end of the year. This produced the country's first 'responsible ministry' and first 'Premier', Henry Sewell, appointed by the Governor with the support of the House in April 1856 (the term Premier was not used officially until the beginning of the Frederick Weld ministry in 1864).

The first ministry was short-lived. Sewell, a non-practising lawyer and an official of the Canterbury Association, announced that he planned to strengthen central government at the expense of the provinces. This provoked strong opposition from and around fellow lawyer and New Zealand Company official William Fox, leader in the House of what came to be called the 'Wellington party', which favoured the provinces. Fox then

––––––

(Continued)

member of this illustrious family had a successful parliamentary career, though Edward Jerningham, by then visibly the worse for excessive use of alcohol, was elected for another term in another Christchurch seat from 1871 to 1875.

became the country's second 'Premier' but his ministry lasted less than a fortnight. He was outmanoeuvred by the 'centralist faction' which had grouped around Edward Stafford, the immensely able Superintendent of Nelson. Stafford's ministry took office in May 1856 and retained power for five years. Fox's light was far from eclipsed, however, and he would return to office as Premier three more times in the next 17 years.

Edward Stafford, who must be given considerable credit for 'bedding in' responsible government and demonstrating that it could work in New Zealand despite a wide variety of competing interests and personalities, was a member of the Anglo-Irish gentry and had arrived in Nelson in 1843 to become a runholder. Success in farming combined with the education he had received at Trinity College, Dublin made him confident about assuming a leadership role in the Nelson settlment. He helped found the Constitutional Association there, and in 1850 he wrote a 'memorial' sent to the British Government demanding full suffrage and responsible government for the colony. He cemented his role in the establishment by marrying Emily Wakefield, daughter of Edward Gibbon's brother William, though she died young in 1857 and he remarried.

Stafford had become first Superintendent of Nelson in 1853 and some of his measures there – the free, secular and compulsory education system and County Roads Act, for example – became models for eventual countrywide legislation. Those who knew Stafford well and had watched the assured way he dealt with Nelson provincial business were convinced that he was the 'coming man' for the whole colony, and he effortlessly became member of the House of Representatives for Nelson in 1855. According to his biographer, Edmund Bohan, Stafford was in his element when confronted by the first parliamentary era, 'with its confusion of personalities, interests and shifting cabals ... His wide knowledge of constitutional history and contemporary government gave him an unmatched awareness of how the new ... system ought to develop, and of the need to pass a body of specifically New Zealand law ... From the start [his] ministers met privately as a working cabinet without the governor, so reducing the Executive Council to a more formal role.'

Stafford was distrustful, however, of the fact that Maori affairs remained in the Governor's hands, and of Gore Browne's over-reliance on the advice of his land purchasing officer, Donald McLean. Stafford was out of the country when the Crown's invalid purchase of land at Waitara was made and returned to find that his parliamentary colleagues were prepared to go to war if necessary to defend the arrangements, which had been made with the wrong chief. In 1861 William Fox and his Wellington-based alliance used conflict that developed in Taranaki to defeat the Government in the House by 24 votes to 23. While Stafford lost on that occasion, he was to witness new ministries coming and going annually – led by Fox, Robert Browning's writer friend Alfred Domett, Frederick Whitaker and Frederick Weld – until he regained the premiership for another four years from 1865 to 1869, and again in 1872.

Meanwhile, the 1860s would be dominated by the second round of the New Zealand Wars (see Chapter 15), and by the effects of the long-awaited discoveries of gold in both islands. Every province in the country was keen to find ample deposits of 'payable' gold within its own boundaries after hearing of the effects of such bonanzas in Siberia, California and Victoria, Australia, in the 1850s. Gold was seen as the magic ingredient that would attract immigrants, transform sluggish economies and deliver instant prosperity to all and great riches to some. To make this outcome more likely, most of the provinces offered rewards as an incentive to attract experienced prospectors and painstaking investigations.

Scientists such as Hochstetter had already reported that geological and mineral configurations were favourable for the presence of gold in some parts of the country – in particular, the Coromandel Peninsula, land either side of Nelson, the West Coast and Otago. Visiting whalers had found traces of gold on the Coromandel in 1842. Ten years later a timber merchant named Charles Ring noticed gold-bearing quartz embedded in a log which he had tumbled down a riverbed behind Coromandel Harbour. Subsequent prospecting turned up further deposits, and the country's first gold rush was under way around Coromandel township, and at Cape Colville and Mercury Bay. It was short-lived, however. Little of the Coromandel gold was in the river silt; most of it was locked up in veins of quartz, from which it was difficult and expensive to extract. Consequently the 'rush' lasted less than a year and the prospectors turned their attentions elsewhere.

Modest quantities of gold were found at Collingwood and Aorere near Nelson in 1857. But the real bonanza turned out to be in Otago. Gold was discovered there in the bed of the Mataura River in 1860, and at Lindis in 1861. The 'rush', however, was sparked by Gabriel Read's strike in the Tuapeka district in May 1861, where he found alluvial gold 'shining like the stars in Orion on a dark frosty night'. Within months the word was out, and thousands of would-be gold miners flocked to the valley still known as Gabriels Gully. Other discoveries followed at Waitahuna and further afield in Central Otago, where towns sprang up literally overnight. Read, a Tasmanian who had worked previously on the Californian and Victorian goldfields, eventually won the provincial prize of £500 for his contribution to the rush of people and prosperity that followed his find.

The Otago goldfields were the most spectacularly productive. But other discoveries occurred throughout the decade: on the West Coast, which had a mixture of alluvial and quartz deposits, from the mid-1860s (and the coast then became the wildest frontier in the country as merchants, publicans and brothel-keepers converged to share the profits), and back on the Coromandel, this time around Thames and further afield, from 1868. By 1871 there were 693 stamper batteries crushing quartz around Thames alone, and the settlement shook day and night as if from continuous earthquakes – except on Sundays when, it was reported, people were unable to rest because of the unfamiliar silence. The bonanzas came to an end in the 1870s, but dredging and sluicing kept the industry going in a modest way in Otago and on the West Coast. The Martha Mine in Waihi produced four billion dollars' worth of gold between 1879 and 1952, and reopened in 1988.

Thanks to a decade of unprecedented prosperity and immigration, the population of Dunedin exploded: from 1700 people in 1858 to 18,500 by 1874. It had by then displaced Auckland as the country's largest city. The full tallies in 1874, for cities and their suburbs, were: Dunedin 29,832, Auckland 27,840, Wellington 15,941 and Christchurch 14,270. Wellington had been boosted by the transfer of the capital there in 1865, a move which coincided with and contributed to a serious economic recession in Auckland. That was eventually relieved by the influx of wealth from the Thames goldfield, which by 1874 had a population of 8000.

Dunedin's new commercial pre-eminence was reflected in the number of mercantile companies and banks newly established there, and by a building boom on a monumental scale, which included the construction of the country's first university, founded by Robert Burns's nephew Thomas Burns in 1869.* Many manufacturing, distribution and retail companies that later went national – Hallenstein Bros, DIC, Sargood, Son & Ewen – established their New Zealand bases in Dunedin. The city also developed a tradition of considerable private endowment of education and the arts, particularly through the gifts of members of the extended Hallenstein family. The latter were descended from or connected by marriage to Bendix Hallenstein, a German-born Jew who established highly successful stores on the Central Otago goldfields before moving to Dunedin.

Nationally, thanks also largely to the gold rushes, the non-Maori population almost doubled in the years 1861–64, from 98,000 to 171,000, and had increased by another two-thirds again by 1874 (255,000). The goldfields also attracted immigrants from countries not previously represented in the New Zealand population. The 1874 census, for example, reveals that 6.06 per cent of the population of Westland and 4.19 per cent of that of Otago were Chinese. By contrast, no Chinese were living at this time in other parts of the country. The Irish presence too had increased considerably, up to 18.95 per cent in Westland, many of whom were diggers who had followed the gold trail from California to Victoria and on to New Zealand. Their presence resulted in Irish issues being debated on the West Coast, and in the arrest and expulsion of some who supported the Fenian cause of Irish independence. It also resulted in a demand for Irish priests and bishops to serve the country's Catholic population, and in an eventual change in the character of the church in New Zealand from a French institution to a largely Irish one.

---

* Other universities opened in Christchurch (Canterbury) in 1873, Auckland in 1883, and Wellington (Victoria) in 1899; Massey (Palmerston North) followed in 1964, Waikato (in Hamilton) in 1965, and Lincoln in 1990.

By the close of the 1860s, the country's earnings from gold were twice those derived from wool, which had been the largest export until that time. If this was all good news for the nation's future economic prosperity – and it was, even though the impact of gold would diminish steadily through the 1870s – it was undercut only by the expense and anxiety generated by the New Zealand Wars in the North Island over the same period.

15

A Time of Turbulence

Despite the skirmishes around Wellington and Wanganui and the Northern War in the 1840s – in all of which Maori had fought on both sides – the two decades following the signing of the Treaty of Waitangi were characterised nationally more by co-operation between Maori and Pakeha than by conflict. As James Belich has noted, a periphery of European settlements on the coast of the North Island became economically interdependent with the Maori hinterland. The two spheres interacted without either side being dominant and Maori were in complete control of their own tribal territories. Most Europeans, however, regarded this state of affairs as temporary. They took it for granted that the Maori population would continue to decrease while that of European settlers increased; and that Maori land would progressively become available to Europeans for agricultural development.

Maori too began to fear this outcome. It seemed to some chiefs that tribal culture and tikanga (customs) might be in

danger of permanent extinction unless active steps were taken
to preserve them. For some, a prerequisite for such preservation
was a ban on further sales of Maori land. A series of meetings
held in the North Island in the 1850s promoted this strategy,
along with the idea that Maori should combine their mana in a
Maori monarch. This movement, inspired by Te Rauparaha's son
Tamihana and his cousin Matene Te Whiwhi, arose in part from
the fact that the presence of Europeans had helped to create a
sense of 'Maoriness'. It arose too from a belief that the key to the
power of Europeans lay in their unity under the British Crown.
If Maori could achieve a similar unity under their own king, it
was argued, they would be able to match European confidence
and cohesion, retain their land and preserve customary law and
traditional authority. In other words, if significant numbers of
tribes were able to coalesce, they would be less susceptible to
divide and rule strategies on the part of Pakeha colonists.

With this object in view, the elderly and ailing Waikato chief
Te Wherowhero was selected first Maori King in 1856 at a
representative gathering of tribes at Pukawa on the shore of Lake
Taupo. He was formally installed in the position in 1858 at his
'capital' at Ngaruawahia and took the name Potatau. In the eyes
of most European colonists who read about this ceremony in
their newspapers, it was an act of Maori disloyalty to the British
Crown, as was any expression of allegiance to a Maori monarch.
In the eyes of supporters of the King movement, or Kingitanga,
however, the mana of the two monarchs would be comple-
mentary. Wiremu Tamihana of Ngati Haua, the 'Kingmaker'
who anointed Potatau, voiced this view at the 'raising-up' ceremony: 'The Maori King and the Queen of England to be joined
in accord; God to be over them both.'

The Kingitanga came quickly to be viewed by Europeans as a
blatant attempt to prevent further land sales at a time when the

populations of Auckland and New Plymouth were spilling over with new colonists. Many settlers, and the Governor, Thomas Gore Browne, began to voice the opinion that Maori needed 'a sharp lesson' to teach them who ought to be in charge of the country. An apparent opportunity for such a lesson arose in 1859 when an Ati Awa chief, Te Teira, offered a 243-hectare block of land at Waitara, near New Plymouth, for sale to the Government. The principal chief of the area, Wiremu Kingi Te Rangitake, objected and said that Te Teira had neither the mana nor the support of Ati Awa to make the sale. But Gore Browne insisted that the transaction proceed, viewing the issue as one of sovereignty. When Wiremu Kingi's supporters peacefully occupied the Waitara block in March 1860, they sparked the Taranaki War.

Governor Gore Browne had called in more than 3000 imperial troops from Australia, and they were commanded first by Colonel Charles Gold and subsequently by Major-General Thomas Pratt. Maori forces, by contrast, fluctuated from a few hundred to around 1500. They were commanded by Wiremu Kingi's 'general', Hapurona. The early stages of the war, from March 1860, consisted of the British storming a cordon of Maori pa that usually turned out to be empty at the time of attack. On 27 June, however, the imperial troops assaulted the manned pa at Puketakauere and suffered 64 casualties while being severely defeated. Maori then tightened their cordon around New Plymouth to the point where the town was under siege and around 100 settlers died from disease in overcrowded conditions. The pressure eased only in September and October when Taranaki Maori and some Maniapoto allies returned to their home bases to help plant crops for the coming summer.

Imperial troops had a victory in November 1860 when they stormed a half-built pa at Mahoetahi. They followed this with sieges against selected pa and extending their own line by building a series of redoubts. This resulted in slow progress against Maori forces, but at enormous cost in time, lives and materials. And so Gore Browne, rather than trying to crush an uncrushable foe, opted instead for a truce in March 1861. The truce held, although fighting broke out again in May 1863 and continued sporadically for a further nine months. By that time, however, the military focus was on Waikato and the far more extensive conflict that had been provoked there.

Sir George Grey replaced Thomas Gore Browne as Governor for a second term in 1861. He was determined to put down what he saw as the threat to British authority represented by the Kingitanga. He persuaded the British Government not to recall to Australia the troops provided for the Taranaki War, and in 1862 he built a military route, the Great South Road, from Auckland to the northern Kingitanga boundary at the Mangatawhiri River in Waikato. At that boundary, a redoubt was built with telegraph communication and strong supply lines back to Auckland. In 1863 Grey used the opportunity provided by the second outbreak of fighting in Taranaki to prise further troops from the British Government. By early 1864 he had as many as 20,000 men at his disposal – imperial troops, sailors, marines, two units of regular colonial troops (the Colonial Defence Force and the Forest Rangers), Auckland and Waikato militia (the latter to be rewarded with confiscated land after the fighting), some Waikato hapu loyal to the Crown and a larger number of Maori from Te Arawa. The Kingitanga, by contrast, was able to mobilise no more than 5000 warriors, some of them from Bay of Plenty, East Coast and Tuhoe tribes, and they never had more than 2000 in the field at one time.

The invasion of Waikato began on 12 July 1863 when Lieutenant-General Duncan Cameron led his combined regular and volunteer troops across the Mangatawhiri River. The first engagement with Kingitanga forces came on 17 July at Koheroa, where a small Maori garrison was defeated. After waiting for reinforcements, Cameron moved against the pa at Meremere, which the defenders decided to evacuate without a fight. It was not until 20 November, at Rangiriri, that the first major battle of the war began.

Rangiriri was designed by Waikato Maori to hold up the British advance down the Waikato River. At the time it was attacked, however, they had not had time to garrison it fully. The first assault left the pa surrounded on three sides. Further frontal attacks failed, and most of the defenders evacuated the position on the night of 20 November. The following morning, after confusion over raising a flag of truce, 180 rearguard defenders were captured. Cameron's forces then surged up the river and occupied the empty Kingitanga capital of Ngaruawahia on 8 December.

The next engagement was at Rangiaowhia, the centre of Waikato's major agricultural region, on 21 February 1864. This action was seen as highly controversial in retrospect. The day was a Sunday, when Christian Maori would not fight and did not expect Pakeha troops to fight either. Further, Rangiaowhia was not a fortified position and many of the inhabitants were elderly people and children. Particular Maori offence was taken at the firing of a whare karakia or house of prayer in which a group of supposed non-combatants were killed, including one elder who had emerged to indicate that they were surrendering.

The final action in Waikato itself was the battle of Orakau on 31 March–2 April 1864. This pa was neither completed nor fully garrisoned, but it withstood three assaults. At this point the Maori commander, Rewi Maniapoto of Ngati Maniapoto, is reputed to have called out defiantly to Major William Gilbert

Mair, 'E hoa, ka whawhai tonu ahau kia koe ake, ake, ake.' (Friend, I shall continue to fight you for ever and for ever.) Orakau was surrounded, however, and on 2 April the defenders cut their way through the British line and attempted to escape. Many were killed in the rout that followed, cut down by swords as they ran from pursuers on horseback; and many of the Maori wounded were bayoneted to death.

The final engagements of the war were near Tauranga in the Bay of Plenty. On 28 April Cameron, with 1700 troops and seventeen pieces of artillery, attacked Gate Pa, defended by 230 Maori. After a heavy bombardment, a storming party managed to get inside the pa, where it was ambushed and forced to flee. Rawiri Puhirake then evacuated his forces and rightly claimed a significant victory. Cameron had his revenge less than two months later, however, when Puhirake and his men were caught and defeated at an unfinished pa at Te Ranga.

The major engagements and dozens of skirmishes of the Waikato War had been responsible for over 1000 Maori and 700 European deaths. Worse than this price, however, Waikato Maori were punished by the confiscation of 1.3 million hectares of land, which further crippled and embittered the vanquished tribes. This action also secured for the New Zealand Government, as it was intended to do, the land with which to reward the militia troops and settle new colonists. What was taken was selected more for its fertility and strategic importance than for the owners' part in the so-called rebellion: some tribes in northern Waikato who had remained loyal to the Government lost land along with those who had not; and the group that had been perhaps most bellicose in both the Waikato *and* Taranaki wars, Ngati Maniapoto, lost nothing (the Government showed little interest in the precipitous hills and valleys of their rohe until it wanted to push the main trunk railway line through there in the 1880s).

King Tawhiao, successor to his father, Potatau, who had died in 1860, took his family and immediate entourage of followers into internal exile in the King Country, thus giving that region its Pakeha name.

The New Zealand Wars as a whole were far from over, however. As fighting in Waikato was winding down, a messianic movement, another syncretic religion, was gaining popularity in Taranaki. Pai Marire (known to Europeans as Hauhau) promised its followers deliverance from European domination. Its founder, Te Ua Haumene, identified closely with the Psalms of David in the Old Testament and wove Biblical and Maori elements into rituals that included incantation and dancing around a niu pole, a gigantic version of the traditional Maori divining stick. Te Ua apparently had no intention that his movement would become warlike (its name meant Good and Peaceful). But his followers, convinced that Pai Marire gave them spiritual weapons to overpower Europeans, also took up martial weapons. They attacked and defeated a patrol of mixed imperial and colonial forces at Te Ahuahu in North Taranaki on 6 April 1864. Just over three weeks later they launched a frontal assault on a redoubt at Sentry Hill, Te Morere, and were heavily defeated. Another Pai Marire group led by Matene Rangitauira led a force down the Whanganui River in May 1864, only to be attacked and defeated at Moutoa Island by tribes of the lower river, who were credited with saving the town of Wanganui.

Before imperial troops were dispersed from the Waikato War, Governor Grey decided to use the Pai Marire disturbances as an excuse to put down what he regarded as Maori rebellion in south Taranaki. He dispatched General Cameron and 3700 men to Wanganui, and this force moved into south Taranaki in January 1865. They had the better of engagements with Maori at Nukumaru and Te Ngaio and halted their advance at the Waingongoro River. Cameron left New Zealand soon after, and his position at the head of this, the last imperial forces campaign in New Zealand, was taken by Major-General Trevor Chute, who led a devastating series of depredations against Maori villages in January and February 1866, laying them waste and destroying crops. A similar campaign by colonial and kupapa forces was led by Thomas McDonnell between August and November 1866. These actions severely crippled Maori communities in the region, who were largely unaware of the purpose of the campaign, and led to starvation and long-enduring anger.

Meanwhile, conflict had broken out in the Bay of Plenty and on the East Coast of the North Island, sparked by the arrival of Pai Marire emissaries in those regions. Kereopa Te Rau, who had lost relatives in the action at Rangiaowhia, was involved in the killing of the missionary Carl Volkner at Opotiki in March 1865. He and his co-religionists were pursued by colonial forces and kupapa Maori. From June to October 1865, there was virtual civil war on the East Coast between Pai Marire and kupapa factions of Ngati Porou. Arawa kupapa joined colonial troops from Taranaki who arrived to fight Pai Marire forces inland from Opotiki and along the East Coast. Later fighting spilled down into Hawke's Bay, where Ngati Kahungunu participated as both Pai Marire followers and kupapa. This series of engagements reached a climax in November 1865 at the battle of Waerenga-a-Hika in Poverty Bay. Four hundred Pai Marire supporters were taken prisoner, many of whom (with wives and children) were banished to a penal settlement on the Chatham Islands.

That action spawned another campaign. One of those arrested at Waerenga-a-Hika, Te Kooti Arikirangi Te Turuki, was a Rongowhakaata man who had fought on the government side. He was suspected of aiding the enemy, however, and banished to the Chathams without trial. After a series of visions which led him to found the Ringatu faith, another syncretic religion, Te Kooti escaped in July 1868, having commandeered a ship which took him and 300 followers back to the mainland. After his request for a pardon was turned down, he waged the most effective guerrilla campaign ever seen in the country. He killed about 30 Europeans and at least 20 Maori men, women and children in the course of raids on Poverty Bay settlements, and was chased by kupapa and colonial troops through the East Coast, Urewera and central North Island for four years. Finally he withdrew to sanctuary in the King Country in 1872, and he was eventually pardoned by the Government in 1883. The shots fired by Gilbert Mair's Flying Arawa column at the retreating Te Kooti in February 1872 are regarded as the last engagement of the New Zealand Wars.

If anyone offered a challenge to Te Kooti's designation as the country's most effective guerrilla 'general', however, it was Riwha Titokowaru of Ngati Ruahine in Taranaki. And his war ran in parallel with that of the Rongowhakaata prophet-fighter.

The basis for the return of fighting to Taranaki in 1868 was the Government's gradual implementation of land confiscations provoked by the previous war. South Taranaki Maori resisted these encroachments non-violently, and then violently. Titokowaru's forces attacked a Patea Field Force of colonial troops led by Thomas McDonnell (by now a lieutenant-colonel). McDonnell retaliated by attacking Titokowaru's home base at Te Ngutu-o-te-Manu in August 1868. The first two of his assaults were abortive, but the third, on 7 September, resulted in a full-scale battle and the defeat of McDonnell's men. Among the casualties was McDonnell's second-in-command, Major Gustavus von Tempsky, the Prussian-born adventurer who had served with the Forest Rangers in the Waikato campaign and participated in Chute's scorched-earth expedition in Taranaki in 1866. He had survived a court martial in 1865 to become, in the minds of the Pakeha public, a dashing hero of the New Zealand Wars. His fearlessness and ability to survive near-misses gave him an aura of invincibility. His death came as shock to his military followers and to his wider audience of admirers throughout the colony.

After the debacle at Te Ngutu-o-te-Manu, McDonnell was replaced by Lieutenant-Colonel George Whitmore, who led the Patea Field Force against Titokowaru at Moturoa, near Waverley. Again the colonial troops were soundly defeated. After this action, Belich has commented, '[almost] the whole of south Taranaki was abandoned to Titokowaru and the colonial army withdrew to the outskirts of Wanganui'. A showdown battle was expected at Titokowaru's new base at Tauranga Ika, near Nukumaru, and McDonnell led almost 2000 men there early in February 1869. But the colonial troops found the pa empty. Because of some personal hara or impropriety (believed to be his liaison with another man's wife), Titokowaru's Maori support had collapsed suddenly and he retreated to the north, fighting rearguard actions en route. He took eventual refuge in inland north Taranaki while government forces reoccupied the south. Eventually he reached a kind of *modus vivendi* with Pakeha settlers and started a business selling them grass seed. Just over a decade after the fighting he was living at Te Whiti-o-Rongomai's and Tohu Kakahi's pa at Parihaka, where he was among the leaders arrested and imprisoned in the wake of the invasion by government troops in 1881.

The latter action was sparked by non-violent Maori resistance to European occupation of confiscated land near Parihaka. This village had attracted more than 2000 inhabitants who were disillusioned by the outcome of the Taranaki wars and who sought cultural and spiritual replenishment from the teachings of Te Whiti and Tohu. Both prophets encouraged further passive resistance to Pakeha settlement, such as pulling out survey pegs and removing fences on the land about to be occupied on the Waimate Plains. Despite Parihaka's pacifist ethos, many Europeans in Taranaki and elsewhere feared that the resistance campaign was a prelude to armed conflict. Native Minister John Bryce used this fear as an excuse to lead 644 troops and nearly 1000 settler volunteers into Parihaka on 5 November 1881. Instead of violence, they were met by singing children offering them food. The pa was destroyed, none the less, and Te Whiti and Tohu and other leaders arrested – but not tried – for sedition. They then endured two years of enforced exile in Otago.

The fate of the Parihaka community had been prefigured two years earlier when another prophet preaching non-violence, Te Maiharoa of Ngai Tahu, had been driven off occupied land in the Upper Waitaki Valley. Te Maiharoa believed that the only land sold to the Crown in the South Island had been that in view of the coast. In 1877 he led a heke or migration of several hundred followers from Temuka to Omarama to reoccupy old tribal grazing land. Two years later the peaceable community he had established there was dismantled and its inhabitants evicted forcibly by police. As they made their way back down the Waitaki Valley through the worst winter storms on record up to that time, several of the very old and the very young died from the effects of the freezing temperatures.

What effects did the New Zealand Wars and the resistance movements that immediately followed them have on the country as a whole? Most European New Zealanders (but not all) viewed them as a decisive demonstration that sovereignty rested with 'the Crown' – that is, with the New Zealand Government of the day – and not with Maori. That, after all, was their view of what the Treaty of Waitangi had been all about. There was little understanding among Pakeha at this time that Maori might feel that the Treaty had been dishonoured by the Crown in its seizure, for example, of confiscated territories; or in the many other dubious ways that governments or companies or individuals had used to acquire Maori lands or resources. The comments of Judge F. R. Chapman, sentencing Rua Kenana of Tuhoe to prison in 1917 for resisting arrest, are instructive. They voice what most Pakeha felt about the idea of Maori resistance in the late nineteenth and early twentieth centuries:

> You have learned that the law has a long arm, and that it can reach you, however far back into the recesses of the forest you may travel, and that in every corner of the great Empire to which we belong the King's law can reach anyone who offends against him. That is the lesson your people should learn from this trial.

That was also the lesson Pakeha felt Maori should take from the outcome of the New Zealand Wars. But had that outcome been so decisive? Large sections of the inland North Island were still, in the 1870s and 1880s, in effect under Maori control. Few Pakeha were prepared to risk entering the King Country until King Tawhiao emerged from exile there in 1881 and formally laid down his arms and those of his followers. Fewer still felt welcome in the Urewera at that time.

For Maori adversely affected by the wars and subsequent land confiscations – principally in Waikato, Taranaki and parts of the Bay of Plenty – life would be considerably more difficult physically because of the loss of economic resources which had previously allowed them to feed themselves and to trade with

Pakeha and in some instances with the wider world.* These peoples also experienced the demoralisation that came with what was viewed as a loss of mana. Tuhoe too in the Urewera had been adversely affected by the Te Kooti campaign. Their support for the prophet and adherence to Ringatu had been punished by the scorched-earth policy adopted by the colonial troops and kupapa pursuing him. In some instances, what could have been seeds of despair eventually became seeds of hope for the future: Tainui tribes, for example, continued to regard the Kingitanga as a shelter for the mana of all their peoples, and loyalty to it gave them a cohesion and a coherence that would sometimes be the envy of other tribes; and Tuhoe eventually found the same benefits from their continuing loyalty to the Hahi Ringatu. Taranaki people had tried to find grounds for renewal in the Parihaka movement, but this had been weakened by the imprisonment of its leaders and, though it enjoyed a resurgence in the late nineteenth and early twentieth centuries, the movement barely survived the deaths of Te Whiti and Tohu in 1907.

Kupapa Maori – most of Te Arawa, Ngati Porou, Ngati Kahungunu and some Whanganui tribes – mostly prospered in the wake of the wars. Their lands and resources were intact, they received favourable government attentions, including ceremonial swords for their leaders, monuments for their dead, and consultation on some matters of public policy. They were also buoyed by the fact that their mana had been enhanced rather than diminished by the wars.

---

* Although it has to be said that the market for Maori crops in Australia had collapsed by the late 1850s, as Australian primary producers caught up with local demand – just as Pakeha producers eventually did in New Zealand. So, even without the effects of the New Zealand Wars, Maori farmers and horti-culturists were likely to have been forced to fall back on subsistence farming.

But all North Island Maori – kupapa, rebels and those like Ngapuhi who had avoided military engagements in the 1860s – were subject to the ravages of disease. And this curse, the effect of pathogens to which Maori still had insufficient immunity, took a higher toll on the Maori population in the second half of the nineteenth century than it had in the first. Epidemics of influenza, measles and whooping cough were reported frequently throughout this period as the rate of European immigration increased. There were also outbreaks of dysentery of massive proportions. The fertility rate declined as women suffered from general ill-health and from the effects of syphilis, gonorrhoea and tuberculosis. Communities, especially those already demoralised by the effects of the wars, which had led to poor nutrition and grossly substandard accommodation in the areas subject to confiscation, visibly shrank.

Nationally, the Maori population dropped from 56,049 in 1857–58 to 42,113 in 1896. As such figures became known they contributed to a widespread belief – among Pakeha *and* Maori – that Maori as a people and as a culture were headed for extinction. Wellington Provincial Superintendent Dr Isaac Featherston echoed liberal European sentiment in the late nineteenth century when he spoke of the responsibility to 'smooth the pillow of a dying race'. John Logan Campbell, who had briefly been Superintendent of Auckland Province and was later the city's mayor, made arrangements in his will for an obelisk monument to Maori to stand on the summit of One Tree Hill. These were not derogatory gestures. They were expressions of respect and regret on the part of Pakeha who admired Maori.

16

A Functioning Nation?

While the wars of the 1860s had been initially a drain on the finite resources of the fledgling colony, some prominent New Zealanders profited handsomely from the outcome. The most notable of these was Thomas Russell, an Auckland lawyer and businessman who was Minister of Defence in two ministries between 1862 and 1864 and law partner of Frederick Whitaker, who led one of them.* Russell, who was in his early 30s when he held the portfolio, has been described by business historian Russell Stone as 'arguably the outstanding commercial figure in nineteenth century New Zealand'.

A 'tall, dark, energetic, intelligent and masterful' man, Russell accumulated a considerable fortune in his 20s through both his law practice and his speculative business activities. Among the latter was his close involvement in the foundation

---

* All four Russell brothers became successful lawyers, and all four founded law firms that survived, with appropriate name changes, into the twenty-first century. Thomas Russell's firm became Bell Gully Buddle Weir.

of the New Zealand Insurance Company in 1859, of the Bank of New Zealand, which took over much government business, in 1861, and, a little later, the New Zealand Loan and Mercantile Company. As Minister of Defence, Russell eagerly prosecuted the Waikato War in order to put Maori in what he regarded as their place, and to open up the Waikato itself to property investment and settlement. In these aims he and his ministerial colleagues fell out with Grey, who believed, correctly, that the post-war confiscation policy was being applied to the most desirable land without any consideration as to which tribes had fought or not fought against the Crown.

Russell profited spectacularly from the war's aftermath when he was out of politics, particularly by persuading the Government in 1873 to sell the enormous Piako swamp to a syndicate of which he was the leading member. This and a number of lucrative government commissions led the Canterbury politician William Rolleston to ask whether Russell 'is not the representative of the Colonial Government, but the Colonial Government ... the representative of Mr Thomas Russell'. Russell overreached himself in a complex network of investments, however; he was lucky not to lose everything he owned and came close to being indicted for fraud. His fortunes were restored by the Waihi Goldmining Company, which went into operation at the time a new cyanide process became available for extracting gold from quartz and brought him considerable profit.

Russell and his partner Whitaker, and their friend and colleague Josiah Clifton Firth, were not untypical of a certain kind of businessman in the colonial era who was prepared to take enormous business and investment risks and dabble in politics to help create the kind of environment in which they and their cronies were most likely to flourish financially. And, in the years preceding income tax and tighter commercial regulations, there were huge fortunes to be made.* The involvement of such figures in national life was inevitable, given the poor remuneration available for Members of Parliament. Even though politics involved about three working months of the year, it was only men of private means who could afford that involvement. Not until 1879 did a working man, Samuel Andrews, a plasterer from Christchurch, win election to the House, and the rates of pay were not raised to an adequate level until 1893.

The Auckland 'society paper' the *Observer* expressed the ideal that drove colonists such as Russell and Firth:

> Here – where the social disabilities, the exclusive caste, the overstrained competition, and the stereotyped conventionalism of the Old World have not yet taken root – there is a clear field for men of talent, skill and energy to climb the social ladder, and to attain to a degree of wealth and social elevation that is possible only to the favoured few in older countries.

What could be gained spectacularly – money or reputation – could also be lost just as spectacularly. William Larnach entered Parliament a decade later than Russell and Firth, representing a Dunedin electorate. Like his predecessors, he took enormous risks that sometimes left him, as he put it, close to 'the edge of the ruinous cliff'. He too narrowly escaped prosecution for some of his less than ethical strategies. When his fortunes were at their height in the early 1870s he built the baronial mansion known as 'Larnach's Castle' on the Otago Peninsula. At various times

---

* Income tax was not introduced in New Zealand until 1891, as part of the Liberal Government's reform programme. Up until that time, government revenue was drawn from a combination of customs and excise duties, stamp duties, property tax, land sales and death duties.

he was Colonial Treasurer, Minister of Public Works and of Mines. When his luck abandoned him in a bank collapse in the 1890s and it was widely believed that his third wife was having an affair with one of his sons, her stepson, Larnach became the first and so far only MP to commit suicide in his parliamentary office.

The dominant politician of the era after the New Zealand Wars, however, and the one responsible for launching the country on its most spectacular development phase, was Julius Vogel, who was Premier twice and Colonial Treasurer in six other ministries between 1869 and 1887. Vogel was a non-observant Jew born in London, who came to New Zealand via Australia in 1861 to work as a journalist. That same year he co-founded the *Otago Daily Times*, the first daily newspaper in the country and eventually the longest-surviving. His considerable appetite for politics and public affairs, which he initially gratified by promulgating his views and panaceas in the papers for which he wrote, led him eventually to seats on the Otago Provincial Council and, by 1866, the national Parliament, which he entered with a strong bias in favour of the provincial system and a plan to separate the South Island administratively and financially from the North.

He eventually modified these views as a result of experience in the House of Representatives, however, and, while not an inspirational speaker, he proved to be a shrewd prober of the Stafford Government's weaknesses, particularly its policies towards Maori. When the Opposition toppled the Government in 1869 and William Fox returned for the third of his four premierships, Vogel became Treasurer. In the view of his biographer, Raewyn Dalziel, he made the portfolio 'the most powerful post in government ... He came into office at a time of economic stagnation [and] adopted a bold expansionist policy with plans to bring thousands of assisted immigrants to New Zealand, to construct roads, railways, bridges and telegraph lines, and to purchase [more] Maori land for European settlement.'

The plan was adopted by Parliament in 1870 and implemented over the following decade. It involved borrowing around £20 million on the London capital market to finance assisted immigration, and to build 1800 km of railway, 4000 km of telegraph lines, and roads and public buildings. It was also popular throughout the country, though the Government was defeated in September 1872, before the beneficial effects were apparent. A month later Vogel was back in office in the Waterhouse ministry, however, and the economy underwent a boom, with full employment and rising incomes up to 1874. Growth slowed in the two succeeding years as export prices fell. Vogel remained in office as Treasurer until 1876, being Premier as well from 1873 to 1875, and again for seven months in 1876, by which time he had been knighted.

Under the Vogel scheme of whole or partially paid assistance, immigrants flooded into the country: around 100,000 between 1871 and 1880. Over half came from England, about a quarter from Ireland, and slightly fewer than that from Scotland. Just under 10 per cent were from Continental Europe, largely Germans (of whom there were more than 4500 by 1878, building on a smaller population that had gone to Nelson in the 1840s), Scandinavians and Poles. Of the 3294 Scandinavians, 1938 were Danes, 667 Swedes and 689 Norwegians. They settled mainly in the Seventy Mile Bush area on the Wellington–Hawke's Bay boundary and left placenames such as Dannevirke and Norsewood; the town of Eketahuna was once called Mellemskov. Another group settled in the Manawatu.

One major object of this immigration programme was to restore a greater balance in the sex ratio of the New Zealand population. In 1871 New Zealand had 89,000 men and 46,000 women over the age of 20 (66 to 34 per cent). This inequality meant that many thousands of men had no prospect of experiencing the settled existence of married family life, even if they wanted to. Many of these single men were absorbed into shearing or back-country farm work, or into milling timber, mining or public works, where they lived in camps and had little or no contact with the opposite sex.

A rich male culture grew up around the lives of such men. In the Coromandel forest, for example, gangs employed by such merchants as the Kauri Timber Company would go into virgin bush to build large shanties in the valleys in which they planned to work. These buildings with split-paling walls and nikau-thatched roofs would become their home for several years. They had bunks around the interior walls, a long table in the centre over an earth floor, and a kitchen and wide fireplace with a wooden or corrugated-iron chimney down one end.

The men worked up on the slopes felling trees and moving trunks by day, and ate, slept and took their days off in the shanties. In the evenings they read by lamplight and candles, played cards, told yarns and sang. Because it invariably led to trouble, liquor was forbidden in most camps – as was spitting, talking about sex and playing cards for money. Alcohol was sought in bush grog shops, and in the towns between contracts or on rare holidays. When the loggers did get to town to spend their wages, like men from other isolated work sectors they spent it on liquor, gambling and prostitutes. Although individuals might be unpopular, there was a strong camaraderie and sense of honour among bushmen. They prided themselves on working extraordinarily hard and in not stealing from one another, and they looked after mates who were sick, injured or sacked. They laid down many of the unspoken conventions of New Zealand male culture in the twentieth and twenty-first century.

To redress the sex imbalance, the Vogel Government offered free passages to British single women. Most of those who came were attracted by the prospect of domestic work at a higher wage than that available at home, and by the prospect of eventual marriage and escape from drudgery (or, rather, escape to drudgery on behalf of one's own family rather than somebody else's). Many failed to achieve that escape. But by 1891 the adult sex ratio was considerably more even: 56 per cent male to 44 per cent female. By this time, 58 per cent of men over 20 were married and 77 per cent of women.

As a consequence of the immigration influx, the non-Maori population of New Zealand had soared to more than 470,000 by 1881. By that year too, the Maori population had dropped to 46,000, and it would continue to decline as a result of disease and low fertility for most of the next two decades. Immigration peaked in 1874, when there were 34,000 assisted migrants, a number that has never since been exceeded. In the mid-1880s, however, those who were New Zealand-born became the majority of the population, and from that time population growth would result more from natural increase than from immigration.

As an integral part of the Vogel programme, transport and communications in New Zealand were revolutionised in the 1870s and 1880s. A telegraph cable had been laid between the North and South Islands in 1866. Ten years later a further line connected New Zealand to Australia, and from there to the wider world. Extensions of road and rail, carried out as part of the public works programme, sped up travel within the country and helped wheat-growers get their grain to markets within the country and to ports for export. In 1874, over 28,000 hectares of the Canterbury Plains was given over to growing wheat. By 1884 that area had jumped to more than 100,000 hectares and oats and wheat made up almost 20 per cent of New Zealand's exports. That proportion dropped as prices declined and frozen meat was developed, but there was another peak of demand and supply in the early 1900s.

The introduction of steamships over this period and their connection with rail links also sped up travel and mail within the country and to and from overseas destinations. In 1859, the fastest journey possible from Dunedin to Auckland took fifteen days. By 1879 that had been reduced to five and a half days, and by 1898, three days. Telephone networks too were established and spreading out from the urban centres from the early 1880s. All these innovations enabled the colony's widely scattered settlements to communicate better with one another, and with the world beyond New Zealand. They were part of the process of creating a single society – or, at least, a single Pakeha society – and, because they allowed more effective centralised administration, they were a factor in the abandonment of provincial government in 1875.

The year after that constitutional milestone was achieved, Julius Vogel resigned from Parliament to take up the post of New Zealand Agent-General in London (he would return to the country and to Parliament in 1884, however). He hoped that the job would allow him to pursue personal business interests and thus to strengthen his own financial position. He was replaced as Premier by a man who could not have been more different in temperament and appearance, the austere, straight-talking farmer Harry Atkinson. Atkinson, part of a tight network of pioneer Taranaki families that included the Richmonds and Hursthouses, had fought in the wars of the 1860s and become a strong advocate of suffocating any Maori resistance to the authority of the Crown. According to his biographer, Judith Bassett, he thought that 'the indigenous population should be utterly suppressed and eventually assimilated by the superior British. If this could be achieved by intimidation that would be preferable to fighting...' There was no suggestion that the Treaty of Waitangi might have any bearing on this.

In national politics, which he had first entered in 1861, Atkinson was a centralist in opposition to the provincialists, and it was largely on this issue that he had joined forces with Vogel. He was relentlessly critical of the provincial councils' 'reckless borrowing and refusal to co-operate either with central government or with one another...' After they were abolished in 1876, it was left to Atkinson and his ministry to oversee their replacement with a local government system of boroughs and counties. He intended, wrote Judith Bassett, that 'central government would have sole responsibility for borrowing money, but that localities would decide how and where it should be spent. He hoped that the new system would result in an even application of the colony's revenues to people's needs.' He was a far more cautious borrower than Vogel, believing that there must be no doubt about a government's ultimate ability to service and pay back loans. As the country drifted into depression, he became even more cautious – not only about borrowing but about public expenditure in general.

One of the functions of provincial governments, which they had fulfilled with varying degrees of conscientiousness, was the provision and support of schools. Abolition meant that this responsibility had to be taken over by central government. The new arrangements were set out in the 1877 Education Act, prepared by the Atkinson ministry and put into effect by the Grey ministry which succeeded it. This provided for 'free, secular and compulsory' primary education throughout the country. There was to be a three-tiered system of administration. At the top was a new department and a Minister of Education (the first of whom was John Ballance, who fifteen years later would become the first Liberal Premier). Below that were district education boards, which largely corresponded to those that existed under the provincial system. At the grass roots were school committees elected by local householders and responsible for management of schools in their own communities. This last element was the weakest in the system, particularly in rural areas where communities were often scattered and communications still primitive. Secondary education, which would not be free until the election of the first Labour Government in the 1930s, was provided by high schools established under separate Acts of Parliament.

Maori children could, if they or their parents so wished, attend local board schools, but they were already catered for by the 1867 Native Schools Act, which enabled primary schools to be established at the request of Maori communities under the supervision of the Native Department. At the specific request of Maori parents, the medium of instruction in these schools was to be English. Most of those parents who expressed a view on this issue in the 1860s thought that Maori was best learnt at home and English in the schools, to give pupils access to a wider world of knowledge. This policy was sometimes taken to extremes in the years that followed, with many children reporting that they had been punished for speaking Maori within school boundaries.

The Atkinson premierships – five of them between 1876 and 1891 – coincided with what came to be called the 'Long Depression'. It began with falling wool prices in 1877 and merged into a period of worldwide recession in which the New Zealand economy did not grow for around sixteen years. It led to regional unemployment, a deterioration in working conditions and a tendency among urban employers to take on women and children rather than men, so that they could be paid at lower rates. Atkinson, as Colonial Treasurer for ten of the depression years, refused to countenance Vogel-type responses. As Judith Bassett writes, he saw 'hard work, thrift and moderation' as the keys to eventual recovery. This was hardly a message calculated to enthuse Parliament or the wider electorate. But Atkinson continued to move into and out of office as politicians with more radical proposals, such as George Grey, were tried and in their turn found wanting.

Former Governor Grey became Premier in 1877. He had entered Parliament two years earlier while holding office as Superintendent of Auckland Province. One of his aims in entering national politics was to save the provincial system, but in this he failed. When Atkinson lost the confidence of the House on unrelated issues, Grey took office with a mixed cabinet of conservatives and liberals, the latter including Robert Stout and John Ballance, both identified early in their political careers as likely Premiers of the future. Parliament turned to the by then 65-year-old statesman because of the residual mana and charisma of 'Good Governor Grey', but his premiership was not a success. The former proconsul found the transition to politician difficult. Grey was not accustomed to being challenged. He was also by this time autocratic and cantankerous, and prone to riding off on hobby-horses of his own. He became extremely hostile towards the operations of a speculative land enterprise called the New Zealand Agricultural Company in which two of his ministers, Stout and Larnach, were involved. Eventually the Government lost the 1879 election, in part because of the persistent effects of the depression.

Grey remained in Parliament as a backbencher until 1894,

though his interests were by then focused more closely on his home on Kawau Island, and on the enormous range of plants and animals he had acclimatised to living there, including wallabies and kookaburras which were still established in the region more than a century later. He was also much taken up with his scholarly pursuits, which had included correspondence with a range of scientific pioneers such as Charles Darwin and T. H. Huxley. Grey's last service to his adopted country was as one of three New Zealand representatives at the Australian Federation Convention in Sydney in 1891, at which he opposed New Zealand's joining the federation – a position supported by the New Zealand Parliament. He died in a London hotel in 1898, a year after reconciling with his long-separated wife, Eliza.

The Long Depression continued to blight the prospects and shorten the lives of the seven ministries which held office through the 1880s. Among the consequences outside Parliament, Raewyn Dalziel identified 'unemployment, poverty, the exploitation of women workers, ragged children in the streets, threadbare men on the tramp, damp dark cottages in mean alleys …' In addition, 'urban growth made social differences more noticeable'.

More women joined the workforce in this decade in an effort to contribute more to family incomes. But, as Keith Sinclair noted, 'the conditions of urban workers steadily deteriorated … Labour was so cheap that secondary industry was actually expanding and the country was able to export small quantities of its manufactures … In 1888 respectable citizens … were shocked to learn from a sermon on "The Sin of Cheapness", delivered by a Presbyterian minister in Dunedin, that "sweated labour" existed in the clothing industry … [A] great many people found it intolerable that such an evil, which they believed had been left behind by the immigrant ships, should so soon be reproduced in "this young fair land".' A royal commission in 1890 reported long work hours, poor pay and, in particular, the exploitation of women and children. The shocked response to this report was one of the factors that boosted the Liberal Party's election campaign in that year.

Even as economic conditions appeared least promising, however, developments in technology were laying foundations for future prosperity from a source previously undreamed of: refrigeration. In February 1882 the steamship *Dunedin* sailed from Port Chalmers with a cargo of 4460 frozen mutton and 449 frozen lamb carcasses from the Totara estate near Oamaru. The vessel reached London three months later with the meat in perfect condition. For New Zealand, the world was suddenly a less frightening place than it had been – though this perception would take time to filter through society at large.

The breakthrough meant that the country had a major new export commodity in addition to wool and grain, and by 1890 it was worth £1 million a year, nearly a quarter of the value of wool exports. By 1910 that figure had jumped to £3.8 million, nearly half the value of wool. This new option radically changed the nature of farming in New Zealand. Previously sheep farmers had been forced to slaughter animals – sometimes by simply driving them over cliffs. Now they could raise sheep for meat *and* wool, which made smaller farms considerably more viable than they had been. It also resulted in a move away from merinos, useful only for their wool, and towards such breeds as Romney, which provided both commodities. The need to slaughter and prepare animals for export and for wider domestic distribution created the country's first large-scale industrial plants, freezing works, which also processed by-products such as skins, tallow and manure. The new trade revived ports in smaller centres such as Bluff, Oamaru, Timaru, Gisborne and Napier.

Refrigeration also allowed the export of butter and cheese, previously produced only for local consumption. This sector was slower to gather momentum than the meat industry, because sheep could be produced on existing farms, whereas land for dairying had to be cleared and broken in over many parts of the country, especially in the Auckland provincial region, which had been focused for so long on extractive industries such as timber, gold and kauri gum. Parts of Southland were able to convert to dairy farming immediately, and the country's first dairy factory opened in Edendale in 1882. As other districts caught up, Taranaki and Waikato joined Southland as the major producers of butter and cheese. The export value of these products began to rise sharply in the early 1900s, reaching nearly 45 per cent of the country's total exports by the early 1920s. As with meat, almost all this produce went to Britain, and New Zealand was well on the way to acquiring its identity as the 'dairy farm of the Empire'.

It is difficult to see how New Zealand could have survived as a viable country had it had to continue to rely solely on wool and grain and extractive commodities for its national income. Wool and grain production could have been sustained, though competition from Australia would have increased. Timber would soon have been exhausted, as it was being harvested unsustainably, and the end of kauri milling was already in sight by early in the twentieth century. The demand and price for gold and kauri gum were unstable, and New Zealand's reserves of the former were limited and the market for the latter would disappear altogether as synthetics became available for the production of varnishes and linoleum. Rather than the country's being forced to wrestle with these considerations, however, the coincidence of refrigeration technology and a guaranteed market in Britain would soon deliver to New Zealanders one of the highest living standards in the world. It was a fortunate outcome, though one that would generate a new set of problems when questions eventually had to be asked about whether the extent and scale of grass farming that New Zealand had opted for was in fact sustainable in the light of the country's soils, climate and land instability.

The 1880s, as well as being the period when major adjustments began to be made to the pattern of farming activities, was the first decade in which the three major issues which had preoccupied early colonial politics were absent. The country by this time had representative and responsible government; the years of overt Maori–Pakeha conflict were over and British sovereignty – now meaning the authority of the colonial government – was a reality throughout the land; and the struggle between central government and the provinces had been resolved in favour of the centralists. Coalitions in Parliament could now form around the social and economic issues that engaged Pakeha New Zealand society as a whole. By 1890 the more radical MPs who sought labour and industrial reforms, better conditions for urban working families and the breaking-up of big estates to give small farmers a chance to participate in the country's agricultural sectors had formed themselves into the Liberal Party under the leadership of John Ballance. They would be the first group in the country's history to go into an election campaign, held at the end of 1890, with a programme that a wide slate of candidates was pledged to support. The effects of this introduction into New Zealand of the kind of party politics that had already emerged in democracies in other parts of the world would be revolutionary and wide-ranging.

17

Maori Lifeways

The national web of roads, bridges, railways and telegraph cables which the Vogel administrations had so greatly extended in the 1870s had not, on the whole, encompassed Maori communities unless they were located close to European areas of settlement. And conditions in those communities varied enormously from district to district and from hapu to hapu – so much so that it is difficult to generalise about Maori life in the later years of the nineteenth century. One reason is that the basis of this life remained whanau (extended family) and hapu. Maori generally did not view themselves as 'Maori', a single race and culture, even after the word Maori had come into common usage from about halfway through the nineteenth century. Consequently there was little incentive for them to behave in a uniform way, other than to continue, in characteristically tribal fashion, to disparage and compete with Maori from other hapu and other places. The very persistence of tribal feeling had worked against the continuation of 'nationalist' experiments such as the

Kingitanga (though the Kingitanga survived, largely as the responsibility of Tainui tribes).

Persistence of tribal feeling as the very essence of Maori identity prevented Maori from acting as a pressure group commensurate with their numbers. Even though four specifically Maori seats were created in the national Parliament in 1867, extending the franchise to all Maori men, tribalism and regionalism prevented the members from acting in concert to promote common Maori objectives (as did the fact that most of those early Maori MPs were not proficient in English, and few Pakeha members spoke Maori).

Despite such diversity, most Europeans, unless they had married into Maori families, rarely distinguished one Maori from another or one tribe from another – a fact especially evident in cartoons of Maori of the period. Maori were simply 'Native' in official language; those of part-Maori descent were almost always identified exclusively with that side if their features or colouring were even slightly Polynesian in character.

One of the reasons for this was that most Pakeha living in, say, the four main centres were by this time unlikely to come into direct contact with Maori, and even in a provincial centre such as Hamilton Maori appeared only to sell vegetables door to door and did not live in the town. Those few Europeans who visited a Maori community were very much aware that they were glimpsing a world quite different from their own. The disposition of such settlements, the provision of communal meeting, cooking and eating facilities, the styles of houses, the materials from which they were built, the nature of the activities that went on in and around them, the language that was spoken, the kind of food that was eaten and the manner in which it was prepared – all these features suggested to Europeans a distinctively Maori way of life and one that seemed indistinguishable from place to place.

Traditional Maori clothing had gone out of general use by the 1850s (and much earlier in communities associated with whaling and trading and those close to European settlements), though it would still be donned, especially cloaks, for ceremonial occasions and cultural performances. As the European settler population had begun to swell in the 1840s, so European clothes, new and second-hand, had become widely available along with blankets, which had the advantage of being usable as clothing and/or bedding. These items were sold by travelling merchants and storekeepers who sometimes exploited the Maori market for excessive rewards, especially in places where whole communities had recently come into money from land sales or the trading of commodities. There was a simultaneous and continuing Maori demand from the same entrepreneurs for pipes, tobacco, axes, spades, cooking utensils – especially billies, camp ovens, kettles, buckets and knives – and for metals with which to make other tools.

Generally in the nineteenth century Maori settlements continued to be built around family and hapu membership, and they ranged in size from half a dozen households to several hundred. Each community was likely to have five kinds of building: whare mehana or sleeping houses; kauta or communal cookhouses; pataka or storehouses; whata or shelters for storing wood (for a long time the only source of fuel for cooking and heating); and, more often as the century drew near its close, wharepuni or community meeting houses. A whare mehana might shelter an immediate family or an extended one. It was common for children to live and sleep with members of the extended family who were not necessarily their birth parents. Such houses would rarely be used for cooking and eating, which would more commonly take place in community facilities. The size and style of these and other Maori constructions gradually changed with the increasing availability of European tools, garments, utensils and other materials. Houses progressively became larger and better ventilated, and chimneys and European-type fireplaces were being added in many districts from the 1870s. It was becoming common by the close of the century for rangatira families to live in well-built and well-endowed European-style houses.

Wharepuni increased greatly in size to the kinds of dimensions that would become common in the twentieth century. The incentive to build larger facilities was greatest where tribes had regular inter-hapu or inter-tribal meetings to sustain – such as Waikato with its Kingitanga poukai or loyalty hui and Tuhoe with its Ringatu tekaumarua or holy days, or those communities in Northland and Wairarapa who became closely involved in the Kotahitanga movement, which attempted to unify Maori politically. Observers noted in the 1870s and 1880s that large and well-catered functions were becoming an increasingly common feature of Maori life now that fighting was no longer available to provide an incentive and a focus for community effort. The larger and more lavish the hui or gathering, the more mana accrued to the host community – prestige in Polynesian terms being measured by what was given away rather than by what was accumulated. And, of course, such occasions required reciprocation by guests, the custom of utu or balanced exchange being as important to the functioning of Maori society in the nineteenth century as it had been in the eighteenth.

Another factor promoting the enlargement of buildings was the availability of pit-sawn timber and European tools. The latter aided construction on a bigger scale and the evolution of increasingly elaborate styles of carving, especially on the East

Coast of the North Island and in Te Arawa territory. A growing familiarity with European architecture also modified the styles of smaller buildings in some areas, even those where traditional building materials were still in use. Some dwellings, such as those in King Tawhiao's settlement at Whatiwhatihoe, had doors at the side sheltered by verandahs.

In most districts, traditional building materials – raupo, muka, ponga, earth sods, bark, nikau branches – continued to be used into the 1880s. Houses were likely to have wooden frames, usually of manuka or tree-fern trunks, and wall material of reed or wood packed against them. Sod walls remained in favour in some South Island communities, partly because wood was not always available and partly because they gave better insulation in a colder climate. There were other marked regional differences. Ponga logs tended to be used vertically for house walls on the mainland and horizontally (a style known as wakawaka) on the Chatham Islands. Roofs were thatched with reed, nikau or tussock, or made from bark. Structures made from these materials were still visible in the early years of the twentieth century, though by then their use was in decline.

Generally, as pit-sawn timber and corrugated iron became available in the last two decades of the nineteenth century, Maori were quick to use them where they could afford to. House styles changed in the process. Those of important or wealthy Maori – the Taiaroa family at Taumutu on Banks Peninsula, for example – became indistinguishable externally from those of comparably wealthy Pakeha rural families. Other Maori opted for rectangular huts and cottages with fireplaces and chimneys, and continued to use communal kauta for cooking and eating. Some Maori leading subsistence lives combined European *and* Maori building materials. Te Puea Herangi of Waikato, for example, used ponga walls and thatching for conventional cottages in her communities up to the 1930s. While people engaged in seasonal work or foraging activities – flax cutting, gum digging, muttonbirding and pigeon trapping, for example – continued to build traditional shelters and camp-sites, these should not be mistaken for so-called substandard permanent housing.

In Pakeha eyes, most Maori accommodation in the nineteenth and early twentieth centuries was substandard. Indeed, the lack of toilet facilities, running water or ventilation, over-crowding in sleeping quarters and unhygienic conditions for the preparation of food – all these features were to be characteristic of Maori communities and individual dwellings until the 1930s, and they contributed to the Maori vulnerability to communicable diseases. 'Maori housing' in European usage was synonymous with poor housing. These features were the first to be criticised and then combated by Maori health authorities when they were appointed for the first time in the early 1900s. They were not self-evidently inimical to Maori lifestyles, however, and there was therefore little immediate incentive for communities to change them. Latrines tended to be built under the supervision of a visiting health officer and then abandoned when he left. But such conditions did contribute to the spread of tuberculosis, typhoid fever, dysentery and diarrhoeal and respiratory diseases, and generally made the outbreak of contagious illnesses more likely to affect whole families and communities. Inasmuch as sickness debilitated people or shortened their lives, then such conditions were a threat to the survival of Maori people and in part the source of the declining population statistics. Once Maori leaders made this cause-and-effect connection, they fought hard to change such conditions.

Some communities sought to anaesthetise themselves from health problems and from grief associated with resulting deaths by excessive use of alcohol – with the result that their members became even more susceptible to ill-health and less capable of coping with the crises that illness brought. In this way whole villages and hapu in some areas were prone to sink into sloughs of despondency from which it was difficult to emerge. Te Uira Te Heuheu, a Tuwharetoa woman who married into such a community in Waikato in 1913, was shocked. 'There seemed to be no sense of direction,' she wrote later. 'Life just drifted by.'*

For a long time the official attitude to problems of Maori health and welfare was to ignore them. There were, in effect, two New Zealands at this time: the Pakeha one, served and serviced by national and local government administration systems; and Maori New Zealand, served by a native schools system and little else, but ignored except when national or local government wanted to appropriate land, income (dog taxes, for example) or manpower. Maori were unable to obtain housing finance until the 1930s. Maori owners were unable to borrow money for land development. Land taken from Maori for public works would not be returned when the public use was over. Few doctors saw Maori patients, hospitals rarely took them and most did not want to. The Auckland health officer, in whose district the bulk of the Maori population lived, stated in 1911 that Maori health should be of concern to Europeans – but only because the unchecked spread of Maori diseases could lead eventually to Europeans contracting them. 'As matters stand,' he wrote, 'the Native race is a menace to the wellbeing of the European.'

---

* Te Uira Te Heuheu's shock, it should be noted, arose from the fact that such conditions were by no means universal. Some Maori communities, especially those with a sound economic base on the East Coast of the North Island, in Hawke's Bay, in Tuwharetoa territory and in parts of the South Island, were coping with their vicissitudes with determination and considerable success.

Despite these fears of contamination, the Maori population was well insulated from non-Maori throughout the nineteenth century and the first half of the twentieth. In 1900, 98 per cent of Maori lived in rural communities that were so scattered as to cause not only geographic separation of Maori from Pakeha, but also Maori from other Maori. The major concentrations were north of Whangarei, in South Auckland, Waikato, the King Country, the Bay of Plenty, inland Bay of Plenty, central North Island, Rangitikei, Whanganui and Taranaki. Families continued to live for the most part in kainga or small villages with a hapu base or, in more isolated districts, in individual family homes outside kainga. The South Island Maori population, numbering only 1400 in 1901 out of a national Maori total of 45,000, lived principally in half a dozen 'kaiks' (kainga in South Island dialect) close to but separate from European settlements in Canterbury, Otago and Westland, or in kainga close to Blenheim, Picton, Nelson and Motueka at the top of the island, which had been colonised by North Island tribes.

Life in such settlements tended to be oriented towards the family, community and hapu. On occasion this orientation would extend to wider tribal units, especially when land matters were being discussed or disputed, or even to waka federations such as Tainui, Te Arawa or Mataatua. The latter was especially likely when wider groupings such as the Kingitanga or Hahi Ringatu were involved, activating more extensive kinship networks and obligations. Effective leaders were kaumatua or family heads, while whole hapu would be spoken for at wider hui by rangatira who usually had a whakapapa claim to leadership, but whose acceptance depended also on retaining the confidence of their kaumatua.

Major decision-making on community matters was centred on consensus-forming discussion among family heads on local marae. In the South Island, kaika had established runanga or councils in which whole communities were likely to be involved, and which would be chaired and spoken for by upoko runaka or community leaders. In rare cases, such as Waikato–Maniapoto and Ngati Tuwharetoa, ariki or paramount chiefs would speak for federations of tribes, but more often tribal spokesmen would be rangatira dominant at a particular time or nominated by the rest of the tribe to represent them for a particular project. Only rarely were such spokespersons women. Male primogeniture was still the concept most often ratified by tikanga.

Within these defined but flexible structures communities organised their rounds of hui, tangihanga (funeral ceremonies) and church functions, arranged marriages to strengthen useful alliances among families and hapu, planned, constructed and maintained community facilities such as meeting houses and dining halls, dealt with local conflict and often resolved it, and discussed the perennial issues raised by prospects of land sales or public works in the vicinity of kainga. When some Maori groups sought greater degrees of rangatiratanga or autonomy in the early years of the twenty-first century, it was not only because they believed such a provision was embedded in the Treaty of Waitangi, but also because such autonomy had been the norm for many Maori communities – even if their exercise of it had been the result of official indifference rather than deliberate government and local government policies.

A few Maori groups were for a time spectacularly and successfully self-reliant, sustaining their members and protecting them from the effects of disease, alcohol and demoralisation felt elsewhere. Te Whiti-o-Rongomai's community at Parihaka, with its largely Taranaki tribal base, was one such successful experiment. From the late 1880s it had its own slaughterhouse, bakery, bank and prison, and it generated electricity for lighting. A similar quest for Maori independence merging Western ideas and technology with Maori needs was launched by the Tuhoe prophet Rua Kenana at Maungapohatu in the Urewera from 1907. Other pa, such as Papawai near Greytown, were not as well equipped technologically as Parihaka had been but were able to nourish their inhabitants and provide lavish accommodation and hospitality for visitors, Maori and Pakeha.

Some communities, like those in the South Island close to European centres of population and mingling with Pakeha in work and sport, were by the beginning of the twentieth century almost indistinguishable in external appearance from a Pakeha village. Others, such as the settlements high up on the Whanganui River and the smaller Tuhoe villages in the Urewera, had changed very little in appearance since the wars of the 1860s.* In these respects as in others, Maori life was characterised by diversity.

Most Maori communities made a precarious living from mixed subsistence farming. The scale of Maori horticulture had diminished greatly from the great days of the 1840s and 1850s when the Waikato, Hauraki, Arawa and Bay of Plenty tribes had been the country's major crop producers and exporters. Later in the century, with most of their good land bought or taken from them, denied access to the government assistance available to Pakeha farmers for land development, Maori in most parts of the country could barely produce sufficient meat, grain, vegetables and fruit to feed themselves. In some places, such as

---

* The Urewera was the last Maori district to be 'penetrated' by Europeans and European influences. For this reason it became a target for ethnologists such as Elsdon Best. These men, most interested in manifestations of 'old-time' Maori culture, tended to ignore or condemn the experiment in acculturation being conducted by Rua Kenana.

the Urewera, communities lived close to starvation. In other areas, such as Maketu in the Bay of Plenty, Maori labour and produce were plentiful.

Paritu, a village on the shore of Wharekawa estuary on the Coromandel Peninsula, was not untypical of turn-of-the-century Maori communities, though the people were of mixed tribal origins – some Arawa refugees from the catastrophic Tarawera eruption of 1886,* others from East Coast and Bay of Plenty tribes who had moved to the district for casual work in the forests, goldmines and gumfields, and still others Tainui people with links to those who had been tangata whenua in the region until scared away by Ngapuhi raids at the time of the musket wars. They grew extensive fruit and vegetable crops, kept some animals for milk and meat and chickens for eggs, and foraged for fish and shellfish, which were plentiful in and outside the estuary. When they needed cash for such groceries as flour, sugar and tea, they dug for kauri gum or took casual work with the timber company Leyland O'Brien, which was logging the Wharekawa watershed, or the Luck at Last Mine, which was extracting gold nearby. They bartered homegrown produce with one another. Community discussion took place around a house and kauta that served as a marae and, unusually, they had a church for Ringatu services. In 1907 a native school opened at Opoutere, a short distance away. Maori was the first language in the homes and Maori values and *mores* prevailed. Everyone involved in this community remembered it as a safe and satisfying place in which to grow up. There was little cash about and few luxuries, but the necessities of life were well provided.

---

* Mount Tarawera erupted on the night of 10 June 1886. At least 147 Maori and six Pakeha died; the villages of Te Wairoa, Moura and Te Ariki were buried, and the fabled Pink and White Terraces destroyed.

At Paritu and elsewhere, when families were unable to be self-sufficient, Maori labourers would rely increasingly on income from seasonal work created by the expanding European rural economy. It was common for Maori gangs in country districts to do fencing, drain laying, shearing, crop harvesting, flax cutting and processing, and scrub cutting, or labouring on road and railways public works. Often whole families or hapu would specialise in specific jobs. In many areas such work was available from farmers or local bodies adjacent to hapu settlements. Where individuals left their own kainga in search of such work they tended to settle in other rural Maori communities, adopting the identity and kawa (protocols) of their hosts, or of the family or hapu into which they married. This served to mitigate the appearance and effects of detribalisation, which – while under way from the early years of the twentieth century – did not become apparent for another generation, as a result of migration for work and the demise of some small communities through depopulation.

A commitment to Maori values remained strong at this time, despite the fact that most Maori had nominally converted to Christianity (the largest number to the Anglican Church, the remainder to Roman Catholicism, Methodism, Mormonism and Presbyterianism, in that order). Mana and tapu were still decisive factors determining who led Maori communities, who deserved respect, and why. The principle of utu still determined what was done or not done. It was still widely believed that hara or faults in a Maori sense created chinks in an individual's personal tapu, and that this in turn left the individual vulnerable to makutu (black magic), illness, madness or death; most instances of actual sickness or death were explained in these terms. Despite a sincere commitment to Christian values, tohunga continued to perform Maori karakia or religious rites and to practise folk medicine, sometimes with disastrous results when dealing with such 'Pakeha' illnesses as measles or influenza (immersion in water was a common feature of Maori ritual which, in the case of influenza, could lead to pneumonia).

In some instances Maori were 'Christian' in some contexts – a wedding or a church service, say – and 'Maori' in others, such as combating makutu or performing rituals prior to planting crops or felling trees. In the latter many Maori saw nothing incongruous about invoking the old gods Rongo and Tane alongside Te Atua, the God of the Bible. Some practised Christian and Maori religions simultaneously: many Waikato Maori adherents of the Kingitanga, for example, were followers of Pai Marire *and* baptised Methodists. This was not regarded as contradictory. Maori had come to view life in terms of taha Maori and taha Pakeha – the Maori and the Pakeha sides of themselves, and of life in general.

The focal point of Maori communal life was the hui. People who could no longer fight one another came together to compete in other ways: to surpass the hospitality of their previous hosts; to issue oratorical challenges and display astonishing feats of memory in the recitation of genealogy and tradition; to debate other people's versions of genealogy and tradition; to display prowess in haka, action song, wielding the taiaha and handling canoes; to celebrate who and what they were.

Hui were an established tradition throughout the country. Ngai Tahu in the South Island kept their identity alive by meeting regularly and debating how to prosecute their claim against the Crown for unkept promises made at the time of land purchases. The people of Whanganui and the King Country met to debate Native Land Court questions, ownership and guardianship of the Whanganui River, where the main trunk railway line should be allowed to go, where roads should be laid, and the extent to which Maori communities should be relocated to take advantage of these new arteries of communication. Ngati Kahungunu hapu met to discuss the Repudiation Movement, which challenged Pakeha land purchases in Hawke's Bay. Tuhoe met to consider whether they ought to allow surveying and gold prospecting in the Urewera. Tainui tribes came together interminably to discuss new proposals for political representation, the mana of the Kingitanga, and the pros and cons associated with the sale and lease of land.

In a sense, though, these were excuses for hui, not the causes. Essentially hui were occasions on which hapu and iwi could come together to renew old relationships, to sing, to dance, to tell stories, to listen to and argue in lengthy whaikorero. Increasingly in the later years of the nineteenth century these occasions were becoming inter-tribal ventures as leaders and followers felt impelled to address the questions of the day. By the 1890s a feeling was coalescing that some form of 'Maori' rather than specifically tribal political activity should be attempted to promote common Maori causes, particularly in dealings with the national Parliament, whose Maori representatives had, on the whole, made little impact.

All such hui were conducted according to Maori kawa, though the details of such etiquette varied slightly from tribe to tribe and district to district. In some places the hosts spoke first during formal welcomes, in others the visitors; in some hosts and visitors alternated speakers, in others they followed one another until each group finished separately. Most tribes forbade women speaking on the marae, though some – such as those on the East Coast – tolerated it. All these customs had evolved and become fixed practices in the pre-1840 years when tribes were largely separated from one another. The general structure of rituals of encounter was recognisable throughout the country, however. Successive waves of visitors would be called onto the host marae, they would pause to tangi for the dead of both sides, they would be greeted by speeches and waiata that asserted the identity of the hosts, and they would reply in kind with speeches and songs of their own. Then they would hongi or press noses with the hosts to indicate that the tapu of visitor status had been removed through the ritual of welcome, and then they would be fed.

The hui ritual that remained most pervasive – and which some referred to as the heartbeat of Maori culture – was the tangihanga or mourning ceremony for the dead. The practice was modified slightly over the years to incorporate some Christian elements and to meet public health requirements. But the fundamental sequence and purpose changed little from the nineteenth to the twentieth centuries. When a person died the body was laid out on the marae of the family or hapu. It was exposed to view – at first on mats, later in open coffins – for days while mourners came to pay respects and to comfort the bereaved. The tupapaku or corpse was addressed in oratory and lament, as were the spirits of the relatives who had predeceased him or her. Fine mats, cloaks and heirlooms would also be on display, to demonstrate the mana of the hapu and to symbolically warm and protect the deceased. From the 1890s photographs were incorporated into the ritual to recall the presence of the dead. At about the same time portraits began to be placed on meeting-house walls, an extension of the concept which regarded such houses as representations of the genealogies of the hapu. This shift was also a striking example of the Maori genius for taking what was useful from Western technology to strengthen Maori concepts and practices.

The duration of tangi varied. Until the end of the nineteenth century they could go on for weeks, even months if the deceased was sufficiently important (the last one of considerable length was for King Tawhiao in 1894, which lasted nearly two months). Public health legislation early in the twentieth century restricted the mourning time and it became customary to hold ceremonies within a week; improving systems of transport and communications also reduced the need to display the body for longer periods. The ceremonies ended with a Christian funeral service, usually conducted by Maori clergymen, of whom the Anglican Church in particular had an ample supply (the Catholics, by contrast, did not ordain a Maori priest until 1944, although the church had had Maori seminarians, one of whom was sent to study in Rome, as early as the 1850s), and a European-type burial service in the course of which many of the deceased's personal possessions were likely to be interred with the body. A year or more later another ceremony would be held to 'unveil' the headstone, and this fulfilled some of the functions of the pre-European hahunga or exhumation rite, which ended the period of mourning. Late in the nineteenth century Maori women began to adopt the Victorian mourning costume of black clothes for tangi, and the practice continued long after Pakeha New Zealanders had dropped the custom.

Although the proceedings of the country's Parliament were remote from the daily lives of most Maori, some legislation had affected them intimately. Since European settlers had been granted so-called responsible government by the British Parliament in 1852, one of the most difficult issues of governance had been devising ways to ascertain ownership of communally held Maori land and hence whom to deal with in sales transactions. The problem increased as the European population increased. Inevitably, too, Pakeha buyers wanted the best agricultural and pastoral land available.

In an attempt to accelerate such transactions the Native Land Court was established in 1865, its functions superseding those of the earlier Native Land Purchase Department. The court held sittings presided over by a judge to investigate claims to land based on ancestral occupation, right of conquest and continuity of use and occupation, to rule on the validity of such claims, and to record the names of successful claimants as owners. Although one of the main reasons for establishing the court's procedures was to facilitate the transfer of Maori land to Pakeha ownership, Maori themselves often displayed a considerable willingness to bring land to the court and to offer it for sale. The reasons were complex. In some cases would-be sellers simply wanted money with which to purchase commodities or expand their capacity to offer hospitality, or the land concerned was unwanted; but in many other cases court sittings and sales were initiated by Maori to prove the validity of their claims over those of rivals. The sittings became, in other words, another forum for the inter-hapu and tribal rivalries that had always characterised Maori life. In some instances spurious claimants launched proceedings simply to annoy an opponent, or to take utu for some wrong inflicted on them previously. In this manner court sittings became an extension of – or at least a sequel to – tribal confrontation.

The Native Land Court also became a major institution in Maori life in the late nineteenth and early twentieth centuries. Some elderly people, repositories of tribal traditions, became almost professional court-goers as claim clashed with counter-claim. More important, perhaps, the court minutes carefully recorded most of the testimony presented and thus became the country's first archive of Maori oral history on a large scale. Families often accompanied elders to sittings in the towns nearest the lands under discussion and camped close to the court. Thus the hearings also became occasions for reunions and hui.

When the national Parliament had instituted four Maori seats in 1867, one of the factors that made this measure acceptable to Pakeha MPs was that it gave the North Island a more favourable balance of seats in relation to the South Island, where gold rushes had ensured a population explosion and consequent disproportionate increase in the number of seats there. In some respects this was an enlightened move, giving adult Maori males universal suffrage twelve years ahead of pakeha men and making New Zealand the first neo-European country in the world to give votes to its indigenous population (it would be another 95 years before Australia did the same). But had those seats been allocated on a population basis, as the non-Maori ones were, Maori would have had fourteen or fifteen. Initially the new electorates were established as temporary ones, reflecting the widely held belief that the Maori population would barely survive the nineteenth century. But they were made permanent in 1876 and, towards the close of the twentieth century, increased in number on – at last – the basis of population.

Early Maori MPs were kupapa and tended to be the nominees and protégés of the powerful Minister of Native Affairs, Donald McLean. They had at first little contact with the 'flax roots' of Maori communities, where national issues, other than the disposal of Maori land, were not a major concern. But by the close of the nineteenth century such members as James Carroll, Wi Pere, Hori Kerei Taiaroa, Tame Parata, Hirini Taiwhanga and Hone Heke Ngapua had begun to surprise and then annoy successive governments by opposing Maori legislation of the day as being not in the interests of Maori constituents. Until the admission of James Carroll into the Liberal Government's cabinet in 1892, Maori members were not effective in changing the course of such legislation. But Maori representation did serve as a Trojan horse to introduce both a Maori presence and Maori considerations into the legislature, and eventually those considerations became part of legislation when more able and more sophisticated members took the seats.

By the close of the nineteenth century, however, the prognosis for the Maori population and culture did not seem favourable. Numbers were falling, as was the Maori percentage of the population as a whole. From constituting 50 per cent of the nation's citizens in 1860, they made up only 10 per cent by 1891. Their remaining lands constituted only 17 per cent of the country, and a great deal of this was marginal and in effect useless. While some communities thrived healthily on their own holdings, most notably those on the East Coast and in parts of the Bay of Plenty, others were demoralised and handicapped by malnutrition, alcohol and disease.

It was an awareness of these negative factors that led Archdeacon Walsh to write of 'The Passing of the Maori' in the *Transactions and Proceedings of the New Zealand Institute*. He summarised: 'The Maori has lost heart and abandoned hope. As it has already been observed in the case of the individual, when once the vital force has fallen below a certain point he died from the sheer want of an effort to live; so it is with the race. It is sick unto death, and it is already potentially dead.' It was in an attempt to rectify those same conditions that a number of Maori leaders from a new generation decided to experiment with new forms of political and social activity. And the patient did not die, as Archdeacon Walsh predicted: he got up from his bed and walked.

18

Party Politics Begins

Sir Harry Atkinson – whose fifth and final administration was defeated by the Liberal Party led by John Ballance in January 1891 – was the most continuous ingredient in the so-called 'continuous ministry'. But the old survivor would not survive this time. In just over a year, after elevation to the office of Speaker of the Legislative Council, he would be dead. The Liberals would be in office for the next 21 unbroken years and the country was about to experience what one historian has called 'a revolution in the relationship between the government and the people ...'

That revolution would become apparent in the way that political *parties* began to condition the conduct of politics, particularly elections. Initially, though, the party apparatus worked on one side only, because the Liberals did not face an organised 'opposition party' until 1909, when Opposition leader William Massey reluctantly recognised the clear advantage of committing candidates and sitting MPs to an agreed set of policies.

The revolution was also apparent in the way that Liberal policies would both lay the foundation for the welfare state and the 'apparatus of modern government' by establishing twelve new government departments.

None of this should suggest that the Liberals assumed office with the backing of a coherent philosophical blueprint, however. Its MPs were not, on the whole, socialists, though one of the party's few 'intellectuals', poet and newspaper editor William Pember Reeves, had socialist ideals, wrote about socialism and would later form close associations with the Fabian Society in England (indeed, he named his only son Fabian). Their unifying belief was in a dominant role for central government in the nation's affairs, but on pragmatic rather than ideological grounds. Private enterprise was weak in New Zealand. Only the Government could assemble sufficient capital to extend the country's transport and communications infrastructure. Most Liberals, according to the major historian of the party, David Hamer, 'simply wanted the benefits of private ownership of property spread more widely...' Further, they were not unhappy with the notion of 'social hierarchy' – they just wanted the hierarchy to be open to the reception of the 'hard-working and morally worthy ... The Liberals' policies aimed at removing barriers to social mobility.'

If the Liberals had one common and dominant preoccupation it was how best to use land, widely recognised as the country's richest resource. For most of them, and in particular Lands Minister John McKenzie, the best use was pastoral farming and the spectacle of 'idle' or unfarmed land, such as that in Maori ownership, a scandal. One of the party's most popular policies, which actually created further political support, was the determination to break up the big estates, formed in the days when 'sheep was king', to allow settlement by smaller landholders able to take advantage of the new refrigeration technology which made meat and dairy farming not only viable but profitable.

The party's first leader, John Ballance, was a northern Irishman who had emigrated to New Zealand via England and Australia and set up in business in Wanganui in 1866. At first he was a retail jeweller, then a newspaper editor and proprietor. He gained both visibility and a local following through his editorials in what became the *Wanganui Herald*, and was in Parliament from 1875 and holding ministerial office, initially under George Grey, from 1878. His impact in and on Wellington was strong and favourable from the outset, particularly in his role as Colonial Treasurer in 1878–79. Ballance fell out with Grey, however; and he had three years out of Parliament in the early 1880s. By 1884 he was an MP again, and a minister, and one of his achievements was helping to persuade the ariki of Ngati Tuwharetoa, Horonuku Te Heuheu Tukino, to gift to the nation the land and mountains in the central North Island that became in 1894 the Tongariro National Park, the country's first national park and one of the earliest in the world.

By July 1889 Ballance was leader of the Opposition. He was not a charismatic man, nor a spellbinding orator. But he was, according to his biographer, 'kindly, courteous and considerate and displayed great patience. He was [also] a man of honesty and integrity. As a result he attracted extraordinary loyalty among his cabinet and party.' He also gained considerable political capital from his first major challenge as Premier. After he lost the 1890 election but before he left office, Harry Atkinson had packed the Legislative Council with his own supporters. Ballance attempted to redress this imbalance, which would have paralysed the Liberals' legislative programme, by making additional appointments of his own. Two Governors,

Lords Onslow and Glasgow, declined to accept Ballance's nominations.

The Premier was forced to appeal to the Colonial Secretary in London, who supported his position and told Glasgow that a governor had to accept the advice of his ministers unless that advice was clearly contrary to the will of the legislature, thus clarifying a vitally important constitutional point. Glasgow obliged and made the appointments – four working men whom Ballance had nominated after close consultation with trades councils in the four main centres. This consultation and its fruit was characteristic of the Liberals' attempts in their early years in office to maintain close relations with trades and labour councils and thus with working people, whom they viewed as an essential part of their constituency, along with small farmers and small businessmen.

While Ballance was temperamentally well suited to maintain the 'liberal–labour' association, much of his time as Premier was blighted by illness. He was widely mourned when he died of cancer in April 1893. A statue of him – regrettably bearing little resemblance to the deceased leader – was erected and still stands in the grounds of Parliament.

Ballance's successor as Premier, Richard John Seddon, is the leader most strongly associated with the Liberals' decades in power. In contrast to his predecessor, Seddon *was* charismatic *and* an orator. He had a huge appetite for the antics, the rituals and the effluvium of politics. He is the first leader of the country who viewed politics holistically – that is, treating every aspect of life as political. And his nickname, 'King Dick', indicates both the manner in which he bestrode his contemporaries and the extent to which he concentrated power in his own hands.

Seddon had been born in Lancashire in 1845, the son of schoolteacher parents. He had no academic talents or aspirations of his own, however. He worked in foundries in England and secured an engineer's certificate before emigrating to Australia in 1863. Dissatisfied with prospects there, he came on to New Zealand in 1866 and joined an uncle on the Waimea goldfield on the West Coast. There he apparently made sufficient money to open several stores and to persuade his Australian fiancée's family to allow him to marry their daughter. In 1872 he obtained a publican's licence for his store at Big Dam and over the next four years acquired a reputation as 'an athlete and fist fighter ... renown[ed] for feats of strength and endurance, and for settling matters – including the payment of debts – with his fists'.

In 1876 Seddon moved his family to the new goldfield and mushrooming township at Kumara and established there a hotel, store and butchery. He plunged into local politics, becoming mayor of Kumara and a member of the Westland County Council and Provincial Council, and it was in those forums that he discovered both his gift for the arm-twisting cajoleries of public affairs and the heady exaltation that he derived from practising them. He also became well known as a theatrical but effective miner's advocate in the goldfields warden's court. By 1879, when he was elected to Parliament representing Hokitika, he had become a West Coast character of considerable proportions, both physically and in his personality. And everything he had learned on the Coast would eventually stand him in good stead as a national politician.

Not at first, though. Although his impact on Parliament was immediate, because of the exuberance of his verbosity and his rapid mastery of standing orders, longer-serving MPs regarded him as uncouth and made jokes about his accent, his malapropisms and his tendency to drop his h's. Initially, too, Seddon concerned himself primarily with constituency issues and made little impact on the country as a whole. At this stage of his career, wrote David Hamer, 'Seddon knew little of New Zealand beyond the West Coast, and it knew little of him.' That would change, however, once he entered the Liberal cabinet in 1891.

The national platform Seddon acquired as Minister of Mines, Defence and Public Works enabled him to transfer to the country as a whole the populist style of politics he had perfected on the West Coast. His portfolios, especially Public Works, gave him an excuse to travel the country, turn first sods, open roads and branch railway lines, make highly colourful speeches in the course of which he gesticulated and slapped his thighs, and in general to be seen and heard. William Pember Reeves, who frequently shared platforms with Seddon, said that audiences warmed to 'the big, smiling man with the flushed face and the powerful voice; they liked the swelling chest, the energetic arm, the flapping coat ... [He] left contentment behind him.'

Seddon also used these opportunities to meet with and speak to local committees of the Liberal Party and cement their sense of loyalty to him. Sometimes, Hamer notes, he behaved outrageously, but he also had 'a very acute sense of when he could get away with this ... [He] was just under six feet in height and [eventually] weighed nearly 20 stone ... he ate and drank without moderation. Totally committed to politics, he had few other diversions ...'

By the time Ballance was mortally ill in 1893, Seddon's gusto and his grasp of parliamentary procedures made him the obvious choice to be acting Premier. He then outmanoeuvred his rivals who wanted the Shetland Islander Sir Robert Stout, twice Premier previously, to succeed 'the Chief', as Ballance had been called. But Stout was out of Parliament and, by the time he was returned in a by-election, Seddon had agreement from his caucus to lead the party into the 1893 general election. When the party increased its majority, winning 51 of the 70 European seats, Seddon was able to portray this result as an endorsement of his leadership 'by the people'. The whole episode was typical of the man, who referred to New Zealand as 'God's Own Country' and who established the tradition of the populist Prime Minister who would, if the occasion demanded it, appeal to 'the people' over the heads of his own parliamentary colleagues.

Because of his success in 1893, and the subsequent electoral success of the party under his leadership, Seddon's position as leader was never again under serious threat until close to the end of his life, when he was suffering from overwork and ill-health and was under some pressure from backbenchers to dislodge the time-servers in his cabinet. In the medium term, however, he strengthened his position by removing potential rivals such as Reeves or by ensuring that others, such as Stout, never entered his ministry.

Seddon was all in favour of the Liberals' programme of reform, especially of land laws and the public service. But unlike Reeves, for example, he was cautious about how far such measures should be taken. A good example of that caution, and of the non-ideological nature of the Liberals' approach to government, is women's suffrage. The granting of votes to New Zealand women in 1893 would come to be seen as one of the most celebrated achievements of the Liberal Government, but it was achieved without the active support of government ministers and in face of opposition by some of them, including Seddon.

New Zealand men over the age of 20 had been given the vote regardless of property qualifications in 1879. In being excluded from that franchise, as one historian has noted, women were classed with 'juveniles, lunatics and criminals'. The cause for female suffrage was taken up by the New Zealand Women's Christian Temperance Union (WCTU) led by, among others, the highly intelligent and persuasive Christian socialist Kate Sheppard. Sheppard and her co-workers were convinced that if women had the vote there would be a national majority in favour of a prohibition on the sale of alcohol; they also believed that the welfare of women and children in general would be uplifted and safeguarded if women could vote and be represented in Parliament.

After failing to secure the passage of a women's suffrage bill in 1887 (Seddon was the MP primarily responsible for its defeat), the franchise department of the WCTU, of which Sheppard was director, took two petitions to Parliament, in 1891 and 1892. They were signed by more than 9000 and 19,000 women respectively. The WCTU also persuaded a former Premier, Sir John Hall, to introduce another women's suffrage bill into Parliament (Hall, a conservative, did so believing that, given the opportunity, most women would vote against the Liberals). The 1891 bill passed the House of Representatives but not the Legislative Council. Influenced by his wife, Ellen, vice-president of the Women's Progressive Society, Ballance was in favour of the bill but thought its effect should be delayed so as to give women time to be 'politically educated' before they cast a vote.

The measure finally passed both Houses of Parliament in September 1893, after Ballance's death, and after the Liberal ministers opposed to it had absented themselves from the House of Representatives. It became law on 19 September, when New Zealand became the first sovereign state in the world to give women the vote (and, it could be argued, the most democratic state in the world, given that suffrage had already been extended to Maori and Pakeha men). Seddon sent a telegram to Kate Sheppard conceding defeat and associating his government with the change ('trust now that all doubts as to the sincerity of the Government in this very important matter [have] been effectively removed'). After winning the next election in November 1893, the Liberals were prepared to embrace the measure with greater enthusiasm.

Other major political advances for women would have to wait, however. They were not made eligible to stand for Parliament until 1919, and the first to do so was lawyer Ellen Melville in Grey Lynn in 1923. The first to be elected was Elizabeth McCombs, who won the Lyttelton seat for Labour in 1933 in succession to her husband, who had died. The first woman to hold a cabinet post was Mabel Howard, who became Minister of Social Welfare in the Fraser Labour Government in 1947. In the same decade as suffrage was achieved, however, there was a series of other 'firsts' for women. In Onehunga in 1893, Elizabeth Yates became the first woman in the British Empire to be elected a mayor; Emily Siedeberg became the first woman to graduate as a medical doctor at Otago University in 1896; and Ethel Benjamin graduated with a law degree from the same university in 1897 (one year after an Act of Parliament had made it possible for women to practise law). For all these gender pioneers, life was not easy. They had to endure endless jokes about the roles they had chosen and constant suggestions, if not downright accusations, that their competence was in doubt because of their sex. The very fact that they did what they did and survived, personally and professionally, was an enormous encouragement to other women to set out on comparable career paths.

For the next 40 years, however, very few women made their way into the professions. Most simply entered the workforce in the years between leaving school and marriage. Those women who did continue working in the first decade of the twentieth century were largely domestic servants in private homes or boarding houses, or worked in small factories making garments or processing foods and drink. The number in such professions as teaching, nursing or librarianship was small. As a further handicap, there was a 'near-universal maxim' at this time that women could not hold authority over men, and this factor further limited potential advancement in almost any job.

There was a considerable improvement in working conditions as a whole, particularly in shops and factories, as a result of labour laws introduced during the Liberal term of office. The Department of Labour was one of the new government departments of the era and was headed by possibly the country's most able civil servant, the scholar and former surveyor Edward Tregear, who was particularly concerned about the conditions in which women and children worked. One of the most important measures on which Tregear worked with his minister, the equally able William Pember Reeves, was the 1894 Industrial Conciliation and Arbitration Act, which set out to replace strikes with arbitration and at the same time encourage workers to belong to registered unions.* The need for such legislation had been highlighted by the great maritime strike, which had paralysed the movement of ships and exports for three months in 1890.

Reeves's success in the Labour portfolio was also his political undoing. When he sought to introduce further union-friendly regulations in 1895, Seddon, uncomfortable with Reeves's intellectual view of political matters and nervous about public toleration of the Liberals' pace of reforms, offered his potential rival New Zealand's only diplomatic post at this time, Agent-

---

* As a result of this law, New Zealand was indeed for some years a 'land without strikes'. See page 308.

General (later High Commissioner) in London. Reeves accepted, and went on to have a distinguished career in England, which included becoming director of the London School of Economics and writing *The Long White Cloud (Ao Tea Roa)*, the first intelligently analytical history of New Zealand. In this volume, Reeves explained the *raison d'être* for the Liberal reforms from the point of view of one who had participated in their planning and execution:

> They were the outcome of a belief that a young democratic country, still almost free from extremes of wealth and poverty, from class hatreds and fears and the barriers these create, supplies an unequalled field for safe and rational experiment in the hope of preventing and shutting out some of the worst social evils and miseries which afflict great nations alike in the old world and the new.

The Liberals' other pioneering measure, alongside female suffrage and labour reform, was one which all cabinet members fully supported: the introduction of an old age pension. Behind this legislation was the memory of one of the 'worst social evils and miseries' to which Reeves referred, the British workhouse in which the indigent elderly were forced to live in spartan institutional circumstances. What the Liberals devised instead was a non-contributory pension scheme which would be available as an entitlement earned by years of paying tax – or being married to someone who had. After four years of debate and political manoeuvring, the pension was introduced in 1898. It was not universal, however (that measure would await the arrival of the first Labour Government in the 1930s). It was restricted to men and women who were destitute, and then only if that state was not the fault of the individuals concerned – in other words, if they were 'deserving poor'. It was complemented a decade later by the country's first widow's pension, which saved from destitution women with children who had lost their husband, father and wage-earner.

Still another measure that would come to be seen as contributing to the foundation of the welfare state was the Liberals' Workers Dwellings Act of 1905. This enabled the Government to buy land at Petone and elsewhere, build houses, and rent them to workers and their families. Although it was not a large-scale scheme, because of budgetary limitations, it represented an attempt to raise the standard of suburban development and to provide diligent workers and their families with affordable good-quality accommodation. It can also be seen as a precursor of the much fuller state housing scheme launched by the first Labour Government in the 1930s.

The Liberals' major programme, which they hoped would generate employment, agricultural production and continued national prosperity while at the same time adding to their support, was the closer settlement of land. They came into office with the declared intention of breaking up large estates and settling small farmers on them. In 1890 less than 1 per cent of all landowners controlled 64 per cent of freehold land. And some of the estate owners, especially in Canterbury and North Otago, had been generating enormous incomes. Thomas Campbell of Otekaike, inland from Oamaru, for example, had annual profits in good years of about £30,000.

The Government did not intend to carve up these properties forcibly, however, and the new opportunities offered by refrigeration and farm mechanisation were incentive enough for many owners to sell out voluntarily. Between 1892 and 1912, the Government bought 223 estates totalling 520,000 hectares; and they settled on them some 7000 farmers and their families. The Government also continued to open up Crown land in the

North Island – much of it purchased from Maori (some 1.2 million hectares for £650,000) – and to build railways, roads and bridges to make that land accessible.

Oakley Sargeson, uncle of the future writer Frank Sargeson, was typical of the settlers who benefited from ballots for Crown land. A plumber in Kaponga, Taranaki, he entered a ballot for land north of Taumarunui in 1912. He drew a 160-hectare hill-country property near Okahukura, available for 'lease in perpetuity' (999 years; later these properties were made available for purchase). The land turned out to be steep-sided with pumice soil, half forested and half in bracken. To convert it for sheep farming, Sargeson had to fell the bush and clear the fern, burn over the remnants, sow grass, fence it, and finally stock it. The whole process took more than a decade of back-breaking labour.

The main architect of the Liberals' land policy was John McKenzie, nicknamed 'Honest Jock', a towering Gaelic-speaking Highlander who in 1860 became part of the chain migration of Scots to Otago. He farmed near Palmerston and won election to the Otago Provincial Council in 1871. Ten years later he became MP for Moeraki and, within a short time, whip for the Stout–Vogel administration and an authoritative speaker in Parliament on land issues – his only real political interest. That expertise brought him the Lands portfolio in the Liberal cabinet and he held it from 1891 until his resignation on the ground of ill-health in 1900, which preceded his death the following year. He was also on occasion acting Premier during Seddon's rare absences.

McKenzie's biographer Tom Brooking credits him with introducing the Government's graduated land tax in 1891 and with designing the Acts that facilitated the state purchase of large estates (backed by the threat of compulsory purchase to encourage the waverers). He also credits McKenzie with introducing the regulations and inspections that ensured the delivery of clean milk to dairy factories and healthy meat to freezing works and butcheries. His 1892 Land Act in particular is memorable for another reason: it 'made the notion of the Queen's Chain more explicit ... McKenzie wanted all New Zealanders to be able to fish the rivers, lakes and coasts and to enjoy unrestricted access to forests and mountains'. This ambition sprang from McKenzie's childhood in Ross-shire, where he had seen the properties of the lairds closed off to the common people. Oddly, though, his first-hand memories of the Highland clearances did not prevent him from taking every opportunity to part North Island Maori from their land. As Brooking notes, McKenzie's 'land for settlements policy assured him a place in the national hall of fame but his Native land policy widened the fracture in the New Zealand dream'.

Along with Labour and Lands, another of the Government's new bureaucracies was the Department of Public Health, the first of its kind anywhere and another of the measures which gave weight to New Zealand's growing reputation as 'social laboratory of the world'. The long-running cause for the creation of this department, and for the appointment of a minister responsible, Joseph Ward, was the widely acknowledged ineffectiveness of the central and local boards of health set up by the Public Health Act of 1872. As health historian Derek Dow notes, these failed because the central boards, based on the old system of provincial government, were barred from raising funds, and the local boards had not been given effective powers. They had been expected to oversee such matters as the quarantining of vessels arriving in New Zealand with cases of infectious disease and vaccinating local populations in the event of outbreaks of disease. Other responsibilities were supposed to include 'removal of nuisances, speedy interment of the dead, monitoring of noxious trades ... animal hygiene as it affected human health [and] requiring earth or water closets to be attached to all houses in towns'.

The last requirement was not easily enforced because of a general absence of effective water and sewerage systems (in 1887, for example, only 10 per cent of houses in Auckland possessed water closets). The best that could be done in most places was arranging 'night soil' collections. Another factor that was often cited to reduce any sense of urgency in the improvement of water supplies and sanitation was the belief – wholly erroneous – that New Zealand had one of the healthiest climates in the world and was therefore less in need of sanitation measures than the crowded cities of the Old World.* In fact, a series of studies in the second half of the nineteenth century revealed that death rates in New Zealand towns were as bad as, and in some cases worse than, those in such cities as Manchester and London. Given that many immigrants had left Europe specifically to escape such conditions, this was disappointing news indeed.

What eventually galvanised the Liberal Government to address such problems systematically was a bubonic plague scare in 1900. The world's third great pandemic of plague spread along the trade routes out of China in the 1890s and eventually killed more than 10 million people, most of them in Asia and India. The disease reached Sydney in January 1900, where there

---

* As far as conditions in Auckland were concerned, a poem published in the *New Zealand Herald* on 11 March 1882 commented:

> The foul putrescence lieth on each side of the street,
> And in each festering backyard, slops swelter in the heat.
> The cess-pits belch forth gases on fever-laden air,
> And fever-damp uprolleth from sewer-gullies there.

were 303 cases that year and 103 deaths. Auckland's considerable trade and transport links with Australia aroused fears that New Zealand would be affected; as if on cue, the country's first plague victim, Hugh Charles Kelly of Upper Queen Street, died on 22 June 1900.

The Government responded to this apparent emergency – 'apparent' because Kelly turned out to be New Zealand's sole plague victim, though this could not be known at the time – with a Bubonic Plague Prevention Act, stiffening quarantine and other measures. But campaigners for a reformed public health system, such as the experienced bacteriologist Dr James Mason, urged the Government to take advantage of the heightened awareness of health issues by making far-reaching changes to the health system. The Government obliged. A new Public Health Act became law on 13 October 1900. It established a centralised department in Wellington with a Chief Health Officer, Dr Mason, and district health officers and offices in Auckland, Napier, Wellington, Nelson, Christchurch and Dunedin.

Mason set out the department's priorities in his first annual report the following year. They included 'continuous vigilance against infectious disease ... sanitary issues, including water pollution, drainage and water supply schemes, the disposal of household refuse and night soil, and the control of meat and milk supplies'. He also referred to measures needed to control tuberculosis, the major cause of death among Pakeha New Zealanders (as it would be subsequently among Maori, once other diseases such as typhoid were brought under control through improvements in sanitation and housing); although it was possible to ameliorate the effects of tuberculosis, particularly by isolating victims in sanatoria or individual huts, the disease would not be eliminated until the widespread availability of antibiotics after World War II.

Prospects for a co-ordinated approach to public health improved further when the department took over hospital administration in 1909. Some of the advantages of the new system became apparent almost immediately when the country had to face its one and only smallpox epidemic in 1913; though the fact that the outbreak was confined largely to rural Maori communities limited the impact of organised vaccination and isolation programmes.

Another major health initiative during the Liberals' term of office, though not directly attributable to them, was the formation of the Society for the Promotion of the Health of Women and Children in Dunedin in 1907. Known as the Plunket Society, after the wife of the then Governor, who was a patron and strong supporter, it was the outcome of a visionary programme for the care of infants devised by Frederic Truby King, superintendent of Seacliff Lunatic Asylum.* King, along with the great physicist Ernest Rutherford, was the first New Zealand-born scientist to make an impact on the wider world. Whereas Rutherford, unable to find a permanent job as a schoolteacher, had left the country in 1895 to seek further opportunities abroad and in 1908 become the first New Zealander awarded the Nobel Prize, King had trained overseas (in Edinburgh), then returned to New Zealand to make his mark there.

Appointed superintendent at Seacliff, the largest asylum in the country, when he was only 31, King transformed the position into his own personal fiefdom and experimented widely with what would come to be known as the practice of psychiatry. As Barbara Brookes has noted, he turned 'a badly designed farm

---

* Seacliff, like some other asylums in the country – Sunnyside, Avondale, Cherry Farm – had the kind of name that suggests a rural estate or cheerful holiday resort; this served to mask what some patients experienced as the horror of having to live in such institutions.

asylum into a working institution with a productive farm and beautifully planted grounds ... [He] promoted fresh air, exercise, good diet, work and recreation as the appropriate treatments for mental illness. He worked towards improved classification of patients [and] took voluntary boarders before provision was made in legislation for voluntary admission ...'

King's work on infant care arose from the need to find a satisfactorily beneficial feeding formula for a baby girl whom he and his wife, Bella, adopted in 1905. Being now responsible, at the age of 47, for the care of an infant of his own, he turned his considerable intelligence to the many issues involved in raising children. His full range of theories about feeding babies, timing of feeding, wider nutrition, toilet training and exercise of discipline were eventually published in his extraordinarily popular book *Feeding and Care of Baby* (1913). Because the medical profession turned its collective back on him, regarding him as an eccentric, King enlisted the help of society women to promote both his ideas and the wider cause of child welfare. His wife Bella and later their adopted daughter, Mary, acted as devoted secretaries for this aspect of his work. Specially trained 'Karitane nurses' visited mothers in their homes to help equip them with all the skills of babycraft and to monitor infant development. The name came from the location of the Kings' holiday home on the Karitane peninsula at the entrance to the Waikouaiti estuary. King used the house as an extension of Seacliff and, after 1907, as a cottage hospital for training nurses in maternal and infant welfare. It became the prototype for Karitane hospitals, of which there were eventually half a dozen nationwide.

In 1912 King was seconded to the Department of Public Health in order to take his message about infant welfare to the country as a whole. Subsequently, through his writings and attendance at international conferences, he promoted his ideas in Britain and Australia. In both countries, his dramatic form of delivery, his exaggeration of the benefits of his methods and his utter lack of self-doubt won him a following every bit as enthusiastic as that which he enjoyed in New Zealand. Although the rigidities of his theories would eventually be challenged and supplanted, King lived long enough to see his infant welfare campaign taken up internationally. In 1921 he was appointed national director of child welfare for what had become, the previous year, the Department of Health, and he subsequently became director of mental health. Sadly, his own mental health declined to the point where he could have been forced to become a patient in one of his own hospitals. Instead, he was cared for at his magnificently gardened home in Melrose, Wellington, where he died in 1938. He had been knighted in 1925 and was the first private citizen in New Zealand to be given a state funeral. To enhance his iconic status, he became in 1957 the first New Zealander to appear on a postage stamp.

After John McKenzie's retirement from public life, the man regarded as Richard Seddon's deputy, and ultimately as his successor as Prime Minister, was the Colonial Secretary and Minister of Industries and Commerce and of Health, Sir Joseph Ward (he had been knighted in 1901 on account of organising a successful royal tour for the Duke and Duchess of Cornwall, the future King George V and Queen Mary). Ward, a Catholic merchant of Irish descent born in Melbourne, represented the country's most southerly electorate, Awarua. He had made what was surely the most dramatic comeback ever seen in New Zealand politics. While he was Colonial Treasurer in the Seddon ministry in the mid-1890s, his own business had collapsed and he was eventually declared bankrupt in 1897. In these circumstances he was, of course, required to resign as Treasurer. But he exploited a loophole in the electoral law by resigning from Parliament and then standing again in the resulting by-election, at which he was re-elected with an increased majority.

Seddon had no reservations about his protégé's fall and rise. Ward had mercantile experience held by few other Liberal MPs and had, on the whole, performed very satisfactorily in the administration of his portfolios, especially in securing an enormous loan in 1895 to finance the Government's land settlement programme. By the early 1900s he was, according to his biographer, an impressive figure with his 'expanding girth, gold watch-chain and waxed moustache ... [He] was inclined to be more pompous and paranoid after his personal trauma, yet he still possessed his enterprise and commercial drive and ... an "inexhaustible stock of splendid optimism".'

That optimism would be fully drawn upon when he did, as expected, succeed Seddon in 1906. The Prime Minister had been visiting Australia in June and was two days out of Sydney on the way home with his wife and daughter when he suffered a sudden heart attack and died. The ship put back to Sydney so that the body could be embalmed for its return to New Zealand. Like his predecessor, Seddon was given a state funeral and a statue in the grounds of Parliament – this one a dramatically good likeness. Ward was in London at the time and a temporary ministry was sworn in under the leadership of William Hall-Jones, who up to that time had been Minister of Justice and of Public Works. As soon as Ward returned in August 1906 he was elected leader of the Liberal Party and thus began his first term as Prime Minister of New Zealand.

While the Liberals would remain in office for a further six years, the steam had gone out of their performance and the reforming zeal was exhausted. This was a consequence partly of their having fulfilled their legislative programme, and partly of the loss of Seddon, who even in his period of declining health had exuded energy and purposefulness. Seddon also proved to have been a far more skilled political manager than Ward, who at times seemed to lack the authority to control his caucus. He was also ridiculed by some of his own MPs, in addition to Opposition ones, for an indulgent preoccupation with imperial affairs (he was absent in London for parts of 1907, 1909 and 1911). 'While the economy prospered,' Michael Bassett has written – and it did, giving New Zealanders one of the highest standards of living in the world – 'Ward's government lacked clear direction. Bold promises of legislation would be lost in controversy, retraction, prevarication and then paralysis.'

At the same time, the Opposition in Parliament was becoming increasingly better organised and controlled under the leadership since 1903 of William Ferguson ('Bill') Massey. In 1909 Massey announced that his supporters within Parliament and those outside in the Political Reform League would henceforth be known as the Reform Party. From this time New Zealand did have a political system based on party politics, and Massey began to impose a degree of discipline on his MPs and candidates comparable with that exercised by the Liberals nearly two decades earlier. Ironically, he was doing this at the very time that Ward's grip on his followers, particularly those from the Labour movement, was weakening.

The problem for Ward was that the entire constituency on which the Liberals had built their original support was breaking up. The Labour part of the 'lib-lab' association was now talking of putting up its own parliamentary candidates. And much of the support from farmers and the small business sector was leaching away to Reform. Farmers had formed their own union in 1899 and shown an increasing determination to promote their interests and those of the agriculture sector. In their view,

'Farmer Bill' Massey was one of them; the townie merchant Joe Ward was not.

In contrast to Seddon's record of leading his party to five election victories, Ward managed only one, in 1908. The 1911 poll produced a deadlocked Parliament. Full of disappointment and feelings of rejection, Ward resigned, to give the Liberal survivors a greater chance of maintaining a slim majority. A ministry was formed under the leadership of the Minister of Agriculture, Thomas Mackenzie, in March 1912. But this collapsed in July when four Liberal MPs voted against the Government in a no-confidence motion. After 21 years, the Liberals were out. Reform, a coalition of farming, urban professional and business interests, was in. One month after this the New Zealand Political Reform League was formally constituted as a political party.

Among the many changes which took place during the term of the Liberal Government was that in 1907 the country ceased to call itself a colony and became a dominion, implying the beginnings of a sense of independent identity. Another was that in 1911 the urban population of New Zealand exceeded the rural for the first time since the earliest years of British colonisation. The population of Auckland alone jumped from 51,000 in 1896 to 103,000 by 1911. These changes provoked a feeling that, despite the continuing reliance on farmers to produce its wealth, New Zealand was no longer a pioneering country composed of Pakeha people quarrying a living from the land and from building the infrastructure of roads and railways. It was now an urban society with a predominantly urban culture.

Over the same period the population of the North Island raced ahead of the South Island's, 56 per cent to 44 per cent by 1911. The long period of South Island ascendancy in population and wealth, generated largely by the gold rushes, was over. The expression 'mainland' to denote the south would now be used only ironically. The drift of people and business to the north would be a continuing feature of the national profile throughout most of the twentieth century.

The coincidence of these demographic and economic changes with anniversaries of the European foundings of dozens of New Zealand's towns and districts in the 1840s and 1850s generated a perception that one major era of New Zealand's history and development was over and another just beginning. Here on the one hand were the now grey-haired and grey-bearded 'pioneers' ('Oh the Pioneers, kiddies,' Janet Frame's mother, who grew up in the 1890s and early 1900s, used to say to her children over and over again, her voice brimming with admiration and nostalgia), and on the other their descendants, by this time more than 60 per cent of the population, who had been born in New Zealand as children and grandchildren of pioneers and who were expected to carry forward the old vision of their country as a 'Better Britain'.

For the first time a 'double patriotism' was emerging which took pride in being both British and New Zealand. One expression of it was the growing interest in New Zealand rugby teams that travelled abroad, as they did to the United Kingdom in 1888–89 (the New Zealand Native Team) and in 1905 (the first All Blacks). The pride in the victories of the latter, and the deep shock and discussion provoked by a controversial loss to Wales, suggested that a large part of the country's emerging identity would be invested in this particular sport, as it would be also in war. Another expression of similar feelings could be found in a modest first florescence of literature which revealed the beginnings of a sense of history (Reeves's *The Long White Cloud* in 1898, Robert McNab's *Historical Records of New Zealand* ten years later, and T. M. Hocken's *A Bibliography of the Literature Relating to New Zealand* in 1909*); and of nostalgia for what was passing away (William Satchell's novels *The Toll of the Bush* (1905) and *The Greenstone Door* (1914)).

With the nostalgia came a strong sense, encouraged by both Liberal politicians and writers in the party's ranks – Reeves, McNab, T. Lindsay Buick and Thomas Bracken (of *God Defend New Zealand* fame) – that the Government's programme had achieved something in New Zealand that offered an example to humankind as a whole. The view emerged that, with votes for women, old age pensions and labour legislation in particular, New Zealand was 'showing the way' to the rest of the world – that Seddon's 'God's Own Country' was, among other things, a social laboratory which other countries could study with envy and profit. Indeed, a whole procession of luminaries – Mark Twain, Beatrice and Sidney Webb, Keir Hardy, Tom Mann, Ben Tillet and Michael Davitt among them – all came to inspect the country and its institutions during the Liberal era. This sense of the country's special mission to the world at large persisted right through the twentieth century and was voiced at various times by political parties of all persuasions seeking either further social innovation or preservation of the *status quo*.

Such feeling was linked also, in the Liberal era and beyond it, to the notion that New Zealand was one of the most loyal – if not *the* most loyal – of Britain's children. And this notion was expressed and exploited by national leaders to persuade their

---

* Hocken and the bibliophile Alexander Turnbull would leave valuable collections of books and manuscripts that became the bases for the country's premier research libraries, the Hocken Library, which opened in Dunedin in 1910, and the Alexander Turnbull Library in Wellington, which opened in 1920.

compatriots to become involved for the first time in wars which were not of New Zealand's making and which were taking place far away from the country's national boundaries.

19

Baptism of Blood?

As the nineteenth century turned into the twentieth, New Zealand had been a British colony for a mere six decades, less than the course of a human lifetime. In that short period, its citizens had achieved a great many things of which they believed they could be proud: stabilisation of relations between Maori and Pakeha to the point where each people lived parallel lives in separate spheres; functioning political and legal systems based on Westminster models; near-universal primary education; transport and communications networks across a land characterised more by mountains and gorges than by plains; a viable meat, wool and dairy industry supplying the British market and generating national income; and social progress in such forms as votes for women, an industrial arbitration system and pensions for the deserving elderly.

The one thing the country had not yet done, and was thirsting to do, was send troops abroad to represent it in combat. There *were* old soldiers in New Zealand – most of them, Maori and

Pakeha, veterans of the New Zealand Wars. There were others who had fought as imperial troops in earlier wars: in the Crimea in 1854, and in many other campaigns on the continents of Africa and Asia. One former officer who lived in New Zealand, Surgeon Captain Robert H. Blackwell, had worked at Florence Nightingale's shoulder at Balaclava; another, Sergeant Major John Bevin of the Otago Mounted Police, had survived the charge of the Light Brigade. And Captain Henry Cecil Dudgeon D'Arcy, born in Wanganui, had won a Victoria Cross in the Zulu War of 1878–79.

Not until the South African War broke out in October 1899 was a force raised in New Zealand and sent abroad specifically to represent the country in combat. In April of that year, Premier Richard John Seddon had offered the British Government 500 troops to put down an uprising in Samoa, and Native Affairs Minister James Carroll, who had fought as a kupapa in the Te Kooti campaign, was keen to lead a 300-strong Maori contingent there. Parliamentary debates and newspaper editorials of the time convey the impression that sections of the country were bored with peacetime (27 years had elapsed since the close of the war against Te Kooti and his followers). Members of permanent militia and volunteer corps were keen to put their rugged training to practical test.

The turn of the century and Queen Victoria's diamond jubilee in 1898 were also generating nascent imperialism and national-ism. Patriotic men wanted to show their mettle in a scrap and to demonstrate the country's unswerving loyalty to Mother Britain, but at the same time to establish traditions and precedents that were New Zealand in origin and flavour. In the case of Samoa, to Seddon's and Carroll's disappointment, the British Government declined offers of assistance. In the case of South Africa five months later, Britain accepted. And the qualities which Seddon had identified as being advantageous for fighting on a Pacific island – European troops accustomed to bush warfare and bush life, and Maori warriors 'loyal, prepared and desirous of … restoring law and order' – might have seemed equally to be assets against the commando tactics of the Boers.

New Zealand was the first colony to volunteer a contingent, of mounted rifles, for this war, and did so two weeks before war itself was declared. The first 200 troops and their horses were despatched only ten days after the declaration. At the send-off at the Wellington wharves an enormous crowd heard Seddon proclaim that New Zealanders 'would fight for one flag, one Queen, one tongue, and for one country – Britain'. An onlooker wrote:

> It was all magnificently fine. The heart of a young nation was going out in throbbing farewell to the flower of its youth, banded together at duty's call to fight for the Mother Land … The bands played, the people sang, and cheer after cheer was sent across the water. Women were weeping now, and there were even sober-sided businessmen whose eyes were just a trifle dim … The sloping sun gleamed on the waters, lit up the streaming flags, and fell upon the thousands of faces that watched as the two lines of steamers, with the troopship in the centre, went slow ahead down the harbour.

Eight weeks later the New Zealanders reached South Africa days ahead of the first Australian contingents, and they were in action in northern Cape Colony by 9 December. On 28 December, Private George Bradford of Paeroa became the first New Zealand soldier to die on overseas duty when he succumbed to wounds as a prisoner of war. His bandolier was recovered and later became the badge of office for successive presidents of the New Zealand South African War Veterans Association (each officeholder would have his name inscribed on a chromium-plated .303 bullet case).

The fundamental cause of the war, as military historian John Crawford has noted, was 'British determination to dominate South Africa and an equally strong Boer determination to resist the extinction of their independence'. The trigger was the rights of *uitlanders* or non-Boers in the Boer South African Republic (Transvaal). Most *uitlanders* were English. They were denied votes and subject to forms of indirect taxation that they considered unjust. By 1899 many *uitlanders* had abandoned their properties and possessions, and the Boers issued an ultimatum for the British to withdraw their troops from Transvaal. The Orange Free State aligned itself with Transvaal and, when the ultimatum expired, the British territories of Cape Colony and Natal were at war with the South African Republic, as was the British Empire as a whole. Richard Seddon was moved to offer New Zealand's participation not only on grounds of imperial solidarity, but also because many *uitlanders* in Transvaal were goldminers of British stock, as he himself had been. He was profoundly moved by Britain's readiness to go to war in defence of a colonial community.

Over three years, 1899 to 1902, New Zealand raised and despatched nine further contingents, the last two of which arrived too late to take part in significant action. In addition to providing their horses, volunteers were expected to take their own equipment, which cost about £25. The third and fourth contingents were funded largely by public subscription, and the fifth to tenth by the British Government. Altogether New Zealand contributed nearly 6500 men to the war effort and over £113,000 of public donations.

From the outset, many Maori were keen to enlist for service in the war. But they were prevented from doing so as a contingent by a British Government directive that 'blacks should not be deployed against whites'. To some Maori this was a source of acute disappointment, and debate ensued over what precisely constituted 'black' and 'white'. Hui such as one held at the Basin Reserve in Wellington on 28 March 1900 protested vigorously against the policy, but to no avail. Maori managed to enlist as individuals, however. Many such as Barney Vercoe, Tom Porter and Paki Withers took advantage of European names and features. They served with distinction, and the experience stood some of them in good stead for promotion within the Pioneer Battalion in World War I more than a decade later.

As New Zealand's first war abroad, the South African campaign impressed itself vividly on the public imagination and provided cameos that were to become archetypical in the national mind. The spectacle of the rugged volunteer, for example, riding off to war with his own horse and equipment, was well captured by Denis Glover in the poem 'I Remember', part of his *Sings Harry* sequence:

> Then Uncle Jim was off to the wars
> With a carbine at his saddle
> And was killed in the Transvaal
> – I forget in just what battle

Indeed, the 'Rough Riders' with their dusty mounts, bandoliers of bullets, weaponry and swaggering gait evoked images every bit as romantic as those of the American frontier. The scenario in South Africa itself intensified the exotic conception people had of the theatre of war. Kopes or small hills overlooked barren, desert-like plains. The daytime temperatures soared and the terrain lacked shade. It was an abrupt contrast with the luxuriant New Zealand landscape and temperate climate. Most New Zealanders found these conditions intensely unpleasant.

For the first half of the war the imperial and colonial forces concentrated on attacking the Boers' fixed positions, relieving towns besieged from the earliest days of combat and in general engaging the enemy's army. The bulk of the action for the New Zealand contingents involved lightning attacks on the Boers' highly mobile units, especially later in the war when the major Boer armies had been defeated and remaining threats to security came from commando bands that were energetic, resourceful and difficult to engage.

As might have been expected from their fitness and keenness, the New Zealand 'troopers' – as they came to be called – fought with distinction. They were remembered especially for their part in actions at New Zealand Hill, Sanna's Post, Diamond Hill and Rhenoster Kop. One in every 48 men received official recognition for distinguished or valuable services. And one trooper, Farrier Sergeant William James Hardham of Wellington, won the Victoria Cross. The number of New Zealanders killed in combat, 59, was relatively low, however. A larger total died from the combined effects of disease (130), accidents (30) and wounds. The accidental deaths included sixteen New Zealanders killed in a train collision at Machavic on 12 April 1902.

Back home in New Zealand, the mood throughout the war remained highly jingoistic. A booklet commemorating the country's contribution of troops and money identified their significance in these terms.

> It is a glorious page in our history. The whole nation is aroused, and the Imperial spirit has taken a firm hold. If this war does nothing else than foster this feeling, it will not have been in vain. The little-Englanders have hidden their diminished heads, party differences have been sunk in the common weal, and the united action of our vast Empire has been an object lesson to the world. The old spirit of the mother is not lacking in the sons.

In sparsely populated rural regions such as the Coromandel Peninsula, parades of local volunteers and the unveiling of post-war monuments did a great deal to create and enhance special feelings of local identity and community cohesion. The Boer War was also in part responsible for the degree of nationalism that decisively ruled out the possibility of New Zealand's federating with the Australian colonies in 1901.

The other face of jingoism was a strong intolerance of anybody who questioned or opposed New Zealand's support for the war. Only five members of the House of Representatives opposed the motion to send New Zealand troops, and only one member of the Legislative Council, Henry Scotland. If Britain were in danger he would defend her, said the London-born Scotland. But she was not. And she was breaking a treaty to deprive the Boers of self-government. Newspapers of the day dismissed this viewpoint as arising from 'advanced senility'. Another parliamentary employee, *Hansard* chief reporter J. Grattan Grey, was dismissed from his job for condemning the war in a letter to a newspaper. Employees of the Westport Harbour Board were threatened with the sack if they continued to voice reservations about the war. In addition to a record of distinguished performance in combat, New Zealand had begun to establish a tradition of harsh treatment of wartime dissenters.

Surprisingly, perhaps, the troops at the front displayed less antagonism towards the Boers and less unqualified support for Mother Britain. Their literature and letters gave the South Africans credit for the manner in which they fought and for their considerate treatment of prisoners of war. Conversely they showed a degree of contempt for some of the overly disciplined procedures of English soldiers, for their rigidly close fighting formations, and for some of the more ridiculous distinctions made between officers and men.

On the home front the public hero of the war was Lieutenant-Colonel Alfred William Robin. Robin was not, as was widely supposed at the time, New Zealand-born. He came from Victoria, Australia, in his childhood. When at the age of 39 he was appointed commander of the first three contingents sent to South Africa, he became the first colonial anywhere to command a unit in defence of the British Empire. All his previous military experience had been in New Zealand and more senior officers in New Zealand with Imperial Army training had opposed his appointment. He performed with great ability, however, in the relief of Kimberley, and at Driefontein, Johannesburg and Diamond Hill. To the New Zealand public he became a symbol of all that was worthy about the country's contribution to the war. He was given a hero's welcome in Dunedin when he returned home in May 1901. Later he became Chief of the General Staff in New Zealand and the Commander of Home Forces in World War I.

The South African War ended on 31 May 1902 with the signing of the Boer surrender at Potchefstroom. The experience of participation provided a hinge for New Zealand's military history, a link between past and future traditions. In a literal sense it spanned the passage of the nineteenth century into the twentieth, and of Victoria's reign into that of Edward VII, which began in 1901. This passage produced new precedents for New Zealanders. It established the principle that the country would involve itself in other parts of the world, and that it would do this to uphold British imperial power rather than simply to protect immediate national interests. There were, of course, elements of self-interest in addition to those of self-sacrifice: it was taken for granted that the Royal Navy would defend New Zealand's coastline if the country was threatened with invasion. Fortunately, this belief was never put to the test.

The war was also the first in which New Zealand troops fought harmoniously alongside Australians, each recognising that they had more in common with one another than they did with British troops, thus laying the foundation for the ANZAC connection that was to be cemented so strongly more than a decade later at Gallipoli, and in North Africa during World War II.

The traditions that grew up about New Zealand fighting men – rugged, enterprising, ready to throw away the rule book when the rules were inadequate – also originated in the South African War. Commentators noted that in many respects, especially in their capacity to handle horses and move rapidly and safely through rough country, New Zealand volunteers had shown themselves to be superior to British regulars. *The Times History of the War in South Africa* went so far as to say that, after they had gained some experience, the New Zealanders were 'on average the best mounted troops ...'

Partly as a consequence of all this, the war also firmly established the New Zealand tradition of amateur soldiering. South Africa had shown that volunteers with minimum peacetime training could enlist in times of crisis and serve under professionals with verve and distinction. Once the war was over, these same men would return to civilian life and leave professional soldiering to a small clique of regulars. This too set a pattern for the next 50 years.

Another effect of the South African War was to create in New Zealand a sharper interest in the broad questions of national and imperial defence. Richard Seddon, who developed a plan to federate Hawai'i, Fiji, Tonga, Samoa and the Cook Islands into New Zealand, was allowed by the British Government instead to annex the Cooks in 1901 and Niue in 1905 – a gesture which could be interpreted as British gratitude for the country's contribution to the South African War. Seddon wanted Samoa too, but New Zealand's assumption of responsibility for part of that territory would have to await the defeat of Germany in World War I. There was nothing in New Zealand's early administration of these islands, through resident commissioners, that suggested a special gift for a colonial role.

Sir Joseph Ward, when he became Prime Minister after Richard Seddon died unexpectedly in 1906, took up military and naval policies with a gusto that embarrassed some of his counterparts from other colonies. At both the Colonial Conference in London in 1907 and the Imperial Conference in 1911, he made some rash promises. One was to offer Britain two battleships to be paid for by New Zealand, only one of which, HMS *New Zealand*, would actually be built. Another was to provide a blueprint for an 'Imperial Parliament of Defence', a proposal rejected by other prime ministers. The message was clear, however: New Zealand expected the Empire as a whole to be prepared for future international conflict, and it wanted to share in both the planning and conduct of future wars.

Implicit in all this was the conviction that the Empire as a whole would never put a foot wrong in matters of principle and foreign affairs, and that anyone who crossed Mother Britain was likely to be wrong and did so at their peril. A pamphlet popular in New Zealand at the time preached that the 'genius of the British race is rooted in justice, truth, honour and consideration for the rights of others. The continued exercise of these principles has given virility to the race.' Another reiterated the New Zealander's 'double patriotism – [that] of his own country and the wider patriotism of the great Empire to which he is proud to belong'. With such principles emphatically in view, the Liberal Government passed the 1909 Defence Act, which established a territorial force recruited from compulsory military training. It was designed to create an adequate system of national self-defence and to allow the country to mobilise rapidly in the event of Empire-wide emergencies.

The first of those emergencies occurred in 1914. After the assassination of Archduke Franz Ferdinand of Austria-Hungary in June, a system of alliances and rapid mobilisations pitted the Central Powers (Austria-Hungary and Germany) against the Franco-Russian alliance. And when Germany swept into Belgium in order to outflank France, thus violating Belgium's neutrality, King George V, who had replaced his father, Edward VII, in 1910, declared on 4 August 1914 that Britain and the British Empire were at war with the Central Powers. While the invasion of Belgium was the trigger, the real motive for British intervention was an attempt to prevent Germany dominating Europe.

Few New Zealanders understood this sequence of events. But most welcomed the fact that the country, as part of the Empire, was now at war with Germany. It seemed that at last an opportunity had arrived to put to the test the virtues and the preparations of the previous decade. John A. Lee remembered the climate of the time. 'I was walking through the country ... and the people cheered. You could understand it – a long period of what was comparative prosperity ... no great events happening for a long time ... [Everybody] rushed of course to enlist. That was the spirit ... [Folks] sang patriotic songs and they cheered ... [They] talked about the great sacrifices of young men that would be made.'

It was left to the parliaments of the individual dominions to decide the extent of their contributions to the war. New Zealand legislators, led by the bluff Northern Irishman William Massey, had no doubts about the need to be involved in the war.

In addition to imperial sentiment, they were influenced by the fact that New Zealand's prosperity rested on its market in Britain and the need to keep the sea trade routes open. They offered the British an Expeditionary Force on 5 August and the offer was accepted by telegraph on 12 August. Volunteers were called for from the territorials and these men went into intensive training under professional officers at camps in the four main centres.

On 15 August a 1400-strong advance party of troops sailed for German-occupied Samoa, and at this point some of the less than satisfactory aspects of New Zealand's preparation for war became apparent. When the New Zealand Government asked the Colonial Office in London about German forces in Samoa, Sir Lewis Harcourt cabled back, 'See *Whitaker's Almanack*.' A search of the *Almanack* revealed nothing about Samoan defences. In addition, the convoy carrying the troops may have passed within 25 km of cruisers which were part of the German East Asiatic Squadron. The operation was successful none the less and the New Zealand commander accepted a German surrender in Samoa on 29 August. It was the first Allied occupation of German territory in the war.

The remainder of the initial Expeditionary Force – some 8500 men and 3800 horses – continued training under the overall direction of Major-General Sir Alexander John Godley. Godley, a nephew of John Robert Godley, one of the founders of the Canterbury settlement, was an English professional soldier on loan to New Zealand to supervise the reorganisation of the country's defence forces. At the outbreak of war he became General Officer Commanding the New Zealand Expeditionary Force, whose Main Body of troops sailed from Wellington on 16 October. At this point it was envisaged that the New Zealanders would be taken to France to counter the German advance along the Western Front. But the entry of the Ottoman Empire into the war on the side of the Central Powers changed the strategic picture and the convoy of New Zealand troops and the Australians who had joined them en route disembarked instead in Egypt, to complete training there and, if necessary, defend that country from Turkish attack.

On 3 February 1915, two months after their arrival, New Zealanders went into action for the first time. A Turkish force that had trekked across the Sinai Desert launched an attack on the Suez Canal at Ismailia. The Nelson Company of the Canterbury Infantry Division filled a gap in the canal defences and repulsed the attack with the assistance of Indian troops. The Turks suffered heavy losses; the imperial forces only eighteen, of whom one, Private William Arthur Ham of Canterbury, died of wounds, thus becoming New Zealand's first casualty in the war.

The greater part of the Expeditionary Force's early time in Egypt was spent in training at Zeitoun Camp near Cairo. Men ran up sandhills with heavy loads, dug and filled in trenches, and launched mock bayonet attacks. They were joined by steady waves of reinforcements from New Zealand, including a 439-strong Maori contingent, and they were linked in training with a combination of Australian brigades and divisions, thus forming the Australia and New Zealand Army Corps: ANZAC.

Before going into action together against the enemy, however, the Australians and New Zealanders turned on some of their Egyptian hosts on Good Friday 1915 in the so-called 'Battle of the Wazza'. This was a riot in one of Cairo's more notorious streets, in which several hundred troops set fire to brothels while thousands more looked on. The action was allegedly taken in retaliation for three grievances: bad alcohol (it was rumoured that the suppliers urinated in it to make it go further); a rise in prices; and the isolation of troops with venereal disease in special compounds. An official inquiry failed to identify any individuals responsible, but Australian witnesses claimed that New Zealanders had been more heavily involved than they had.

Three weeks later the war began in earnest for New Zealanders. The ANZACs were transported to Lemnos in the Aegean Sea, and from there to Gallipoli for a major assault on the Dardanelles, the Hellespont of the ancient world. This operation, planned by British First Lord of the Admiralty Winston Churchill, was designed to open the straits to the British and French navies to allow an attack on Constantinople and thus relieve Turkish military pressure on Russia. The area, the boundary between Europe and Asia, was renowned for heroic battles. Troy had stood on the Asian side near the entrance to the straits, and Xerxes had built his bridge of floats over the narrows in the fifth century BC to mount the Persian invasion of Greece.

From the outset, however, the ANZAC part of the Gallipoli campaign went terribly wrong. The 'spearhead' troops ahead of them were landed three kilometres north of the planned landing-place. When the ANZACs followed them ashore at what came to be called Anzac Cove at around 9 am on 25 April, they encountered almost sheer cliffs instead of climbable slopes, and the Turkish Army's 19th Division commanded by Mustafa Kemal Bey, later known as Kemal Ataturk, the founder and father of the post-war Turkish republic. The combination of obstacles proved insurmountable. The Australian and New Zealand losses were high (one in five of the 3000 New Zealanders who landed that day became casualties). It was all the troops could do to dig in on the slopes and prevent themselves being driven back into the sea.

Hold the position they did, however, for what became a prolonged stalemate of equally balanced forces. Trooper Gordon Harper of Christchurch wrote to his family on 15 May:

> The hillside [is] studded with dug-outs, and like an ant heap, swarming with men, and the foreshore piled up with stores and ammunition ... The whole time, on the ridges on either side of us, the terrific fusillade [keeps] up without ceasing ... almost impossible to hear one[self] speak ... [Across] the sea is the rugged island of Imbros, and near it a huge mountain island (Samothrace) rising sheer out of the sea, behind which the sun sets ... and provides us with many beautiful sights. It is a strangely peaceful setting for the horrors of war, those green hills and fields, red and yellow with poppies and wild flowers, and the blue Aegean coming right to their feet ...

As the weeks went by with no essential change in positions, conditions deteriorated until they were as close to hell as men could conceive – living, as one New Zealander said, 'like dirty rabbits' in cramped trenches and dug-outs. ANZACs and Turks, Ian McGibbon wrote,

> faced each other sometimes only metres apart, in a state of increasing discomfort. Searing heat and the swarming flies (made worse by unburied corpses in no man's land) tormented the men, conditions exacerbated by water shortages. Disease, especially dysentery, flourished in the insanitary conditions among men already debilitated by weeks of inadequate food. These physical problems were compounded by the psychological pressures stemming from the consciousness that no place in the tiny perimeter was safe from artillery fire. With the Turks overlooking them, snipers [too] were an ever-present hazard.

The position was not a great deal more favourable for the English, French and Indian troops on other parts of the peninsula, except that they were not dug in on slopes as precipitous. Several assaults were planned in an attempt to break the deadlock. In one, in May, on flatter terrain near Cape Helles to the south, the New Zealand Brigade lost 800 men in what was described as an 'ill-conceived attack' across a notorious piece of ground known as the Daisy Patch.

The other major Allied offensive, in August 1915, was an attempt to push troops to the summit of the peninsula and open the way for attacks on Turkish positions on the Dardanelles side; this too was a costly failure. New Zealand troops led by Lieutenant Colonel William Malone and his Wellington Regiment captured the ridge of Chunuk Bair on 8 August – the furthest point inland reached in the whole campaign. But it was lost to a massive Turkish counter-attack on 10 August and Malone and most of his men died. One New Zealander, an Auckland bank clerk named Cyril Bassett, a signaller, won a Victoria Cross for his part in the Chunuk Bair action. According to other survivors numerous deeds of collective and individual heroism went unrewarded because the officers who could have written citations became casualties.

By December 1915 the Allied forces were no closer to clearing the Dardanelles than when they landed eight months before. If anything, they were further from that objective because of the subsequent reinforcement of Turkish positions. Worse, the Turks had brought in heavier artillery capable of demolishing even the strongest Allied positions. The extreme heat of summer had given way to punishing winter conditions, which included a massive blizzard that covered the New Zealand positions with ice and snow in late November. It was no surprise when the order to evacuate was given in mid-December. It was carried out secretly and virtually without casualties, and was the only aspect of the campaign that could be called successful.

The debacle of the campaign as a whole, however – the fault of the planners and the strategists, not the frontline troops – made it imperative that something by way of positive achievement be salvaged from the carnage. Over 400,000 British and 79,000 French troops had been committed to the assault; half of these became casualties. The cost to New Zealand was 2721 dead and 4752 wounded out of a total of 8450 men – a staggering 88 per cent casualty rate. The remains of those killed were left there; many were never found. Historian John North wrote:

> It may be doubted whether in the whole history of war an army has ever been called upon to endure severer strain. They were everlastingly fighting with their backs to the sea. They were in complete isolation. No one could ever expect relief or rest. Every man [felt] condemned to stay there until death, wounds or sickness overtook them, and the world does find it difficult to remember so large a debt of suffering.

For the New Zealand and Australian public at home the experience of Gallipoli had also been traumatic. It was the first time lengthy casualty lists were published in the newspapers. On top of this was the inconceivable fact that the Allies had been defeated. The effect of this double tragedy on two countries of small populations was to make the experience sacred. Only in that way could such a vast human sacrifice be made comprehensible and acceptable. Anzac Day, 25 April, was established as an annual day of commemoration. For the next three generations it would be the focal point of national mourning for all wars, and for expressions of patriotism. The necessary myth evolved quickly in both countries that they had 'come of age' on the slopes of Gallipoli. Fred Waite, official historian of the New Zealand contribution, put it this way: '[Before] the war we were an untried and insular people; after ANZAC, we were tried and trusted.' But at what frightful cost.

It was thought by troops at the time that nothing in warfare would equal the rigours and the horrors of Gallipoli. But that was because they did not know of the squalor that awaited them on the Western Front, in France and Belgium. And in April 1916 New Zealand soldiers were committed to that battlefield for another round of carnage, this one lasting two and a half years. In the lines of trenches that ran, in effect, from the North Sea to Switzerland, troops encountered swamp-like mud, snow and ice in winter, frightful slaughter in the course of offensives such as those at Passchendaele and the Somme, the stench of unburied men and horses, and new refinements in technological barbarity such as poison gas. Advances, on the rare occasion they occurred, were measured in hundreds of metres; in four years of Allied effort the front moved no more than 100 km.

There, as in Gallipoli, New Zealanders took a full share in the fighting – and a full share of the casualties that would so baffle and anger the post-war world. At the Somme in September 1916, 1560 New Zealanders died; at Messines in June 1917, 3700 casualties; in October 1917 at Passchendaele, in the space of a few hours, the New Zealand Division lost 640 men killed and 2100 wounded. It was slaughter on a scale unprecedented in human history and, considering the negligible result, utterly wasteful.

Other New Zealanders had returned to the Middle East after Gallipoli and they were part of Allied forces that pushed the Turks out of Egypt and Palestine over the next three years. They included the New Zealand Mounted Rifles, the last of the country's troops to go to war – and fight – on horseback. They lost 500 men killed and 1200 wounded.

Back home, the prevailing jingoism and the pain experienced by bereaved families combined to generate intense hostility towards those suspected of being shirkers or disloyal. People of German descent were treated badly – butchers' shops were wrecked, barbers forced to close their premises and, in Christchurch, the bells of the Lutheran church were smashed. Many Continental European immigrants, especially the Dalmatians from the Austro-Hungarian Empire, were interned as aliens. Even the Tainui Maori leader Te Puea Herangi was ostracised because of distant German ancestry.

Treatment of conscientious objectors was also harsh. When a national register was taken in 1915, men of military age were asked to declare whether they were willing to do military service. Of the 196,000 eligible, 33,700 said they would not undertake service of any kind, and 44,300 were willing to serve only at home. While a proportion of these would have been malingerers, a large number were men of principle and integrity who could not accept the morality of war in any circumstances – especially a war fought 20,000 km away and offering no immediate threat to New Zealand's security. Unless they belonged to a church, 'the tenets and doctrines of which declare the bearing of arms and the performance of combatant service to be contrary to divine revelation', they had no grounds for exemption once conscription was introduced in August 1916.

Hundreds of genuine conscientious objectors were imprisoned and subjected to physical and dietary punishments in an effort to make them relent. They were also deprived of civil rights, including the right to vote, for ten years. Half a dozen, including Archibald Baxter (who wrote a moving anti-war memoir, *We Will Not Cease*), were shipped to the Western Front and exposed to fire and to a series of barbaric 'field punishments'. In Waikato, Te Puea Herangi led a campaign of passive resistance against Maori conscription, which had been imposed on Waikato–Maniapoto tribes only. Police raided her headquarters at Mercer four times and arrested nearly 200 of her followers. Maori from most other areas, apart from Taranaki, had enlisted willingly, however. They took part in combat at Gallipoli and formed a Pioneer Battalion of sappers in France.

For a country of its size – a population of less than one million in 1914 – the New Zealand contribution to World War I was massive. Nearly 20 per cent of the eligible manpower was recruited; of all the Allied countries, only Britain's proportion was higher. The number sent overseas was over 100,000, and of these nearly 17,000 were killed and more than 41,000 wounded. In cities, towns and villages across the country war memorials went up to list those killed. Scarcely a surname was not represented, and some small communities lost their entire crop of young manhood, some families all their sons. As one historian commented, the next generation did not need to be told that the angel of death had passed over the land: they had heard the beating of its wings.

Anzac Day, marking the anniversary of that first Australian and New Zealand landing on the Gallipoli Peninsula at dawn on 25 April 1915, was the occasion that both countries chose to commemorate all their dead from the war – and, subsequently, from *all* wars. As Ian McGibbon has noted, the high casualty rate and eventual failure of the Dardanelles campaign served only to enhance its sanctity in the public mind. In New Zealand, after persistent lobbying by the Returned Soldiers' Association (later the Returned Services' Association), the day was declared a public holiday in 1920 and 'Sundayised' – meaning that shops and hotels would be closed – in 1922.

A ritual for the day evolved from the standard military funeral. It would begin with the Dawn Parade – a march of former servicemen in the early morning darkness to the local war memorial. Members of the wider community would join them there, but with pride of place given to the veterans. Then would follow a short service: prayers, hymns and a dedication concluding with the final verse of Laurence Binyon's poem 'For the Fallen'. The last post would be played, followed by a minute's silence. For all New Zealanders who attended these ceremonies over the succeeding decades, the element that carried most reverberation was the Binyon dedication. And participants would disperse, thoughtfully, with the words of that dedication still suspended in the early morning air:

> They shall not grow old, as we that are left grow old:
> Age shall not weary them, nor the years condemn.
> At the going down of the sun and in the morning
> We will remember them.
> We *will* remember them.

20

Farmers in Charge

One of the first consequences of World War I came as a surprise to most New Zealanders. At the Paris peace conference in June 1919, Prime Minister William Massey signed the Treaty of Versailles as a representative of one of the Allied powers which had defeated Germany and the Austro-Hungarian Empire. This gesture was unexpected because New Zealand, as a dominion of what was still referred to as the British Empire, had automatically been in a state of conflict with the Central Powers once Britain had declared war on them. The public assumption in New Zealand had been that Britain too would make peace on the dominion's behalf. In one sense, that of preparing the terms of the settlement with Germany, that is what occurred: Britain, France and the United States reached the agreement that Germany was forced to sign. But each dominion of the Empire signed the Versailles treaty as a separate and independent country, and this opportunity was the first of its kind ever offered to New Zealand.

At the same conference New Zealand became a founding member of the fledgling League of Nations, the international body which would advocate collective security, arbitration of international disputes, and arms limitations. William Massey was not enthusiastic about either the treaty or the league. He continued, in Barry Gustafson's words, 'to look to Britain and the British Empire to guarantee New Zealand's future economic and military security'. He had not welcomed the Liberal Government's annexation of Niue and the Cook Islands, and he was not especially pleased that the League of Nations would give his country mandate responsibility for Western Samoa, which had been liberated from German occupation by New Zealand troops in 1914.

Massey did not in any way see himself as leading his country off down a new road towards independence in foreign affairs and trade. Ironic as it may seem, he took the measures he did because the British Government wished him to do so. And in demonstrating this reluctance he was setting a precedent for a theme that would characterise New Zealand's behaviour for another three decades: being offered increasing degrees of independence from Britain that New Zealand neither sought nor wanted.

All of this was understandable in view of the Prime Minister's background and the nature of the interests he represented in politics. When he succeeded to the leadership of the country in 1912, ending two decades of Liberal Party rule, he had already been in Parliament for eighteen years. He had been born in Northern Ireland in 1856 and immigrated to New Zealand to join his family there when he was fourteen. He farmed successfully at Mangere and was a committed member of the Presbyterian Church and the Orange and Masonic Lodges. He had also, through his chairmanship of the Mangere Farmers

Club and presidency of the Auckland Agricultural and Pastoral Association, become *de facto* spokesman for the farming lobby in Auckland – hence his nickname of 'Farmer Bill'.

It may well be true that, in the words of one historian, Massey 'never had an original idea in his life. Nor ... did he ever question his belief that New Zealand should always remain a loyal, Protestant, family-centred, rural society where every man was his own landlord.' But it was equally true that he exhibited 'tenacity and clarity in debates and in time revealed his astuteness as a tactician and organiser'. In 1896, after only two years in Parliament, he had become Opposition whip. As the Liberal Government accumulated years in office, what conservative opposition there was in the House of Representatives to its state interventionism coalesced around Massey. During Seddon's lifetime, he made little impact against a Prime Minister who had become something of a demi-god. But once Joseph Ward was in charge Massey seemed to grow in assurance and presence. By 1912 he had become a nationally known figure reminiscent of King Dick himself, inasmuch as he had a burly frame and a powerful platform manner. And, as an Ulster Protestant, he presented an inevitable contrast with the Catholic Ward. He came to power supported by a coalition of farmers, urban professionals and businessmen, and he intended to legislate in the interests of these sectors, who felt abandoned by the Liberals.

The first challenge Massey faced as Prime Minister was offered by organised labour, in the form of two major strikes which, according to Miles Fairburn, brought New Zealand 'closer to class war than at any other time in its history'. These strikes, of goldminers at Waihi in 1912 and watersiders in Wellington in 1913, were not precipitated by the new Reform Government – and, indeed the Waihi strike was under way before Reform took office. But it is difficult to avoid the impression that Massey and his cabinet welcomed the opportunity to deal decisively to the 'Red Fed' unionists whom they believed were responsible for such unrest and whom they suspected of wanting to bring down the whole infrastructure of New Zealand's capitalist society.*

The industrial troubles that came to the boil in 1912 and 1913 had their origins in what Erik Olssen has called 'a complex interplay of changing work patterns, a rapidly expanding work force [and] the bankruptcy of traditional union strategies ...' Olssen also notes that the first decade of the twentieth century had seen employees in New Zealand attempt 'the control and management of the labour force ... on an unprecedented scale' and that 'real wages did not rise between 1900 and 1913, except for miners, while expectations did'. Another historian of the period added that by 1912 New Zealand workers had experienced, for the first time, a decade of inflation, and that this had generated a very real sense that they were losing out to other sections of the community. All these factors contributed to a cultivation of worker discontent on a scale previously unseen in New Zealand.

Dissatisfaction with the country's system of compulsory arbitration had become especially strong. It had spawned the formation in 1909 of the first Federation of Labour, a national confederation of unions that grew out of the New Zealand Federation of Miners. The Liberal Government's much-vaunted

---

* The name 'Red Feds' had nothing to do with communism, although it *was* perhaps related to the red flag that was the symbol of the international socialist revolution (celebrated in James Connell's 1889 song that begins, 'The people's flag is deepest red ...'). The term was coined by the Wellington newspaper *Evening Post* early in 1912. It followed the publication on red paper of a circular outlining the Federation of Labour's attitude to a local tramways dispute.

Industrial Conciliation and Arbitration Act, which had come into force in 1894, required unions to register in order to qualify for its protection. It operated at two levels. Local conciliation boards (later 'councils'), with equal employer and employee representation and an independent chairman, ruled on disputes in their own districts; if either side refused to accept a board decision, the dispute was referred to the Arbitration Court, whose judgements were binding. The latter was made up of a judge, who acted as chairman, and one representative each of unions and employers.

For a time the system appeared to work well. It stimulated the formation of trade unions and eliminated strikes from the New Zealand industrial scene for eleven years. Workers seemed generally satisfied, as early court decisions, often upholding union submissions, improved wages and conditions. In 1906, however, there was evidence of dissatisfaction with the arbitration system among some unions. That year Auckland tramway workers went on strike to protest against the unfair dismissal of one of their members. In 1907 there were twelve strikes, and twelve more in 1908. By 1910, 240 workers were on strike, and this rose to 1089 in 1911, 2985 in 1912 and 13,871 in 1913.

For posterity, the most significant of the early strikes was in 1908 at the Blackball Mine on the West Coast of the South Island. This was led by Pat Hickey, a fiery and charismatic New Zealand-born miner who had worked previously in a coal mine in Utah, where he joined a union affiliated to the International Workers of the World* and learnt that 'class warfare was

---

* The International Workers of the World, known as IWW, was a syndicalist movement established in Chicago in 1905 with the motto 'the world's wealth for the world's workers'. IWW followers were also known as 'Wobblies', allegedly after an attempt by a Chinese-American restaurateur to pronounce

(Continued)

inevitable, class solidarity essential, and revolutionary industrial unionism the only defence and hope for the "wage slave"'. The Blackball strike originally aimed to increase the miners' 'crib' or mealtime underground from 15 to 30 minutes. It represented a challenge to the arbitration system since Hickey believed that the most satisfactory results could be obtained by direct industrial action. The miners' union was fined for striking illegally, but none the less kept its members on strike. After three months the employers relented. They increased 'crib-time' to half an hour and reinstated miners who had been dismissed for organising the strike.

This outcome encouraged a belief in the value of direct action among some unionists who felt that the arbitration system was too slow, too cumbersome, or downright unfair to workers in its decisions. Miners' unions from all over the country met to form a national federation, with Australian immigrant Bob Semple of Runanga as president and Hickey as secretary. The following year this organisation became the Federation of Labour, opened its membership to all unions and elected Paddy Webb, another Australian import, as president, while Semple became the national organiser paid to travel around the country calling on unions to de-register from the Arbitration Act. The federation took over the Shearers' Union journal *The Maoriland Worker* and turned it into a national socialist paper under the editorship first of Bob Ross and then of Harry Holland, both of them Australians by birth. Pat Hickey turned out to be the only New Zealander prominent in a movement that would be dominated by unionists

------

(Continued)

    'IWW'. In the disparaging popular idiom in New Zealand, IWW was said to stand for, 'I won't work'. It was the IWW element in New Zealand unionism that generated most suspicion and fear among Reform Party ministers and MPs.

born elsewhere, including the Scottish-born Peter Fraser, who arrived in New Zealand in 1911 and was working for the Federation of Labour by May of that year.

Shortly after Fraser's arrival the federation showed its syndicalist inclination by promoting the concept of 'One Big Union'. This was based on the IWW doctrine that workers would gain control of the economy by gaining control of industry. All the craft unions and workers yet to be unionised would be organised into about eight large unions based, according to one model, on agriculture, mining, transport, distribution, manu-facturing, construction, printing, journalism and the Public Service. Each sector would have a departmental headquarters, and all eight would be co-ordinated from a central headquarters. The debate over this concept was the major issue in socialist circles and publications in New Zealand in 1911 and 1912.

The two events which, more than any others, were to put syndicalism to the test were the Waihi and waterfront strikes. Both turned out to be disasters for the radical trade union movement. In Waihi, the goldminers had affiliated to the Red Feds, and the advocacy of Bob Semple on their behalf had won them improved pay and working conditions. This led a majority of the union to vote for withdrawal from the Industrial Conciliation and Arbitration Act so they would have the right to strike. One group in the union, the engine drivers, however, decided to form their own union and register it under the Act. This led the miners to fear that such registration would be used to force all workers in the mine back to arbitration. The miners threatened to strike unless the company sacked the engine drivers. The company refused and the miners went on strike. The company responded by closing the mine.

By the time the Reform Government came into office in July 1912, there was considerable disorder in Waihi caused by the conflict between the Red Fed supporters and the so-called 'scab-unionists' (those who continued to work despite the calling of a strike). When the company reopened the mine and employed only members of the newly formed 'scab-union', several battles ensued in the streets of the town. Massey, after consultation with his Attorney-General, Alexander Herdman, and the Commissioner of Police, the authoritarian John Cullen, sent in the police ostensibly to restore order, but in fact to crack down on the striking unionists. In one of the resulting mêlées, the miners' union hall was stormed by police and George Frederick Evans, a Red Fed supporter, was clubbed to death after he had allegedly shot at one of the attacking constables, thus becoming New Zealand's first martyr to industrial action. The newly registered union then conducted a 'campaign of terror' against the Red Feds, who were eventually run out of town. This brought the dispute to an end.

Such a major setback caused the syndicalist wing of the labour movement to withdraw, reorganise and reflect. At a so-called 'Unity Conference' in Wellington in January 1913, two new organisations were established: a United Federation of Labour, which supported strike action for individual disputes but not as a mechanism for bringing down governments, and a Social Democratic Party (SDP), which was to work through the political system for the 'socialisation of the means of production, distribution and exchange'.

In October of that year, however, employers, fearing a continuation of 'revolutionary' union tactics, engineered a lockout at the Wellington wharves. When the United Federation of Labour then declared a general strike and persuaded the excluded workers to occupy their workplace, the Government recruited young farmers as special constables ('Massey's Cossacks') to both protect and work the wharves and to put down trade union demonstrations. Law and order was preserved, but at a price. According to Barry Gustafson, the use of and the brutality of the special constables 'poisoned relations between town and country and helped polarise New Zealand politics for a generation'. The general strike was called off for lack of national support.

From this point on the key figures in the Labour movement – Semple, Fraser, Holland, Michael Joseph Savage and others – began to put their energies into political rather than industrial action. And this new focus of activity led, after the most disorderly general election campaign in memory in 1914, to the formation in July 1916 of the New Zealand Labour Party, which combined all the disparate political and trade union elements into a single organisation to fight elections. The party retained the SDP goal of 'the socialisation of the means of production, distribution and exchange', including the nationalisation of land, and labour representation committees as the unit of organisation and control at the electorate level. From this time on the Labour movement would work politically as a single and relatively united body.

The Massey Government was given the credit – or the blame – for the suppression of revolutionary trade union activity in New Zealand in its early years in office. In fact, however, these revolutionary tactics failed because New Zealand was largely free of class consciousness and was not a large enough society to support the kinds of syndicalist tactics that worked well on the far larger factory floors of Europe and the United States. Outside the mines, most workplaces and most unions were relatively small. Further, most members of what working class did exist in New Zealand aspired, on the whole, to join the middle class. They wanted to own their own homes, they wanted their children to receive the best possible education, they wanted the security of long-term – if possible, life-long – employment. All these objectives seemed as achievable via the policies of a conservative government as of a liberal one. And it was this perception of diminishing ideological boundaries that eventually led to a permanent coalition between Reform and Liberal. Few people in New Zealand from any background wanted to 'smash' the capitalist system: most just hoped to make that system more responsive to their wants and needs.

This fundamental reality accounts for the Labour movement's joining mainstream parliamentary politics – and perhaps, if so many of the movement's leaders had not been immigrants, they might have recognised the inevitability of this strategy earlier. It also accounts for Labour's taking so long to achieve political power. The proportion of votes for Labour candidates under various labels in 1914 was 10 per cent. By 1919, in the first election contested by the New Zealand Labour Party, it rose to 24 per cent. But then the party made no real headway for a further twelve years. Even in 1931, at the depth of the Great Depression, when all the indicators were in its favour, it mustered only 35 per cent. Real progress was not made until the party abandoned its programme of socialisation, particularly its threat to nationalise land, and until it had convinced the electorate at large that it was not made up of fanatical reformers. By the time Labour took office in 1935 it had become apparent that the party, like most of its supporters, wanted to 'improve capitalism, not ... abolish it'.

The half-dozen independent Labour members in Parliament after the 1914 general election declined to join the Coalition Government which Massey (unwillingly) and Ward formed in August 1915. Massey had little choice. With 41 seats out of a total of 80, to the combined Liberal–Labour total of 39, the Government had a bare majority once the Speaker had been selected. It was insufficient to ensure smooth government through the war years. And so, although the leaders of the major parties 'detested each other on personal, political and religious grounds', they attempted to work together for the national good. The Labour MPs formed a caucus and elected Alfred Hindmarsh as their chairman, then took their place for the first time as the official Opposition. Before the next general election could be held in December 1919, delayed by the war, further influential Labour members would join the caucus as a result of by-elections: Harry Holland (who became leader after Hindmarsh died in the 1918 influenza epidemic), Peter Fraser and Bob Semple. The 1919 election brought in the man who would eventually lead Labour into office as the 'kindly face' of social-ism, Michael Joseph Savage.

The conduct of the war, and an agreement to withhold new laws unless both major parties were in favour of them, led to virtual legislative paralysis from 1915 to 1919, when the coalition was dismantled. In addition, Massey spent a great deal of time at sea and abroad – five visits to Britain in the course of the war and its immediate aftermath. He attended meetings of the Imperial War Cabinet in London, collected honorary degrees and the freedom of ten British cities, and visited New Zealand troops in France (one of whom was his youngest son, who was severely wounded at the Battle of the Somme). On some of these expeditions he was accompanied by Ward, while James Allen, Minister of Defence, was left as acting Prime Minister.

The completion of one of these trips, when Massey and Ward disembarked from the vessel Niagara at Auckland in October 1918, became the subject of controversy and inquiry. Also on board were people suffering from the virulent strain of influenza that was to kill 200 million people worldwide. Because it was necessary for the Prime Minister and Deputy Prime Minister to resume their duties in Wellington, the ship was not placed in quarantine. A subsequent royal commission was to conclude that there was a 'strong presumption' that the *Niagara* brought the 'flu to New Zealand. Eventually, the country lost over 6700 people to the epidemic, a disproportionate number of them Maori. This figure represented more than a third of the casualties suffered by the country in the war, which ended the month after the *Niagara*'s arrival.

While political partisanship was diminished for most of the war by the existence of the coalition and the need to support the war effort, there were two major ripples across the surface of national unity. One was the Labour-led anti-conscription campaign, which resulted in four Labour MPs or soon-to-be MPs being imprisoned for sedition, among them the future World War II Prime Minister, Peter Fraser. The other was a storm of religious bigotry generated by the Protestant Political Association.

Up until the war years, most visitors who commented on religious affairs in New Zealand had been struck by the lack of the sectarianism – especially Protestant versus Catholic antagonism – that was so pronounced in Britain, the United States and Australia. Indeed, despite being a predominantly Protestant country (the Catholic proportion of the population was only around 13 per cent), New Zealand had already had two Catholic Prime Ministers, Frederick Weld and Sir Joseph Ward, and a host of other Catholics in influential political positions. In 1917, however, former Baptist minister Howard Elliott formed the Protestant Political Association (PPA) with the active support of the Grand Orange Lodge, of which William Massey was a member. It was opposed to 'rum, Romanism and rebellion', and it used such events and issues as the 1916 Easter Rebellion in Dublin, Joseph Ward's Catholicism and Catholic opposition to the Bible-in-schools campaign to whip up anti-Catholic feeling. By 1919 Elliott claimed to have 225 local branches and a national membership of 200,000. The PPA campaigned on behalf of Reform candidates in the 1919 general election and were instrumental in depriving Ward of his seat and helping return Massey's Government with a 29-seat advantage over the Liberals, the first and only time Massey won a decisive majority in Parliament. The PPA also supported the prosecution for sedition of the Catholic Assistant Bishop of Auckland, James Liston, after he had spoken in the Auckland Town Hall on Saint Patrick's Day in 1922 about the Easter uprising. Liston was acquitted.

That incident was a last gasp of PPA-inspired bigotry, however. Britain's granting independence to Ireland while retaining the province of Ulster in 1921 took the wind out of the PPA's sails, and its membership went into steep decline. It is also probable that, as one historian put it, Massey succeeded in giving 'right wing Protestants a sense of security they had not previously enjoyed ... Their paranoia thus receded.'

Up to 1920, Massey's administrations had been sustained largely by a prolonged economic boom. One symptom of that prosperity was the considerable amount of money the Government made available to settle returned servicemen on the land, with additional funds for land clearance and development and provision of rural infrastructure such as roads, bridges and electricity. Circumstances changed in 1921, however, when the prices Britain was able to pay for New Zealand's primary produce began to fall and the country slid into recession. Many farmers and soldier settlers who had saddled themselves with debt to buy farms when money was readily available now found that they could not afford to service their loans. This was one of the factors which led so many ex-servicemen, including Rewi

Alley and his companion Jack Stevens, to walk off the land, and which left such poignant relics in the landscape as Mangapurua's 'bridge to nowhere'.

Massey attempted to gain a degree of control over economic circumstances by establishing strong producer boards. But his farming and business constituents agitated for lower taxes, decreased government spending and rejection of demands for higher wages, none of which the Government could deliver. In the 1922 election Reform lost its majority. The party retained 38 seats against the Liberals' 24 and Labour's 17. Although there were now no significant ideological differences between Reform and Liberal, continuing personal antipathies prevented another coalition. And the Liberals and Labour were by this time too far apart to combine forces. So Massey retained the prime minister-ship, leading a minority government.

At the following year's Imperial Conference in London, the dominion prime ministers and Britain formally recognised the right of all the dominions to conclude their own trade treaties with foreign governments. This agreement was further formal-ised in the Balfour Definition* at the 1926 Imperial Conference, which stated that the dominions 'are autonomous communities within the British Empire equal in status, in no way subordinate one to another in any aspect of their domestic or external affairs, though united by a common allegiance to the Crown and freely associated as members of the British Commonwealth of Nations'.

New Zealand, represented by Massey at the 1923 conference and by his successor, Gordon Coates, in 1926, took no part in the formulation of these positions – indeed, Coates thought the

---

* Sometimes confused with the 'Balfour Declaration' of 1917, which stated the British position in favour of a national homeland for Jews in Palestine.

Balfour Definition 'a rotten formula' that would serve only to weaken the ties of Empire when New Zealand preferred those ties to be intensified. The country none the less took advantage of the new interpretation of its status by concluding commercial treaties first with Japan in 1928, and then with Belgium in 1933. When the Balfour Definition was recast in the Statute of Westminster and passed by the British House of Commons in 1931, however, New Zealand, unlike Canada, Eire and the Union of South Africa, declined to ratify it.

This persistent reluctance to accept the growing independence on offer from Britain has been linked by some historians to a 'withering of the country's spirit'. Another symptom of such 'withering' has been identified as the exodus of much of the nation's talent, which went abroad throughout this era in search of more fertile soil in which to flourish. Some of these talented people – the brilliant physicist Ernest Rutherford, for example, the first scientist to split the atom, the classicist Ronald Syme and the ethnologist Peter Buck – left because New Zealand lacked the institutions and colleagues which would enable them to make full use of their talents at home. Thus Rutherford worked at the Cavendish Laboratory in Cambridge through the 1920s and 1930s, Syme at Oxford and Buck at the Bishop Museum in Honolulu.

The case of writers and artists was somewhat different. Here it was a lack as much of an understanding audience as of supportive institutions and colleagues that drove people abroad, usually to London, which was widely viewed as the metropolis to New Zealand's province. Short-story writer Katherine Mansfield, for example, left New Zealand for the last time in 1908. Her career blossomed in London in the years immediately after World War I and the best of her stories are sharp evocations of the family life and Edwardian middle-class culture that she had left behind in New Zealand. She was both admired professionally and disliked personally by members of the Bloomsbury group in London, and Virginia Woolf viewed her as a serious competitor. But her early death in France from tuberculosis in 1923 meant that she herself witnessed and enjoyed very little of that *succès d'estime*. She was known in New Zealand, but not *well*-known until the 1950s and 1960s.

Painter Frances Hodgkins is a comparable figure in the art world. She left New Zealand for good in 1913 and by the 1920s and 1930s had made a name for herself as one of the outstanding British avant-garde painters of her generation. Hodgkins worked in France and, wrote Linda Gill, her 'pictorial language was transformed as she assimilated modernist ideas. Colour remained all-important: with her muted subtle harmonies Hodgkins became one of the most remarkable colourists of her time. Her work became more abstract, with simplified forms and surfaces enriched with patterning.' Unlike Mansfield, she lived long enough to appreciate some of the esteem she attracted (she died in 1947 aged 78). But her work provoked misunder-standing and even hostility in New Zealand until the latter half of the twentieth century.

Others who took similar professional paths included the artist Raymond McIntyre, who painted in London from 1909 until his death in 1933, and writer Jane Mander, who lived and worked in New York and London between 1912 and 1932 and wrote half a dozen novels, including the classic *The Story of a New Zealand River*. Those of her books which reached New Zealand were, like the later work of Frances Hodgkins, reviewed with hostility, largely because of what was regarded as 'immoral' content. The poet R. A. K. Mason remained in New Zealand and lived long enough to be recognised by the 1960s as a founda-tional writer, but he was so disillusioned by the lack of any kind of understanding reception to his first book of poems, *The Beggar* (1924), that he is said to have pitched the unsold copies into the Waitemata Harbour.

Oddly, the most commercially successful New Zealand writer of the period remained virtually unknown by her own name. Edith Lyttleton wrote popular fiction as G. B. Lancaster and had more than a dozen novels and 250 stories published, largely in London and New York, between 1904 and 1944. In 1933 her novel *Pageant* topped the American best-seller list for six months. Lyttleton wrote her early work on her parents' sheep station in Canterbury and later travelled widely, especially through Australia and North America. She died in 1945 without any mark of recognition from her own country, but she had been awarded the Australian Gold Medal for Literature in 1937.

If writers and artists were unclaimed and unacclaimed in New Zealand at this time, prime ministers who died in office were not. William Massey succumbed to cancer in May 1925 at the age of 69. He had not become a hero or a 'character' of King Dick proportions, but he was admired and respected for the length of time he had been in office and for the fact that he had successfully steered the country through years of industrial unrest, war and economic downturn. He was given a state funeral and buried on a promontory overlooking Wellington Harbour, where a large memorial was unveiled in 1930. In 1926 the country's new agricultural college in Palmerston North, later its fifth university, was named after him.

After an interim administration led by Massey's Attorney-General, Sir Francis Dillon Bell (nominally the country's first New Zealand-born Prime Minister), Joseph Gordon Coates of Kaipara was elected to the leadership of the Reform Party and thus to the prime ministership. He too was New Zealand-born and, like Massey, a farmer. He had represented the Kaipara electorate since 1911 after experience running a family farm at Matakohe and serving in the local territorial mounted rifles. His biographer Michael Bassett described him as a 'tall (six-foot), handsome, broad-chested man with auburn hair ... [He had] an educated voice with clipped, well-formed vowels, but all his life he had a taste for the vernacular.' Coates was no orator but he did have the quality known in the military as 'command presence'. In the course of two years' service in World War I he won a Military Cross and bar in action in France and ended the war as a major.

Massey put him in cabinet from 1919 and Coates eventually became a highly respected Minister of Public Works and of Railways, the more noticeable because of the lacklustre calibre of the cabinet as a whole. Coates oversaw the completion of the country's main trunk railway lines, got major hydro-electric projects under way on the Waitaki and Waikato Rivers, and financed the construction of further roads, made necessary by the massive increase in car ownership. He rapidly established a reputation as an 'active, hard-working minister ... who was fair, but brooked no nonsense'. He also had a special affinity with Maori people and issues and took over the portfolio of Native Affairs from William Herries in 1921. In this capacity he worked in close co-operation with his friend, but political opponent, Apirana Ngata. Coates was notably less partisan than most MPs and popular among his colleagues from all parties. The press enjoyed his 'breezy informality'.

Helped by the brilliant advertising agent A. E. Davy ('Coats off with Coates'), the new Prime Minister led his party back into office with a landslide victory in November 1925: Reform 55 seats, Labour 12, National (formerly Liberal) 10, and three independents. However, as his biographer notes, Coates was unable to live up to the high expectations generated by this result. He retained too many of Massey's poorly performing ministers and he lacked the political skills needed to manage both his party and his caucus. His one major measure, the Family Allowances Act, did not please many of his own supporters. And the effects of a major drop in farm export prices in 1926 were laid at the door of his Government. Labour also took steps at this time to increase its own electoral appeal by dropping its land nationalisation policy and undertaking to guarantee freehold. In a 1927 by-election Labour acquired its first farmer MP, William Lee Martin, an indication that it was beginning to broaden its electoral appeal.

The 1928 election was as much a disaster for Coates as the previous one had been a triumph. The recycled Liberal Party, now calling itself United and organised by Coates's former ally A. E. Davy, won 32 seats. Reform support was slashed by almost half to 28, and Labour won 19. There was one independent. United's leader, the also-recycled Sir Joseph Ward, was 72 years old and disintegrating from the effects of diabetes. He became Prime Minister again 22 years after he had first assumed the office. His success was due at least in part to the fact that he appeared to misread his speech notes and promised to borrow £70 million in a single year to solve the country's economic ills.

'What followed', Michael Bassett wrote, 'was pure farce. Ward cracked hearty and optimistic as of old, but very little of the £70 million was, or could be, borrowed.' The former bankrupt could no longer be considered the country's 'financial wizard', and nobody now claimed this title for him. The economy steadily deteriorated throughout 1929 and early 1930 as commodity prices fell again and the country began to experience the effects of global depression. Unemployment mushroomed. Ward became progressively more ill and left governance to his political lieutenants and one of his sons, Vincent. New Zealand's disgracefully inept administration of Western Samoa resulted in a riot in Apia on 28 December 1929, in the course of which twelve men died, including the high chief and Mau leader Tamasese. The Governor-General, Sir Charles Fergusson, was at first unable to find any cabinet ministers or public servants available to deal with the crisis. Fergusson left New Zealand in February 1930 relieved to escape from the 'official torpor' which had effectively paralysed the business of government.

Finally, in May 1930, Ward was persuaded to resign and hand over authority to one of his protégés, Hurunui MP and Agriculture Minister George Forbes. He died three months later. Thus it was left to another farmer Prime Minister, the third in sixteen years, to try to negotiate the country through the shoals of the Great Depression.

21

Maori Survival

In the face of negative statistics and gloomy prognostications, the Maori population had not only survived into the twentieth century but begun to grow again. And with that growth in people came a corresponding increase in Maori social and cultural vitality in many parts of the country.

The national census of 1901 showed a rise in the number of Maori from 42,000 in 1896 to 45,000. As a result of both inter-marriage with Europeans and previous exposure, Maori in general were at last acquiring immunity from the diseases that had taken such a terrible toll over the previous half-century. Fertility was improving and the birth rate climbing. Although infant mortality rates remained high, as they were for the country as a whole, more Maori children were being born and more were surviving.

Political consciousness, too, was fermenting on marae all over the country in the last decade of the nineteenth century. There was increasing talk of claims for land unjustly confiscated or (in the South Island) bought without subsequent observation of the agreed terms of sale; of seeking redress for breaches of the Treaty of Waitangi; of petitioning the Crown to alleviate Maori grievances (two deputations had gone to Britain for this purpose in the 1880s and been referred back to the New Zealand Government, which declined to accept that the Treaty had any judicial or constitutional force*); and of experimentation with new political structures. Inter-tribal hui were being widely held to debate these and other issues. In the national Parliament, a Maori MP, James Carroll, was acquiring considerable influence within the ruling Liberal Party – as a senior cabinet minister, he would eventually serve, on two occasions, as acting Prime Minister. And a group of young Maori, who would become sophisticated in things Pakeha as well as Maori, were completing their education and laying the foundations for new styles of Maori leadership.

James Carroll, known to Maori as Timi Kaara, had been born in Wairoa in 1858, son of a Ngati Kahungunu mother, Tapuke, and a Sydney-born Irish father. After schooling in Wairoa and Napier he joined kupapa troops in the pursuit of Te Kooti and his forces through the Urewera and was mentioned in despatches for his bravery. He later joined the Native Affairs Department and worked in both its Hawke's Bay and Wellington offices. In 1879 he became interpreter in the House of Representatives, an experience which gave him an intimate association with Maori MPs, a detailed knowledge of parliamentary procedure, and confidence in speaking publicly in both Maori and English.

---

* Successive late-nineteenth-century governments had been influenced by the ruling in 1877 of the Chief Justice, Sir James Prendergast, that 'the whole treaty was worthless – a simple nullity [which] pretended to be an agreement between two nations but [in reality] was between a civilised nation and a group of savages . . .'

Carroll first stood for Parliament in his own right in 1883, challenging the sitting member for Eastern Maori, Wi Pere. He lost narrowly. He was successful in 1887, however, and held the seat until 1894, when he contested and won the European electorate of Waiapu, later Gisborne. He thus became the first Maori to hold a non-Maori parliamentary seat. He was a member of the Liberal Government cabinet from 1892 and Minister of Native Affairs from 1899 to 1912. As Alan Ward commented, Carroll administered this portfolio 'with unsurpassed authority'. It would not be held again by a Maori MP until 1928, when Apirana Ngata became minister.

As Alan Ward has also noted, Carroll's ebullient and successful lifestyle 'led him firmly to believe that Maori could succeed very well in European society'. He wanted Maori parliamentarians, for example, to compete with Pakeha on European terms and, where possible, to beat them, as he had done in winning his European seat and in frequently running rings around his political opponents in parliamentary debate. He joined in social occasions with gusto, delivered superb stories and impromptu speeches, and followed horse racing with an impressive knowledge of form and pedigree.

As a member of the Liberal cabinet, Carroll came to accept that Pakeha settlement of undeveloped Maori land in the North Island was inevitable, but 'he sought a place for Maori to lease land and use the revenue to invest in their own farming, just as [Pakeha] settlers did'. Carroll's attempts to circumvent the growing influence of the Kotahitanga movement produced the Liberal's Maori Councils Act of 1900, which proposed elected committees to supervise Maori community and tribal affairs with powers comparable with those exercised by ordinary local authorities. These councils were seen in some Maori eyes as exercising the 'tino rangatiratanga' or separate

Maori authority guaranteed in the Treaty of Waitangi.

The councils were expected to supervise sanitation and suppress customs which European health authorities regarded as dangerous (the use of tohunga, lengthy tangihanga and the like). It was hoped, too, that they would provide accurate information on Maori births, deaths and marriages and population movements. The proclamation of this system did defuse support for Kotahitanga, but in the long run the experiment was not a success. Councils were embraced with temporary enthusiasm in some districts and ignored in others. Even in areas where they met with initial approval they eventually lapsed through a combination of lack of enduring enthusiasm, unfamiliarity and impatience with Pakeha committee procedure, and lack of commitment to the inter-tribal co-operation that the system tried to promote. By 1910 most councils had ceased to function.

At the same time as James Carroll was serving his apprenticeship for what would become an exceptional public career, traditional modes of leadership persisted in most areas of Maori occupation. Where hapu had not been broken up by mortality or alienation of land, hereditary rangatira families still tended to be spokespersons for their communities. Families with ariki claims – the kahui ariki in Waikato, the Te Heuheus of Ngati Tuwharetoa, the Taiaroas in the South Island – still threw up leaders who acted on behalf of federations of tribes. But patterns of leadership were changing. Increasingly the way was opening for men and women with acquired vocational skills, quick wits and eloquence to make bids for community and tribal leadership against or alongside those whose claims were hereditary, especially for those who had received secondary education or trained for a church ministry.

Some of the new breed were prepared to go further than lamentation of Maori grievances on marae. They determined to use the system of government to obtain redress and to secure better living and working conditions for their people. In the South Island, such members of Ngai Tahu used adversity and a sense of injustice to regenerate tribal spirit and loyalty. Conditions on which they had sold much of their land – that reserves be put aside, hospitals and schools built and landmark boundaries observed – had mostly been ignored. Ngai Tahu with education and some familiarity with the Pakeha world exerted pressure on their rangatira and on tribal runanga to seek compensation from the Crown for these grievances. They formed a parliamentary-type body to represent the entire tribe and sent letters, petitions and deputations to Parliament. They elected a succession of members of Parliament for Southern Maori who had the specific task of prosecuting their kerema or claim – the first instance of Maori agitation resulting in the election of an MP for a particular purpose.

In Waikato, after failing to persuade the Government to set up a national Maori parliament with himself at its head, King Tawhiao established his own Kauhanganui at Mangakawa, near Matamata, in 1892. It too debated land claims, especially the question of compensation for the Waikato lands confiscated by the Government in the 1860s. The Kotahitanga or Maori unity movement, which originated in Northland and was based on upholding the principles of the Treaty of Waitangi, picked up membership throughout the country, mainly among traditional rangatira such as Te Heuheu Tukino, and held its own 'Maori Parliament' meetings from 1892 to 1902, latterly at Papawai marae in Wairarapa under the leadership of Tamahau Mahupuku. It seemed for a time that tribalism was being submerged in a feeling that resembled Maori nationalism. That feeling did not persist, however. The Kingitanga Kauhanganui became increasingly a forum for the Ngati Haua tribe alone; and the Kotahitanga movement was overtaken by another, which came to be called the Young Maori Party.

The Young Maori Party was not, strictly speaking, a political party (and some would go further and argue that it was neither young nor, in its origin and orientation, especially 'Maori'). It was an association of professional men that grew out of the education most of them had received at Te Aute College, an Anglican secondary school in Hawke's Bay. In particular, it was a product of the activities of pupils and of the Te Aute Old Boys' Association in the 1890s. The group was initially known by the cumbersome and pretentious title of the Association for the Amelioration of the Condition of the Maori Race. Members had come under the commanding influence of the school's headmaster, the Revd John Thornton, who believed that 'when a weaker nation lives side by side with a stronger one, the weaker, poorer and more ignorant one will die out if it does not emulate the stronger'. This was the ideal he imprinted on his Maori pupils: if the Maori were to survive, they would have to adopt the features of Western nations that had made the latter pre-eminent throughout the world and in particular dominant over indigenous peoples.

The more able and ambitious of Thornton's pupils left Te Aute in the 1880s and 1890s determined to improve the health, literacy and technological progress of the Maori people. They tried to do this at first by holding consciousness-raising meetings among themselves, at which they discussed papers with such titles as 'The decline of the Maori race: its causes and remedies'. These were full of Christian fervour and read like sermons. 'To them Maori society was degraded, demoralised, irreligious, beset with antiquated, depressing and pernicious customs. Their task ... was to reconstruct this society to make the race clean, industrious, sober and virtuous.'

While still being educated they went out into Maori communities to preach their message of survival through social and
religious reform. Some of them devoted school and university
vacations to walking tours that took them to rural villages and
marae. On one such trip in June 1889, Maui Pomare, Reweti
Kohere and Timutimu Tawhai visited a dozen Hawke's Bay
settlements over a month, where they led prayers and lectured
elders on how to improve their spiritual welfare and material
circumstances. Most prominent in the group were Apirana
Ngata of Ngati Porou, Te Rangi Hiroa (Peter Buck) and Maui
Pomare of Ngati Mutunga, Reweti Kohere and Tutere Wi Repa
of Ngati Porou, Edward Pohua Ellison of Ngai Tahu and
Frederick Bennett of Te Arawa (though Bennett went to
St Stephen's Native Boys' School in Auckland, a brother college
to Te Aute).

Ngata was ultimately the most successful of the Young Maori
Party leaders. He was born near Te Araroa on the East Coast of
the North Island in 1874. He was brought up in the household
of his paternal great-uncle, the kupapa chief and fighter Ropata
Wahawaha. At the age of ten he went to Te Aute, and from there
won a scholarship to Canterbury College, where he came under
the influence of the polymath professor John Macmillan Brown.
In 1893 he became the first Maori to obtain a university degree
when he graduated BA. Then he moved to Auckland, where he
worked for a law firm and studied for an LLB, which he gained
in 1897. Committed by this time to a crusade to save the Maori
people, Ngata became full-time travelling secretary for the
Young Maori Party. In particular he encouraged and supervised
the setting up of Maori tribal committees under the Maori
Councils Act of 1900 and he lobbied sympathetic Members of
Parliament, especially James Carroll, who had devised the Act.
In 1905 he himself would enter Parliament as member for

Eastern Maori, a seat he would hold for the next 38 years.

Pomare and Buck, both from Taranaki, were early Maori medical graduates – the former from a Seventh-Day Adventist college in Michigan in 1899, the latter from Otago University in 1904. Both worked as native health officers before entering Parliament, Buck as member for Northern Maori in 1909, Pomare for Western Maori in 1911. Buck's political career was brief. He contested a European seat unsuccessfully in 1914, then served overseas with the New Zealand Army for most of World War I. After the war he was appointed Director of Maori Hygiene, but his interests turned increasingly towards ethnology. He left the Health Department to work for the Bishop Museum in Honolulu in 1929, and subsequently became its director and held a chair in anthropology at Yale University. He was knighted in 1946. Pomare served continuously as a cabinet minister in successive Reform Governments from 1912 to 1928, being responsible successively for the Cook Islands, Health and Internal Affairs. He died in 1930 during a visit to Los Angeles.

Both men believed strongly that Western culture and Pakeha people were to be permanent features of New Zealand life, and that the most promising future for Maori lay in progressive adoption of Western practices, institutions and technology. In particular they advocated health and hygiene measures to halt the population decline, literacy and extension of agricultural assistance for the development of Maori land. They also sought a strong degree of individualism in Maori life, the adoption of the Protestant work ethic and the abolition of what Pomare referred to as the 'pernicious' customs of tohunga-ism, tangihanga and the hui.

In his annual report to the Health Department in 1906 Buck wrote: 'The [Maori] communism of the past meant industry, training in arms, good physique, the keeping of the law, the sharing of the tribal burden, and the preservation of life. It was a factor in the evolution of the race. The communism of today means indolence, sloth, decay of racial vigour, the crushing of individual effort, the spreading of introduced infections, diseases, and the many evils that are petrifying the Maori and preventing his advance.' Like Pomare, Buck believed that Maori ought to volunteer in large numbers to fight in World War I, first because it would be good for them to submit to the organisation and discipline of the armed forces, and second because such a contribution would prove that Maori had earned the right to equal citizenship status with Pakeha, and the consequent right to call upon the resources of the state for such purposes as development of agricultural land.

Once war broke out, Pomare became minister in charge of Maori recruitment and chaired a committee made up of the other Maori MPs. They stumped the country to raise volunteers for what became the Pioneer Battalion, but which in Maori was called Te Hokowhitu a Tu – the army of Tumatauenga, god of war. Peter Buck set a personal example by sailing for Egypt with the first contingent and serving in the war with distinction, rising to the rank of major. Once Maori casualties began to occur at Gallipoli and later in France, the recruitment committee was forced to redouble its efforts to obtain the necessary reinforcements.

The campaign was not an unqualified success. Although some 2200 men volunteered, about 20 per cent of the eligible group, almost half became casualties and the committee found it difficult to maintain the promised reinforcement quotas. Some tribes – Te Arawa, Ngati Porou, Ngai Tahu (on the whole, those who had been kupapa) – contributed disproportionately; others such as Waikato and Taranaki, with confiscation grievances, scarcely at all. Later drafts had to be filled by

Cook and Niue Islanders, and even then did not come up to strength. Pomare was especially embarrassed and annoyed that Waikato in his own electorate mounted a passive anti-conscription campaign.

The overall Maori contribution to the war effort, however, had the effect sought by the Maori MPs. It showed Maori to be, in Pomare's words, 'the peer of any man on earth', and it made it more difficult for the country's Pakeha leaders to argue in favour of excluding Maori from full participation in the national life. It also raised hopes among Maori ex-servicemen that conditions of wartime equality with Pakeha soldiers would continue into peacetime. They did not. Legislation forbidding the sale of alcohol to Maori and excluding them from housing and farm development finance persisted after the war. Few Maori soldiers were eligible for rehabilitation assistance. These were among the conditions that drove many ex-servicemen into the ranks of the Ratana movement.

This organisation had very different roots from those of the Young Maori Party. It was neither elitist nor traditionalist in origin, though it did draw on Maori precedents for prophetic movements. It arose from a vacuum that developed in some Maori areas in the early years of the twentieth century. On the one hand were the Young Maori Party 'modernisers', working at parliamentary and Public Service level to improve the lot of Maori nationally. On the other were community leaders operating according to traditional conventions. There was a growing number of Maori, however, who were not touched by either of these brands of leadership: those who lived in places where traditional leadership structures had fallen away, and those living in communities outside their own tribal rohe. Many such people were unmoved by and uncomprehending of the kinds of directions offered by the Young Maori Party. They were leaderless, yet seeking leadership, but of a kind that was Maori rather than tribal; and they found it in Tahupotiki Wiremu Ratana.

Ratana was a ploughman from the Rangitikei district south of Wanganui. He began his spiritual mission in the course of the 1918 influenza epidemic when he was 45 years old. As he sat on the verandah of his family home looking out to sea, a small cloud arose from the water and hovered over the house. From it Ratana heard the voice of God telling him that He had selected Maori to be His chosen people in place of the Jews, and that Ratana's mission was to unite Maori and turn them towards God.

In the wake of this experience Ratana prepared himself for his new role. He read the Bible closely, and a book called *Health for the Maori* by J. H. Pope (one of the texts most valued by the Young Maori Party). Then he began to preach the kotahitanga or essential unity of Maori people and to practise faith healing, initially among his own family and then among a wider congregation as news of his gifts began to spread by word of mouth and in newspaper reports. People began to visit him from all over the country as his reputation grew.

Unlike most Maori leaders of the time, Ratana, although he belonged to Ngati Apa, did not have a recognised hapu or tribal base; nor was he well educated in the Western sense, or even especially charismatic. He was a man of ordinary appearance and manner driven by an extraordinary mission. Much of his success can be understood in the light of the social climate in which he preached, especially the fact that Maori people at large were at that time reeling from the physical and psychological effects of the influenza epidemic, which took four and a half times as many Maori lives as non-Maori (5516 to 1200). Further, many Maori returned servicemen had become impatient with the conservatism, inertia and technological backwardness of rural Maori communities. They sought leadership that offered, among other things, material progress for Maori.

Ratana provided leadership that met these diverse needs. From his reading of the Bible he offered – like Maori prophets who preceded him, including his kinswoman Mere Rikiriki – an Old Testament explanation for the displacement and suffering of Maori as God's chosen, and he promised deliverance from these tribulations. Although emphatically Maori in his use of language and metaphor, he rejected many traditional practices and values such as tribalism, tangihanga, tapu, tohunga-ism and carving. His faith-healing successes were so spectacular that a settlement grew around his house and came to be known as Ratana Pa. The museum there took on the appearance of a New Zealand Lourdes as it filled with discarded crutches, wheelchairs and spectacles. Now called the Mangai (for 'mouthpiece of God'), Ratana began to travel to carry his preaching and healing to all parts of the country. He had a special appeal to those he called the Morehu – the growing number of detribalised, non-chiefly common people, most of them at this time subsistence farmers, farm labourers or rural town workers.

From 1922 the Ratana movement that had formed around the Mangai became increasingly preoccupied with politics. It campaigned for statutory ratification of the Treaty of Waitangi as a panacea for most Maori difficulties, and collected 30,000 signatures on a petition calling for this. When the Mangai's oldest son contested Western Maori in the 1922 general election, he astonished political observers by coming within 800 votes of unseating the experienced Maui Pomare. Clearly the face of Maori politics was changing: Ratana and his followers by this time constituted a political force as well as a spiritual one. In 1928 the Mangai declared the end of his spiritual mission and the beginning of his temporal one. He vowed to place his chosen representatives – known as the Four Quarters – into all four Maori seats.

Before any substantial progress was made towards that goal, however, Apirana Ngata was to get one final and spectacular opportunity to implement the policies of the Young Maori Party – or what remained of those policies three decades after they had first been announced. For two of those three decades Ngata had been in Parliament, but his Liberal Party had been out of office since 1912. Between 1912 and 1928, he had seen, as a direct result of government policies, Maori land holdings reduced from over 3 million hectares to 1.8 million. And of that 1.8 million, an estimated 310,800 hectares were unsuitable for development and 300,000 were already leased to Pakeha farmers.

Ngata had worked virtually on his own as an Opposition member to explore organisational and legislative measures that might surmount the difficulties associated with the administration and development of Maori land. With his own Ngati Porou people he had evolved land management by incorporated committees, of which the Mangatu Incorporation would eventually be the most successful. Ngata also pioneered a system of consolidation that allowed exchanges of interests to group land blocks into economic holdings. These experiments were limited largely to the East Coast and Urewera until the mid-1920s, when other tribes began to adopt them with the encouragement of the Native Land Court. By that time Ngati Porou owned nearly a quarter of a million sheep and had their own dairy company, finance company and co-operative store.

When the Liberals were returned to office again in 1928 as the United Party and Ngata at last became Minister of Native Affairs, he was able to devise legislation to assist Maori farmers on a national basis for the first time. His Native Land Amendment and Native Claims Adjustment Act allowed the advance of public money for clearing and developing Maori farms – up to three-fifths of the value of the property, allocated through local land boards. These loans would be repaid through subsequent agricultural production. The scheme was operated largely by Maori labour under Maori leadership, and Ngata was assiduous in recruiting the mana and talents of local Maori leaders such as Te Puea Herangi in Waikato, Whina Cooper in the Hokianga and Taiporoutu Mitchell in Rotorua. The *raison d'être* for the whole scheme was to ensure that Maori retained their land and used it to enable them to live healthy and fulfilled lives in their own rural rohe.

The other part of Ngata's programme for Maori recovery was cultural revival. While still in Opposition, he had persuaded his friend Gordon Coates, Reform Prime Minister and his predecessor as Minister of Native Affairs, to set up the Maori Purposes Fund Board to provide grants for educational, social and cultural activities (the money came from unclaimed interest earned by native land boards). Together, Coates and Ngata also prepared the Maori Arts and Crafts Act of 1926 which set up a carving school in Rotorua. They collaborated too in the establishment of the Board of Ethnological Research to finance the investigation and recording of Maori oral and material culture, and Ngata himself undertook a study of Maori waiata which was eventually published in four volumes, with additional editorial work by Pei Te Hurinui Jones and others, as *Nga Moteatea*.

Once Ngata replaced Coates as Minister of Native Affairs, the same kinds of measures continued with increased momentum. He made use of large hui – such as that in Ngaruawahia for the opening of Mahinarangi meeting house in 1929 – for inter-tribal discussion on broad questions such as how Maori could best share in the opportunities offered by Pakeha society and technology, and on specific topics such as social welfare, land development and the future of Maori language, arts and crafts. In this manner he was able to prepare people for aspects of the programme he planned, gauge reaction to them, and often shrewdly plant initiatives so that they appeared to come from the people themselves rather than from the Government or the Department of Native Affairs.

The effect of Ngata's cultural policies allied to his land development scheme was a flowering in aspects of Maori culture. There was a sharpening and strengthening of the arts of oratory and waiata on marae throughout the country. Haka and action song were revived for competitive display at inter-tribal hui and competitions. Maori sports meetings intensified competitiveness and strengthened hapu and tribal cohesion. New meeting houses and dining rooms were built in large numbers throughout the North Island in the 1930s and 1940s, many of them carved by graduates of the Rotorua Carving School, such as Pine and John Taiapa. Grants from the Board of Ethnological Research laid the foundation for further research into aspects of Maori culture, particularly in association with the Polynesian Society, of which Ngata was an enthusiastic member.

In alliance with Ngata and drawing on resources he made available, many tribal leaders began cultural revivals of their own. Te Puea Herangi of Tainui, for example, established a carving school at Turangawaewae (after her leading carvers had been trained at Rotorua), built a series of meeting houses and other community facilities throughout the Waikato and King Country, revived the construction and ceremonial use of canoes, composed waiata and action songs and trained her Te Pou o Mangatawhiri concert party for performances throughout the North Island. The effect of all this, she noted, with due acknowledgement to Ngata, was 'to make Waikato a people once again' – to enhance tribal identity and cohesion, to make functional what had previously been dysfunctional.

Te Puea had been born at Whatiwhatihoe in the King Country in 1883, a granddaughter through her mother Tiahuia of the second Maori King, Tawhiao. She achieved prominence within the Kingitanga when she led the campaign against the conscription of Waikato Maori in World War I. Her claims to leadership as a member of the kahui ariki were greatly strengthened by her sharp intellect, quick wits, high degree of articulateness in Maori and near-ruthless determination to achieve the goals she set herself.

All these qualities were in evidence when she established Turangawaewae Marae at Ngaruawahia from 1921. In the late 1920s the coincidence of her need for further resources with Coates and Ngata's plans for Maori cultural and agricultural development brought her into fruitful contact with the governmental and Public Service network, which Waikato had shunned since her uncle King Mahuta had sat on the Executive Council representing the Maori people (1903–09). From the late 1920s Te Puea was a national Maori figure, Turangawaewae began to take on the character of a national marae, and she had access to the resources of the state with which to achieve her objectives and heighten her mana (though some conservatives in Waikato referred to her disparagingly as 'Mrs Kawanatanga' on account of her association with politicians). Ngata's land development scheme was the most dramatic example of this process – it offered a means by which Waikato Maori communities could subsist on their own territory, mainly through dairy farming, and conserve their traditional living patterns. In association with this security she consolidated a calendar of Kingitanga hui in the 1930s and 1940s which gave these communities activities to plan for and look forward to the year round.

Like other successful local Maori leaders, Te Puea was an innovator who appealed to precedent. It is difficult to judge the extent to which she chose this role or the role assumed her. What is clear is that, having decided on a course – moving to Ngaruawahia, building a meeting house, re-establishing carving and rivercraft, returning to farming – she would always find justification in tradition, most often in the whakatauki or proverbs of Tawhiao. Even when breaking with tradition – by standing and speaking in public, for example – she always made it clear that her own actions should not be taken as grounds for discarding tikanga. When she devised new programmes – such as raising money by concert tours or by inviting political participation in her hui held to open Mahinarangi meeting house in 1929 – she cloaked them with traditional Maori ceremonial so as to arouse, quite deliberately, nostalgic memories of past tribal achievements.

Te Puea's natural aptitudes – in particular her perceptiveness about tactics and the quick-wittedness with which she wrong-footed rivals – were strengthened by her mastery of the arts of delegation and organisation. Her meticulous keeping of records ensured that she was always well informed, and often better informed than her rivals. She knew instinctively when to persist in one tactical direction and when to alter course. She was adept at extending her own talents and compensating for the skills she lacked by recruiting lieutenants to act for her in specialised ways. Her use of Maori and Pakeha mediators made valuable paths for her into both worlds to an extent she could not have achieved on her own. And at points where people were no longer useful or let her down she was rarely handicapped by sentiment: she simply discarded them.

The immediate consequences of Te Puea's leadership can be judged by comparing the legacy she left with the conditions she inherited. She began tribal work in 1910, when Waikato were largely fragmented and demoralised. In 40 years of relentless effort she found ways for them to return to a system of rural-based extended families and communal patterns of living, influenced by traditional leadership and with a calendar of distinctively Maori cultural activities. In addition to these more general goals, she was largely responsible for the considerable measure of Pakeha acceptance that the Kingitanga had won by the time she died in 1952. She has been called 'possibly the most influential woman in our political history' and it would be difficult to dispute this assessment. The fact that her great-niece Te Atairangikaahu achieved such widespread support as Maori Queen and head of the Kingitanga from 1966 was in no small measure due to the precedents Te Puea had set. And Dame Te Atairangikaahu, while not as extroverted a figure as her great-aunt, further consolidated the mana which earlier leaders of the movement had husbanded so carefully.

It was while Te Puea was approaching the height of her influence that the most florescent era in national Maori affairs to that time came to an end. In October 1934 Apirana Ngata resigned his cabinet portfolio. A royal commission investigating the administration of the land development scheme had found the minister guilty, not of any major impropriety, but of disregarding accepted Public Service procedures, not adequately accounting for the expenditure of state funds, and possibly favouring the interests of his own tribe. None of these matters was criminal. But, unsupported by his own colleagues and under fierce attack from the Opposition, Ngata decided to step aside. It was a sad end to a ministerial career which had seen him at one point, in 1930, holding the position of acting Prime Minister.

There would not be another Maori minister in charge of Maori affairs for a further 38 years. The land scheme itself was regarded as sufficiently successful to be carried on by subsequent administrations, however.

Throughout the period of Ngata's ministry New Zealand had moved steadily into the grip of worldwide economic recession: the justifiably named Great Depression. Maori rural workers had begun to suffer as farmers, their income from agricultural products falling, and local bodies laid off contract and casual workers. In rural towns the small number of Maori salaried workers were the first to be displaced by staff reductions. There was a feeling in government, and among the public at large, that Maori – unlike Pakeha – could simply 'go home to the pa' for food and shelter. By 1933 Maori made up an estimated 40 per cent of the total unemployed and they were paid lower benefits than non-Maori.

The situation was relieved after the election of the first Labour Government in 1935. One of its first measures was to abolish the unequal benefit rates. And the expansion of economic activity in the late 1930s brought a degree of temporary prosperity to the land development scheme and created additional employment in rural areas. The introduction of social security benefits greatly increased the spending power of extended families with their provision of additional income for children and for the aged. Labour also modified earlier requirements that had made it difficult and sometimes impossible for Maori without adequate documentation to secure child allowances and old age pensions. A study in one district noted that 'From the Maori [social security] has removed some of the grinding poverty which has been ... the major anxiety of their lives.'

The political consequence of this transformation was that Maori would support Labour parliamentary candidates for the next three decades; and, because of an alliance made between Labour and the Ratana movement, that meant support of Ratana MPs. By 1935 two of Ratana's 'Four Quarters', his son Tokouru (Western Maori) and Eruera Tirikatene (Southern Maori), were already in Parliament as independents. On 4 February 1936, the Mangai visited the new Prime Minister, Michael Joseph Savage, and formalised an association between their two movements in a manner that was characteristically Maori.

> Ratana ... placed on the table before him four objects: a potato, a broken gold watch, a greenstone tiki and a huia feather ... The potato was the ordinary Maori, needing his land. The watch was the law relating to the lands of the Maori. Only the machinery of the law could repair the law. The greenstone tiki stood for the traditions and mana of the Maori. And the huia feather, the sign of a paramount chief, would be worn by Mr Savage if he would look after his Maori people. The Prime Minister accepted the proposal.

The Prime Minister also took on the portfolio of Native Affairs, as did subsequent Labour Prime Ministers, though not unbrokenly, until the era of Norman Kirk in 1972. Ratana electoral support increased as a result of the pact. Paraire Paikea took Northern Maori in 1938. And in 1943 Tiaki Omana did what most observers believed was impossible: he toppled Ngata in Eastern Maori. The Mangai's prophecy was fulfilled, the Ratana hegemony was now complete. The alliance was cemented by the policies of the Labour Government that found favour with Maori, and by the continuing success of Ratana candidates at the polls – a consequence far more of those policies than of the calibre of the MPs.

22

Depression and Recovery

George Forbes was perhaps New Zealand's most unlikely Prime Minister. He was a bull-necked farmer from Cheviot who had captained the Canterbury rugby team from the position of half-back in 1892. Assessing his career, W. J. Gardner would say that his greatest political strength was an ability to go down on the ball in the face of dangerous rushes. In other words, he was tough and stubborn but not inspiring. Forbes had entered Parliament taking the Hurunui seat as a Liberal in 1908 and was party whip from 1912 to 1922. In 1925 and 1926 he was briefly Leader of the Opposition. His perceived virtues were honesty ('Honest George' was his nickname in farming circles), doggedness and loyalty.

His weaknesses arose from doubts about his intelligence and ability to take initiatives. His colleague Keith Holyoake, who was at one time the youngest member of Forbes's caucus, used to say that the only reason his leader had graduated from Lyttelton Primary School was that the school had burned down. In cabinet he sometimes bamboozled his colleagues by making dogmatic but wholly incorrect pronouncements (that two-thirds of something was more than three-quarters, for example). As events would prove, in May 1930, when he became Prime Minister on the retirement of Sir Joseph Ward, Forbes was the wrong man in the wrong place at the wrong time.

The Great Depression, already apparent for nearly two years, worsened dramatically and apparently inexorably. One historian has noted that, between 1928 and 1931, 'export prices fell by 40 per cent. There was a consequent fall in government revenue, which shrank by five million pounds in 1930 and eight million pounds in 1931 – half the normal revenue. The government ... could see only one answer and that was to balance the budget by cutting costs.' This was Forbes's response to the crisis, for he had taken the portfolio of Finance in addition to his prime ministerial responsibilities. Public works expenditure was slashed, and staff would later be laid off and taken on again at considerably reduced relief rates. Public Service wages were cut by 10 per cent in 1931 and again in 1932. The Court of Arbitration was given the power to lower wages and minimum rates disappeared. Old age and war pensions were cut and family allowances abolished. The result was unemployment for tens of thousands and reduced purchasing power for others. Shopkeepers began to go bankrupt as customers could no longer pay bills.

While Forbes was out of the country for the 1930 Imperial Conference in London, Parliament passed the Unemployment Act, which promised relief payments for those who registered. When he returned in January 1931 Forbes announced that there would be no pay without work. This meant that, in order to receive payments, the unemployed, regardless of their skills or former occupations, would chip weeds, make roads, work on

345

farms, join forestry projects or participate in other 'make-work' schemes, many of them operating far away from towns and cities. A famous 1931 Labour Party poster shows a photograph of Richard Seddon overlooking one of the men pulling a chain harrow, a job normally performed by horses. The shade of King Dick says, 'This! In God's Own Country!'

When the unemployed register opened in February 1931, 23,000 put their names down at once. This number had risen to 51,000 by June. And from that point on, regardless of government policies – and possibly because of them – the number of jobless continued to rise, to a peak of around 80,000 in July 1933. Among these were 20,000 general labourers, 5000 farm workers and 7000 building tradesmen. These registrations did not include Maori or women or young men under sixteen. It is probable that, at the height of the Depression, the actual number unemployed was over 100,000, or around 40 per cent of the male workforce.

In September 1931 Forbes told an all-party political conference that, as in wartime, the country needed a coalition government to face a common enemy, share responsibility and nurture national unity. Labour declined to co-operate, but Gordon Coates, leader of Reform, though he disliked Forbes intensely, saw merit in the proposal and advantage for his party. Thus United and Reform formed the Coalition Government, with Reform taking many of the key portfolios, including Coates as Minister of Public Works again and as minister with responsibility for unemployment. He made little headway in the latter portfolio, however, as he was up against William Downey Stewart, who had taken Finance and was no less orthodox than Forbes had been in that role. The general election in December returned the Coalition with 51 seats to Labour's 24. But discontent with the rising number of unemployed was building.

By 1932 the vigorous Unemployed Workers Union had 13,000 members. The Communist Party had become active in this organisation and elsewhere, particularly in setting up women's committees. In April and May meetings of the unemployed in Auckland, Wellington and Dunedin precipitated riots. In Auckland, mounted police were used to clear the streets and special constables recruited to protect damaged buildings and act as a deterrent to further violence. Labour MP John A. Lee had been speaking at a meeting inside the Auckland Town Hall which, because of lack of room, had been forced to exclude thousands of unemployed waiting outside. Frustration at this exclusion had sparked the riot. Lee saw the aftermath.

> Queen Street was looted from end to end. Law and order were down and out. Men were being marshalled from the navy to patrol the streets. The looters, being ordinary decent citizens moved to desperation by distress, exploded in violence and then just as suddenly disappeared, not anxious to be seen in the street of anarchy, although they would gather in Karangahape Road for a repeat the next night ... If [they] had not been democratically minded they would have had the government out that week.

In Wellington, the unemployed had wanted to hold a mass meeting at the Basin Reserve.

> [But] the authorities refused them. So they got permission from a private property owner to use a big vacant section somewhere up ... Cuba Street way, and they were all peaceably having their meeting there when without warning the police rushed them. They came charging through the gates, over the fences and belted hell out of them ... and of course the crowd scattered. Well, that incensed the people of Wellington and that night they started to flock in the thousands ...

Several nights later, near the Cenotaph,

> I heard a voice cry out, 'Let's smash the bloody town up'...[They] started to advance up Lambton Quay belting windows with oranges or bananas and as they broke the windows, particularly of hardware shops, they'd pick up spanners and iron bars and different gear like big tools...And as they went up Lambton Quay you could hear the windows crashing, it was a horrible sound... and if you wanted to go against the crowd you just couldn't. They just surged right up behind those rioters, right up through the Quay.

Although in every instance the number of people responsible for damage was small compared with the number of onlookers, many New Zealanders feared at this time that the country was on the brink of anarchy. Expressions of contempt and even hate for politicians were widespread: it was said of Gordon Coates, for example – untruthfully – that he was drinking heavily and had told a deputation of unemployed workers to 'eat grass'. The Government passed the Public Safety and Conservation Act which gave the police draconian powers to detain people. But there was no further violence. It was as if the country had looked over an abyss and then decided by common consent to draw back.

Just how bad, though, did living conditions become over this period? Tony Simpson has described the Depression as 'a grey and ill-defined monster, an unspeakable disaster' that 'cast a long shadow, a blight on everything it touched ...' After 1933, when the Government required at first single and then married men to go into rural work camps to qualify for relief payment, those workers often found themselves in extraordinarily unpleasant places. One such was Aka Aka, south-east of Waiuku, where the *Auckland Weekly News* reported:

The floors of the tent are earthen, uncovered by boarding, and on Wednesday many of them were dampened by rain soakage. The surroundings ... were very muddy. Then men bathe in the drains, wash in a horse trough, and if it rains have to don wet clothing the next day, for there is no drying room. Men recently arrived at the camp and unused to navvying may earn only five shillings a week ... Nearly always they are ankle-deep and knee-deep in water, and often waist-deep.

And, of course, life was difficult for dependants living on reduced incomes. '[Wives] had to make do as best they could,' wrote Erik Olssen, 'improvising clothing out of sugar sacks, trying to feed their families, scrounging and begging. They also had to keep their homes clean and tidy to impress the voluntary inspectors who checked to make sure that families really needed assistance.' While there was help for the poor, again they had to be the *deserving* poor.

The Depression was not an unmitigated disaster for all New Zealanders, however. There were some who, because of their occupations or private means, scarcely noticed its passage. And there were others who succeeded in making the experience positive, a source of adventure and spiritual or cultural enrichment. On the whole these were single men with minimal responsibilities, but not always. When Fred Miller, a South Island journalist, was laid off by his newspaper, he took his family to Central Otago for three years where he panned for gold (and, for part of that time, housed his wife and children in a cave). The motto he coined as a result of those years was 'Pain is inevitable, misery is optional. Stick a geranium in your hat and be happy.'

Frank Sargeson launched his writing career by working on a relief gang one or two days a week, and spending the rest of the week growing fruit and vegetables, fishing and writing. He considered himself fortunate to have escaped being an office 'work slave'.

He also observed that economic difficulties had the curious effect of turning people towards a 'country way of life: you see numbers of relief workers and sustenance people providing for themselves by forgetting about their specialised jobs and developing ... a Crusoe-like resourcefulness. These people have learned to put up with inconvenient baches, to keep and milk cows, to grow their own vegetables ... Do they know that sow thistle and kumara leaves taste as good as cabbage and spinach? Or that some of the seaweed round our coasts is as good to eat as Irish dulse ... [The Depression] can't have been without its benefits.'

The Depression had another effect which Sargeson said he had not expected, but found stimulating: '[A] great variety of people [were becoming] very conscious of the miseries and hardships which were inflicted on people, and inflicted unjustly, because it was through no fault of their own that they suffered.' Combining with others to address these injustices put 'a sort of comradeship into life which may have been [there] at one time, but which I think [had] been lost.' Sargeson found this comradeship in part through reading and writing and meeting other writers who shared his preoccupations, such as Roderick Finlayson and A. R. D. Fairburn, and in part through joining the Young Communist League.

A small but influential number of New Zealanders joined one or other branches or denominations of the Communist Party as a result of experiencing the Depression, thinking analytically about its causes, and wanting to help ensure it would not recur ('breathes there a man with soul so dead/ who was not in the 'thirties red' ran a parody of Walter Scott not long afterwards). They included Sargeson, poet R. A. K. Mason, Connie Soljak and

Peter Purdue (who would marry), Connie Rawcliffe (later Birchfield), Elsie Freeman (later Locke), and others. Most of these people, including Sargeson at first, believed that the Depression was final and inevitable proof that capitalism could deliver neither prosperity nor social justice, and that it would have to be replaced by an alternative system such as communism. Russia was looked to at this time as the home and proving-ground of Marxist communism, and as the source of informed analysis of what was wrong with capitalism. Others joined communist organisations because they seemed to provide the only forums in which people could address difficult issues, such as social inequity and racism. Most drifted out of the movement once the worst effects of the Depression had dissipated. Others hung on until the Russian invasion of Hungary in 1956 and the revelations of the brutalities of Stalinism, or even until the invasion of Czechoslovakia in 1968. Those who remained faithful to a 'party line' beyond these events, whether Russian or Chinese determined, were few indeed.

It might have been supposed that the Depression delivered miseries enough to New Zealanders in the early 1930s. But, for some, a worse catastrophe was in store. Because New Zealand sat astride tectonic plates, it was and always had been prone to earthquakes ('the Shaky Isles' was a favourite term of Australians to describe their trans-Tasman neighbour). Two in the nineteenth century, in 1848 and 1855, had almost destroyed the fledgling town of Wellington. On 3 February 1931 the country's worst recorded quake devastated Napier, Hastings and wider Hawke's Bay. One survivor, Dorothy Campbell described it.

> [We] were thrown on the ground & there we were with it heaving up & down like the waves of the sea & roaring & crashing & banging, so much so that we literally could not hear the chimneys come down or the crockery breaking … We were facing the sea

> & I saw an island jump ... about fifteen feet out ... and at the
> same time a reef of rocks which I had never seen before appear
> between the island & the mainland ...

Shaking and strange marine effects were felt and seen in many parts of the east coast of the North Island. The future writer Ruth Park was in a dinghy on the inner Hauraki Gulf when the sea disappeared,

> as though the water had been yanked away underneath ... I saw
> things I had never seen before ... The seagrass was all combed
> one way, as though the retreating water had tried to take it with
> it. It jumped with dying life. The air glittered with leaping fish ...
> snapper, dogfish, mullet and clouds of sprats that had taken to
> the air in their hysteria. Afar, a huge ray lifted first one wing and
> then the other in a mad shuffle ...

Napier and Hastings were left in smoking ruins and 256 people died, making the quake the worst human disaster in the country's history.* Damage at the time was estimated at more than £10 million. Whole hillsides disappeared, rivers were dammed, great fissures appeared in the earth and ran for kilometres. For weeks some 30,000 people were deprived of food, water, electricity, telephones and transport. The Government, temporarily distracted from national economic woes, appointed two commissioners to oversee the enormous task of reconstruction.

The person most responsible for trying to revive the fortunes of the country as a whole, however, was Gordon Coates, first as Minister of Works and minister with responsibility for unemployment and subsequently, from January 1933, as Minister of Finance. Coates tried to explore more imaginative ways of

---

* 257 passengers and crew died in the Air New Zealand crash on Mount Erebus
in 1979, but that disaster occurred outside New Zealand's territorial limits.

addressing the problems that Forbes had simply allowed to accumulate. As Michael Bassett notes, he 'introduced his Small Farms (Relief of Unemployment) Bill to help [put] workers on to the land, and later in the year [1933] Parliament passed his Reserve Bank of New Zealand Bill which established a central bank – partly state-owned, partly private – to assist banks to pool their reserves and to take over the issue of banknotes.' Coates also set up what would later be called a 'think-tank', a group of bright young left-wing economists, R. M. Richard (Dick) Campbell, W. B. (Bill) Sutch and Horace Belshaw, who gave him alternative advice to that available from the Treasury. It was their recommendations that led to the creation of the Mortgage Corporation of New Zealand to help farmers refinance their loans at lower interest rates. Subsequent measures were introduced to 'reduce farmers' overheads in the hope of restoring profitability to the rural sector', and so to the whole economy.

These measures did produce beneficial results. But Coates's political allies were suspicious of the personnel in the think-tank and appalled at what they regarded as the minister's excessive state intervention in economic matters. William Downey Stewart, whom Coates had replaced as Finance Minister, complained that 'the Prime Minister is too passive and the Minister of Finance too active'. As far as Forbes was concerned, that was a fair judgement.

The only thing that would 'solve' the Depression and the problems it brought, of course, was the recovery of export prices. And by 1935 that was well under way and the number of unemployed was already dropping. This salvation came too late for the Coalition Government, however, which had exhausted the patience and the confidence of too much of the electorate. Labour, by contrast, bore no responsibility for the failed policies of the preceding years. And, with the death of its firebrand orator Harry Holland on the slopes of Taupiri mountain in October 1933 – he was attending the burial of the Maori King, Te Rata – the party was now led by Michael Joseph Savage.

'Mickey' or 'Joe' Savage, as he was variously known, was no threat to anybody. Australian-born, he had entered Parliament in 1919 and proved himself a sound if unimaginative worker for his Auckland constituents and his party. His socialist credentials were impeccable – he had first stood for Parliament in 1911 under the banner of the old Socialist Party – but his appearance and mannerisms and emphases disarmed the paranoia of those who were not socialist. Indeed, his definition of social security was 'applied Christianity'. His colleagues had elected him leader in Holland's place because of his benignity, and because they could rely on him to represent their body corporate in the most faithful, predictable and platitudinous manner. The real sources of power in the party for policy-making and discipline were former syndicalist Peter Fraser and former shopkeeper and commercial traveller Walter Nash, the 'money man'. But it suited them as well as the Labour caucus as a whole to have Savage out front, being everybody's favourite bachelor uncle. Labour no longer planned to smash capitalism, as it had wanted to do two decades earlier. Like the electorate at large, it wanted to make capitalism work better. In particular, it wanted to ensure that, in a country with the rich food resources of New Zealand, nobody would have to go hungry, or without work, education or health care. Labour was promising a benign socialist millennium to match its benign leader. And the electorate was now ready to take the party at its word.

In November 1935, therefore, the Labour Party won the election delayed by the Depression in a landslide: 55 seats, counting the Ratana members who would soon join their caucus. The Coalition, which had contested the election as the National Political Federation (and would in May 1936 become the National Party) won 19. A new conservative Country Party took two seats and there were four independents. Labour was in office for the first time, and with a powerful mandate for change. And change was what the new Government would deliver, on a scale unprecedented in New Zealand's history up to that time.

Labour's intentions had been signalled in 1934 by the pamphlet *Labour Has a Plan*, written by the party's most articulate and eloquent publicist, returned serviceman and MP John A. Lee.* New Zealand could be made the centre of a new civilisation, Lee proclaimed. A Labour Government would 'use our own physical resources and amplify the progressive genius that has been dormant in these past decades and erect the new socialist state that will once again cause New Zealand to inspire the world ...'

The new Government set out at once to institute a series of measures – some symbolic, some substantial – to meet the expectations its propaganda and its victory had raised. A Christmas bonus was issued immediately to the unemployed. The Labour caucus voted unanimously to nationalise the Reserve Bank. Old age pensions were restored and increased. Teachers' colleges, closed as an economy measure, were reopened. Secondary education, like primary, was made free of charge. A state-owned radio network was established and parliamentary debates broadcast for the first time. Farmers got a guaranteed

---

* Articulate Lee may have been, a fine writer and an arresting soapbox orator. But he disliked and was disliked in turn by Savage, excluded from the cabinet (though given an under-secretaryship) and eventually expelled from the party in March 1940 in the wave of emotion that welled up after Savage's prolonged dying.

dairy price. Industrial arbitration was restored and union membership made compulsory; this led to the formation of a new Federation of Labour with a sound financial and membership base from which to represent workers nationally. The Arbitration Court was instructed to introduce a 40-hour working week and provide a minimum wage capable of supporting a married couple and three children (the assumption remained that the primary role of women was that of homemaker). A state housing scheme was launched, initially administered by John A. Lee, with the goal of providing for every New Zealander what Walter Nash called 'a home fit for a Cabinet minister'.* And the Reserve Bank was instructed to finance this scheme with interest-free credit.

The Coalition Government had managed to balance its budgets in the three preceding years, and the incoming Government found it had inherited a surplus. This it spent largely on public works schemes which, along with recovering export prices and the slow return to prosperity, helped to soak up the previously unemployed. The former Red Fed organiser Bob Semple, now the snappily dressed Minister of Public Works and of Transport, was one of the characters of the Labour cabinet and never at a loss for a dramatic gesture. In the Ngauranga Gorge, he symbolised the new administration's optimism and

---

* It was widely believed that the state house building programme earned a fortune for Fletcher Construction and its Scottish-born founder, James Fletcher. In fact, Fletchers initially incurred heavy losses on the contract as a result of tendering too low and were saved from financial collapse only by the Government's willingness to guarantee a company overdraft. Under the successive direction of Sir James Fletcher's son and grandson, J. C. and Hugh, the expanded company, eventually Fletcher Challenge, went on to become the largest in New Zealand in the 1980s, with a wide range of construction and manufacturing subsidiaries, including Tasman Pulp and Paper and Pacific Steel.

the power of machinery over the pick and shovel by getting into a bulldozer and wrecking a pile of wheelbarrows. In Parliament, he frequently had MPs almost collapsing with laughter at his pungent epithets ('snivelling snufflebuster' was one, and 'the honourable member doesn't so much speak as open his mouth and let the wind blow his tongue around').

The Government's crowning achievement, however, was what Savage told delegates to the 1938 party conference would be social security 'from the cradle to the grave'. The Social Security Act, passed by Parliament in September 1938, gave the country a virtually free health system (covering doctors' visits and hospitalisation), a means-tested old age pension at 60 and universal superannuation at 65. This package was received rapturously by Labour's supporters, and by some who would now become Labour's supporters (such as most Maori electors). As Erik Olssen has written, 'the extent of the change which occurred ... is difficult now to recapture. Savage and his Cabinet appear[ed] to have put New Zealand back on its true course as the most advanced and humane society in the world ...'

There would be unforeseen problems in future years: an erosion of the Government's subsidies to general medical practitioners, an inability to bring dentistry into the free health scheme, an explosion in the costs of public health, particularly those associated with hospitals. Eventually, the effectiveness of 'big spending' would be questioned and concerns raised about the extensive intrusion of government into the lives of its citizens, along with a fear that welfare states sapped individual responsibility and initiative. But in the late 1930s social security was valued so highly because it helped erase recent memories of genuine hardship and it seemed a fulfilment of a social blueprint which the Labour movement had been developing for more than two decades.

Among those to benefit most spectacularly from all Labour's measures – in social security, education and housing – were Maori. Up to the 1930s, typhoid fever, dysentery, diarrhoeal and respiratory diseases took a disproportionate toll on the tangata whenua population. In 1938 the Maori death rate per 1000 people was 24.31; that for non-Maori 9.71. The Maori infant mortality rate was 153.26 per 1000 live births, as against 36.63 for others. No real progress was made in reducing these figures until the Labour Government's health and housing reforms had begun to take effect, and until Maori health became the respon-sibility of the Health Department's district health officers. This last measure succeeded because it presented 'a direct challenge to bring the state of Maori health to a standard more comparable to that of Europeans, and medical officers could no longer look to anyone else as being responsible for doing this'.

If one individual was responsible more than any other for improvements in Maori health it was Dr Harold Turbott, first as South Auckland medical officer and later as Director of School Hygiene. Turbott lobbied the Labour Minister of Health – and later Prime Minister – Peter Fraser for special appropriations for Maori health projects. His most efficacious programmes were providing water tanks and privies for Maori homes, and persuading Maori on a wide scale to seek treatment for tuber-culosis and to accept a degree of isolation for this treatment, often in well-ventilated portable huts provided by the Health Department. Turbott also directed district health nurses towards a greater degree of preventative work, especially with children, and he developed good working relations with local leaders such as Te Puea Herangi.

The combination of all these measures, along with the general lifting of Maori incomes in the post-Depression years, brought spectacular improvements in Maori health over two decades. The death rate for tuberculosis dropped from an estimated 50 per 10,000 of population in 1933 to 10.6 in the early 1950s and 3.82 in 1956–60, by which time antibiotics had become available to treat the disease. The incidence of typhoid fell away and infant mortality rates dropped, though not as spectacularly. The general life expectancy for Maori rose from 46.6 years for men and 44.7 for women in 1925–27 to 57 and 59 by the mid-1950s.

Labour's education policies also had beneficial effects for Maori. Up to the 1930s, Maori education in both state and denominational schools reflected the ideology that had animated Apirana Ngata's land development schemes: that the future of Maori was to be worked out in rural areas. This view had been reflected in a major policy statement by the Director of Education in 1931: '[The] best means for [Maori] to realise the full benefits of civilisation is through the cultivation of land … These considerations lead us to the final conclusion that … we should provide fully a type of education that will lead the lad to be a good farmer and the girl to be a good farmer's wife.'

A consequence of this policy, which ignored the achievements of the Young Maori Party generation of leaders, was that the curriculum in Maori schools emphasised agriculture and (to a lesser extent) manual and vocational training for boys, and domestic skills for girls. Few Maori pupils moved beyond primary level (about 8.4 per cent in 1935, compared with nearly 60 per cent of all pupils), most of them defeated by the absence of Maori-oriented secondary schools, by the need to pay fees, by the requirements of the Proficiency exam (which was a condition for entering secondary education) or by parental discouragement. At this time too Maori parents and grand-parents were discouraging children from learning the Maori language. The widespread belief – among Pakeha *and* Maori –

was that proficiency in English would make upward social mobility for Maori more likely and better prepare youngsters for a world in which Maori culture was going to be a diminishing influence. This was the era when the number of native speakers of the language began to diminish sharply.

Educational opportunities for Maori improved dramatically under Labour. Expenditure on education as a whole was greatly increased, rural schools were consolidated and their facilities improved, and school transport added. Secondary education was made free, the Proficiency exam abolished and the minimum school-leaving age raised to fifteen. The Government also built native district high schools for the first time, which placed greater emphasis on vocational training than on farming skills. As a result of these efforts, the number of Maori at secondary schools increased to 30 per cent of those eligible by 1951 – still not satisfactory, but a considerable improvement on the 1935 figure. Further progress would have to await the Maori movement into towns and cities over the following decades.

By the time the 1938 general election fell due, the Labour Government was, for the time being, indefatigable, even though the National Party was now better organised and had a new leader in Southland businessman Adam Hamilton. Labour's share of the vote rose 10 points to just under 56 per cent. Though it lost some seats, it gained others and ended with 53 to National's 25. Independents held the other two.

In the course of its second term, Labour was determined to take advantage of the nation's centenary, which fell on the 100th anniversary of the signing of the Treaty of Waitangi in February 1840. The Government hoped to generate national pride, indicate a growth of national maturity and highlight favourably its own association with the celebrations. The outbreak of World

War II eventually put restrictions on the amount of money devoted to the centenary and a damper on the main event, the Centennial Exhibition in Wellington, which was supposed to showcase cultural, agricultural and industrial progress. But a government-appointed National Historical Committee produced an excellent series of publications, including a serial pictorial journal aimed largely at schools, *Making New Zealand*, and a dozen book-length surveys of 'the nation's development', of which the best were by J. C. Beaglehole (*The Discovery of New Zealand*), who would later win fame as the world's greatest authority on James Cook, F. L. W. Wood (*New Zealand in the World*), Oliver Duff (*New Zealand Now*) and E. H. McCormick (*Letters and Art in New Zealand*). McCormick, who would go on to become the country's leading cultural historian, also edited the series as a whole after Duff had been poached to become the foundation editor of the *New Zealand Listener*, a national weekly magazine under the control of the country's broadcasting service for the next 50 years.

Ironically, despite the intention of generating national pride, the Centennial Council rejected an application that the Thomas Bracken hymn *God Defend New Zealand* be made the country's national anthem. It opted instead for the retention of *God Save the King*, for which movie-goers still stood at the beginning of cinema sessions, as the anthem. As a consolation prize, Bracken's effort was designated 'national hymn'. Independence from Britain was not a national priority at this time.

There was evidence of rather more nascent nationalism, perhaps, in Labour's adoption of a degree of independence in foreign affairs. The Government sent former MP and ex-Cockney policeman Bill Jordan to London as High Commissioner and New Zealand representative at the League of Nations (at this time the country's only other diplomatic post was

Canberra). At League meetings in Geneva, Jordan was admired by some for his 'blunt speech and simple moral judgment', though not by the British delegation, whose advice he was not prepared to accept automatically. Thanks to one of his votes, made with the approval of the cabinet in Wellington, New Zealand joined the Soviet Union as the only two countries to oppose recognition of the Italian conquest of Abyssinia. This led the National Opposition to accuse Labour of endangering imperial solidarity. But the Government stood firm and insisted that 'all aggressors be [opposed] by the League, even when they were powerful states such as Japan'. The only thing wrong with the League of Nations, Labour believed, was that it ended up betraying the ideal of collective security.

New Zealand's willingness to express and invest confidence in the League was in part a response to the rise of totalitarianism in Europe and Asia – which alarmed not only the Government but the Labour movement as a whole. And, by the time it was apparent in 1938 that the League was insufficiently functional to prevent another global war, Labour knew that it would have to reconsider its long-held reservations about the role of the British Empire and the British Navy in world affairs and in the affairs of New Zealand. In 1939, when Peter Fraser was in London for the kind of ministerial meeting that had replaced the old Imperial Conference, he was relieved to be assured that the defence of Australia and New Zealand against attack by Japan would be second in Britain's priorities only to the containment of the German naval fleet. In other words, imperial protection rather than the League of Nations was still New Zealand's best option for security. That hypothesis would almost immediately be put to the test.

23

Conformity and Non-conformity

Maori and Pakeha societies, running on separate but parallel tracks in New Zealand in the years preceding World War II, each displayed considerable internal cohesion and conformity. Each also served as the 'exotic other' to highlight and confirm its own identity and distinctiveness.

Adherence to Maori values persisted in Maori communities to an extent that surprised such Pakeha observers as journalist Eric Ramsden and Native Land Court Judge Frank Acheson. They noted that mana continued to be the quality that determined status, though increasing importance was being given to mana that was earned by achievement rather than being simply inherited. The personal tapu of persons of rangatira rank – Te Puea Herangi of Tainui or Hoani Te Heuheu of Ngati Tuwharetoa, for example – still invited respect in Maori contexts, where people continued to place weight on personal identification through their whakapapa.

Discussions at hui were held almost exclusively in Maori, and at this time there was no shortage of native speakers in the kaumatua age-group to assume this responsibility (though the fact that outside such exclusively Maori areas as the Urewera many younger Maori were no longer learning the language would result in gaps on the paepae after the passage of two more generations). Such deliberations would be structured according to the conventions of whaikorero, and would centre on the constant preoccupation with whenuatanga (land), rangatira-tanga (leadership), whakapapa (relationships), mana and mana motuhake (Maori authority). Speakers were surrounded and protected by marae ceremonial conducted according to the protocol of the tangata whenua.

Tribalism continued to be a dominating feature of Maori life, to the joy of those who *felt* tribal, and to the exasperation at times of those who felt *Maori*, such as Bishop Frederick Bennett, since 1928 the first Bishop of Aotearoa, or who were Pakeha. After spending nearly half a lifetime building up material for his *Dictionary of New Zealand Biography* (1940), Parliamentary Librarian G. H. Scholefield concluded: 'Maori history is sadly distorted and vitiated by the highly developed tribalism and the intense rivalries of the generations that the Maoris have spent in New Zealand ... [The] spirit of tribal pride moves even the broadminded Maori to ignore ... the vicissitudes of their own tribes and chiefs.'

What was a debilitating and destructive handicap from one point of view (in the case above, a Pakeha one) was a source of strength from another. Tribalism provided much of the group vitality and competitiveness of Maori life. And most Maori continued to draw their strength and identity not from being Maori, but from being a known and knowing member of a particular hapu or tribe, and from being embraced by the people, history and traditions of that tribe. John Rangihau of Tuhoe, who grew up in such a situation at Waikaremoana in the 1920s and 1930s, expressed it this way:

> [My] feelings ... are my Tuhoetanga rather than my Maoritanga. Because my being Maori is utterly dependent on my history as a Tuhoe person ... It seems to me there is no such thing as Maoritanga because Maoritanga is an all-inclusive term ... I have a faint suspicion that [it] is a term coined by the Pakeha to bring all the tribes together. Because if you cannot divide and rule, then for tribal people all you can do is unite them and rule. Because then they lose everything by losing [the] tribal history and traditions that gave them their identity.

The dominant cultural identification of Pakeha at this time was still 'British', a continuing reflection of the fact that, for more than 95 per cent of the non-Maori population, their countries of origin were England, Scotland, Ireland and Wales, in that order. Lord Jellicoe, the Governor-General, noted in 1924 that New Zealanders were 'extremely proud' of their British nationality. 'They claim, in fact, to be even more British than their kin of the Motherland, and that no doubt accounts for the intensely loyal spirit which characterises the Dominion.'

The only variegations in this pattern were the festivities marking St Patrick's Day or Burns' Night, in which New Zealanders of Irish and Scottish stock celebrated their more specific heritages. But even the anti-Irish feeling that had been nurtured by the Protestant Political Association during and after World War I had evaporated in the wake of Irish independence in 1921: if the British Government approved the foundation of the Irish Free State, how could anybody professing 'Britishness' object?

One symptom of the intensity of British feeling was the continuing lack of interest New Zealand showed in ratifying the 1931 Statute of Westminster, which had granted the dominions complete autonomy in foreign as well as domestic affairs and put their parliaments on an equal footing with Westminster. Most New Zealanders probably agreed with National MP Charles Bowden when he declared his opposition to the statute and said he would rather be a 'British subject' than a 'national of the British Commonwealth'.

Such certitude in the matter of identity had been confirmed by the length of time that New Zealand had been a British colony, by a continuing inflow of predominantly British immigrants, by the heightened feelings of imperialism – or, at the very least, that 'double patriotism' engendered by World War I – and by Britain's continuing role as receiver of New Zealand's exports and provider of its imports. New Zealand, as an island nation, had no borders with other countries or cultures to mitigate a sense of racial solipsism – and to describe this feeling as 'racial' is no exaggeration. One of the government census reports of the 1920s noted that 'the importance of racial purity has long been recognised [in New Zealand]. History has shown that the coalescence of the white and the so-called coloured races is not conducive to improvement in racial types.'

The obverse side to this confidence in racial and cultural identity, however, was a fear and dislike of nations and cultures that were not British. Such a fear was at times xenophobic. Despite the very small numbers involved, the presence of Indians working in market gardens around Pukekohe in the 1920s precipitated the establishment of a 'White New Zealand League'. Poet Anton Vogt reported riding a tram around Wellington's Basin Reserve in 1936 and talking Norwegian to his father as, standing, they hung onto the roof straps to retain their balance. Another passenger got to his feet – a trade union official, as it turned out – and knocked Vogt senior to the floor with a blow to the jaw. 'Speak English, damn you,' said the assailant, glaring down at his victim. While it is probable that few other New Zealanders, confronted with this scene, would have resorted to violence, it is likely that many would have been unnerved by hearing a 'foreign' language for the first time.

An example of xenophobia made legal was the fact that, as a consequence of New Zealand's adopting the British Nationality and Status of Aliens Act 1914, any New Zealand woman who married an 'alien' lost her British citizenship and became herself an alien, without the right to vote. Miriam Soljak, a New Zealander of Irish descent who had married a Dalmatian immigrant, spent most of her adult life fighting for the repeal of this legislation. It was not until after New Zealand had ratified the Statute of Westminster in 1947 that New Zealand married women were given their own independent nationality.

Most non-British immigrants, living or growing up in a country in the formation of whose national identity their own ethnic group had played no part, merged as rapidly and as smoothly as possible into the ranks of mainstream culture. It would be a source of irony that, during World War II, the two most senior officers in the New Zealand Division fighting Germany would be named Freyberg and Kippenberger. Because the families of both men had long since left behind any trace of their Germanic origins, however, nobody in New Zealand thought of them as other than British officers and gentlemen – and, indeed, after his brief time in New Zealand as a dental technician, Bernard Freyberg had enjoyed a distinguished career in the British Army. Members of Wellington's small Italian community would attract more public suspicion during the war than those with German names.

People whose looks, language and culture made it obvious that they were not British in origin, nor even European, generally faced a far more difficult life. And the group which suffered most from prejudice and misunderstanding was the Chinese, who had been entering New Zealand from Canton since 1865, initially to work the Otago goldfields. Although their number was almost insignificant and most were single men, the New Zealand Parliament passed several Acts in the late nineteenth century specifically to discourage Chinese immigration. A poll tax of at first £10 and later £100 had to be paid by each Chinese person entering the country, and ships were permitted to bring in only one Chinese passenger per 200 tons of cargo.

Once in New Zealand, the Chinese who persisted despite the poll tax and considerable prejudice proved themselves to be law-abiding and hard-working citizens. Some, such as Sam Chew Lain, the Lawrence publican, and Chew Chong, who eventually opened the first butter factory in Taranaki, became widely respected business people. Most, however, graduated from the goldfields to market gardening and retailing fruit and vegetables, occupations which other New Zealanders eventually came to regard as 'appropriate' for their Chinese compatriots. But there was general opposition – from Pakeha and Maori – to mixed-race marriages involving Chinese, while Chinese men were discouraged from settling their families in New Zealand. When subsequent generations of New Zealand Chinese moved into professional careers, there was a further round of disapproval.

The poll tax was eventually abolished in 1944 by the Fraser Labour Government. Deputy Prime Minister Walter Nash called it a 'blot on our legislation ... [The] Chinese are as good as any other race [and] we will not in future countenance any discrimination against them.' It was to be a further 58 years before another Labour Government, that of Helen Clark, apologised to Chinese New Zealanders for both the tax and the wider discrimination it reflected.

Other non-British peoples – Indians, Dalmatians, Lebanese – were also subjected to social discrimination, especially in employment and accommodation, but individually rather than, like the Chinese, as a group. Many Dalmatian men in Northland married into Maori families and thus integrated into New Zealand society by that route. Jewish New Zealanders too faced discrimination, even though they had been in the country since the earliest days of European settlement, and in many instances – Nathans, Levins, Hallensteins, Myers and others – played a prominent role in commercial and cultural activities. One Jew, Sir Julius Vogel, had become Premier; another, Chief Justice Sir Michael Myers, had acted as Administrator of New Zealand four times between the departures and arrivals of governors-general. As late as the 1940s one of the highlights of the annual Wairoa Agricultural and Pastoral Show Parade was the local farmer who donned a mask with an enormous nose, a top hat and a long black coat to appear as 'Ikey the Jew'.

Unlike its worst manifestations in Europe, anti-Semitism in New Zealand tended to be covert and subtle, arising partly from the tenets of Christianity, which suggested that the Jews as a people had been responsible for the death of Christ, and partly from the conviction that Jews were 'mean' with money and 'looked after their own' ahead of broader social responsibilities. No amount of largess by the Fels and Hallenstein families of Dunedin, or contributions to local body administration by the likes of Ernest and Moss Davis in Auckland, would diminish prejudice of this kind. It was even on occasion voiced by officials responsible for the administration of policies on immigration and the settlement of 'aliens'. One such official was to write in 1946 that 'the worst thing about [Jews] is that they cringe and fawn when they are weak and bully and exploit when they have power ... [and] there is always the Jew's uncanny ability to see always one move ahead of his competitors'. Views of this kind did not significantly diminish until the decades after World War II when New Zealand society became more pluralistic and less prone to uninformed and pejorative stereotyping. There was by that time, too, the example of the Holocaust in Europe, which revealed the shocking extreme to which anti-Semitism could be taken.

While Maori and Pakeha interacted on a small scale in rural towns and Pakeha and Maori continued to intermarry, Pakeha representations of Maori still tended to be as uninformed, and in some cases as pejorative, as those of other non-British peoples. In other cases it was simply patronising. An editorial in Wellington's *Evening Post* newspaper in the mid-1920s noted how tragic it was that the life of a prominent city lawyer had been lost while he attempted to rescue a 'half-caste girl' at Otaki Beach, as if a person of mixed race was not worth saving. And articles and books of the 'coon humour' variety, the most popular of which was *Maori Tales*, portrayed Maori in prose and cartoons as simpletons who were comic in their inability to cope with modern civilisation (and this at a time when Apirana Ngata was one of the most highly qualified members, Maori *or* Pakeha, of the House of Representatives).

The artists and writers who patronised Maori, by contrast, were at least motivated mainly by humanitarianism and compassion. Many of them had a kind of *fin de siècle* interest in characters they described in such terms as 'the last of the old type of better Maori'. The leading practitioners of this perception and style were the artists Charles Frederick Goldie and Louis John Steele, and the journalist and historian James Cowan, each of whom regretted the extent to which Western culture had intruded on and – in their eyes – fragmented 'authentic' Maori culture.

In their view, much about pre-European and nineteenth-century Maori had been noble and dignified. There had been old-world courtesies, codes of honour, psychic and spiritual perceptions, handsomeness and virility in 'pure-bred' chieftains and warriors, and winsomeness and dusky beauty in maidens of similar pedigree. According to this view, throughout the late nineteenth and early twentieth centuries Maori had been in physical, cultural and moral decline as a consequence of abandoning old ways and of prolonged contact with alcohol and disease. Cowan tended to view his elderly informants as survivors from a pristine age, as men and women who exemplified the most worthy features of their culture, which were destined for extinction. He described one of them, Hauauru of Araikotore, in this manner:

> [He] is a picturesque figure who, in my memories of the past, personifies much of the departed savage glory of the Maori race. He typified the splendid dying manhood of his people. Born in the New Zealander's Stone Age, he survived [as] flotsam of the primitive world stranded on the shores of modern progress ... A Homeric personality was that of this old cannibal warrior, a savage but a gentleman, full of courteous friendly feeling for the whites whom he had once fought and bitterly hated, and full of the hospitality of the true Maori rangatira ...

Such a view was limited on several counts. First, it sentimentalised Maori life to the point of unreality. At whatever moment writers chose to 'freeze' history there would always have been Maori whom they would regard as 'good' and 'bad', courteous and discourteous, traditionalists and innovators, activists and idlers. Second, it suggested that everything worthwhile about Maori life lay in the past and would soon be lost irretrievably. And, third, it tended to blind observers to the fascinating and innovative adaptations that Maori were making at the very time Cowan was writing and Goldie painting.

Such views were, however, well-intentioned. They did at least place positive value on Maori perceptions and customs. Yet Cowan's verbal and Goldie's pictorial images served with their gauze of romanticism to place Maori and Maori considerations into a kind of never-never land, safely beyond the political and social preoccupations of contemporary New Zealand life. In such a vision, Maori need not be claimants on the national purse and conscience, their social and economic difficulties need not be the responsibilities of the country as a whole. They recede to being merely a colourful element from New Zealand's past, surviving in the mountainous and rural hinterland.

The imaginative equivalent of Cowan's descriptive writing was the fiction of authors such as William Satchell (*The Greenstone Door*), F. O. V. Acheson (*Plume of the Arawas*) and A. W. Reed in his novelisation of the Rudall Hayward film *Rewi's Last Stand*. These men depicted romantic Maori figures – noble heroes, beautiful and tragic heroines, unrequited love – through a haze of poetic imagery. The figures they created bore little relation to life and conditions in twentieth-century Maori communities, and for the most part they made no distinction between Maori of different regions and tribes – distinctions that would have been crucial in Maori eyes.

From the 1930s more able writers such as Frank Sargeson, A. P. Gaskell, John Mulgan (in his novel *Man Alone*) and especially Roderick Finlayson would devise more credible Maori characters and situations that were closer to the realities of Maori life. There was still, however, in the words of Patricia Grace, 'the temptation . . . to find in the Maori virtues that are missing in the Pakeha and to use him as a criticism of Pakeha society'. Stereotyping continued ('happy-go-lucky, lazy people, mostly not too bright . . . or the big-brown-eyes and little-bare-feet touch'), and these writers experienced severe difficulties in conveying Maori English. Fiction involving Maori did not lose these elements of awkwardness or reflect the varied patterns of Maori experience until imaginative writers who were also Maori, most notably Witi Ihimaera, Patricia Grace and Keri Hulme, emerged in the 1970s.

In non-fiction, apart from the ethnologists such as Elsdon Best and Peter Buck (both of whom, like Cowan, tended to equate Maori adaptation to Western influences with pollution of a formerly 'pure' cultural stream), the earliest perceptive writers on Maori matters were the journalist Eric Ramsden, who made earnest and frequently successful attempts from the 1920s to interpret Maori preoccupations to non-Maori audiences and Pakeha authorities; and I. L. G. Sutherland, New Zealand's first recognised social scientist. Sutherland and his successors, Ernest and Pearl Beaglehole and James Ritchie, highlighted for the first time reasons for lack of Maori advancement in socio-economic as well as cultural terms, while recognising the intrinsic worth of Maori concepts and values.

There was no comparable body of literature to mirror Maori views of Pakeha over the same period. But what has been published by way of reminiscence by such writers as Eruera and Amiria Stirling and Reweti Kohere suggests that there was a Maori stereotype of the Pakeha as someone who was self-centred, materialist, acquisitive, unfeeling about their extended family and callous in their treatment of the dead. By highlighting and caricaturing European qualities that were distasteful in Maori eyes, Maori commentators such as Apirana Ngata and Te Puea Herangi also communicated indirectly the qualities they most valued according to their own *mores*. These examples suggest that a wide and continuing gap existed between the lifeways of Maori and Pakeha.

There were further gaps, too, *within* the otherwise coherent domains of Maori and Pakeha cultures. The positive effect of conformity – a society in which there was widespread agreement about what was right and what was wrong, about what constituted appropriate and inappropriate behaviour – gave pre-war New Zealand considerable social cohesion. The negative effect was that people who did not conform in their views or behaviour were either treated harshly or lived in fear of disclosure and retribution.

Women, for example, both Maori and Pakeha, still had nothing like the freedom available to men in the choice of an occupation, or even in deciding whether to be married or unmarried. Right into the 1930s New Zealand society, in Miles Fairburn's words, continued to believe that a woman's place was in the home.

> Mothers were taught to be professional child carers, and girls learnt home craft in schools. Women, especially working class women, were given limited scope for fulfilment outside family life. Women's occupations had diversified ... since the turn of the century. Domestic service, the traditional mainstay, diminished in relative importance and office jobs, nursing, teaching, and working in shops had increased. But the proportion of female school leavers designating the 'home' as their destination remained very high ... Very few women still worked after marriage. The fraction of all women actively engaged in the workforce remained at around 17 per cent to 18 per cent from the turn of the century until the 1930s ...

Women who chose to live outside these expectations, such as the sex hygiene campaigner Ettie Rout, whose book *Safe Marriage* was banned in New Zealand in 1923, and the writer and sexual liberationist Jean Devanny, faced condemnation and ostracism (Rout eventually committed suicide in Rarotonga in

1936, and Devanny emigrated to Australia). Even so innocuous an activity as writing poetry in preference to doing housework provoked horror, as Janet Frame's mother, Lottie, discovered in Oamaru in the 1930s. In such New Zealand towns, even among families who were poor, pretension and social ambition were rife and women's domestic reputations could be made or lost according to how well they scrubbed their front doorsteps.

Thoughout these years, the justice system was especially punitive towards male homosexual behaviour (though not, surprisingly, towards the female kind, which was not recognised by law and probably not conceivable in the public imagination). The Crimes Act of 1908 outlawed sodomy and any form of 'indecent' behaviour between men. Penalties were severe: usually gaol terms with hard labour, most often in New Plymouth prison which was, conveniently, built alongside a quarry.

In the face of such sanctions, homosexual men who were aware of their sexuality had to choose among several options. They could embark on a life without any form of sexual expression (and that was most often the advice given to them by ministers of religion, who conveyed the further bad news that God also opposed same-sex transactions). They could disguise their nature by marrying, having sexual relations that they found difficult and distasteful, and fathering children. They could emigrate to a country which had a degree of toleration of homosexual activity (and for most New Zealanders, like the writers James Courage and Lionel Grindley, this meant living in London). Or they could accept the risks inherent in active homosexual behaviour and the constant state of anxiety that accompanied such risks. Some New Zealand men, at different times of their lives, adopted more than one of these strategies.

That the risks involved in active homosexuality were high was illustrated by the experience of Charles Ewing Mackay, a Wanganui lawyer who became mayor of the borough in 1913 (he had previously stood for Parliament in 1908 and 1911). Mackay's achievements were considerable. He was responsible for building the much-admired Sarjeant Gallery, he enlarged the borough and its resources, and set in motion plans to build a museum and library to complement the gallery. He was unusual in New Zealand local body affairs for being as interested in cultural activities as in commercial and administrative matters.

Mackay was unpopular in some quarters, however, particularly among the ranks of the town's Returned Services' Association, which he prevented from holding a separate welcome for the Prince of Wales when he visited Wanganui in May 1920. Some RSA members persuaded a visitor to the town, the fellow returned serviceman and future poet Walter D'Arcy Cresswell, to act as *agent provocateur* and invite overtures of intimacy from Mackay. When these duly occurred, Cresswell told Mackay that he had to resign the mayorality or else he, Cresswell, would report the indiscretion to the police. In a panic Mackay drew a pistol and shot Cresswell, wounding but not killing him.

In the subsequent trial for attempted murder, Cresswell, who was also homosexual but failed to disclose the fact, was wholly exonerated ('no blame could be attached to [him] and the action he took would be commended by all right-thinking men', thundered the Chief Justice, Sir Robert Stout). Mackay pleaded guilty and was sentenced to 15 years' imprisonment with hard labour. His name was sanded off the Sarjeant Gallery foundation stone and his portrait removed from the borough council chambers. His wife successfully petitioned for divorce and he was never again allowed to see his daughters. After his early release from prison in 1926, Charles Mackay went to Europe and became a journalist. In May 1929 he was covering a clash between communists and police in Berlin when he was accidentally shot.

Another public figure who had married but retained homosexual associations was the public servant Alister McIntosh, foundation Secretary of External Affairs and from 1945 permanent head of the Prime Minister's Department. McIntosh was widely admired for his sagacity and his support of library and cultural projects, such as the 1940 centennial publications, and for the sound advice he gave to four Prime Ministers, Peter Fraser, Sidney Holland, Walter Nash and Keith Holyoake. In 1965, in what was to be the pinnacle of his career, he was nominated for the position of first Secretary-General of the Commonwealth and widely regarded as having the inside running for election at the Commonwealth Prime Ministers' Conference in London that year. At the eleventh hour his nomination was withdrawn after the New Zealand Prime Minister, Holyoake, had been visited by British security officials. They apparently advised that McIntosh's sexuality made him vulnerable to blackmail and therefore a security risk in the position. The British Government would not now support his candidacy. Advised of this, McIntosh himself withdrew, citing health reasons (he had an inner ear disorder which affected his balance and his hearing). Instead, the New Zealand Government sent him to Rome as the country's first ambassador to Italy. He was knighted in 1973 on the advice of the Kirk Labour Government.

Other homosexuals in government departments whose personnel required security clearance were forced to remain sexually inactive and to conceal any clues as to their inclination. In one case an External Affairs officer serving abroad was caught by police soliciting sexual companions in a public lavatory. He was repatriated and transferred to a department in which security clearance was not required.*

The writer Hector Bolitho, like the novelist James Courage, moved to England in the 1920s in part because of his sexuality, and his popular books on members of the Royal Family earned him the designation 'biographer royal'. James Courage, by contrast, wrote short stories and novels in London, his first being published in 1933. Some of them dealt with themes of sexual orientation and same-sex relationships and one, *A Way of Love*, was banned in New Zealand for this reason.

Other homosexual writers chose to live in New Zealand and negotiate the difficulties. Frank Sargeson changed his name from Norris Davey because of a conviction for indecent assault in Wellington in 1929. He lived much of the rest of his life in Takapuna in fear that the conviction would become public knowledge, or that his homosexual activities might again bring him before the court as a result of police surveillance. Travelling to Wellington to receive the prestigious Katherine Mansfield award for short stories in 1965, he forced himself to remain awake all night in the train because his sleeping-car companion turned out to be a detective and Sargeson feared entrapment.

His friend Bill Pearson, a writer and academic, was another who navigated these shoals but managed to survive without the stress of an arrest and conviction. According to another friend, 'the fear of being outed, the public shame, the potential

---

* Homosexuality *per se* ceased to be formally a ground for declining security clearance in certain jobs in the Public Service in 1989, three years after the passage of the Homosexual Law Reform Act. What then became unacceptable was 'heterosexual or homosexual behaviour, such as deviant or promiscuous behaviour, which may provide susceptibility to blackmail or exploitation or indicate personality instability'.

loss of unsympathetic colleagues, the loss of his job and a jail sentence – all this haunted Pearson and drove him underground'. He attempted to write a novel about a homosexual schoolteacher on the West Coast, based on his own experience in Blackball in 1942, then turned it into a story with a heterosexual protagonist because he feared that his original plot would disclose his own sexuality. The book that resulted, *Coal Flat*, eventually published in 1963, has thus been described as 'a gay novel in straight drag'. It was not until 1986 that Fran Wilde's Homosexual Law Reform Act decriminalised homosexual acts and lifted the burden of secrecy and anxiety which had blighted the lives of so many gifted men – and, no doubt, of many who were less gifted than ordinary.

Other New Zealanders declined to be covered and protected by the blanket of conformity. The pre-1930s writers, such as Alan Mulgan in his 1927 book *Home: a New Zealander's Adventure*, had on the whole accepted that New Zealand's place in the world was defined and determined by its historical and colonial relationship with Britain. In the 1930s, however, dissenting voices subversive of that consensus began to be heard more often.

One was that of the scholar Ian Milner, whose father, Frank Milner, Rector of Waitaki Boys' High School, was one of the most John Bull-ish characters in the country. '[We] stand on the threshold of a new order,' wrote the younger Milner in the Canterbury College *Review* in 1932, 'looking about [us] for suitable weapons in case the door has to be broken down. You will find this new spirit informing the work of our best younger poets …' And so it was. The best of them were R. A. K. Mason, Allen Curnow, Denis Glover, Charles Brasch, A. R. D. Fairburn and Robin Hyde. They were joined in this stance by the fiction writers Frank Sargeson, Roderick Finlayson and (again) Robin Hyde, and the essayist Monte Holcroft. Part of their fundamental viewpoint was signalled in Glover's 1936 poem 'Home Thoughts':

> I do not dream of Sussex downs
> or quaint old England's quaint old towns –
> I think of what may yet be seen
> in Johnsonville and Geraldine

These writers, who came to be known as 'cultural nationalists' or, to distinguish them from the aspirations of Maori, 'settler nationalists', stood in silhouette against the colonialist themes and preoccupations of the generation that preceded them, and against the Georgian ornateness of the writing of their predecessors (for example, Eileen Duggan, Alan Mulgan and Hubert Church). In Erik Olssen's judgment, they 'rejected the view that they should celebrate natural beauty ... and instead chose to explore the human predicament ... [Their] dominant tone was caustic.' The new breed of writers were seeking in their own genres what Allen Curnow called 'an uncompromising fidelity to experience'. They were pursuing a 'New Zealand-centred truth' based on the notion that 'we [are] a nation with a history and a will of our own'.*

In the words of one cultural historian, this movement should be seen as part of the 'task of staging settler cultural legitimacy ... [Their] narrative of settlement emerges as the battle of humans against the elements, unmediated by any significant prior occupation. The history of struggle between Maori and Pakeha [was] displaced by the myth of Pakeha struggle with the land ...' It is perhaps not surprising that the 'headquarters' of cultural nationalism should have been Christchurch, where the

---

* Painters too – Colin McCahon, Rita Angus, Christopher Perkins, Lois White – were undertaking a comparable rejection of romanticism: 'clarity and harshness now dominated the genre'.

absence of Maori and the 'vast open spaces' combined to offer an opportunity for a different kind of European acclimatisation than might have occurred in the North Island.

More immediately influential, however, Christchurch was the home of the left-wing journal *Tomorrow* (1934–40), edited by Kennaway Henderson, and of the Caxton Press, founded and funded by poet and printer Denis Glover. *Tomorrow* and Caxton published all the writers who would come to be seen as making up the cultural nationalists' school. Caxton in particular was publishing the best of New Zealand poetry, fiction and essays from the mid-1930s until well into the 1950s. Its influence was detected and admired beyond New Zealand. The London editor John Lehmann referred to it as 'a focus of creative activity in literature of more than local significance'. It brought together 'a group of young writers ... who were eager to assimilate the pioneer developments in style and technique that were being made in England and America ... to explore the world of the dispossessed and under-privileged for their material and to give their country a new conscience and spiritual perspective ...'

Uppermost in Lehmann's mind when he wrote this was Frank Sargeson, a North Islander but also one of *Tomorrow*'s regular contributors and Caxton's 'star' authors, whom Lehmann himself would publish in London. And Sargeson was in many ways typical of the Caxton stable. He had been born in 1903 in Hamilton into a middle-class Methodist family. His father would go on to become the town's longest-serving town clerk. Sargeson, chafed by what he regarded as his parents' bourgeois values, left home in the mid-1920s and, after qualifying as a solicitor in Auckland, spent a year in England and Europe.

When he left Auckland in 1927, he said, he felt like a European in New Zealand; he left London a year later feeling like a New Zealander in Europe. An intensive spell of reading and study at the British Museum in Bloomsbury had served only to remind him of 'the intolerable weight of so much civilisation ... I knew that I was only indirectly part of it all ... [For] better or worse, and for life, I belonged to the new world.' So he returned to New Zealand where, after a short spell in the Public Trust Office in Wellington, followed by nearly two years on his uncle's King Country farm, he became a full-time writer at a time when possibly only one other person, Monte Holcroft, was making the same attempt. From 1931 until his death in 1982, Sargeson lived a monastic life in a bach at Takapuna, writing in the mornings and tending his garden and entertaining friends in the latter part of the day. He became the first person in New Zealand since Edith Lyttleton to try in a sustained way (Holcroft had retreated to journalism) to earn a living primarily from writing fiction.

And he succeeded. His earliest stories were published in *Tomorrow* and later in a Caxton collection, *A Man and His Wife*. His full oeuvre would eventually total 20 books of stories, novels, plays and autobiography. He became the first New Zealand writer other than Katherine Mansfield and G. B. Lancaster to be published widely outside New Zealand. And he did what those earlier writers had not attempted to do: introduce the New Zealand vernacular to world literature in English. Equally important, he became an active mentor to the two generations of fiction writers who followed him: A. P. Gaskell, Greville Texidor, Maurice Duggan, John Reece Cole, David Ballantyne, C. K. Stead, Kevin Ireland, Maurice Gee and Janet Frame.

Frame, who would eventually – like Duggan and Ireland – live in Sargeson's backyard army hut when she emerged from psychiatric hospitals in the mid-1950s, spoke of her surprise and delight at discovering New Zealand writing in three seminal books published by Caxton in the mid-1940s. One was *A Book of*

New Zealand Verse 1923–45, edited by Allen Curnow, the second was *Beyond the Palisade*, the first volume of poems by the precocious eighteen-year-old Dunedin writer James K. Baxter, and the third was *Speaking for Ourselves*, a collection of stories edited by Sargeson. 'It was almost a feeling', Frame wrote, 'of having been an orphan who discovers that her parents are alive and living in the most desirable house ...'

Hundreds of other New Zealanders had a comparable experience as they discovered the work of Caxton authors in beautifully designed and cleanly printed books in the 1930s and 1940s; and, later, in the work of these and other writers published by Blackwood and Janet Paul and the Pegasus Press in the 1950s and 1960s. It would be true to say, however, that the writing of the cultural nationalists did not begin to make an impact on New Zealand at large until teachers and academics began to feature it in secondary and tertiary curricula in the 1960s. From that time such work became one of a number of influences that made it more likely that subsequent generations of New Zealanders would have a 'New Zealand-centred' view of the world in place of that which had preceded it – which was characterised by Curnow as being, for Pakeha, redolent of the 'great gloom [that] stands in a land of settlers with never a soul at home'.

For less exquisitely sensitive people than writers, of course, there were ample ways of keeping gloom at bay – and, indeed, of abolishing introspection altogether. New Zealand men were still avid followers of rugby football and horse racing: 'That we may worship in the liturgical drone of the race-commentator and the radio raconteur', Michael Joseph prayed in his poem 'Secular Litany', 'Saint Allblack, Saint Monday Raceday ... Pray for us.' And many more of them, men and women, were still regular church-goers.

Just how *high* church attendances were during this period is difficult to calculate. Anglicans were still by far the largest Christian denomination, reflecting the fact that they were both the first group to evangelise in New Zealand and the majority of immigrants. In 1936 they had 625,618 nominal adherents, almost 40 per cent of the total population of more than 1.5 million. Of these, the church itself calculated that around 45,500 were active participants. Presbyterians made up 23.44 per cent, a continuing reflection of the substantial minority of Scottish immigrants; Catholics 13.13 per cent, a position they had held steadily for six decades and would continue to hold for the next six; Methodists 8.05 per cent; and Baptists 1.57 per cent. There is evidence that the larger Protestant denominations were experiencing a slow decline in attendances at this time, but Catholics and the smaller churches were not. Catholics were still obliged to send their children to Catholic schools, which meant that most of them were locked more tightly into a parish structure than non-Catholics.

Church historians Allan Davidson and Peter Lineham note that the major denominations had by this time 'settled into a particular role in New Zealand society, accepted and even respected by most people ... [Most] New Zealanders were in some senses adherents of the Christian faith.' Oliver Duff, who cheerfully described himself as 'heathen', reinforces this view in one of the country's centennial publications in 1940:

We still go to church to get married. We go to get buried. We have our children christened. We swear by God and the Bible. We turn back to religion in sorrow and in trouble ... [Religion goes on] building churches and schools and hospitals and orphanages, maintaining through all its lapses and failures the dignity of man, preaching (and generally practising) charity ... although the pace [has] slackened, there [is] no indication at all that the impulse [is] coming to an end.

One factor which may have affected church attendance but did not signify a decline in conviction was the growing popularity of radio in the 1930s – and church services had quickly become an established feature of broadcast programmes. 'A number of churchmen held regular services "on the air",' Davidson and Lineham reported, 'most notably "Uncle Scrim", C. G. Scrimgeour, who with "Uncle Tom" Garland formed a "radio church", the Church of the Friendly Road and drew very large listening audiences.' Another popular sermoniser on Sunday morning programmes was the Revd Harry Squires, Wellington City Missioner from 1939. To the modern ear, much of this radio evangelising sounds shallow and trite. But it was effective in its day. Listen to 'Uncle Scrim', for example:

> No one knows more than I that we all strike trouble along life's road. No one appreciates more than I that it is easy to give advice, but really we meet so many along the road who need encouragement ... and practical sympathy, that I never tire of entreating travellers of the Friendly Road to keep their eyes open for those less fortunate travellers who need just that little act of kindness, that kind word of cheer, which puts new heart into those who find the road heavy going ... Look up! It is when the lights of earth are dimmest that we can see the most stars.

Scrimgeour was, in fact, far shrewder and more worldly than these sentiments suggest. He became Controller-General of Commercial Radio in 1936, fell foul of the Labour Government with his forays into political and social comment, and proved himself to be anything but reverent and avuncular when he stood unsuccessfully against Prime Minister Peter Fraser in the 1943 general election, the same year he was dismissed from his broadcasting post.

Scrimgeour had done early 'home mission' work among the

Maori and, as he himself observed more than once, religion and spirituality permeated Maori life more intimately than it did the life of non-Maori, even though their formal church attendance may have been lower. Services were held frequently in the course of hui and tangihanga, Maori committee meetings customarily opened and closed with prayers, and the very status of training for the ministry or receiving ordination tended to confer kaumatua rank in the Maori world.

As with non-Maori, the Anglican Church had the strongest following throughout the first half of the twentieth century: over 30 per cent of declared Maori affiliations. The Ratana Church had increased its membership spectacularly through the 1920s to claim second place and a proportional peak of 20 per cent in 1936. In the 1940s it would drop back to third place behind Catholics, who remained steady on 13 to 14 per cent. The other major affiliations in order of size were Methodist, Latter-Day Saints (Mormon) and Ringatu.

Of the specifically Maori churches, Te Kooti's Ringatu was the strongest behind Ratana with around 6 per cent in the 1930s. Numbers for the smaller denominations – Pai Marire, Wairua Tapu and the followers of Te Whiti o Rongomai and Tohu Kakahi at Parihaka – fell away sharply between the 1930s and 1950s. Statistics for Maori religious adherence can be misleading, however. They do not show that many people belonged to a Christian denomination *and* a Maori church. Declared affiliation would usually depend on whether the circumstances were judged to be taha Maori or taha Pakeha, and the collection of census information was decidedly Pakeha.

If church organisation reflected the fundamental separation of Maori and Pakeha domains before World War II, rugby football did not. Apart from warfare, in fact, the one national activity to which Maori contributed was rugby. The first Maori to represent New Zealand overseas had gone on a tour of Britain and Australia in 1888–89 as the 'New Zealand Native Team' (they were not all Maori; New Zealand-born Pakeha also qualified as 'native' in this context). Other specifically Maori tours followed from 1910. Within New Zealand there were Maori clubs, internal Maori tours, a Maori Advisory Board of the New Zealand Rugby Football Union from 1922, and from 1928 the country was divided into four Maori districts to compete annually for a trophy donated by the Prince of Wales.

Maori were also welcomed into the country's national representative team, the All Blacks. Those who distinguished themselves, such as legendary fullback George Nepia of Ngati Kahungunu, acquired the status of national heroes in their playing days. In this sphere there was little reluctance to recognise or accept Maori talent – except in New Zealand tours of that other great rugby-playing nation, South Africa. On such occasions Maori players were stood down, the first time from a New Zealand Army team in 1919, the second from the All Black tour of 1928. These exclusions created some ill-feeling throughout the country, although not among Maori players themselves, if Maori rugby administrators are to be believed. Change, when it did come in the 1970s, was forced by the wider New Zealand community, not the New Zealand Rugby Union.

For New Zealand men as a whole, Maori and Pakeha, playing and following rugby was the great common denominator they could share as players and supporters and as a sure-fire topic for socially bonding conversation. In most New Zealand schools before the war it was the only male winter sport available, and in many of them participation was compulsory. And, as Jock Phillips has noted, rugby was, along with drinking in public bars, one of the twin pillars of New Zealand male culture. Interest in the game embraced people from every class and occupation, and from both town and country – 'urban professionals right through to farmers and working class ... it became a universal experience for nearly all New Zealand men'. Cricket too had a following, local and national, but nowhere near as large or as socially diverse as that enjoyed by rugby. Consequently New Zealand's international cricket performances were usually memorable only for the dimensions of the defeats.

Interest in horse racing, again largely but not exclusively among men, was almost as high, and outstanding horses – Carbine, Kindergarten, Desert Gold and Gloaming – acquired the status almost of rugby heroes. The greatest of them all, Phar Lap, was born in Timaru in 1927 but never raced in New Zealand. His great triumphs were in Australia and the United States, where he died unexpectedly in 1932. News of this catastrophe displaced accounts of the Depression riots in many local papers. New Zealanders had followed his fortunes like those of a favourite son. After his death, Phar Lap's heart and hide went to Australian museums and his skeleton to the Dominion Museum in Wellington.

Racing, however, with its ranks of owners, trainers, riders and club officials, was not as demotic as rugby. As Graeme Dunstall has said, 'the private bar and the Members Stand pointed to a continuing distinction between the respectable and the rough ...' Although support inevitably dropped during the Depression, broadcasts of race meetings on commercial stations eventually ensured a continuing wide following for racing and trotting, and almost every public bar in the country had 'bookies' operating illegally to take bets and reward those who backed winners (by the mid-1940s, bookmakers' turnover, untaxed, was estimated nationally at £24 million). Betting at race meetings was administered by local totalisators, which had been operating in New Zealand since the 1880s. Not until 1951 would the system be centralised through the national Totalisator Agency Board, known as the TAB, which became one of the institutions of New Zealand's recreational life.

The number and frequency of race meetings were drastically reduced with the outbreak of war in 1939. In many local communities the race courses themselves were taken over for military training. But there was no reduction in the popularity of the sport, nor in the number of horses kept in training. Eventually, after considerable public agitation, the New Zealand Racing Conference allowed meetings to be run again in the later years of the war with the excuse that such meetings were for the collection of 'patriotic funds'. The war would represent, none the less, an inescapable interruption in almost every feature of national and community life.

24

At War Again

Despite the carnage that had occurred on the battlefields of World War I, imperial feeling had remained strong throughout New Zealand, even if its expression would never again be as jingoistic as it had been in 1899 and 1914. When a crisis at Chanak threatened the Dardanelles in 1922, the New Zealand cabinet took three minutes to decide that the country would go to war again if necessary, and over 13,000 New Zealand men enlisted virtually overnight for service in another expeditionary force. No war eventuated on that occasion.

The election of the Savage Labour Government in 1935 did not indicate a change in direction, even though the cabinet wanted to put whatever weight it had behind the League of Nations. The Labour movement as a whole had long declared its doubts about the value of imperial policies and its dislike of war as an instrument of national politics, and, of course, four Labour ministers – Peter Fraser, Bob Semple, Paddy Webb and Tim Armstrong – had been imprisoned for sedition because of their opposition to conscription in the previous war. From the time of their elevation to government, however, Labour spokesmen, including Prime Minister Savage, had declared that Britain's interests were New Zealand's interests – in trade, economics, defence and culture. 'When Britain is in trouble, we are in trouble' was one of Savage's mantras (along with his trademark, 'Now then …').

The Government created a Council of Defence in 1937 and prepared a 'War Book' or dossier on the administrative changes required to put the country on an immediate war footing. When Germany invaded Poland on 1 September 1939 and New Zealand declared war on Germany on 3 September – this time, independently of Britain – the country was prepared politically, bureaucratically and in spirit, even if the armed forces had been allowed to run down badly in the previous decade. The attitude of most citizens was articulated in a quavering voice by the dying Savage in a radio broadcast on 5 September:

> With gratitude for the past and confidence in the future we range ourselves without fear beside Britain. Where she goes, we go; where she stands, we stand. We are only a small and a young nation, but we march with a union of hearts and souls to a common destiny.

This was no exaggeration. Only one political party opposed participation in the war. This was the tiny New Zealand Communist Party, which had just begun to publish its national newspaper, *People's Voice*, and was, according to one historian, 'faithful to the false promise' of the German-Soviet Non-Aggression Pact of August 1939. This source of opposition, and that expressed through the left-wing journal *Tomorrow*, largely collapsed after Germany invaded Russia in June 1941. There would also be a small number of conscientious objectors, around

800 of whom would be detained, most of them after the introduction of conscription for Pakeha males in June 1940. Some who spoke out against the war from the outset, however, such as Methodist minister Ormond Burton, were arrested in September 1939.

In addition to the calmer expressions of loyalty to Britain and the Empire than those heard in 1914, there was one other major difference in the Government's approach to the coming conflict. The cabinet was determined that New Zealand should retain its national identity in Allied policy-making, and insisted that its expeditionary force remain a discrete unit and not be dispersed throughout the British Army. A British officer with close New Zealand family associations, Major-General Bernard Freyberg, was appointed commander of the New Zealand Division and secured a charter that stressed that his primary responsibility was to the Government of New Zealand.

Voluntary enlistment for the war began on 12 September 1939, and the first echelon of 6600 troops sailed for training camps in Egypt in a convoy of six ships which left Wellington Harbour on 5 January 1940; the second left on 2 May. They included a smaller number of men who had enlisted for the Royal Navy and the Royal Air Force. Ormond Burton, decorated for bravery at the Western Front in World War I but now imprisoned in Mt Crawford gaol, watched them go with tears in his eyes.

> The great ships passed immediately below the prison garden. Some twenty-five years before I had been with the cheering transports that swung out from Mudros to the beaches of Gallipoli where the gallant companies were torn to bloody shreds by the bursting shrapnel and the hail of machine-gun fire.
>
> In my mind's eye I could see the battles that were to come and how the strong and exultant young men who crowded these decks

would be broken under the barrages. I found it very moving, as one always must when one senses the willingness of men to suffer and die for a cause that seems to them right. So, standing in the garden in my prison dress of field grey, I gave the general salute with my long-handled shovel – very reverently.

The naval and air force volunteers went on to England for training; the troops found themselves encamped close to where their fathers and uncles had trained in Egypt for World War I. Another generation experienced the discomforts of the desert, the delights of Shepheard's Hotel, the Muski, Groppi's and Shafto's, and had themselves photographed on camels with the Sphinx and the great pyramids of Giza in the background. The major camp was at El Maadi, eight miles south of Cairo, where the command headquarters became known as Bludgers' Hill. As subsequent transports arrived in Egypt, an *esprit de corps* built up that led Freyberg to believe that the division was ready for combat by March 1941, when a German invasion of Greece was imminent.

Meanwhile there had been a change of political leadership and direction of the war effort at home. Michael Joseph Savage had, after a prolonged illness, died of cancer on 27 March 1940. His body was returned to Auckland by train, with frequent stops en route for mourners to express their grief. He was buried at Bastion Point on 31 March after his cortège had driven along a route lined by 200,000 observers. Peter Fraser, his deputy and a strong Minister of Education and of Health, succeeded him. In this respect the country was singularly fortunate. While Fraser, a dour Scotsman, would never be loved as Savage had been, he was far more intelligent and shrewd, and a more able political operator (he had the ability to 'see round corners', his private secretary would say).

Fraser imposed firm controls on the wartime economy in an

effort to accomplish what he believed the administration during World War I had neglected to do – to conscript the country's wealth in addition to its manpower. In July 1940 he established a War Cabinet in which the Opposition was represented by its leader, Adam Hamilton, and former Prime Minister and World War I veteran Gordon Coates. The National Party changed leaders in November 1940 and Hamilton's successor, Sidney Holland, an abrasive small businessman and hobby farmer from Canterbury, demanded a coalition government. Fraser, who doubted his ability to work harmoniously with Holland, refused. Holland eventually joined the War Cabinet, responsible for the administration of the war effort but not domestic affairs, and the wider War Administration, of which the War Cabinet was the executive.

In fact, the politicians on whom Fraser relied most for support were his deputy and Finance Minister Walter Nash, who eventually went to Washington for sixteen months in 1942–43 as New Zealand's resident minister, to keep the Roosevelt administration aware of New Zealand's position and needs, and Coates, who, before he died suddenly in May 1943, was Minister of Armed Forces and War Administration in the War Cabinet. The nominal Minister of Defence, Fred Jones, worked at Fraser's close direction. Paraire Paikea of Northern Maori became Minister in Charge of Maori War Effort, and William Perry, a member of the Legislative Council and immediate past president of the Returned Services' Association, took Coates's portfolios after the latter's death. Another important figure, trade unionist Fintan Patrick Walsh, never sat in cabinet but ran the administration's Economic Stabilisation Committee. The key civil servants were Alister McIntosh and Treasury Secretary Bernard Ashwin. Over all these personnel and activities, however, Peter Fraser held a tight rein. He persuaded

Parliament to postpone the general election due in 1941. When it was eventually held, in 1943, Labour won comfortably, but only because domestic discontent at rationing and restrictions on such things as petrol and travel was outweighed by the overwhelming support of servicemen overseas.

In Greece, the New Zealand Division was in combat for the first time against German forces in April 1941 (they had previously been involved in limited actions against Italians in North Africa). This campaign represented a disastrous start to the country's overseas war effort. Misunderstanding the significance of an exchange of cables, the New Zealand Government believed that Freyberg had approved the viability of the operation when he had not, and Freyberg believed that the New Zealand Government had approved it, unaware that that approval was based on his own putative support. As it transpired, the Allied forces – eighteen Greek divisions and one each from Australia and New Zealand – were heavily outnumbered by 27 German divisions, and by 800 German aircraft against the Allies' 80.

From the time fighting began in early April, New Zealand troops were on the back foot, though they fought strong rearguard actions at the Servia Pass and Mount Olympus, in mountainous conditions for which they had not been trained, and later across the Thessaly Plain to Thermopylae. The decision to evacuate was made on 21 April and accomplished by 1 May. New Zealand had lost 291 men killed and 1826 taken prisoner; a further 387 were seriously wounded.

Sadly, many New Zealand troops and officers moved directly from one defeat to another. Most of the Commonwealth and Greek evacuees from the Greek mainland were transported to Crete, which they believed to be an assembly point on their way back to Egypt. But by the beginning of May they learned that they were to play a major role in the defence of the island, which had considerable strategic value for both sides in the war. Allied forces would be under the command of General Freyberg. Numbering around 32,000 men, they were again under-equipped, and they were to fight alongside some 11,000 poorly trained Greek troops. There was no air support.

The German airborne invasion began on 20 May 1941 with an unopposed aerial bombardment followed by a mass release of parachutists and troops in gliders. The sight of this mass of men silently dropping out of the sky was almost hypnotically beautiful. Once stirred into action, however, Allied soldiers began to pick off the parachutists as they floated to earth. The German losses from this phase of the campaign were appallingly high. Sufficient soldiers were landed to secure some positions, however, and they directed the full force of their attack at the three airfields on Crete's northern coast, and at the harbour at Suda Bay. It was the loss to the Germans of one of these airfields, Maleme, in controversial circumstances in which senior New Zealand officers made ill-judged decisions, that allowed the invaders to land transport aircraft and more troops, and consequently gain a substantial foothold on the island.

After less than a week of fierce fighting, in which Captain Charles Upham won the first of his two Victoria Crosses, Freyberg decided that the battle was lost and began to make plans to evacuate as many troops as possible from beaches on the southern coast. New Zealand troops and their British, Australian and Greek counterparts then began an arduous and dangerous trek over the island's central range in an effort to reach the points of embarkation. Total Allied casualties amounted to 15,743 men. Of these, 671 New Zealanders were killed, 967 wounded and 2180 taken prisoner. This was a high cost for a country whose population allowed it to contribute, at this point, only one division to the entire war. And it would have been even higher had Peter Fraser not been in Cairo at the time and persuaded the Royal Navy to take off a further 3700 men.

Afterwards there were recriminations in plenty. The New Zealand Government came close to losing confidence in Freyberg, some of whose senior officers went behind his back to raise doubts about his competence. Senior British officers and British Prime Minister Winston Churchill continued to express confidence in him, however, and this swung the pendulum back in Freyberg's favour. With the passage of time, some historians have suggested that the task of defending Crete may have been beyond Freyberg's capacities, and that he appeared to lack the imagination to consider the implications of an airborne invasion (he continued to act as if he believed that the major German threat would come from the sea).

Of all the New Zealand battles in World War II, none engraved itself more deeply on the national consciousness than that for Crete. It was the Gallipoli of its era (and both campaigns, of course, were conceived and overseen by Churchill). As Glyn Harper has noted, 'there a scratch force made up largely of New Zealanders and Australians came tantalisingly close to inflicting Germany's first land defeat of the war. It was a tragedy and a serious defeat for the Allies but by only the narrowest of margins.' The links between New Zealanders and Cretans were further strengthened by the fact that some soldiers, such as Dudley Perkins, returned to the island to fight with partisans for the remainder of the war. Perkins, known as Vasili ('the Lion'), was eventually shot in a German ambush in February 1944. He was but one of hundreds of examples of mild-mannered civilians who discovered that, faced with wartime conditions, he was possessed of great courage and considerable military skills.

The New Zealand Division's lengthiest contribution to the

war was made in the North African campaigns from 1941 to 1943. This region was of vital strategic importance because of its proximity to the Suez Canal, the Middle East oil fields and the mid-Mediterranean base of Malta. The first engagements in which New Zealanders were involved came as part of the British Army attacks on Italian positions in Egypt and Libya in late 1940 and early 1941. The arrival of General Erwin Rommel and his armoured Afrika Korps greatly strengthened the Axis forces, and British Army units were driven as far back as Egypt by April 1941.

Back from Greece and Crete, New Zealand troops were in action against German and Italian forces in the North African desert from November 1941. The conditions were trying – hot and fly-ridden during the day and freezing at night, while wind-blown sand played havoc with machinery. Nevertheless the division forced its way westwards, helping push the Axis troops almost back to the Libyan border. There was a series of battles around Sidi Rezegh and Belhamed as an attempt was made to relieve Australians besieged at Tobruk. In one of these engagements, on 23 November, one New Zealand battalion lost over 100 men. There were further casualties and around 700 New Zealanders taken prisoner when Rommel overran 5th Brigade headquarters on 27 November. Two days later two New Zealand battalions were overrun by the Germans, as was a third on 30 November. By this time Rommel's supplies were depleted, however, and his forces withdrew to El Agheila, west of Tobruk. The New Zealand Division returned to its Egyptian base to recover. It had lost 4620 men in that series of battles. A further 80 drowned when the *Chakdina*, carrying wounded men away from Tobruk, was sunk on 5 December.

While New Zealanders were resting and training in Egypt and then Syria, Rommel's men had again attacked British forces and driven them back to the Egyptian border. Tobruk fell to the

Germans and Italians on 21 June 1942. New Zealand troops rejoined the battle and almost the entire division was cut off and surrounded by Axis troops at Minqar Qaim in late June. The solution was a desperate night-time breakout, which succeeded, but at the cost of almost 1000 casualties and the temporary loss of General Freyberg, wounded by a shell splinter. Early in July the division attempted to take Ruweisat Ridge, which dominated the El Alamein position. But this action ended in disaster with over 1400 New Zealanders killed, wounded or captured. One of the few pieces of eventual good news was that Charles Upham had become the only combatant to win a bar to his Victoria Cross.

The setbacks experienced by the Allies in mid-1942 resulted in changes in the British command, most notably in Lieutenant-General Bernard Montgomery's taking charge of the 8th Army. His professionalism and determination lifted the morale of Allied forces as a whole, and New Zealand troops were especially relieved when Freyberg returned to lead the division. Montgomery launched the crucial Battle of El Alamein on 23 October 1942, and by 4 November the Axis forces were in retreat, with New Zealand units among those in pursuit. By January 1943 New Zealand troops had reached Tripoli, and by March they were fighting the rearguard Axis positions in Tunisia. During one such action on 26 March Moana-nui-a-Kiwa Ngarimu of Ngati Porou earned a posthumous Victoria Cross at Tebaga Gap.

> He was killed on his feet defiantly facing the enemy with his tommy-gun at his hip. As he fell he came to rest almost on top of those of the enemy who had fallen, the number of whom testified to his outstanding courage and fortitude.

The following month, at Takrouna, Sergeant Haane Manahi came close to earning another VC for the 28th (Maori) Battalion when he led his men through intense fighting to retake a position that had been lost. The battalion as a whole won the admiration of other units in the New Zealand Division, other Allied troops and the Germans and Italians for the determination of their fighting in North Africa, especially in hand-to-hand combat. Brigadier Howard Kippenberger, most popular of the senior New Zealand officers and commander of the New Zealand forces at Takrouna, commented that Maori were 'splendid troops' but 'needed an iron hand' to keep them under control.

The fight for Takrouna was the last in which New Zealanders participated in North Africa. The Axis forces collapsed in May 1943 and 238,000 troops surrendered. The New Zealanders began the almost 3000 km journey back to their Egyptian base. Unbeknown to them, the Government back home had been debating in the latter part of the campaign whether or not to leave them in the Middle East. The situation back in the Pacific had changed, and there was now a fear that another Axis power – the Japanese – might threaten the mainland of New Zealand itself.

New Zealand's security in the Pacific had long been based on the twin propositions that the British Navy would sail to the region if the safety of New Zealand and Australia was threatened, and that the British naval base at Singapore was able to paralyse or deter any threats originating in Asia (and Admiral of the Fleet Lord Jellicoe had identified Japan as the most likely source of aggression as early as 1921). By June 1940, however, the New Zealand Government knew that this basis for security in its region was flimsy. The British Government, alarmed by German victories in France, told New Zealand that, if France did fall, Britain would be unable to deal simultaneously with the German, Italian and Japanese navies and would have to rely on the United States to safeguard its interests in the Far East.

The Singapore base was not completed until 1941 and almost immediately showed itself unable to meet the expectations invested in it. On 8 December 1941 the Japanese attacked the American naval base at Pearl Harbor in Hawai'i and simultaneously moved against other American and British territories in South-east Asia. The British naval commander at Singapore, Admiral Sir Tom Phillips, took the battleships *Prince of Wales* and *Repulse* north to try to intercept Japanese landings in northeast Malaya. Both vessels were sunk by shore-based bombers. The shock was complete when Singapore fell to the Japanese on 15 February 1942.

This series of disasters resulted in Walter Nash being sent to Washington as, in effect, the country's first ambassador there, to reinforce New Zealand representations already made to President Roosevelt and strengthen the likelihood that the United States would indeed guarantee the security of Pacific countries.* A debate was simultaneously ignited in New Zealand about whether the country's troops should be left in the Mediterranean theatre of war in pursuit of a 'Europe first' policy (it was regarded as axiomatic that there would be no future for New Zealand if Britain fell to the Axis powers), or brought home to defend New Zealand against Japanese invasion. Australia made an early decision to bring home two of its three divisions from the Middle East, and the third followed after the Battle of El Alamein. After debate in cabinet and in

---

* This move and the appointment of support staff to Washington in 1942 was the beginning of the country's diplomatic service. Prior to the war, New Zealand had representation only in London and Canberra; by war's end four new posts had been established along with a new Department of External Affairs headed by Alister McIntosh. Nothing could have signalled more strongly the Labour Government's determination to act independently of Britain in foreign affairs.

Parliament, which took into account the 'Europe first' arguments, shipping problems and dangers, and the fact that American troops were already in New Zealand in large numbers by June 1942, the Government decided to leave the New Zealand Division where it was and allow it to take part in the Italian campaign which followed the collapse of Rommel's army in 1943.

New Zealand troops were also despatched to the Pacific, however. A garrison was maintained at Fiji until relieved by American forces in June 1942. After the crucial battles of the Coral Sea (May 1942) and Midway (June 1942), in which the Americans turned back the Japanese naval advance, New Zealand reorganised its Pacific division as an amphibious unit to assist in American assaults on islands held by the Japanese. Its troops took part in mopping-up operations at Vella Lavella in the Solomons, losing 32 killed and 31 wounded. In October 1943 they invaded the Mono and Stirling Islands in the Treasury Group at a cost of 40 killed and 145 wounded. In February 1944 they captured Nissan and other islands to the north. Although the war had another year to run, the threat to New Zealand was clearly over and this division was disbanded.

New Zealand airmen had participated in the war with Japan earlier than soldiers and sailors, however. It was a Maori pilot, Sergeant B. S. Wipiti, who was credited with shooting down the first Japanese plane over Singapore. He was one of a squadron of Royal New Zealand Air Force pilots training there with the RAF. Others, more than 100, had already fought with distinction in the Battle of Britain in 1940 and were the largest group of Commonwealth pilots in that action. Another New Zealander, Keith Park, was in command of 11 Group, which bore the brunt of the Battle of Britain. New Zealand pilots were also part of Britain's Bomber Command and Coastal Command, and they fought with distinction over Europe, the Atlantic, North Africa and the Middle East. In the Pacific, they saw most action over the Solomon Islands. By war's end, more than 12,000 had served as pilots, gunners and mechanics, of whom 3285 had died and around 500 been taken prisoner.

The third service to recruit New Zealanders for combat was the Royal Navy (the Royal New Zealand Navy was not formed until 1941). From 1940, 7000 reservists (RNVR) went to Britain to serve subsequently on Arctic, Atlantic and Mediterranean convoy escorts, in the Fleet Air Arm, in submarines and in the Merchant Marine. New Zealanders largely manned the Royal Navy's light cruisers *Achilles* and *Leander*. *Achilles* first went into action spectacularly at the Battle of the River Plate on 13 December 1939, which led to the scuttling of the German pocket battleship *Admiral Graf Spee* off Montevideo, Uruguay. *Leander* was first assigned convoy duties in the Pacific and then sent to join the Red Sea force in 1940. Minesweeping activities off the New Zealand coast were stepped up after several local ships were sunk from 1940. In November of that year the German raider *Komet* intercepted and sank the passenger steamship *Holmwood* off the Chatham Islands. The 29 passengers and crew were eventually landed at Emirau Island in the Bismarck Archipelago.

New Zealand-manned cruisers came back to the Pacific for the war with Japan. *Achilles* was badly damaged by bombs in a raid that killed 13 of its crew, and *Leander* lost 28 men when torpedoed off Kolombangara Island in July 1943. *Achilles* returned to action for attacks on Japanese bases and patrols off the Japanese mainland shortly before and after the end of the war. Other members of what was by this time the Royal New Zealand Navy served in corvettes off the Solomons and manned minesweepers and Fairmile launches in other parts of the Pacific.

From November 1943 the New Zealand Division in the Mediterranean became part of the British 8th Army's push to clear German forces out of Italy. The war was not yet over, but German defeats in North Africa and Russia were clear indications that the tide had turned and an Allied victory in Europe was ultimately assured. The very month that the New Zealanders began their northerly advance up the long leg of Italy from Bari to Trieste, Churchill, Stalin and Roosevelt were meeting in Tehran to plan the shape of the post-war world.

There were still battles to be fought and lives to be lost, however. In November and December 1943, New Zealand forces bogged down at the Sangro River were trying unsuccessfully to break through the Germans' Gustav Line. Early in February 1944, as part of the newly formed New Zealand Corps, they were thrown into costly action at Cassino, near the southern end of the Gustav Line. It took almost three months of fighting and a high rate of casualties to reduce the town to rubble by 18 May, when the Germans at last pulled out.

From that time, the war for New Zealand troops was a matter of pursuing German forces as they withdrew. Spirited fighting occurred north of Rome and just south of the River Arno. Then the front moved across the Apennines, from Rimini to Ravenna and on to Bologna. In the north-east, the New Zealanders had to adapt to a very different style of warfare to that which they had become accustomed to in North Africa: bridge building and river crossing, fighting through canals and ditches, house-to-house engagements. They were held back for some months south of Bologna, which other forces entered in April 1945. They moved across the River Po, and from there on to Padua and Venice, both of which turned out to be in the hands of Italian partisans. They then began a race for Trieste in an unsuccessful attempt to prevent Tito's communist partisans from incorporating the province of Venezia Giulia into the new Yugoslavia.

In late April and early May 1945, while the New Zealanders were eyeballing Tito's men, Prime Minister Peter Fraser was impressing delegates at the first meeting of the United Nations Organisation (UN) in San Francisco. Fraser had an ambitious, global vision for the post-war world and New Zealand's place in it. He had already opened new diplomatic posts in Washington and Ottawa, and another would soon follow in Moscow. He had concluded an agreement with the Australian Government – the so-called Canberra Pact of January 1944 – in which both countries undertook to consult on international matters, particularly those affecting Pacific countries, to be involved in decisions regarding the disposal of 'enemy' territories, to advance a trusteeship system for colonial dependencies and to set up a 'South Seas Regional Commission' to promote further economic and social development in the Pacific (this last led to the foundation in 1947 of the South Pacific Commission).

Fraser and the Australian Prime Minister, John Curtin, had not established a rapport – Curtin considered the New Zealander too impractically idealist, and was still smarting from the fact that his neighbour had failed to bring home its division from the Middle East when Australia took that step. But Fraser formed an especially close and mutually respectful relationship with the Australian Minister of External Affairs, the robust and sometimes uncouth former High Court judge, Herbert Evatt. This relationship bore fruit at San Francisco, when both men pressed for mechanisms to protect small nations from aggression and opposed – unsuccessfully – granting veto powers to members of the Security Council. Fraser also chaired the committee which set up the Trusteeship Council and engineered the placement of Western Samoa within this system as a first step on the road to political independence.

On the international stage, at this and other UN meetings and conferences of Commonwealth prime ministers, Fraser cut a far more resolute and charismatic figure than he appeared at home, where he was often preoccupied by the trivia of political administration. Leaders of other countries, including Churchill, admired his sagacity and his firm stands on matters of principle. And the value he placed on the United Nations as an international arbiter and potential protector of small and weak countries set a precedent that New Zealand Labour governments in particular would follow and indeed emphasise in the later years of the twentieth century.

Germany surrendered on 8 May 1945, V-E Day, and New Zealanders in towns and cities awoke on the morning of 9 May to the sounds of whistles, hooters and car horns. Scenes that followed in the course of the day were unusual in a country that did not normally favour public displays of emotion. '[Trams] were packed with people and everybody travelled free,' one Wellingtonian recalled. 'People met at various points in the city and danced and sang and there was ... general hilarity everywhere.' The impulse was the same in rural areas. Congregations gathered at isolated churches to give thanks; even larger crowds gathered at country hotels.

For most New Zealanders, the war in Europe was *the* war. Germany had had to be defeated and Britain secured before civilisation – and New Zealand's principal market for exports and major source of imports – could be considered safe. In all, 194,000 men and 10,000 women had served in the country's armed forces, 140,000 of them abroad. And most had been involved in 'Hitler's war'. More than 11,500 had been killed, the highest casualty rate per head of population in the Commonwealth.

By the time of the German collapse, the Japanese too were in retreat, fighting their way back to their fortress of islands. When the end came there too, in atomic explosions at Hiroshima and Nagasaki in August 1945, it was sooner than expected – but expected none the less. V-J Day on 15 August inspired scenes of jubilation, but none so joyously uncontrolled as those which had marked V-E Day. A sense of climax, however, was followed by anti-climax. The only immediate change that the close of hostilities brought was the end of casualty lists. Many of the conditions of war persisted. Petrol, meat, butter, sugar and tea continued to be rationed. Men and women overseas could not be brought home at once; some had to wait until 1946 before they could be reunited with their families. When those reunions took place, they were often among tired men and women, spiritually and physically spent after six years of deprivation and sacrifice.

The sense of anti-climax included, for some, feelings of downright disappointment. Only in times of crisis are men and women inclined to extend themselves to exceptional limits; only when challenged in extraordinary ways does the human spirit soar. Troops in combat enjoyed physical fitness and a sense of comradeship for possibly the first and the only times in their lives. And they witnessed or shared in acts of heroism. It was strange, the writer John Mulgan noted, that war which accustomed men to death also brought with it 'so full and rich a sense of life'. For thousands of men and some women, it had been the one great epic in their lives, the time when they felt most conscious of being alive and of having a worthy role to play. The return to the mundaneness and petty squabblings of civilian and domestic life was often accompanied by disenchantment.

This war would also be New Zealand's last great common denominator, the last intense experience that tens of thousands of people would share, and one whose rationale was accepted by the country as a whole. For the time being, it strengthened the convictions that made New Zealand life and cultures coherent and harmonious. In the coming decades, however, the certainties would erode and the harmonies be interrupted by static. The settled society New Zealand had become in the century from the 1840s to the 1940s would now be subject to unsettlement.

Unsettlement

25

Cracks in the Plinth

The immediate effect of World War II and its aftermath was to turn New Zealanders in on themselves – as individuals and as families – and to confirm some of the most profoundly imprinted social patterns of the pre-war years. Joseph Adelson's analysis of North America in the 1940s and 1950s rings true also for New Zealand.

> We sought, all of us, men and women alike, to replenish ourselves in goods and spirit, to undo, by an exercise of collective will, the psychic disruptions of the immediate past. We would achieve the serenity that had eluded the lives of our parents; the men would be secure in stable careers, the women in comfortable homes, and together they would raise perfect children ... [It was] the idyll of suburban domesticity, which would redress the grievances of the past and ensure a perfect future.

The sheer magnitude and force of these domestic ambitions produced national trends. One was the rapid development of city suburbs and suburban culture, concentrated on the nuclear family and on house and garden. The nation bred at an unprecedented velocity. From 16 births per 1000 population in 1935–36, the rate rose to over 26 per 1000 by the late 1940s and this was maintained until 1961 – the so-called 'baby boom' that would necessitate a massive expansion in the number of schools and teachers through the 1950s and 1960s. Another trend was the growth in philosophical and political conservatism, leading to disenchantment with the tired, elderly leadership of the Labour Government. This brought National to power in 1949 and kept the party in office for 29 of the next 35 years. At the same time there was an American-led build-up of the Cold War mentality and a minor outbreak in the 1950s of something resembling McCarthyism. There was also the growth of a more overt form of materialism than had been apparent previously, centring on a desire for better homes and more consumer goods: washing machines, refrigerators, family cars, fashionable clothing – the phenomena that came to be known collectively as 'keeping up with the Joneses'.

Belief in the appropriateness of the values underlying such things was reinforced by a series of events which some saw as portents confirming New Zealand's position in the world as unusually blessed. There was Edmund Hillary's triumphant conquest of Mount Everest in 1953, for example, as a member of a British expedition, followed immediately by the coronation of a young monarch – the newspapers spoke of the promise for the whole Commonwealth of a 'new Elizabethan age' – and a visit from that Queen and her consort to New Zealand in 1953–54, the first time a reigning monarch had set foot on New Zealand soil. Other events cited for their oracular value included the appearance of Opo the dolphin in the Hokianga in 1956 and her playful interaction with humankind (some local Maori identified the dolphin as the spirit of Kupe, as presaged in the full name of the harbour, Te Hokianganui-a-Kupe, the great returning-place of Kupe); and the three to one defeat of the Springboks in the All Blacks' test series at home the same year.*

In the 1940s, many features of pre-war life seemed to have survived reassuringly intact. Most New Zealanders still spoke of Britain as 'Home' and saw nothing wrong with superannuated British aristocrats or military men being sent here to represent the King of New Zealand in New Zealand. They certainly saw nothing odd in having the country's head of state live 20,000 km away in London. On New Year's Day 1946, the outgoing Governor-General, Sir Cyril Newall, a much-decorated former Marshal of the Royal Air Force, reminded young New Zealanders that they were 'heirs to a partnership in an Empire whose contribution to the welfare of mankind was second to none'. Sir Cyril was replaced by Sir Bernard Freyberg, who did at least have a New Zealand connection though he was British-born, like all of his predecessors.** In that same year New Zealand still possessed a Department of 'Native' Affairs, whose function was to assist the country's first indigenous people and, by organising the development, lease and sale of their land, contribute to what almost all New Zealanders believed were the 'best race relations in the world'.

Yet cracks were already appearing in the foundation of

---

* It could be said, of course, that the Ballantyne's department-store fire in Christchurch in 1947, which killed 41 people, and the Tangiwai rail disaster on Christmas Eve 1953, in which 151 people died, represented portents of another kind.

** The country was not to have a New Zealand-born Governor-General until Sir Arthur Porritt in 1967. His successors too were New Zealanders, and – unlike Porritt, who was the Queen's physician – had spent their working lives in New Zealand.

national unity and coherence. The Fraser Government, narrowly re-elected in 1946, was already discussing with its civil servants ways in which the country's defence arrangements could be transferred from the waning world power that was Britain to a United States that was by this time showing serious interest in its potential responsibilities as a nation with a Pacific seaboard. British politicians were by the late 1940s beginning to give serious thought to ways in which Continental-wide security could be guaranteed, to prevent yet another round of blood-drenched wars on European soil. This consideration would lead in the 1950s and 1960s to specific proposals for a European Economic Community that would have no reason to retain Britain's historical and sentimental links to its Commonwealth primary producers. And Maori, who had lived predominantly in rural communities for the whole period of their interaction with Pakeha, had begun during the war to move into towns and cities, a trickle that would become a torrent in the 1950s and 1960s. This demographic change would alter the ethnic composition of New Zealand urban communities and eventually require a rewriting of the social contract between the two peoples.

Perhaps most dramatic of all, in the 1960s television and cheap jet travel would open New Zealand to the world and the world to New Zealand. All kinds of domestic cultural features – from cuisine to clothes to literature – would change as a result of new global influences and of New Zealanders being able to travel widely and return home. And the development of the contraceptive pill would revolutionise the nature of personal and sexual relations.

One of the small seeds that eventually helped to develop social and cultural change was a direct consequence of the war and the upheavals in Europe that preceded and accompanied it:

the displacement and dispersal of talented people – 'like a ripened crop from a vigorously shaken tree'. New Zealand was fortunate to benefit from this diaspora of talent, particularly in the case of Jewish refugees from Hitler's Europe, who were admitted only in their hundreds but, as one of them said, 'punched well above their weight'.

Perhaps the best known was the Viennese philosopher Karl Popper, who left Austria in 1937, one year ahead of the disastrous Anschluss with Germany, to take up a position as lecturer in philosophy at Canterbury University College. '[New Zealand] is not quite the moon, but after the moon it is the farthest place in the world', he wrote, voicing the reason some refugees chose to travel so far – in the case of Jews, to the very edge of their diaspora. At Canterbury, according to the university's official history, 'Popper's impact on academic life was greater than that of any person before or since.' Between 1938 and 1943, Popper also wrote what may well be the most influential book ever to come out of New Zealand: *The Open Society and Its Enemies*, a classic definition, through a study of Plato, Hegel and Marx, of the values that underlie non-totalitarian societies. For all the praise heaped on him subsequently, Popper was given no strong encouragement to remain in New Zealand and in 1945 accepted a post at the London School of Economics.

Another intellectual leviathan who did stay, the German–Jewish scholar and poet Karl Wolfskehl, arrived in Auckland in 1938. A relative of Heinrich Heine and a cousin of Sigmund Freud's wife Martha Bernays, Wolfskehl had abandoned Germany the day after the Reichstag fire in 1933 and lived in Italy for five years before burgeoning anti-Semitism there drove him on to New Zealand as the 'refuge [most] remote from the sickness of Europe'. Described as 'a walking encyclopaedia who could always supply a missing quotation or an apposite ... myth', he formed influential associations with such New Zealand writers as Frank Sargeson and A. R. D. Fairburn. According to Sargeson, Wolfskehl brought with him a whiff of the antiquity and high culture of Europe and 'could immediately be recognised as a figure from the previous century: dark clothes, cravat or great bow, a crop of hair, artist's wide-brimmed hat ...' He was progressively isolated by blindness and depression, however, and his late letters and poems are full of the gloom of exile. He died in Auckland in 1948 at the age of 79.

Younger refugees fared rather better. Margot Philips became an important painter, Maria Dronke a well-known actress and voice teacher, Peter Munz a leading historian, Harry Seresin a restaurateur and theatrical entrepreneur, Fred Turnovsky (manufacturer) and Denis Adam (insurance broker), patrons of the arts, and Paul Heller an expert on international aviation law. Beyond individual contributions to national life, however, these people introduced a wide circle of New Zealanders to European food and wine and manners, and strongly supported artistic activities such as theatre and chamber music. They were a major leavening agent in the culturally more diverse New Zealand society that began to open up after the war.

Among the non-Jewish refugees, Count Kazimierz Wodzicki arrived in the country in 1941 as consul-general for the Polish government-in-exile in London. After the war he stayed on to become New Zealand's first professional ecologist and do valuable work for Victoria University and the Department of Scientific and Industrial Research. He and his wife, Maria, were the major movers in the project which brought 700 refugee Polish children and around 100 adults to New Zealand in 1944.

While such talent flowed into New Zealand from Europe, however, much of the homegrown variety continued to leave the country, or not return after the war, in order to secure career advancement. This was sometimes because, as in the case of the pre-war anthropologists Raymond Firth and Reo Fortune, their subjects were not at that time taught in New Zealand universities. The loss of Peter Buck, the only Maori ethnologist of distinction, to the Bishop Museum in Honolulu and Yale University was an especial tragedy. Of this phenomenon, the American scholar Margaret Mead was to say: '[It] is New Zealand's role to send out its bright young men and women to help run the rest of the world. And they go, not hating the country of their birth but loving it. From this . . . base they make their mark on the world.'

Mead may have been exaggerating the degree of 'love'. But she was thinking of the likes of Katherine Mansfield, Buck and Fortune (to whom she was briefly married), all of whom wrote and spoke respectfully and affectionately of their homeland once they were no longer living there. Another expatriate, John Mulgan, who had gone to Oxford in the 30s and joined Oxford University Press (OUP) shortly before the war, expressed similar feelings when he encountered his fellow countrymen fighting Germans in the North African desert.

> They had confidence in themselves . . . knowing themselves as good as the best the world could bring against them, like a football team in a more deadly game, coherent, practical, successful. Everything that was good from that small remote country had gone into them – sunshine and strength, good sense, patience, the versatility of practical men.

Mulgan, to the intense regret of all who knew him, died by his own hand just before the war ended. But others of his generation, such as journalist Geoffrey Cox and writer and publisher Dan Davin (who took Mulgan's place at OUP and became a kind of unofficial high commissioner for New Zealand culture in

Britain) remained on that side of the world and enjoyed careers of distinction. They were followed by such scholars as Robert Burchfield, who became editor of the Oxford English Dictionary, and they interacted in Oxford with a so-called 'New Zealand mafia' already there, classicist Sir Ronald Syme, medievalist Norman Davis, publisher Kenneth Sisam and language scholar Jack Bennett.

Scientists too went abroad for further study – space engineer William Pickering, physiologist Maurice Wilkins, chemist Alan MacDiarmid, cardiologist John Williams, astrophysicist Beatrice Tinsley, and many others – and often found that the only way they could advance in their careers of teaching and research was by joining well-endowed universities or institutes in Britain or the United States. Psychologist John Money also moved to America in 1947 to do a doctorate and stayed on to become a world-renowned sexologist at Johns Hopkins University in Baltimore, a sucessor, some said, to Frend and Kinsey.

The dramatic expansion of New Zealand universities in the 1960s, and hence of university jobs, would help reduce the immediate post-war 'brain drain', though by that time relatively low academic salaries were creating other kinds of recruitment and retention problems. But opting for the enlarged platform of opportunities offered by countries with bigger populations and more substantial resources would always remain an attractive option to a proportion of New Zealand scholars. Writers and artists, on the other hand, tended, in the wake of Frank Sargeson's example, to remain in New Zealand, like poet James K. Baxter; or, as in the case of Charles Brasch or Janet Frame, to return to it after a period abroad. From the 1960s, when international travel was so much faster and cheaper, it became possible for writers and artists to have their so-called OE (overseas experience) but still be primarily based in New Zealand. Unlike in the first half of the century, the great New Zealand painters of the second half, Colin McCahon, Toss Woollaston, Ralph Hotere – who, like their writer counterparts, had dismissed romanticism – did their major work at home.

While local art and literature did not begin to flourish strongly until the 1970s, the post-war Labour Government, thanks largely to Peter Fraser's personal interest and his good relations with the head of the Department of Internal Affairs, Joseph Heenan, did make real progress in laying the foundations for national cultural institutions. The National Orchestra (later the New Zealand Symphony Orchestra) was established in 1946 with costs to be borne by the National Broadcasting Service (which would, in return, retain broadcasting rights). That same year the New Zealand Literary Fund was set up on the recommendation of historian J. C. Beaglehole and Heenan to provide subsidies for local writing and publishing. One of its earliest grants went to the quarterly literary journal *Landfall*, established and edited by Charles Brasch, scion of a family of wealthy Jewish merchants well known for their support of culture. For the rest of the twentieth century and beyond, *Landfall* would more than any other single organ promote New Zealand voices in literature and, at least for the duration of Brasch's editorship (1947–66), publish essays, fiction and poetry of the highest standard. Another precedent was set in 1947 when Frank Sargeson was given a literary pension drawn from Art Union lottery funds. A further sum was set aside in the Internal Affairs budget, at Fraser's instigation, for scholarships for New Zealand artists, actors and musicians to study abroad.

The major constitutional development of the post-war years went almost unnoticed at the time by the public at large. On

25 November 1947, the New Zealand Parliament finally ratified the Statute of Westminster, which gave the country complete autonomy in foreign as well as domestic affairs. In one sense this was no more than formal recognition of a position that had existed since World War I. But the measure had considerable symbolic value. New Zealand was no longer a colony, nor a 'dominion'. It was a fully independent member of the British Commonwealth. That it had taken so long to get the statute before the New Zealand Parliament (all the other dominions had ratified it earlier, most of them in 1931) indicated how reluctant New Zealanders were to take this step and how imperial feelings persisted into and through the years of World War II.

Between 1946 and 1949, Labour's electoral tide went out. The Government had become less interested in continuing social reform and more focused on trying to retain the ebbing support of the floating voter. Internal Affairs and Social Security Minister Bill Parry was speaking for many of his contemporaries in cabinet, the former Red Feds, when he told a meeting of civil servants in 1947: 'I don't understand you young blokes. Labour has achieved the programme it battled for, it *was* battling for before some of you were born ... Everything is done.'

National, by contrast, led by the brash Sidney Holland and his energetic farmer lieutenant Keith Holyoake, was hungry for power and an opportunity to bend the country's institutions in other directions. 'If you want to condense our policy,' Holland told an audience in 1948, 'it is the private ownership of production, distribution and exchange.' But Holland, like most New Zealand politicians, was pragmatic, not ideological. Although his party's programme would be aimed primarily at businessmen and farmers and their supporters, he had decided by 1949 to retain social security. Two previous election losses had brought him to the conclusion that the welfare state was an institution most New Zealanders wanted to retain.

Other policies that verged on being bipartisan, at least at the level of party leadership, related to defence and foreign affairs. As the 1949 election approached, Peter Fraser was determined to reintroduce conscription. He had become convinced that Russian intransigence in the United Nations and elsewhere would lead to futher global conflict, most likely centred on the Suez Canal and oil reserves in the Middle East, and he wanted New Zealand armed forces to be better prepared for combat than they had been in 1939. While the Prime Minister convinced his cabinet of this necessity, he failed to carry his caucus and the Labour Party at large. His compromise was to submit the conscription proposal to public referendum at the same time as the election. Conscription won, but Labour lost (it was, after all, a policy favoured by National too): 34 seats to 46. And National, after being out of office for fourteen years, would retain power for sufficiently lengthy periods in the coming decades to believe that it was, after all, the natural party of government.

One of the new Government's earliest measures was the appointment of a 'suicide squad' of new members specifically to vote the Legislative Council or upper house out of existence. This was a surprising move to come from a conservative Government, and many of Holland's cabinet and supporters assumed that it would lead to the creation of a more effective senate (indeed, a committee set up under the chairmanship of Education Minister and former law professor Ronald Algie proposed exactly that). But Holland and his successors were never convinced that there could be circumstances in which the will of an elected House of Representatives should be thwarted, and consequently the New Zealand Parliament has remained unicameral since 1950.

Crises of greater magnitude gained the Government's attention, however – one external, the other internal. Chinese communists had won their civil war in 1949 and created the People's Republic of China. That victory, coupled with the descent of an 'Iron Curtain' across Eastern Europe after World War II, gave credence to the myth and the fear of communist expansion. When, in 1950, the New Zealand Government was asked by the United States to support American-led United Nations intervention in the Korean civil war, it agreed to do so – the first of several actions the country was to take in the 1950s in the interests of 'containing' international communism.

A body of 1100 men, subsequently raised to 1550, sailed for Korea in December 1950 as 'Kayforce'. It was in effect an artillery regiment with all the services necessary to maintain it on a war footing. The New Zealanders went into action for the first time on 21 January 1951 south-east of Seoul and were involved in sporadic conflict until mid-1953. The Royal New Zealand Navy was also committed to the war, and its entire fleet of six frigates and 1350 of its men served in Korean waters. By the time of the ceasefire in July 1953, Kayforce had lost 38 men killed and 79 wounded and had one soldier taken prisoner. The navy lost two men killed and one wounded. This contribution won New Zealand credit in both the United Nations and the United States and earned the country a visit in 1953 from Richard Nixon, the American Vice-President.

Anxiety about communism also lay behind the Government's strategy for dealing with its second potential crisis, the waterfront dispute of 1951. National had come to office threatening to abolish compulsory unionism, though this was not favoured by employers. In particular, the new Government was worried about the power of the more militant unions, grouped in the Trade Union Congress in opposition to the more moderate

Federation of Labour. The federation faction was led by the deeply conservative and authoritarian Fintan Patrick Walsh, whom one historian has called 'the nearest thing [New Zealand had] to an American-style industrial gangster'; the congress was headed by Jock Barnes and Toby Hill of the Waterside Workers' Union.

The dispute itself began when shipowners refused to give watersiders a 15 per cent pay increase. Watersiders retaliated by banning overtime work, and the employers began to lay off wharfies who declined overtime. When the union refused arbitration, the Government activated the 1932 Public Safety and Conservation Act, which included a prohibition on publicising the waterside workers' case and penalties for those who paid or fed or otherwise assisted families disadvantaged by the strike. The armed forces were moved in to work the wharves and maintain the flow of exports to Britain. The striking union was deregistered and its funds seized. All this was done with the support of Walsh's Federation of Labour, but some other unions went out on strike in support of the wharfies. The dispute – called a 'strike' or 'lockout' depending on where sympathies lay – lasted 151 days.

The Labour Opposition handled the issue poorly in Parliament. Walter Nash, who had succeeded to the leadership on Peter Fraser's death in 1950 even though he was himself almost 70 years of age, made the mistake of saying that Labour was 'not for the waterside workers, and we are not against them …' And when the Opposition suggested that the Government lacked the support of 'the people' in its tough crackdown, Holland called their bluff and ordered a snap election. The electorate, worried about alleged communist domination of the militant unions and told that the election was about 'who governs, elected governments or trade unionists', returned National with an increased majory, 54 seats to 26.

Anxieties about communist expansion, especially in South-east Asia, also underlay the Government's decision in 1951 to join the ANZUS defence pact with the United States and Australia. In this agreement, each of the member countries undertook to come to the aid of the other two if they were threatened with aggression or invasion. In fact, of course, it represented the preparedness of the United States to defend New Zealand and Australia. It also implied – as did the Manila Pact or SEATO (South-East Asia Treaty Organisation) agreement – that Australia and New Zealand would support American military initiatives in the region.

This obligation would be called upon in 1965, when the Americans sought allies for their war in Vietnam. Before that, in 1956, New Zealand sent troops to Malaya as part of a Commonwealth brigade fighting communist insurgents there. The Special Air Service squadron – an elite commando-type paratroop group – was formed for this mission and patrolled dense Malayan jungle for two years. It had numerous engagements with guerrilla bands until it was replaced by a full infantry regiment, and it was retained as the New Zealand armed forces' ready-response elite unit. The Royal New Zealand Air Force also committed two squadrons and the navy volunteered a vessel at the Singapore naval base. By the end of the 'emergency' (as it was called) in 1960, the New Zealand Army had lost ten men killed and 21 wounded, and the air force five dead and two wounded.

Involvement in this campaign and participation in the treaty signings which preceded it indicated that, for the immediate future, New Zealand would regard South-east Asia as the frontline for its policy of 'forward defence'. The existence of ANZUS and SEATO, allied with the refusal of New Zealand to support Britain militarily in the Middle East over Egypt's seizure of the Suez Canal in 1956, also signalled that the United States, not Britain, would now be the country's major partner in bilateral defence arrangements.

One clear symptom of the extent to which the New Zealand Government had adopted the Cold War mentality of its American allies was the appearance of McCarthyism in Wellington over the same period as this phenomenon plagued the United States more publicly. It was to have damaging and in some cases catastrophic effects on the careers of some civil servants who were believed to be communists or just of left-wing political persuasions. The implication was that they could not hold such views and remain loyal to the Government and the country that employed them.

There had been hints of such attitudes in the twilight years of the Fraser Labour Government. The American Federal Bureau of Investigation had raised doubts about the allegiances of economist William Ball Sutch at the time he was secretary-general of the New Zealand mission to the United Nations. The accusation, passed on to the New Zealand Government and Department of External Affairs, was that Sutch had been conducting clandestine meetings with Russian delegates at the UN.

Over the same period, in the late 1940s, British security agencies became concerned about Desmond Patrick Costello, first secretary and then chargé d'affaires at the New Zealand legation in Moscow. Costello, a brilliant linguist, had attended Cambridge University in the early 1930s and there was suspicion that he had been recruited to spy for the Russians (as had, it later became apparent, his fellow Cambridge students Kim Philby, Guy Burgess, Donald Maclean and Anthony Blunt). Certainly Costello had joined the Communist Party while he was a student in England, and in 1940 he was dismissed from a lecturer's post because of his close association with a student convicted of a breach of the Official Secrets Act.

Paddy Costello, as he was known to his friends, found his way into the New Zealand Army during World War II and, together with the former Rhodes Scholars Dan Davin and Geoffrey Cox, onto the intelligence staff of General Bernard Freyberg, commander of the New Zealand forces. From there he was recruited by Alister McIntosh for the Moscow legation because of his fluency in Russian. In addition to his student activities, what appears to have aroused the suspicion of British security officials was the extraordinarily well-informed intelligence reports that Costello sent to Wellington on such matters as the development of the Soviet atomic bomb. It was believed that he would not have been able to glean such information ahead of other security and diplomatic missions unless he had an unusually close relationship with Soviet authorities.

Prime Minister Fraser and External Affairs Secretary McIntosh protected both Sutch and Costello from external demands that they be sacked. After National assumed office late in 1949, however, new Prime Minister Sidney Holland was more responsive to both British and American warnings about communist 'spies'. He forced Costello's 'resignation' in 1954 (with difficulty, because Costello was not of a mind to co-operate), and he and other National ministers prevented Sutch from becoming head of the Department of Industries and Commerce, until the Nash Labour Government came into office in 1957.

The accusations which raised a question mark over Sutch's loyalty to New Zealand were especially ironical in view of his deserved reputation as the country's leading economic and cultural nationalist. He was widely seen as being, along with long-time Treasury Secretary (1939–55) Bernard Ashwin and industrialists Sir James and J. C. Fletcher and Wolf Fisher, one of the twentieth-century 'nationbuilders' who set out to diversify the New Zealand economy and reduce its almost total dependence on pastoral products. Economist Brian Easton has written:

> Sutch saw the need to foster industry and employment within New Zealand, and to earn foreign exchange by exporting a diversity of goods and services to many countries, as well as conserving foreign exchange through import substitution. Production had to be of high quality, be well designed, and make full use of human resources. Thus he was a tireless advocate for the development of a national culture. People were at the core of his developmental vision: children were a key to the future, and women were entitled to equality both as a right and because they contributed to the broad social and economic development. Full employment, education and the welfare state provided human resources. He saw a role for the state, but it was a Fabian one, for he advocated decentralisation and was concerned with human rights.*

The loyalties of other New Zealand officials were challenged over the same period that Sutch was under the observation of the FBI in New York. Ian Milner, son of the ultra-imperialist Rector of Waitaki Boys' High School, Frank Milner, left the Australian Department of External Affairs under suspicion of having spied for the Russians. The strongest evidence for this suspicion emerged in 1954 in a 'confession' to Australian security

---

* New Zealand security officials, including those of the New Zealand Security Intelligence Service established in 1956, continued to have suspicions about Dr Sutch's loyalties. In September 1974, when Sutch was chairman of the Queen Elizabeth II Arts Council, he was observed holding clandestine meetings in Wellington with a staff member of the Russian Embassy. Police arrested and charged him under the Official Secrets Act with obtaining information that could be helpful to an enemy. In February 1975 a jury acquitted him of that charge, and he died in September that year.

officers by Vladimir Petrov, a defector from the Russian Embassy in Canberra. This accusation was seen at the time as adding weight to previous suspicions about Milner's loyalties, which had resulted in his being placed under surveillance by British and New Zealand security authorities in the 1930s and 1940s. Petrov also claimed that there was a spy in the New Zealand Prime Minister's Department, which immediately brought other officials under suspicion.

In New Zealand, Cecil Holmes, a communist working for the National Film Unit in Wellington, was dismissed in 1948 after accusations that he had promoted 'communist-inspired' agitation within the ranks of the Public Service Association. A court later found that the sacking was unlawful, because Holmes was only a probationer, but rather than seek reinstatement he left New Zealand for Australia. In the Holland era, an External Affairs employee who had worked with Costello at the Moscow legation, Douglas Lake, lost his job on suspicion of being a communist. This decision created some embarrassment for the Government, as Douglas Lake's brother, Harry, was a National Member of Parliament and, from 1960 to 1967, National's Minister of Finance.

Several other left-wingers, including two Wellington law graduates, were forced out of External Affairs on the ground that their political and ideological opinions allegedly cast doubt upon their loyalties and sense of discretion (one went on to become president of the Wellington District Law Society). On matters such as these, Prime Minister Holland was inclined to accept the recommendations of what McIntosh regarded as poorly researched and unduly paranoid police reports, including one which identified a group known as the Vegetable Club – which met in the office of a Wellington law firm to discuss politics and distribute vegetables at wholesale prices – as a probable communist cell on account of the left-wing views of many of its members.

One civil servant frequently came under suspicion during the McCarthyist period but survived none the less. Jack Lewin came to prominence as president of the Public Service Association and was involved in the Cecil Holmes case. Lewin too was a left-winger, and he was a pugnacious and sometimes discourteous advocate for union causes. But there is no public evidence that he was ever a communist. He retained his Public Service career in part because of the protection of ministers who admired him, such as Walter Nash, and in part because he was exceptionally able in his work. He completed a distinguished career as Government Statistician and, finally, head of the Department of Industries and Commerce.

Little hint of the Government's 'cloak and dagger' considerations or activities leaked out to the public at large, who at this time mostly valued conformity and predictability in the behaviour of fellow citizens.* Clothes of the day tended to be drab by previous and later standards, and short-back-and-sides haircuts were part of the national male uniform, while rugby, racing and beer did represent for most men the extent of recreational options. As Miles Fairburn has noted, creativity was largely recognised only in 'sport, war, growing grass [and] do-it-yourself hobbies and pastimes ...' Even rugby, which did generate passion, especially during the Springbok tour of New Zealand in 1956, was played unimaginatively – in 1959, thanks to 'the Boot', fullback Don Clarke, the All Blacks won a test against the British Lions by six penalties to five tries (tries at this time being worth only three points). There was little variety in food and,

---

* Indeed, the very existence of the Security Intelligence Service was treated as a state secret until Keith Holyoake returned to office as Prime Minister in 1960.

apart from a small number of Chinese restaurants in the main centres, nowhere to eat out other than hotels or 'greasies' – dining rooms that served fish and chips or steak and chips.

Home recreation of the time was limited largely to gardening, reading and radio. The 1950s was the last decade in which magazines – *New Zealand Woman's Weekly*, the orange-covered *Free Lance*, the pink-covered *Auckland Weekly News* – played a major role in the country's national life, along with radio. Housewives – and this was still the career destination of the vast majority of women – tuned into the 'soaps': *Dr Paul* and *Portia Faces Life* in the mornings, *Aunt Jenny's Sunlight Stories* in the afternoons. Children hurried home from school to hear the late-afternoon serials, *Superman* and *The Air Adventures of Biggles*. Whole families gathered around for the evening favourites: *Dad and Dave, Journey into Space, Take It from Here*. The personalities of radio – celebrities whose sole claim to recognition was that they performed well in that medium – became much-loved national figures: Aunt Daisy, Selwyn Toogood, Winston McCarthy. Each came to be known by his or her signature phrase.

The only apparent interruption to the even tenor of New Zealand life in the 1950s was the atmosphere of moral outrage and panic that surrounded hearings of the 'Special Committee on Moral Delinquency in Children and Adolescents' and the release of the committee's Mazengarb Report in 1954. The inquiry was launched as a result of police and newspaper allegations of adolescent sexual activity in Wellington's Hutt Valley. The Minister of Social Welfare, Mrs Hilda Ross, had no doubt about what was behind the depravity. 'Laxity, terrible laxity, has produced the scandal which is now before us,' she warned. 'If minds are fed with lustful images flowing from trashy magazines and unclean reading matter, then the nation [can] expect the degradation revealed in the police files.'

The report, named for the committee's chairman, lawyer Oswald Chettle Mazengarb, was sent to every home in the country that had a child on the family benefit. Its thrust was to confirm existing social and moral values. It laid the blame for loose sexual behaviour on the absence of working mothers from the home and on 'oversexed or morally degraded' young women, who allowed young men to have their way with them. The committee unanimously condemned the availability of contraceptives to adolescents (none of the girls involved in the incidents which sparked the inquiry had become pregnant) and asked Parliament to legislate for a ban, which it did. The committee also asked that girls who permitted males to be sexually intimate with them be charged with an offence, a recommendation the politicians did not take up. Figures printed in the report revealed that juvenile offending in 1954 was scarcely worse than at any other time in the previous two decades and, indeed, was better than it had been during the war years.

Apart from the temporary drop in overseas reserves which triggered the Labour Government's 'Black Budget' in 1958, and its highly unpopular reimposition of severe import controls, the 1950s was generally a prosperous decade – especially after the Korean War created a sales boom for New Zealand wool. Agriculture remained the country's dominant industry, though the manufacturing and forestry sectors were beginning to expand, particularly after David Henry opened the New Zealand Forest Products mill at Kinleith in 1952, and J. C. Fletcher the Tasman Pulp and Paper plant at Kawerau in 1955. City suburbs mushroomed, initially without vegetation or parks, which gave them a raw and impermanent feel and led to the detection of such social problems as 'juvenile delinquency', as defined in the alarming but rapidly forgotten Mazengarb Report, and to 'suburban neurosis', a term coined to describe the depression some young wives experienced as a result of isolation from adult company and purposeful activity. Politicians shared the desire of the nation as a whole to enjoy the good times and not rock the boat. When American rock and roll reached New Zealand via film and radio towards the end of the decade, it represented a minor revolt of youth against the comfortable and secure world of their parents. As a rebellion, it did not persist: *real* rebellion awaited the 1960s and 1970s.

26

Land under Pressure

Poet-politician of the 1890s, William Pember Reeves, was speaking for most of his Pakeha compatriots when he wrote:

> We stand where none before have stood
> And braving tempest, drought and flood,
> Fight Nature for a home.

In Reeves's view, Maori had been and still were irrelevant in the development of the land. That task was being undertaken by Pakeha settlers who were in combat with nature, and their ultimate mission was to turn as much of New Zealand as possible into an agricultural landscape, thus realising Julius Vogel's vision for New Zealand as the 'Britain of the South' in function and appearance. Those parts of the country that were not suitable for farming might, it was hoped, yield up other resources such as minerals and timber.

The consequence of this view was that, for more than a century, mature native forest was regarded both positively as a source of timber or firewood and negatively as an impediment to agriculture; coal and gold as mineral resources to be exploited as rapidly as possible; rivers and lakes, from the early twentieth century, as potential sources of hydro-electricity; and land as a surface to be covered as far as possible with grass, which was in turn to be converted into protein in the form of meat, butter or cheese, or into wool. No thought was given to the replacement of native trees *with* native trees, although from the 1920s the New Zealand Forest Service began to experiment with plantings of exotic trees, such as *Pinus radiata*, for future harvest, especially in areas such as the central North Island plateau where successive volcanic eruptions seemed to have rendered the land unsuitable for grass farming.

Not until the middle years of the twentieth century would serious questions be raised about whether the strategies New Zealanders had adopted to generate food, shelter, income and energy from their country made the best possible use of the land. Indeed, most would have agreed with the agricultural scientist and Director-General of Agriculture, A. H. Cockayne, who likened New Zealand's land area to 'a magic hat which, while still retaining its original size, allowed the conjurer to draw out a seemingly never ending stream of objects ...'*

Yet there had been a few – very few – cautionary and prophetic voices. In 1940 Herbert Guthrie-Smith, writing a preface for the third edition of his magnificent work of environmental history, *Tutira: The Story of a New Zealand Sheep Station*, posed

---

* One wonders whether A.H. Cockayne's father, the great botanist Leonard Cockayne, would have agreed. Cockayne senior wrote, with a very different emphasis: 'The innate patriotism which compels us to feel that our country stands high above all other lands, must also make us love its natural characteristics, so that ... of all the trees or shrubs or herbs which we cherish, none can ever rank so high as those which slowly took their shape on New Zealand soil ...'

questions that his fellow farmers might have found surprising. '[Am] I absolutely happy [about] my substitution of domestic breeds of animals for native lizards and birds; my substitution of one flora for another; my contribution towards more quickly melting New Zealand through erosion into the Pacific ... Have I then for sixty years desecrated God's earth and dubbed it improvement?' He did not answer these questions but left them dangling for the troubled consideration of his readers. They were in the nature of a final testament, for weeks after asking them he was dead.

In the late 1940s, the writer Frank Sargeson, visiting the King Country farm his uncle had broken in from bush more than 30 years earlier, found Oakley Sargeson full of doubts as to whether the life-long experience had been worth it. The grasses he had sown so carefully were being overrun with weeds. Land at the back of the property was being recolonised by bracken fern and scrub – and then by the 'second growth' trees which eventually sheltered the growth of larger ones. The fences on steep slopes were being wrecked by landslides. 'And from the high boundaries there were the long, long views across the waves of ridges ... with more bush removed, and more faces grassed, and more, many more scarrings from slips and slides ... [All], as my uncle remarked, challenging us to take note that the big question of grass-farming country of such character was still not answered let alone understood. Or even asked.'

Writer Helen Wilson, casting her mind back in 1955 over her life of more than 80 years, wrote that her country had been 'too desperately poor to deny the present for the benefit of the future' – meaning that thoughts of immediate gain rather than conservation for future and sustainable use had determined such decisions as the use the country made of its timber and over what period of time. Another forty years on, scientist Geoff Park would pose the key question more bluntly: 'what happens ecologically when humans decide to channel a whole eco-system's productive energy into themselves?' For that was precisely the decision that four or five generations of colonial nationbuilders in New Zealand had made.

The most crucial area in which this focus had been apparent was in the so-called 'grasslands revolution' – the process by which a combination of bush clearance, the introduction of vigorous strains of exotic grasses and mixed use of herbicides and fertilisers had resulted in the conversion of 51 per cent of the country's surface area into grasslands (and the percentage would have been even higher but for the alpine spine of the South Island). These measures, allied with the temperate climate which allowed farms to carry stock all year round, was the key to the high levels of meat, wool, butter and cheese production which gave New Zealand a standard of living 'ranked between the fifth and the third highest in the world' from the 1920s to the 1970s ('and this Arcadian state', the poet M. K. Joseph had observed, 'is built on butter fat').

All this had been achieved, however, in a country charac-terised by a paucity of fertile soils, instability and high rainfall. Initial prosperity had been based on the artificial fertility produced by burn-offs and the inherent but shallow 'virgin fertility' of the soil itself. Once these were worked out, most farms, especially those in hill country, remained fertile only through the application of ever-larger quantities of fertiliser. New Zealand had access to enormous quantities of inexpensive phosphate from 1919 as a result of its joint mandate (with Britain and Australia) over Nauru and nearby Ocean Island. Both islands were ruthlessly stripped of guano and rock phosphate, without any regard for the welfare of their inhabitants, to feed the farms of the mandate member countries. After World

War II, the aerial top-dressing industry enabled that fertiliser to be spread widely, cheaply and efficiently. New Zealand's annual application peaked in 1985 at more than 3 million tons, or 2 per cent of the world's total. At that point it began to fall away because the fourth Labour Government removed the subsidies that had encouraged such high usage.

The question which agricultural scientists had begun to ask by the 1970s was whether New Zealand farming was being pushed beyond its ecological limits. Part of this concern arose from the increasingly self-evident observation that grass was unable to hold land on hill-country farms and some river flats in the way that forests had, and that as a consequence, as Herbert Guthrie-Smith had noted, large quantities of New Zealand were being flushed away each year by erosion. Another source of alarm was the growing realisation of the continuing toxic effects on the food chain of such herbicides as DDT and 2,4,5-T mixed in with superphosphate top-dressing. The equation was further complicated by a calculation that New Zealand sheep and cattle produced as much organic waste as 150 million people, and by documentation of the deleterious effect that dairy effluent was having on rivers, lakes and estuaries.

The potentially negative effects of so-called 'scientific farming' were acknowledged in the authoritative 1990 book *Pastures: Their Ecology and Management*, edited by R. H. M. Langer, emeritus professor of plant science at Lincoln University. This warned about the environmental degradation caused by traditional farming methods and advocated a greater use of indigenous grasses and, wherever possible, preservation – or re-creation – of indigenous landscapes and trees. It even reassessed the value of gorse, a prime target of pesticides, pointing out the plant's ability to fix nitrogen and to act as a nursery for regenerating bush. While these considerations were being weighed, farmers were beginning to plant trees in significant quantities, especially such rapidly growing and high-return species as *Pinus radiata*, while others in drought-prone Hawke's Bay, Marlborough and Central Otago were beginning to replace animal farming with horticultural crops such as grapes and olives. The evolving effect was one of more careful and more thoughtful husbandry.

None of these changes in farming was occurring in isolation from the rest of the country, however. Traditional uses of land and water were coming under intensive scrutiny in the second half of the twentieth century as the result of a convergence of factors. None was more important than New Zealand's first national conservation campaign, which heightened awareness of the need for conservation of natural resources in general and turned the country away from its pioneer phase of simply 'quarrying' those resources into extinction. That campaign was the battle to save Lake Manapouri in the South Island, which grew out of a political decision made in the late 1950s.

Hugh Watt, Minister of Works and Electricity in the Nash Labour Government, was keen to establish more local industry and more hydro-electric power generation. He regarded the two great achievements of his term of office as signing off in 1958 the Tongariro power project, which would divert part of the headwaters of the Whanganui River through a tunnel and out into Lake Taupo via the Tongariro Power Station, and securing the following year an agreement with an Australian company, Consolidated Zinc Proprietary, to develop Lake Manapouri's hydro-electric potential to fuel an enormous aluminium smelter in the South Island. The latter agreement collapsed, however, when the company decided in 1960 that it could not after all afford to build the power station. That part of the project was taken over by the incoming National Government, which oversaw the construction of a massive power project that took water from the West Arm of Lake Manapouri, drove it vertically down through underground turbines and out a long tailrace tunnel into Deep Water Cove at Doubtful Sound – all this supposedly to provide cheap electricity for the Comalco aluminium smelter being built on Bluff Harbour.

In 1969, when the West Arm turbines went into operation, it was revealed that empowering legislation passed in 1960 allowed for the level of Lake Manapouri to be raised by up to eleven metres, to permit the generation of an additional 200 megawatts of electricity, and that, because of the connecting waterway, such an action would also raise the level of Lake Te Anau. Only at this point did scientists and recreational users of the lake start to make environmental impact assessments, and what came to light appalled them. Lifting the lake level to the maximum provided for in legislation would inundate 160 km of lake shoreline and drown 800 hectares of shoreline forest; it would cause almost continuous landslides on steep slopes around the lake from the combination of wave action and a rise in the ground water level; it would introduce tree trunks and branches into the lake which would become a hazard for boaties, fishermen and swimmers; it would drown all of Manapouri's beaches and 26 of its 35 islands. All these changes and the addition of rotting plant material would destroy the ecology of the lake, as that of Lake Monowai had been destroyed when it was raised for electricity generation by only two metres. Finally, it was estimated that the severe reduction in the flow of the Waiau River into Lake Manapouri would cause silting of the riverbed and flooding of adjacent farm lands.

The revelation of these likely consequences of raising the lake sent shock waves through the Te Anau district, through Otago and Southland, and eventually through the country as a whole. What scientists and lay people had difficulty coming to terms with was that the effect of millions of years of evolution which had shaped the lake's character and ecology could be wiped out so comprehensively for such a small gain in electric power. It seemed disproportionate. Further, the aesthetic despoliation was likely to reduce the district's income from tourism by as much as $10 million a year. And the lives and livelihood of farmers in the Waiau Valley would be under threat.

Concern about all these factors lay behind the Save Manapouri Campaign, launched in Invercargill in October 1969. Very soon a well-known farming advocate and community leader named Ron McLean was its leader, and he took to the road to establish branches – eventually a total of nineteen regional committees – all over the country. Perhaps the most extraordinary feature of the campaign was that, because it raised the fundamental question of how the nation should use its natural resources, it drew people from every possible political and ideological background: 'left-wingers' such as Sir Jack Harris and Dr Ian Prior, conservative former National supporters such as McLean, scientists such as Alan Mark, members of the Forest and Bird Protection Society, the country's longest-established conservation group. Farmers and Chamber of Commerce stalwarts found themselves rubbing shoulders with trade unionists and students.

The National Government of the day – and the Opposition, whose ranks still included Hugh Watt, who had been so proud of the project – were taken wholly by surprise. The then Minister of Works and Electricity, Percy Allen, blustered that any change in the project would require renegotiation of the contract with Comalco, and he was not sure whether the company would agree to that. The campaign was waged over the next three years through public meetings, newspaper advertisements and features, remits to the conferences of all political parties, and a substantial petition to Parliament asking the Government to decline to raise the lake.

The issue eventually became a party political one when Labour, over Hugh Watt's objections, undertook not to raise the lake if it won the 1972 election. The promise was honoured, and Hugh Watt became Prime Minister Norman Kirk's deputy and Minister of Works and Development (but not, this time, of Electricity). It transpired that the additional electricity sought by raising the lake was to boost the national grid and was not essential for Comalco's operation. The integrity of the lake was guaranteed, and in 1973 Joe Walding, Minister for the new portfolio of Environment, appointed Ron McLean and five others to be foundation Guardians of Lakes Manapouri and Te Anau. There were no further proposals to raise the levels of those or other natural lakes. A valuable precedent had been set.

The greatest benefit arising from the Save Manapouri Campaign, however, may have been that it started a national debate on environmental issues, involving national and local body politicians, scientists, professional planners and members of the public. And that debate, fed by literature and television reports of similar issues arising in other countries throughout the developed world, especially the United States, persisted long after the campaign itself had been won. Early national spin-offs included the overhaul of water management in the Water and Soil Conservation Act, the attempted elimination of air pollution in the Clean Air Act, and the protection of marine life in the Marine Reserves Act, which eventually resulted in the establishment of reserves in half a dozen locations on the New Zealand coast and around the Kermadec and Poor Knights islands.

The fundamental problem which had underlain the Manapouri campaign remained, however. Some state agencies were committed to developmental policies that took no heed of environmental considerations. This became the basis for another set of disputes that broke out in the early 1970s over the use of native forests. The protagonists were senior executives of the New Zealand Forest Service, who wanted to continue to log mature native trees for timber, and environmental groups such as Forest and Bird who argued that the natural and ecological values of such forests outweighed the commercial gains from harvesting – and in the process destroying – them. The last remaining unprotected giant kauri on the Coromandel Peninsula (in the Manaia block) and in Northland (in the Warawara Forest) were saved after appeals to the Government, which involved a repetition of arguments put forward to preserve the Waipoua Forest in the 1940s and early 1950s. Forests of giant podocarps at Pureora and Whirinaki were also protected after public protests, which involved some activists tying themselves to the upper branches of trees. These protests and those against plans for the large-scale harvesting of beech forests in the South Island produced two new and eventually powerful lobby groups, Friends of the Earth and the Native Forest Action Council. The beech forests too eventually gained protection and an emphasis on 'natural, intrinsic and scientific values' was written into reserves and national parks legislation. Further, over a period of three decades, the amount of land held in such parks and reserves was doubled.

The Clyde Dam proposal, to raise the level of the Clutha River in Central Otago to generate more hydro-electricity and contribute to irrigation, was yet another public works project driven by government departments that aroused controversy. It involved flooding the Cromwell Gorge and inundating historic and scenic sites and orchard land. The Muldoon Government was eventually able to pass the empowering legislation in 1982, but only by enlisting the support of Parliament's two Social Credit members* – which turned out to spell electoral doom for them and to contribute to National's loss of office two years later. In the wake of this battle a wary public sought, and eventually achieved more than a decade later, stricter environmental controls for such projects and far more transparency in the processes that governed them.

The cause of marine conservation and the movement to ban nuclear weapons from the South Pacific were boosted in July 1985 when agents of the French secret service (the DGSE) bombed and sank the Greenpeace organisation's flagship vessel *Rainbow Warrior* in Auckland Harbour. The ship had been about to sail to Moruroa in French Polynesia to protest against continuing nuclear testing by the French on that isolated atoll. The effect of the DGSE's intervention, however – the first act of state-sponsored terrorism in New Zealand – was to increase substantially Greenpeace's local membership and enlarge support for the anti-nuclear movement, already galvanised by Labour Prime Minister David Lange's proclamation that New Zealand would prohibit the passage of nuclear-armed or -propelled vessels through its territorial waters. The French Government subsequently paid New Zealand compensation for the bombing.

Another watershed in the development of environmentally sound policies was the effect of Cyclone Bola on the East Coast of the North Island in March 1988. This event caused $112 million worth of damage on unstable hill-country farms – the

---

* Social Credit, a rare 'third party' in New Zealand politics, absorbed much of the country's protest vote from the 1960s to the 1980s. The organisation, based on the economic doctrines of Major C. H. Douglas, succeeded in putting four members into Parliament – but never more than two at any one time.

kind of country whose suitability for farming Oakley Sargeson had questioned exactly 40 years earlier. As a result of the storm and its disastrous aftermath – further eroding hillsides, washing tons of soil out to sea via some rivers and blocking others and flooding surrounding land – large areas on the East Coast and elsewhere were taken out of pasture farming and planted in exotic forests.

It was the fourth Labour Government, however, which was in office at the time of the *Rainbow Warrior* bombing and of Cyclone Bola, that subjected the country's environmental policies and practices to the closest possible scrutiny, while Geoffrey Palmer was Minister for the Environment. State development agencies, such as the Forest Service, the Department of Lands and Survey and the Ministry of Works and Development were disestablished. Commercial functions of those departments were transferred to state-owned enterprises, charged with operating commercially and making a profit. Subsidies for forest clearance and land development were abolished. A Department of Conservation, to advocate *for* conservation and administer land with high conservation values, was created out of parts of the old Forest Service, Lands and Survey and the Wildlife Service. A new Ministry for the Environment was established with a policy role and a Parliamentary Commissioner for the Environment to play a monitoring role. At the same time government and local government planning and environmental procedures were completely overhauled in the Resource Management Act, initiated by Palmer but not endorsed by Parliament until 1991, when the Bolger National Government was in office and a new minister, Simon Upton, was responsible for its passage and implementation.

The Resource Management Act was gigantic: it replaced almost 60 other laws, including the Town and Country Planning

Act and the Water and Soil Conservation Act. When it was introduced into Parliament in 1989, Environment Ministry staff noted that the country's planning laws had 'evolved in a piecemeal fashion, resulting in a set of complex, overlapping and sometimes conflicting rules. As a result, outcomes for the environment are often inadequate ... In a world where concern for the environment grows stronger every day, New Zealand has recognised that the clean-up must begin at home.'

The Act as eventually passed covered the 'use, development and protection' of air, land and water. It put in place a three-tiered (national, regional, local) management system and a scheme for allocating rights to use land, air and water. Before any such proposed use, its potential effects on the environment had to be assessed and a wide range of other interests, including intrinsic values and the principles of the Treaty of Waitangi, had to be addressed. Maori who held 'mana whenua' or authority over specific rohe had to be consulted. Above all else, however, the Act aimed to promote sustainable management of resources. That core principle subsequently found its way into other legislation, including that governing the use of forests and fisheries (the latter being now subject to a transferable quota system).

Another important step towards environmental responsibility New Zealand took at about the same time was signing the Framework Convention on Climate Change at the Earth Summit in Rio in 1992. This committed the country to work actively to reduce carbon monoxide emissions contributing to the 'greenhouse effect', and thus to global warming. Since that time, however, successive governments have shown a preference for using carbon sinks to absorb greenhouse gases rather than reduce emissions, and one environmental lawyer has put this behaviour into the category of 'well-meaning but empty policy statements'. A proposal to levy New Zealand farmers for research into the effects of animal gas emissions proved massively unpopular.

Inevitably too there was criticism aplenty of the Resource Management Act after its first decade of operation: that its processes were too costly and time-consuming; that developments needed rapidly for the healthy functioning of communities were unreasonably delayed; that tangata whenua and objectors to development had too much influence; that some environmentally damaging projects came to fruition anyway, despite the safeguards; that regulatory bodies are only as competent as the individuals who sit on them. Given that the Act was always going to be a referee among competing interests, however, it was inevitable that few parties would be entirely satisfied by its operation. On balance, it does subject the country's use of finite resources to more rigorous, more fair and more transparent monitoring than was possible previously. And, while developers and those who profit most from development would prefer a return to the manipulable circumstances of the less regulated era, most organisations and individuals concerned with environmental protection and sustainability value the Act and its operation highly.

27

A Revolution Begun

Although the legislation that would eventually ignite the Save Manapouri Campaign was drafted in 1960, its full significance would not be recognised for another nine years. Consequently the decade began quietly enough and the first events to engage public attention seemed to promise continuity in New Zealand life rather than social change on an unprecedented scale.

Among those events of 1960 were victories on the same day of Peter Snell (800 metres) and Murray Halberg (5000 metres) at the Rome Olympics and their breaking of world records for these and equivalent distances soon after. It seemed that the afterglow of Hillary's conquest of Everest in 1953 was to be complemented by a New Zealand global pre-eminence in middle-distance running (as it was, for a short period). Even though there were protests against the racially selected All Black team to tour South Africa that year – 'No Maoris, No Tour' – the Nash Labour Government declined to intervene and it was business as usual for the New Zealand Rugby Football

Union and most of the rugby-loving public.

Even a political shift did not seem like change. Walter Nash led Labour into the 1960 general election in his 79th year. After more than three decades in Parliament, Nash basked in public adulation as the 'grand old man' of New Zealand politics and as the country's 'elder statesman'. He was liked, even loved by some, for a cluster of qualities that could be seen as both admirable and exasperating. The British High Commissioner during his prime ministership, Sir George Mallaby, recalled Nash affectionately in his memoirs.

> Squat and foursquare he stumped boldly through life, indefatigable, talkative to the point of tedium, but always saved by a touch of humour or a visitation of grace ... The annual dinner of the local rugby team was to him as interesting and as exciting as a state banquet for the Queen Mother [in 1958], and he gave himself equally and tirelessly to both, talking on, reminiscing, holding the floor, while men half his age prayed in silence for their beds.

The electorate, however, and many in the Labour Party, thought it was time for Nash to take a well-earned retirement, and that meant that his Government, still attracting political flak for overreacting to the balance of payments crisis in its 1958 'Black Budget', had to go too. In the general election at the end of 1960 National was elected by 46 seats to Labour's 34. And the party's leader, Keith Holyoake, began his long reign over New Zealand politics – twelve continuous years as Prime Minister, exceeded only by Seddon's fourteen and Massey's thirteen.

Holyoake was an able and energetic farmer who had originally entered Parliament as its youngest member (aged 28) in a by-election for Motueka in 1932. He lost the seat in 1938, and returned representing Pahiatua in 1943. Had it not been for that five-year absence he might well have beaten Sidney Holland for the National Party leadership in 1940. He became Holland's deputy, however, and after the 1949 election Minister of Agriculture, and an unusually successful one. In 1954 he became the first New Zealander designated Deputy Prime Minister, which up until that time had been an informal arrangement. His succession to the leadership and prime ministership only ten weeks before the general election in 1957 left him too little time to establish himself in those roles and Labour won narrowly, 41 seats to 39.

By the time he resumed leadership of the country in 1960, Holyoake, by then aged 56, certainly seemed more vigorous than the faltering Nash – though voters were divided on whether the 'mannered façade, the fruity voice [and] the booming bonhomie' were assets or liabilities.* In the pre-television era, he shone in platform presentation and debate, and was a powerful speaker in Parliament and a master of its standing orders. As television became a more potent medium for political discourse through the 1960s, however, Holyoake's larger-than-life mannerisms came to be seen as exaggerated and pompous.

Holyoake's greatest strength as a politician, and the one that kept him in the top job for more than a decade, was his ability to seek and find consensus among his colleagues in cabinet and caucus. The party campaigned on a 'Steady Does It' slogan in 1963, and that summed up Holyoake's *modus operandi* for the whole of his second prime ministership. He saw his role as 'chairman of the board' and conservator of the *status quo*, and

---

* In his poem 'Election 1960', James K. Baxter likened Nash to 'King Log … an old time-serving post/ Hacked from a totara when the land was young'; and Holyoake to 'King Stork', who, in the fairytale 'The Frogs Desire a King', devoured his subjects and made them submissive with fear – a judgement which proved to be excessively severe.

because his first years in office saw sustained prosperity that posture struck a responsive chord in the electorate.

By the second half of the 1960s, however, circumstances had begun to alter and with them the public mood. A variety of factors leavened the change. One was a collapse in wool prices which reduced overseas earnings and led to a tightening in the economy and increased unemployment. A more major one, however, was television, which New Zealanders had long been told they would never get because their country was overly endowed with mountains and valleys. Despite the geographical problems, transmission had begun in Auckland in 1960 and nationally in 1961. Over time the television set would become a standard appliance in every home and the medium would make New Zealanders more conscious of world politics and conflicts, and more vividly aware of national politics, as news and current affairs programmes gradually became more comprehensive and more professional in their presentation. One effect was an eventual decline in the career prospects of politicians who did not shine in the medium, such as the Leader of the Opposition, Arnold Nordmeyer, Holyoake himself and his deputy and later successor, 'Gentleman Jack' Marshall. Conversely the medium would bestow a rapid rise in the visibility and authority of younger politicians who handled it well, such as Norman Kirk and Robert Muldoon.

Another feature that changed the political climate was the war in Vietnam. The Holyoake Government's view of defence was identical to that of its immediate predecessors. It was based on three principles: 'forward defence', which meant keeping aggressors as far from New Zealand shores as possible; collective security, which recognised that New Zealand was too small in size and resources to defend itself alone and therefore needed defence pacts with larger powers such as Britain or the United

States; and close co-operation with its nearest neighbour, Australia. These principles lay behind the earlier despatch of New Zealand troops to Korea in 1950, Malaya in 1956 and Malaysia in 1964, and they also ensured that when the United States asked for a contribution to its war against communist forces in Vietnam the New Zealand Government was likely to agree. And agree it did.

Prime Minister Holyoake went on television in May 1965 to announce that New Zealand would send an artillery unit to Vietnam to assist the South Vietnamese Government and its American and Australian allies. (Interestingly Britain, which was associated with these countries as a member of SEATO, supported the Americans in principle but declined to send troops – a further indication of the extent to which New Zealand was no longer in close collaboration with what had been the Mother Country.) 'If South Vietnam falls, I am sure that other countries of South-East Asia ... will be the next targets for communist expansion,' Holyoake intoned, thus accepting the Americans' domino theory. Subsequently the New Zealand contribution to the war would be enlarged to include infantry rifle brigades, a Special Air Service troop and a medical team: 3890 men in all.

There were several notable features to this development. One, it was the first time a New Zealand leader had appeared on prime-time television to make an announcement of national importance. Second, the Labour Opposition did not support the troop commitment, identifying the conflict as a civil war and thus ensuring that for the first time New Zealand was pursuing a major foreign policy without bipartisan political support. And third, the Vietnam war, which was never declared as such, was to divide New Zealand as never before. Hardline anti-communists felt that the country's contribution was token –

which it was – and insufficient, while anti-war activists, encouraged by the Opposition's stance, believed that the country should play no part in the conflict other than a humanitarian one. Within days of the Prime Minister's initial announcement his suite in Parliament Buildings was invaded by protestors – the beginning of a seven-year-long protest campaign which, as in the United States and Australia, would divide families, communities and the nation as a whole. Television, which would bring the realities of the war nightly into the living rooms of the nation, as well as the spectacle of local or international protests against the war, served only to heighten the controversy.

The potent combination of protest and television coverage of it sparked what conservative commentators such as William Buckley would call a 'contagion of protest'. For the rest of the decade and on into the 1970s, there seemed to be a super-abundance of causes that would bring people out into the streets: the arrival of Lyndon Baines Johnson, the first visit to New Zealand of an American president in office (1966); visits from American Vice-President Hubert Humphrey and Secretary of State Dean Rusk; students protesting against the level of university bursaries; the Russian invasion of Czechoslovakia; the decision to install an Omega navigation beacon in the South Island; the closure of some parks in Auckland to public use; the proposal to raise Lake Manapouri to generate additional electricity; the continuation of sporting contacts with South Africa; and, through the 1970s, issues of Maori, women's and homosexual rights.

While all these causes simmered away, coming and going from public view, the lifestyles of the young – and in some cases the not so young – were mutating in highly specific ways and at an unprecedented rate. The widespread availability of the oral contraceptive to married and unmarried women made pre- and extra-marital sex more acceptable and marital sex less fraught. Popular music was becoming louder, more exciting, more promiscuous – a process given impetus by the Beatles' visit to New Zealand in 1964, which spawned a rash of imitative local bands such as the Librettos and Ray Columbus and the Invaders (though music on offer by the end of the decade made the Beatles look and sound innocuous). It became fashionable to experiment with recreational drugs, especially marijuana, which began to be grown in quantity in New Zealand for the first time. With the abolition of six o'clock closing of hotel bars in 1967 and an eventual relaxation of restaurant licensing laws, alcohol became available at more civilised hours and in more civilised circumstances than it had been in the days of the 'six o'clock swill'. Long hair, previously regarded as effeminate on men, spread like an epidemic, affecting even All Blacks. Clothes became more colourful and imaginative; the mini-skirt and trouser suit arrived for women, flared trousers and brightly coloured shirts and ties for men.

The heroes of radio were steadily eclipsed by the dominant faces on television: chef Graham Kerr, current affairs star Brian Edwards, who, astonishingly, began to interrogate public figures on behalf of the public, and a rising politician named Robert Muldoon, who shot from backbench obscurity to national visibility in 1967 when he was given responsibility for overseeing the introduction of decimal currency. The same year Muldoon became National's Minister of Finance and from that time his face was rarely *off* the screen. The immediacy of television was seen again in April 1968, when the inter-island ferry *Wahine* grounded on Barrett's Reef in Wellington Harbour and subsequently sank with the loss of 51 lives. The drama unfolding on television shocked the nation as a whole.

While television was also the chief purveyor of new global

ideas and trends in such subjects as conservation and opposition to war, a simultaneous source of new ideas and information was the increasing contact that individual New Zealanders were now enjoying with Britain, Europe, North America and Asia. The key to this explosion of travel opportunities was the jet aircraft. The grandparents of the '60s generation had taken as long as three months to transplant themselves from Europe to New Zealand, and for most of them there was no return voyage because of the unavoidable time and expense involved. The World War II baby-boomers coming to maturity in the 1960s and 1970s could make the same journey in just over 24 hours.

Regular jet services between New Zealand and the United Kingdom began in 1963, when BOAC flew its first Comet 4 aircraft into and out of Whenuapai Airport in Auckland. As the decade progressed, the Comets were replaced by Boeing 707s and the number of routes and airlines flying them increased dramatically. New Zealand bought out Australian shares in the TEAL company in 1961 and this airline became Air New Zealand in 1965. By the end of the decade it was ordering DC-10 jets for the American and Asian routes, and from 1973 it won the right to fly to London.* With Air New Zealand and other overseas airlines operating in and out of the country – including Pan-Am, UTA, BOAC (later British Airways), QANTAS, American

---

* Air New Zealand operated with an outstandingly good safety record until one of its DC-10s on a scenic flight to Antarctica slammed into Mount Erebus on 28 November 1979 with the loss of all 257 passengers and crew. A subsequent commission of inquiry conducted by High Court judge Peter Mahon placed the weight of the blame on the airline's administration, which had changed the route on the plane's computer navigation system without telling the flight crew. Mahon's report, accusing the airline of an 'orchestrated litany of lies', was criticised by the Privy Council for exceeding its terms of reference and breaching principles of natural justice. As a consequence Mahon resigned from the High Court.

Airlines – New Zealanders were spoiled for choice and competition kept prices relatively low. The rate of travel shot up as young New Zealanders in particular claimed what came to be seen as a right: OE or overseas experience. And they brought home first-hand information on how other world centres, especially London, were living the 'Swinging Sixties' and their aftermath.

As that decade began to merge with the 1970s, it seemed to some as if the maelstrom of change was gathering momentum rather than diminishing. Book censorship had been liberalised by the Indecent Publications Tribunal, set up in 1963, and previously forbidden works by such writers as D. H. Lawrence and Henry Miller were now readily available for those who were interested. New Zealand writing began to display new life and vigour and the local offices of London-based publishers – Collins, Heinemann, Hodder & Stoughton – began to publish New Zealand fiction and non-fiction in some quantity, forcing the two established New Zealand publishers, A. H. & A. W. Reed and Whitcombe & Tombs, to expand their own lists. Among the writers who began prolific careers in this decade are the poets Bill Manhire, Ian Wedde, Vincent O'Sullivan, Lauris Edmond and Sam Hunt; the story writers and novelists Owen Marshall, Elizabeth Smither and Fiona Kidman; the playwrights Roger Hall, Robert Lord and Greg McGee; and the children's writer Margaret Mahy. They joined those working from the previous decade and earlier – Maurice Gee, Marilyn Duckworth, Bruce Mason, Alistair Campbell, C. K. Stead, Janet Frame – who were establishing that it was possible to build a career in New Zealand based on serious writing. Ronald Hugh Morrieson had lived long enough to see his macabre novels based on small-town New Zealand life published in Australia, but not long enough to see them taken up in New Zealand after his alcohol-related death in 1972. Barry Crump was still around and keeping his hand in writing popular fiction in the '70s, but nothing matched the quality or the commercial success of his 1960s best-seller *A Good Keen Man*. The poets Fleur Adcock and Kevin Ireland were writing in England but continuing to publish in New Zealand, to which Ireland would eventually return in 1986.

New Zealand painting too began to flourish as the protégés of the McCahon and Woollaston generation – Don Binney, Pat Hanly, Gretchen Albrecht, Robin White – were taken up by dealer galleries who promoted their work with a zeal not seen previously. Woollaston and McCahon themselves benefited from the florescence as their foundational work began to be taken seriously for the first time by the public at large and to fetch prices that represented a fairer return on their talent and effort. New Zealand literature and history began to be taught seriously for the first time in universities, and when new universities were established in Hamilton (Waikato) and Palmerston North (Massey), it was the first such increase since the turn of the twentieth century. Even conservative institutions such as the churches were affected: the Catholic Church experienced local controversy over its new post-Vatican II vernacular liturgy and a papal ban on the oral contraceptive; and members of the Presbyterian General Assembly brought Professor Lloyd Geering to trial – unsuccessfully – on a charge of heresy.

In the early 1970s, two broad but powerful forces coalesced from social and ideological seeds released in the late 1960s: the counter-culture and women's movements.

The counter-culture in New Zealand developed out of that of the Yippies in the United States, which in turn was a product of the civil rights and anti-war campaigns there. Books such as Jerry Rubin's *Do It*, Abbie Hoffman's *Revolution for the Hell of It* and a variety of titles by Buckminster Fuller, found a ready market among the New Zealand baby-boomers, many of whom were disenchanted with the very things that their parents had sought to establish after World War II – the security of the nuclear family, suburban *mores*, lifetime jobs, conformity, predictability.

The most influential leaders of the movement in New Zealand – though they were 'leaders' because of their fluency and charisma, not in any sense of running a structured organisation – were Auckland protestor Tim Shadbolt, whose book *Bullshit and Jellybeans* (1971) was the local equivalent of the Rubin and Hoffman volumes; Alister Taylor, who published Shadbolt's book and other subversive volumes such as the *Whole Earth Catalogue* and *The Little Red School-Book*; James Ritchie, a Waikato University ethnologist and psychologist who had strong professional links with Berkeley in California and the American counter-culture movement; and poet James K. Baxter, who, a few years before his death in 1972, left suburban comfort to establish urban communes in Auckland and Wellington and a rural one at Jerusalem on the Whanganui River.

Baxter was both an appealing and a tragic figure. His poetic gifts, so vividly on show in *Beyond the Palisade* when he was eighteen, had continued to enlarge in range and power. By the 1960s he was, with Allen Curnow, the country's pre-eminent poet. But he was always troubled by a Calvinist conscience that made it impossible for him to enjoy the fruits of his libidinous and alcoholic propensities. He converted to Catholicism in 1958 and soon after swore off alcohol, and in 1968, after two years on the Otago University's Burns Fellowship, he left his family to work with the 'mokai' – the unprivileged or tribeless young people who were having difficulties coping with the materialism and the competitiveness of urban culture. While Baxter was influenced by all the ingredients of the counter-culture, including its literature and its strong anti-war message – he had come, after all, from a family of pacifists – he sought to develop a New Zealand lifeway that embraced Maori spirituality and social concepts. His early death at 46 prevented the fulfilment of that vision. But among the rich legacy he left his country was some of its most haunting poetry:

> Alone we are born
>   And die alone;
> Yet see the red-gold cirrus
>   Over snow-mountain shine.
>
> Upon the upland road
>   Ride easy, stranger:
> Surrender to the sky
>   Your heart of anger.

Being by its very nature informal and unstructured, the counter-culture movement never sought to institutionalise itself. The nearest it came to official sanction was when the Kirk Labour Government announced its 'ohu scheme' in 1973, to help groups to live and work communally on rural land, kibbutz-fashion. The programme was not in the long term a success, in part because almost all the participants found living communally considerably more difficult than they had imagined, and in part because in some instances a refusal to commit to a disciplined work ethic and a liking for recreational drugs, especially marijuana, proved inimical to the need to provide food and shelter and emotional security for the adults and children who made up the ohu 'families'.

Apart from a brief eruption of geodesic domes in rural areas, the most pervasive effect of the movement was as a source of new ideas about living on land sustainably and working co-operatively in non-hierarchical ways. These ideas fed gradually into mainstream New Zealand culture, but were concentrated more specifically in the programmes of the Values Party of the 1970s and 1980s and its ideological successor, the Greens, who achieved parliamentary representation in the 1990s thanks to the introduction of proportional representation, itself an idea promoted by the counter-culture.

Women's liberation in New Zealand also grew out of the American civil rights and anti-war movements. Women there, 'fighting to free other peoples, found themselves relegated to making tea, typing and providing sexual comforts for men ...' And so they began, in the late 1960s, a process of 'consciousness raising' to heighten an awareness of oppression and to engender a feeling of solidarity with others of their sex. The ground for such a movement in New Zealand was fertile because of what most women – and many men – could see was the second-class status of women in such areas as employment opportunities, rates of pay, excessive domestic responsibilities and education. Again, overseas literature was important in helping individual women recognise and analyse the problems, and in developing a belief that oppressive circumstances could be changed. Betty Friedan's *The Feminine Mystique* and Germaine Greer's *The Female Eunuch* were especially influential, as was a visit to New Zealand by Greer in 1972, during which she was arrested and fined $40 for using the word 'bullshit'.

New Zealand women organised themselves into small leaderless groups for consciousness-raising meetings. By 1972 around 20 women's liberation groups were operating throughout the country, spawning a forest of new acronyms. NOW (National Organisation for Women) was a good one, as was WOW (Wellington Organisation for Women). A Southland Organisation for Women presented problems, however, and was quietly abandoned as an option. Most visibly, as far as the wider community was concerned, the movement organised four biennial United Women's Conventions, in 1973, 1975, 1977 and 1979. In addition to providing New Zealand women with valuable networking opportunities, the conventions enabled locals to hear directly from some of the great figures in the international women's movement, such as Margaret Mead and Robin Morgan. The conventions were aimed at women in the mainstream, but they eventually proved impossible to manage because of internal dissension within the women's movement, particularly between gay and straight women, and between Maori and Pakeha.

The most visible public faces of the movement in New Zealand were journalist and researcher Sue Kedgley, whose striking good looks and gypsy outfits dispelled any notion that women's libbers were sexless and embittered androgynes; Sandra Coney, a founding editor of the feminist magazine *Broadsheet*; Ngahuia Te Awekotuku, a Te Arawa Maori activist; Marilyn Waring, the charismatically intelligent and (usually) high-spirited backbench National MP; and the unlikely named Phillida Bunkle of Victoria University, who, with Rosemary Seymour at the University of Waikato, was most responsible for pioneering women's history and women's studies in New Zealand tertiary education. As the women's movement grew, Bunkle would write, 'more and more women began to insist that they did not want equality in a man's world [but] the femini-sation of society'. By asserting such values as nurturing and co-operation, feminists would seek to 'overthrow the values of male dominance'.

Like the counter-culture, the main achievement of the women's movement was its role in changing the attitudes of mainstream New Zealand society, but in this case to sex roles, equality of opportunity and equal pay. Many women in the Labour movement in particular carried its values into party and parliamentary politics, the fruit of which was such measures as the wider provision of daycare facilities for children, which allowed growing numbers of women to enter the workforce, and securing equal pay in principle in the 1980s. The fact that the early years of the twenty-first century AD would deliver simultaneously a woman Governor-General, a woman Prime Minister, a woman Chief Justice and a woman Attorney-General was one measure of the progress the movement had achieved in New Zealand.

Much of the excitement generated by the late 1960s and early 1970s seemed to come to fruition in the election of the third Labour Government in 1972. Keith Holyoake had retired from the prime ministership – though not from politics – at the beginning of the year, and his deputy John Marshall succeeded to the leadership. Marshall, however, like Holyoake before him in 1957, had insufficient time to establish himself in the position before the election. Alongside Norman Kirk, still in his 40s and by this time slimmed down and looking vigorous and hungry for responsibility, the 60-year-old National leader seemed tired and dispirited. It was no real surprise that he led his party to defeat.

Kirk, a former stationary engine driver, had enjoyed a meteoric rise in politics since becoming mayor of Kaiapoi at the age of 30. He entered Parliament in 1957 representing Lyttelton, and quickly established himself as an articulate and forceful MP in a way that Walter Nash and his successor as leader, Arnold Nordmeyer, were not and never had been. Kirk replaced Nordmeyer in 1965, then led Labour to defeats in 1966 and 1969. By 1972 he was ready for high office, however, and the electorate was ready to put him and his party into government. Kirk had been groomed by his minders, grown his hair and by this time wore suits that fitted him. In addition to being dynamic, he now appeared statesmanlike. He was also a stronger nationalist than his political opponents and had developed into an eloquent rhetorician. 'Circumstances dictate that, while we preserve the warmest ties and closest sentimental attachments between our country and the United Kingdom, we recognise that we have come of age and must now stand on our own feet to reject the role of the dependant and at every opportunity seize the initiative,' he affirmed.

The realisation of many of the aspirations of the '60s was apparent in the new Government's withdrawal of the last of the New Zealand troops from Vietnam, cancellation of the planned 1973 Springbok tour, sending a New Zealand frigate to Moruroa in 1973 to protest against French nuclear testing there, and the encouragement of ohu to allow committed people to return to the land for their livelihood. The Commonwealth Games held in Christchurch in 1974, when Richard Tayler in the 10,000 metres won a gold medal for New Zealand on the first day, were seen by many commentators as a festival celebrating the country's new self-confidence and optimism. Talented New Zealanders who had left home to work abroad were starting to return in significant numbers.

The mood did not persist, however. Norman Kirk failed to recover properly from an operation for varicose veins and died from heart complications in 1974. His successor, a decent but tentative man, Finance Minister Bill Rowling, was unable to harness the energies of the country and of his Government. In addition, he faced Robert Muldoon as Leader of the Opposition, put there by his colleagues largely on account of Marshall's inability to counter Kirk. This time it was Rowling's turn to be outmanoeuvred in debate and in strategy. Two massive and unexpected increases in oil prices underlined New Zealand's vulnerability to interruptions in the supply of overseas fuel and fed inflation at an unprecedented rate. In 1975 an apparently panicking electorate called the National Party and its pugnaciously confident leader back to govern the country.

The warm positivism of the Kirk era was replaced by defensive negativism. 'The New Zealand way of life,' wrote journalist Colin James, 'became antagonistic, mean and grudging.' The power of the country's executive in relation to Parliament increased noticeably, particularly the power of the Prime Minister, who also took the Finance portfolio. National, while continuing to profess loyalty to Britain – and Muldoon sent the Royal Navy a New Zealand frigate in 1982 to allow the British to deploy another vessel in the Falklands War in the South Atlantic – carried on the country's search for markets outside Europe: in Australia (with whom New Zealand signed a Closer Economic Relations agreement in 1982), the United States, Asia and the Middle East. It also developed the country's manufacturing and energy-producing industries. The need for all these measures had been increased by Britain's entry into the European Economic Community (as it was then) in 1973.

Within New Zealand, however, some citizens were doing very well – in business, property speculation and the new cornucopia of horticulture, especially kiwifruit, which had been selectively bred out of the humble Chinese gooseberry and found to have a lucrative overseas market. Wealthier suburbs in Auckland looked and *were* even wealthier; ownership of yachts, cruisers and top-of-the-market cars increased. Urban shop windows displayed more luxury items. New Zealanders' spending power was boosted by an extravagant Muldoon-devised superannuation scheme, which gave 80 per cent of the average wage to married people aged over 60. Diversity of culture and of appearance became more acceptable. The New Zealand cricket team, revitalised by the introduction of the era of the one-day game, began to win matches and to win series against traditional adversaries, especially in the period of Richard Hadlee's pre-eminence as an all-rounder. A rash of formerly exotic foods – European, Asian, Pacific – became available in restaurants, and nightclubs proliferated. It was possible by this time, if one had the wherewithal, to enjoy a night life in New Zealand cities. The incidence of prostitution increased under the guise of strip clubs and massage parlours and Auckland and Wellington at least had what could be called 'red-light districts'.

At the same time there was a boom in local crafts, and writing and painting continued to swell in confidence and competence, thanks in part to increased government patronage – and in particular to a sympathetic National Minister for the Arts, Allan Highet. An indigenous film industry, whose first faltering initiatives had come from Rudall Hayward and John O'Shea, began to polish such actor stars as Sam Neill and to produce such directors as Vincent Ward, Jane Campion and, eventually, Peter Jackson. Colin James commented:

[We are] producing films, novels, plays and art and craft that are self-confident without being self-conscious. While our politicians have been locked into Europe ... our artists and poets have been reaching towards a self-sufficient definition of European-descended New Zealand. Our habits, our customs, our attitudes [are being] measured for the first time against New Zealand touchstones ... We have a vibrant if uneven local theatre; a developing book publishing tradition; the beginnings of a significant film industry; and a fine and inventive sense of craft that is spilling into art. Give us one, maybe two more generations ... and we will feed no more through [Europe] ... It is good, it is exciting to be a New Zealander now.

Throughout the 1970s the country was making a gradually stronger commitment to biculturalism in Maori–Pakeha relations, and to multiculturalism. In the education system, in the administration of some state institutions such as the Arts Council and the Historic Places Trust, the nation began to down-play its Anglo-Celtic heritage, which had previously been the only basis for public policy-making in the culture and heritage sectors.

These moves were partly a belated recognition of ethnic diversity within New Zealand. The population contained nearly 400,000 Maori and 100,000 Pacific Islanders by the end of the decade,* plus a growing number of Asian immigrants, including former Vietnamese and Kampuchean boat people. But the changes were brought about largely by Maori activists, who were determined that Maori ought to be able to behave as Maori in wider New Zealand life rather than submerge their identity in favour of Pakeha *mores* and values. By 1979 both major political parties had accepted this argument in principle, although the major institutions of the state – especially the law and the Public Service – were slow to adapt and to understand its consequences.

---

* Western Samoa gained independence from New Zealand in 1962, and the Cook Islands became self-governing in free association with New Zealand in 1965. New Zealand continued to be directly responsible for Niue, and for the Tokelau Islands, which had been inside its territorial boundaries since 1948. The country's Pacific Island population was made up principally of immigrants from these territories and from Tonga, and their descendants.

28

Return of Mana Maori

Apirana Ngata and his contemporaries in the Young Maori Party had been largely content to see Maori living in rural communities separately from Pakeha. They believed that this situation provided the best opportunity for Maori culture, identity and confidence to recover after the trauma of nine-teenth-century European colonisation and, in some regions, the effects of the New Zealand Wars and subsequent land confiscations. The farm development scheme and cultural revival programme of the 1930s were designed by Ngata to protect and reassert mana Maori in traditional rohe or tribal territories. While Ngata and Peter Buck hoped that other Maori would follow their example and seek higher education and a place in the country's professions, they saw that path as being open to an elite who would constitute a national Maori leadership rather than as a choice that the Maori population as a whole could or should opt for. They also worried that most Maori were not adequately prepared to resist the 'temptations' of town life

– alcohol, unsupervised access to members of the opposite sex, potential contact with a Pakeha criminal underclass.

After World War II, the Maori demographic and cultural landscape would change in ways that Ngata and his contemporaries could never have envisaged. There was an aptness in the fact that he, Buck, Te Puea Herangi, Bishop Frederick Bennett and other leaders all died between 1950 and 1952, just as a new set of circumstances was evolving. A steady and increasing rate of Maori urbanisation would mean that in the second half of the twentieth century Maori and Pakeha would come into widespread contact with each other for the first time since the 1860s. With that contact would come challenges, prejudice and conflict – and, eventually, an opportunity for Maori to participate for the first time in mainstream New Zealand social, political and cultural life. And these new conditions would require major recasting of the social contract between Maori and Pakeha, and between Maori and the Crown. That readjustment would be one more of the ways in which New Zealand in the later part of the twentieth century parted company with circumstances that had prevailed previously. And this in turn would require Maori and Pakeha to shed one set of reassuring myths and develop others to replace them.

For Maori, the dominant pre-war myth had been that people derived their identity from whakapapa and turangawaewae (a home place), and that those umbilical connections were best preserved by living close to one's extended family, home marae and urupa (cemeteries). An associated myth, nurtured in particular by Ngata and the tribal leadership of his generation – Te Puea, Hamuera Mitchell, Eru Ihaka and others – was that living close to the land, one's own land, was the best way of preserving whanau and hapu life, and that in most areas farming, especially dairy farming, offered the best means of retaining traditional family and community links. The myth would be challenged by some of the next generation who served abroad in World War II, especially those who made up the officer corps of the 28th (Maori) Battalion. These men, like their fathers and uncles in the preceding war, got a taste of other ways of life in other places, assumed wartime responsibilities far beyond those for which their age and previous experience had prepared them, and returned with altered expectations for themselves and for their people. Among them were men such as Arapeta Awatere and James Henare, both of whom had commanded the battalion, and others such as Rangi Royal, Charles Bennett, Bill Herewini, Moana Raureti, Harry Dansey and John Rangihau. They no longer believed in the inevitability or even the sustainability of the Maori rural idyll. That idyll was also challenged by the fact, apparent from the late 1940s, that family dairy farms were going to be too small to compete with the larger and more highly mechanised farm units owned and operated by Pakeha with access to more investment capital than was available to their Maori counterparts.

For Pakeha, the matching myth was that New Zealand had the best race relations in the world, a verdict Pakeha politicians trumpeted at every possible opportunity. That situation prevailed, it was believed, because the Treaty of Waitangi had been 'the fairest treaty ever made by Europeans with a native race', according to *Our Nation's Story*, the set of books to which all New Zealand schoolchildren were exposed in the 1920s and 1930s, and because Maori were, in the words of one Native Affairs Minister, William Herries, 'the finest coloured race in the world'.

According to these viewpoints, the only time trouble arose between Maori and Pakeha was when Maori wilfully misbehaved or showed something less than the gratitude expected of them for the gift of civilisation. 'No other country in the world has such a record,' the acting Minister of Native Affairs lectured Te Puea Herangi in 1940. '[Yet] I regret to say that many of our Maori brethren do not fully appreciate all that has been done for them in a brotherly, loving way.' Even governors-general indulged in such sermons. Lord Galway, presenting Te Puea with a CBE at Ngaruawahia in 1938, told his Tainui audience: 'It is a personal responsibility of each one of you to see that the conduct ... of every man of the race is in every way above reproach. Any failings ... might lead to the loss of that helpful assistance now being given to you and tends to alienate that sympathetic understanding which is so necessary to further progress.'

Te Puea found such statements breathtaking in their impertinence and ignorance. Would Pakeha audiences have been addressed in this manner? she asked. This was the Crown which had frequently breached the Treaty of Waitangi and, according to a 1927 royal commission, confiscated an excessive amount of land from Tainui for simply trying to protect its borders and its Kingitanga. And here were its representatives, one of them a viceroy, saying that, if individual Maori did not behave as Pakeha believed they should, then they would be further deprived of the already meagre resources which governments of the day chose to share with Maori.

All the myths about interaction between the two peoples were about to be fully tested for the first time. Most Maori tribes retained traditional recollections of one or even two migrations: that which brought their people from an ancestral homeland in the Pacific, and that which took them from an earlier place of settlement to the one in which the hapu was currently living based on its meeting houses, urupa and wahi tapu. From the time of World War II, however, most Maori families underwent a third migration, which took its members from small, largely rural communities into the towns and cities of the nation, where the living conventions were defined by Pakeha.

That new shift brought both compensations and trauma: eventual security and wider educational and employment opportunities for some, and cultural and emotional dislocation for others. Some families, removed from the social and cultural structures that had given their lives meaning and direction for generations, and lacking any alternative structures to substitute or compensate for these changes, collapsed into dysfunction, alcohol and drug abuse, physical and emotional health problems, violence and crime.

The relocation began in earnest during World War II, when manpower regulations and the Maori War Effort Organisation opened up a diversity of labouring and manufacturing jobs not generally available previously to Maori men and women. In addition, the recreational options of city life created in some country areas what anthropologist Joan Metge called a 'fantasy contagion'. In 1936 only 11.2 per cent of the national Maori population had lived in urban areas. By 1945 this had risen to 25.7 per cent, and by 1996 to over 81 per cent. Maori had become, in little more than a generation, an overwhelmingly urban people.

The impact can best be visualised by consideration of the effect on individual cities. There were 1766 Maori in Auckland in 1935, for example. By 1945 there were 4903, and by 1951, 7621. In the same period the Wellington Maori population jumped from 341 to 1570. At the same time suburbs that had previously seen few Maori became predominantly Maori (and later Pacific Island) in their ethnic composition: Otara in South Auckland, Frankton in Hamilton, Porirua East in Wellington. Even South Island cities such as Christchurch and Invercargill began to acquire substantial Maori populations as North Island Maori moved there for employment, particularly in freezing works.

There was no single cause for the momentum which this migration built up over three decades. In periods of national prosperity, like the early 1950s, the ready availability of well-paid but unskilled jobs was one attraction. It led to Maori men in particular taking manual jobs in large numbers in provincial towns and cities, in labouring, construction and meat works, for example – the kinds of jobs that would leave them vulnerable to unemployment in times of national economic downturn. Nor was the migration caused simply by the positive appeal of such work. There was also a negative factor in the economic decline of Maori rural communities, brought about because Maori land alone was unable to provide for what was by this time a burgeoning Maori population.

This is not to suggest that Maori farming as a whole was a failure – far from it. Some incorporations, such as Mangatu on the East Coast, and some individual farmers did spectacularly well. Nor was Pakeha farming by contrast an unqualified success. But the overall situation of Maori farming, particularly on the small dairy units developed under Apirana Ngata's scheme, was uneconomic by the 1950s. This provided an added incentive for farm workers and their families to move to towns and cities, and this depopulation made rural communities even less viable and urban migration still more appealing. It was a combination of rural population displacement, urbanisation, and a relative lack of educational, trade and professional quali-fications among Maori workers that created a brown proletariat in New Zealand cities – a situation that some commentators viewed as a potentially dangerous ingredient in urban race relations. Professor J. G. A. Pocock, for example, wrote in 1965:

> [We] may be going to have ghettoes – the current term for urban areas where a distinctly pigmented minority have to live with bad houses, bad schools and unrewarding jobs – and, when faced with

such ghettoes, the Pakeha may find that he is more prejudiced than he likes to believe ... whakama may cease to be the mere feeling of shyness and inadequacy which it is now, and become instead a truly bitter sense of rejection; ideologies of alienation and ambivalence may arise, and the voice of some Maori (or Islander) James Baldwin may some day be heard.

This is an anticipation, by a quarter of a century, of the inflammable social ingredients described in Alan Duff's seminal novel *Once Were Warriors*.

As Pocock recognised, the social and cultural consequences of the relocation of the Maori population were considerable. Migrants newly arrived from rural areas were faced with a set of Pakeha suburban *mores* not evident in Maori communities. There were difficulties with managing salaried incomes for the first time, with budgeting, savings and investments, and with accommodation, hire purchase and door-to-door salesmen. There were instances of overt discrimination in employment, accommodation and hotel bars that arose from Maori and Pakeha having to interact widely for the first time. Such instances generated publicity only when they involved well-known professional figures, such as Kingseat Hospital Superintendent Henry Bennett, who was refused a drink in a hotel private bar in Pukekohe because he was Maori.

Urbanisation also created the need to redefine aspects of Maoriness: the nature of the extended family in the urban context; how to hold hui in the city; whether to take tupapuku (corpses) 'home' to rural marae or to conduct tangihanga in a city living room or garage; how, and whether, to keep live links with rural tribal bases; the tribal status of people who were one or two generations removed from live iwi associations. There was also the need, for the first time outside conditions of war, for people from differing tribal backgrounds to devise ways of co-operating with one another to solve specifically Maori issues. Differences of kawa had to be resolved, traditional suspicions and antagonisms discarded or submerged.

Tangata whenua people already swallowed up by urban expansion – Ngati Whatua at Orakei, for example, Tainui at Mangere or Ngati Toa in Porirua – were unwilling to let people from other tribal backgrounds make use of existing marae. This, coupled with the absence of marae in new suburbs, led to the conception and development of urban marae. In addressing these problems, Maori discovered that detribalisation could lead to multi-tribalism, and an intensification of a sense of Maoriness grew out of such urban marae projects as Te Unga Waka at Epsom, led by Whina Cooper, Hoani Waititi in West Auckland, led by Pita Sharples, and Maraeroa in Porirua East, led by Ned Nathan. Some peoples, such as Tuhoe in Panmure, also built urban marae that were specifically tribal.

Urbanisation accentuated aspects of Maori insecurity in relation to non-Maori. In 1951, 57 per cent of the Maori population was 20 years old or younger (as against 34.8 per cent of Pakeha), which indicated a greater proportion of young dependants and non-wage-earners. At the same time the Maori birth rate was considerably higher than that of non-Maori: 43.6 per 1000 in 1955 as against 26. Most significant, almost all the Maori workforce was in unskilled and lower-income employment, especially in agriculture and related industries (33 per cent in 1951) and manufacturing (23 per cent). Only 3.6 per cent of Maori workers at that time earned £700 or more, compared with 18.6 per cent of non-Maori. And in 1956 only 6.56 per cent of the Maori workforce held professional, managerial and clerical positions, as against 26.69 per cent of non-Maori.

All these factors combined to make Maori more vulnerable as a group than Pakeha when wool prices fell a decade later and ended full employment. They created a cycle of circumstances that was self-reinforcing and difficult to break: lower standards of educational attainment led to lower-income jobs or unemployment, which led to lower standards of housing and health, which led to higher rates of crime, which led back to lower educational attainment, and so on. Attempts to define these factors and their magnitude, and to devise new policies to deal with them, were not made until well into the 1960s. By that time some dysfunctional Maori families were two generations into the poverty trap, living on welfare in substandard accommodation, their children playing truant from school, a prey to alcohol and other forms of substance abuse and possibly sexual abuse, habituated to violence and criminal activities, without any sense of identity or belonging or of empathy with other people – and, as a consequence, contributing disproportionately to all negative Maori statistics.

This was also the period when many families living in cities ceased to have active links with their iwi and hapu, and lost all live connection with the Maori language, the practice of Maori ritual and the observance of tikanga Maori. The language was in a relatively healthy state in the early 1930s. By the 1970s it was in serious danger of extinction as elderly native speakers died and were not replaced by younger ones. The policy of not speaking Maori in schools, requested by Maori parents and school boards in the 1860s, had done some damage to the transmission of the culture, but not nearly as much as that caused by the later breakdown of family and tribal links in the post-war years. In addition, there was a tendency for those of grandparent age to view the future of the language – and of Maori culture itself – with pessimism. A commonly heard saying of the time was, 'You'll have better prospects if you korero Pakeha.'

Those who grew up from their earliest years in a cultural vacuum, in which they felt ill-equipped to be Maori, yet knew by the way people treated them that they were not Pakeha, were also those who were most vulnerable to non-achievement and crime if they were associated with other risk factors. From the earliest days of European colonisation, it was this period, and these experiences, that held most risk for the survival of Maori culture. And this phenomenon was not even recognised officially, let alone seriously addressed, until the 1970s.

Changing social and economic conditions in Maori life led to continued experimentation with different styles of leadership. The rangatira or hereditary basis for hapu and iwi leadership survived, especially in such tribes as Tainui and Ngati Tuwharetoa, but it was largely a rural phenomenon. An increasing number of urban-based leaders, such as Pita Sharples of Ngati Kahungunu and Ranginui Walker of Whakatohea, accumulated authority based on achievement. Graham Latimer of Te Aupouri became a national figure as a result of his lengthy chairmanship of the New Zealand Maori Council. And some, such as Whina Cooper, made the transition from tribal to multi-tribal mana.

Born Josephine Te Wake at Te Karaka on the Hokianga Harbour in 1895, Whina was the daughter of a leading Te Rarawa chief, Heremia Te Wake. From him, she inherited mana, considerable ability and an expectation that she would assume a leadership role among the Kai Tutae and Ngati Manawa hapu of Te Rarawa. After education at Whakarapa Native School and St Joseph's Maori Girls' College in Napier (where Sir James Carroll paid her fees), Whina was in succession a teacher, a storekeeper and a farmer in the northern Hokianga. She took her father's place after he died in the 1918 influenza epidemic. By the late 1920s, based at Panguru, she was known as the most forceful community leader in the district. When Apirana Ngata was seeking local tribal support for his land development scheme, Whina was an obvious ally, and she introduced and supervised the scheme in her area. She extended both her expertise and her influence as a result of a second marriage in 1935 to William Cooper, a Ngati Kahungunu friend of Ngata who had represented Maori on the royal commission investigating Maori land in 1927.

After Cooper's death in 1949, Whina observed the large number of Maori abandoning rural districts for the cities and decided to move to Auckland to become involved in voluntary welfare work. She patrolled hotels, looking especially for Maori parents who were not coping with alcohol or who were neglecting their families. In 1951 she was elected first president of the Maori Women's Welfare League, which was set up that year by the Department of Maori Affairs on the initiative of Rangi Royal, a senior welfare officer. Whina held the position for six years. After establishing local branches throughout the country, and making a considerable impact with the education of Maori mothers in such matters as child-rearing and house-hold budgeting, Cooper turned the league into the only national Maori forum then in existence, and into the major non-political pressure group for representations to governments on Maori issues (both these roles would later be subsumed by the New Zealand Maori Council, set up by the Holyoake National Government in 1962). She was also especially active in securing adequate Maori housing in Auckland, in building urban marae and in fundraising for voluntary welfare programmes, especially those organised by the Catholic Church.

In 1975 Whina Cooper established Te Roopu o te Matakite and led the Maori Land March from Te Hapua in the far north to Parliament in Wellington, dramatising a national Maori determination not to lose further land to Pakeha or Crown ownership. She remained a prominent Maori protest figure in the 1980s and 1990s, still adopting new causes and formulating representations to ministers of Maori Affairs as she approached 100 years of age. She had long since departed from traditional patterns of Maori leadership in that her influence in later years sprang from her reputation as an urban and national Maori figure – as Te Whaea o te Motu or Mother of the Nation – rather than from her localised or tribal position. She died in 1994 aged 98.

Another training-ground for non-tribal Maori leadership was the Public Service. After World War II a large number of former Maori Battalion officers moved into Maori-related posts in government departments. Many of them completed university diplomas or degrees with rehabilitation assistance. To some extent, these men provided an extension of the Young Maori Party model in that they accepted the need for Western education and administrative skills so as to function influentially within the system of government. Unlike their predecessors, however, they had seen the Maori language and culture survive into the second half of the twentieth century and they were impatient with anything less than full equality with Pakeha citizens. One of their number, Rangi Logan, voiced their feelings in the 1946 general election campaign: 'We more than did our share at El Alamein and elsewhere ... [We] shed our blood in two world wars.' If these acts had done nothing else, he declared, they had at least purchased the right to equality of opportunity.

These men generally accepted the *raison d'être* for the Department of Maori Affairs and the hierarchical structure by which it functioned. They accepted the concepts behind the land development schemes, incorporations and post-war welfare services. They also accepted that, to make a significant impact on the Pakeha-dominated systems of party politics and the Public Service, they had to lobby as Maori presenting Maori causes. To be seen as Waikato stating Waikato views or Ngapuhi representing Ngapuhi would have been to exercise relatively little influence over government policy and legislation. In this they were assisted by their Maori Battalion service, which helped them to view Maori as a people rather than as a group of competing tribal units, and by the detribalisation that accelerated after World War II as more and more families left their traditional rohe and intermarried in the cities with Maori from other regions.

These same Maori bureaucrats would be challenged a generation later, in the 1960s and 1970s, by a group of largely urban-based Maori dissidents, most of whom had backgrounds in tertiary education. They included Ranginui Walker and Patu Hohepa of the Auckland District Maori Council, Robert Mahuta of the Tainui kahui ariki, Koro Dewes and Sydney Mead of Victoria University, Tipene O'Regan of Ngai Tahu, and leaders of protest groups such as Nga Tamatoa and Te Ahi Kaa, Syd and Hana Jackson, Atareta Poananga and others. All these people spoke out for Maori interests more emphatically and more abrasively than their predecessors, and they would question whether the Public Service and local authority structures, with Pakeha reserving for themselves key decision-making positions, were the most appropriate ones to deal with the needs and aspirations of an indigenous Pacific people.

A major source of discontent among almost all Maori leaders after World War II was that successive governments were slow to perceive the changing conditions and needs generated by Maori urbanisation, and to respond to representations by Maori to address those needs. Labour made some concessions by passing the Maori Social and Economic Advancement Act in

1945, which allowed for the establishment of local tribal committees and the first Maori welfare officers appointed to work with urban Maori. Labour also dropped the expression 'Native' from all official usage in 1947 and substituted 'Maori'.

When National came to power under Sid Holland in 1949 they did so without any Maori MPs and without any previous interest or conspicuous expertise in Maori affairs. On the advice of officials, however, they did allow the setting-up of the voluntary Maori Women's Welfare League, and in 1962 they accepted a recommendation of the Hunn Report and passed the Maori Welfare Act, which set up the New Zealand Maori Council, a pan-tribal organisation above the tribal committees established by Labour. The feature of the legislation that most appealed to National was that the Maori Council would provide a form of largely National-supporting Maori leadership that would counter the Maori MPs, all of whom had been Labour since 1943. As expected, the first three chairmen of the council, Sir Turi Carroll (nephew of Sir James), Pei Te Hurinui Jones and Graham Latimer, were all National Party supporters. What National did not expect, however, was that, despite the conservative leadership, the council would campaign strongly for the recognition and implementation of the Treaty of Waitangi.

The Hunn Report of 1960 was a milestone for its time. It had been commissioned but not actioned by the Nash Labour Government: Walter Nash, who had become Prime Minister and Minister of Maori Affairs in his late 70s, was by this time a notorious procrastinator and simply put the report away in a drawer. It represented, and this may have made it unwelcome in the eyes of the minister, the first official recognition that Maori urbanisation was occurring and that the unpreparedness for it was creating difficulties in New Zealand towns and cities. Jack Hunn, Secretary of Maori Affairs, assumed, however, like so many of his predecessors, that the future of New Zealand's two major cultures was to blend and that this was a desirable process.

Articulate Maori spokespersons attacked the report on the grounds that Maori themselves had been insufficiently consulted in its preparation and did not want to 'blend' with Pakeha culture. The National Government initially accepted Hunn's recommendation that suburban Maori houses should be 'pepper-potted' among general state houses, but later abandoned the policy when Maori made it clear – as did many Pakeha who did not want Maori neighbours – that they disliked it. The report's most successful outcomes were the setting-up of the Maori Education Foundation to help pupils through secondary and tertiary education, the extension of trade training facilities for Maori, and the provision for hostel accommodation and pre-employment courses for young Maori new to city life.

While all of these measures did some good, especially trade training, in total they were to prove an inadequate response to the magnitude of the problems created by urbanisation. In particular, there were no government initiatives at this time to arrest the decline in Maori language and the erosion of Maori culture. Nor did governments initially favour such policies, because they accepted the blueprint of integration. It was assumed, erroneously, that those who grew up feeling 'less Maori' than their parents and grandparents would by that very fact become 'more European'. Instead, many such people simply grew up in a cultural vacuum and felt directionless and detached from the society into which they emerged as adults; and these formed a large proportion of those subsequently represented in crime statistics.

It was also taken for granted by most Pakeha, including the political leadership of the day, that 'integration' in fact meant 'assimilation'. And assimilation required Maori to become Pakeha. Integration would have implied an equal obligation on the part of Pakeha to learn Maori language and customs, and there was no official encouragement to follow this path. Instead, Maori were expected to learn the English language and Western ways of living, and many Maori parents and grandparents accepted this as inevitable. As a result Maori values and institutions had a lower status in New Zealand life than their Pakeha equivalents. Even Maori who wanted to pursue Maoriness as part of urban life were in many respects prevented from doing so because Pakeha-oriented institutions – in education, in the health system, in the legal system – could see neither the value nor the necessity of such measures. When Maori in the Public Service, such as John Rangihau, advocated such measures, they were quickly dismissed as separatists and as potential sources of social divisiveness. The agencies of the state were committed to reflecting Western values, criteria, practices and priorities rather than Maori ones.

The more such factors were recognised and articulated in Maori quarters in the 1960s and 1970s, the more they came to be resented and resisted. And this resentment led to the rise of urban protest groups: Maori organisations which articulated Maori considerations and needs, but which adopted Western rather than traditional modes of expression, such as demonstrations, picketing, petitions to Parliament, press releases and appearances on television.

The first such group to make its influence felt was formed in the late 1960s in Auckland, where Maori numbers were by this time greatest and where the unpreparedness of the Government, local bodies and individual Pakeha for Maori urbanisation was most vividly apparent. Nga Tamatoa (the Young Warriors) grew out of the Auckland University Maori

Club but its membership included young manual workers. Like the Maori Organisation on Human Rights, established in Wellington by Tama Poata slightly earlier, it was initially a reaction to the National Government's 1967 Maori Affairs Amendment Act, which gave the Maori Trustee additional powers to take control of Maori land, and which provided for land owned by fewer than four persons to pass into individual titles. The Act was immediately attacked by Maori opinion as a high-handed measure lacking the support of the very people it purported to help.

Rapidly, both protest groups widened their campaign to include the teaching of Maori language in schools, Maori control of Maori land and Maori monies (trust boards could act in financial matters only with the permission of the Minister of Maori Affairs), legal assistance for Maori offenders appearing unrepresented before the courts and for Maori in prisons, an end to annual celebrations commemorating the signing of the Treaty of Waitangi, and the severing of sporting links, especially the rugby association, with the apartheid-conditioned Republic of South Africa. They were joined by Te Reo Maori, centred on Victoria University, which concerned itself primarily with the promotion of Maori language and literature and with the performance of the media, especially television, in dealing with Maori issues.

Whina Cooper's Te Roopu o te Matakite (later called Te Matakite o Aotearoa) grew out of the Maori Land March of 1975. Separate groups formed to campaign for the return of the Raglan golf course to Maori ownership (the land had been seized by the Government and a community displaced in order to build an emergency landing-strip during World War II), and for the return of Bastion Point in Auckland to Ngati Whatua ownership. This last led to a seventeen-month occupation of the Point in

1977–78, and to the arrest of 200 protestors in May 1978 after the largest police operation in the country up until that time. In 1979 the Labour MP for Northern Maori and former Minister of Maori Affairs, Matiu Rata, resigned his parliamentary seat and contested it as leader of the Mana Motuhake Party, which presented a modest programme for a greater degree of Maori self-determination. He did not regain the seat, but Mana Motuhake achieved second place to Labour in all four Maori electorates, the most spectacular launch of a new political party since the appearance of the Ratana movement. Over the next decade Labour would progressively erode support for Mana Motuhake by adopting most of its policies.

The combined effect of the activities of all these groups was to focus media attention on Maori issues in a way that had never occurred previously, gradually to radicalise such establishment organisations as the New Zealand Maori Council, Maori parliamentary representation and the mainline churches, and to bring about major changes in the operations of such government departments as Education, Social Welfare, Justice and Maori Affairs. Kohanga reo or 'language nests' were set up for pre-schoolers, one-year teacher training courses were established for Maori speakers, public funds became available for the first time for the renovation of marae buildings, legal aid was offered for Maori offenders, and the Race Relations Act 1971 outlawed discrimination and established the Race Relations Conciliator's Office to promote public education on ethnic issues, deal with complaints about discrimination and to mitigate racial and cultural conflict.

While all these measures were being discussed and implemented, the literature on Maori history and culture was burgeoning, indicating both a new Maori market for such publications and a growing interest in tangata whenua culture on the part of Pakeha. Work by Maori writers – Hone Tuwhare, Witi Ihimaera, Patricia Grace, Ngahuia Te Awekotuku and Keri Hulme among them – was published more often. Maori artists – Para Matchitt, Cliff Whiting, Ralph Hotere – attracted increasing public attention. A Maori writers and artist's organisation began to hold annual hui on marae around the country. Marae which had been derelict for decades were revived and renovated. By the late 1970s there was talk of a 'Maori renaissance' and ample evidence that a movement of this kind was gathering momentum.

Perhaps the single measure with the most pervasive influence, though not greatly commented on at the time, was the establishment of the Waitangi Tribunal by the Rowling Labour Government in 1975. This was set up to deliberate and rule on alleged breaches of the Treaty of Waitangi that occurred from that date. Little public notice was taken of its operations until 1985, when its powers were made retrospective to 1840. From this time, it became the focus of Maori resource claims against the Crown and the source of major settlements that would reinvigorate tribal activity over large parts of the country. It was one of a series of measures which so changed the face of New Zealand life in the 1980s and 1990s that their cumulative effect could legitimately be called a revolution.

29

A Revolution Confirmed

If the 1960s was the decade in which New Zealand's turning away from traditional allegiances and patterns of association first became unmistakably apparent, then the 1980s was the time when new directions were confirmed. The unprecedented disruption wrought by widespread opposition to the 1981 Springbok tour ensured that official New Zealand teams would never again play rugby with South African sides in the era of apartheid. And the 1984 general election turned out to be as much of a watershed for the whole country as those which had brought to power the Liberals in 1891 and Labour in 1935. And again it was Labour who would initiate both the deconstructing and the rebuilding.

Sir Robert Muldoon's National Government of 1975 to 1984 was the last to involve itself in the New Zealand economy in a big-spending and heavily interventionist way. At different points in its term it imposed a wage and price freeze, controlled rents, directors' fees and dividends, and tried to force down interest rates. It invested heavily and ultimately unsuccessfully in a programme to make synthetic petrol, ammonia urea and methanol out of natural gas – the so-called 'Think Big' strategy designed to make New Zealand self-reliant in energy and soak up unemployment. And it instituted a superannuation regime that the country simply could not afford. These were all policies and tactics favoured by the man who had chosen to be both Prime Minister *and* Minister of Finance, and who was so strong-willed that nobody in his cabinet or caucus was capable of challenging him or deflecting policies he was determined to follow.

By 1984 Muldoon's hold on considerable power was shaky, however. He had already had to sack one minister, Derek Quigley, for publicly questioning the value of the 'Think Big' strategy and the Prime Minister's insistence on a high level of economic control. Two other National MPs, Marilyn Waring and Mike Minogue, were threatening to cross the floor and vote against the Government. And so Muldoon, showing the effects of both illness and alcohol, made an impulsive decision to call a snap election, which the Government lost. The swing of the electoral pendulum not only brought Labour to power again for only the fourth time in half a century, but also swept out of office a generation of politicians whose views and values had been formed by the Great Depression and participation in World War II.

Ministers in the new government, led by former Auckland barrister David Lange, were mainly in their 40s and brought new perspectives to bear on both government policies and New Zealand's place in the world. They turned away from the kinds of economic strategy that had been standard in New Zealand since the 1930s. One of their number, Michael Bassett, an historian by profession, described their perspective in these terms: '[The] era of big government had largely been played out. The world economic downturn in the 1970s rendered further expensive extensions to the welfare state unaffordable, especially in New Zealand, where poor economic stewardship [had] caused the country to subside swiftly down the OECD performance ladder. In any event, doubts were growing inside the Labour Party about the effectiveness of big spending.'

The leader of and major spokesman for the doubters was Finance Minister Roger Douglas, who had a background in business and accountancy. Persuaded by his arguments, the Labour cabinet set in motion reform of the Public Service, a transformation of some departments into state-owned enterprises charged with making a profit, and the sale of others, such as the telephone and banking sections of the former Post Office, New Zealand Steel and the Shipping Corporation. Where traditional Labour had sought to be as widely involved as possible in the business of running the country, the new Labour Government was ready to devolve or sell as much of its inherited business as it could.

Economic controls were also shed in an enactment of the kinds of policy that Quigley had been trying to sell to his National colleagues. Agriculture and consumer subsidies were phased out ('It's possible to grow bananas on Mt Cook,' Roger Douglas had famously announced, 'but is it worth spending the money it takes to do so?'). The financial market was deregulated, the New Zealand dollar floated for the first time, controls on foreign exchange were removed, new banks allowed to open their doors. Douglas also introduced a sales tax on goods and services, initially set at 10 per cent and subsequently raised to 12.5 per cent, and a heavy surtax on superannuation, which the previous Government had made universally available at the age of 60 and set at 80 per cent of the average wage. The marginal tax rate was reduced from 65 cents in the dollar to 33. The combined effect of all these measures, which amounted to a wholesale adoption of a monetarist programme, was eventually to reduce inflation dramatically, bring down national debt and increase economic growth.

Local government too was reorganised drastically. As minister responsible for this sector, Michael Bassett reduced some 500 local authorities and special purpose boards to less than 100. Geoffrey Palmer, Deputy Prime Minister, Minister of Justice and of the Environment, devised a Bill of Rights to protect civil liberties and the Resource Management Act, eventually passed in the term of the subsequent National Government (1991), to ensure greater environmental protection, more sustainable use of resources, control of development and acknowledgement of Maori traditions and values in local body planning processes.

There was a political price to pay for both the scope and the pace of these changes, however. Because of the suddenness of the 1984 election campaign, Labour had not laid out a coherent economic plan for the consideration of voters. The policies that were eventually enacted came as a shock to many Labour supporters, and to some MPs and cabinet ministers. Whereas Roger Douglas had been refining his monetarist ideas for years and had presented them previously in an unauthorised 'alternative' budget, many of his colleagues were strong on social policy but economically illiterate. They initially allowed the Douglas-inspired programme to proceed, because they were ill-equipped to argue with it and scarcely recognised at first the nature of what was occurring. By the time they had concluded that the social cost of the policies was too high – in tearing the heart out of small communities by post office closures and loss of forestry jobs, for example – it was too late: the policies were entrenched. The only other option then became fighting a rearguard action against a programme which they and many supporters outside Parliament viewed as inimical to Labour values. Former Labour Party president and by this time back-bench MP, Jim Anderton, left the party over this issue and formed first the New Labour Party and then the Alliance, a grouping of small parties which also included Mana Motuhake and the remnants of Social Credit.

In addition, while Labour won re-election in August 1987 (with a measure of cross-over National Party support), a stockmarket crash later that year, triggered by falls on overseas markets, resulted in company collapses and a heavy loss of funds by small-scale private investors. This in turn led to a loss of confidence in the Government's authority in financial matters.

A major split developed too between Douglas, who wanted to press on with deregulation, reduction of the tax rate and asset sales, and Prime Minister Lange, who was becoming less confident about the value and legitimacy of the Government's economic programme. A powerful orator in the soapbox tradi-tion, Lange had been Labour's greatest asset in two successful election campaigns. By 1988 he nursed so many reservations about the effects of his Government's policies on traditional Labour supporters that he sabotaged Douglas's introduction of a low, flat tax rate and called for a pause in the programme of restructuring and reform. After more than a year of feuding with Douglas and his strongest supporters, Lange resigned when the cabinet backed Douglas and one of his associate ministers Richard Prebble, whom Lange had sacked. The now visibly damaged Government staggered on for another year under the leadership of first Geoffrey Palmer and then briefly the more populist Mike Moore. Ironically, the National Government that took office at the end of 1990 under the genial farmer Jim Bolger initially persisted with so-called 'Rogernomics' policies under the even more markedly monetarist Finance Minister, Ruth Richardson. Richardson, a 'conviction politician', persuaded her colleagues to reduce spending on welfare significantly, increase pharmaceutical charges and charge market rentals to Housing New Zealand tenants. In addition, National failed to lift the superannuation surcharge as they had promised, because of what they judged to be the parlous state of the economy.

The effect on the electorate of successive governments of different colours enacting controversial policies for which they had neither sought nor obtained a mandate was to increase considerably the widespread mistrust of politicians (a poll in 1975 had revealed a 32 per cent public trust of politicians and Parliament, but by 1992 that had dropped to 4 per cent). Calls mounted for electoral reform. After a royal commission recommended that a mixed-member proportional system (MMP) like that operating in Germany would better suit New Zealand's needs, a majority of the electorate voted for that option in a binding referendum in 1993. The National Government undertook to implement it in 1996. The new system would provide 120 MPs (up from just under 100), 60 of whom would represent electorates and 60 from party lists. The proportionality of Parliament would be determined by the percentage of party votes won by each party. To win any list seats a party had either to elect at least one member for a constituency seat or pass a threshold of 5 per cent.

Prior to the 1996 general election, there was a good deal of manoeuvring as some MPs defected from established political parties and formed groups which they hoped would be able to garner 5 per cent of the vote. Roger Douglas and Richard Prebble peeled off from Labour and set up the Association of Consumers and Taxpayers (ACT), attracting some support from like-minded former National supporters such as Quigley. At the other end of the spectrum, former Labour MP Jim Anderton welded his group of small parties into the Alliance, which generated policies closer to those of traditional Labour. Breakaway National Maori MP Winston Peters had founded New Zealand First – more conservative than Labour but somewhat more liberal than National, according to conventional political values. Despite a measure of disintegration, National and Labour remained the largest parties in Parliament.

The first MMP general election in 1996 achieved some of the advantages claimed for the change of system. The number of Maori in Parliament increased from five to fifteen, leading, inevitably, to renewed calls for the abolition of the Maori seats; the number of women rose from 21 to 35; and there were three Pacific Island MPs and one New Zealand Chinese. In addition, a far wider range of political and philosophical views was represented than had occurred under the first-past-the-post system. All these ingredients would make political management a more taxing task than it had been previously.

The time it took National to form its coalition with New Zealand First, who held the balance of power with seventeen seats, had the effect of eroding public confidence in the new system, however. So did the antics of some of New Zealand First's MPs, including the party leader, in the years that followed. National dropped Jim Bolger as leader before the Government's term was over, in part because it had doubts about the manner in which he was dealing with Peters. He was replaced by Jenny Shipley, a former teacher who had held the Health and Social Welfare portfolios and who then became the country's first woman Prime Minister. But she failed to win a general election as party leader. After falling out with her coalition partner, she kept National in office for a further two years by cobbling together a second coalition of New Zealand First fragments and an independent MP expelled from the Alliance, and retaining the support of ACT and the one United MP. But the prognosis for both the Government and the MMP system was not good by the time of the next general election in 1999.

Labour was by this time led by Helen Clark, who had succeeded Mike Moore after he took Labour to a second defeat in 1993. After a shaky start as Opposition Leader, when it seemed more than once that her colleagues might replace her, she had developed into the most commanding figure in Parliament. It was no real surprise that she led Labour and its pre-announced coalition partner, Jim Anderton's Alliance, to victory in 1999. The manner in which the new Government quickly completed coalition formalities and the fact that the agreement lasted almost until the following election – when the Alliance implod-ed with internal dissension – went a long way towards restoring public faith in a political system that had been on trial in the previous three years and found wanting.

Despite the controversies generated by Labour's 1984–90 reforms, few of them were reversed by subsequent administra-tions. The Bolger National Government even retained Labour's anti-nuclear policy, which had forbidden visits to New Zealand ports by nuclear-armed or nuclear-powered vessels. This new strategy, which grew out of a 'people's peace movement' in the 1970s and 1980s and opposition to French nuclear testing in the Pacific, was strengthened by the considerable overlap in mem-bership between that movement and the Labour Party. It strained relations with New Zealand's traditional allies, Britain and the United States. It also ended – at the insistence of the Reagan-led American administration – New Zealand's partici-pation in ANZUS, and hence in shared intelligence and exercises with American forces. The determination of both David Lange and the wider New Zealand electorate to persist with this policy of 'independence' was only increased when, in 1985, French secret service agents sank the Greenpeace flagship *Rainbow Warrior* in Auckland harbour. Both the American and British Governments of the time declined to condemn this act of terrorism by one of the leading members of the Western alliance. New Zealand was learning that there was a price to pay for being independent from that alliance, but it showed no inclination to change its stance in the face of bullying or 'punishment'.

Some former ministers in the Lange Government hinted subsequently that the Government as a whole had never intended – nor had the cabinet – to break the alliance with the United States, an action which inevitably had consequences for trade prospects in addition to defence implications. In their view, the anti-nuclear policy was embraced by the Prime Minister to cement his own ties with the Labour movement – 'to enter his inheritance as its leader', as Michael Bassett put it. While other ministers were preoccupied with the considerable burden of reforms in their own portfolios, the Prime Minister allowed negotiations with the American administration to drift to the point where the relationship was unsalvageable and the break with ANZUS became inevitable. However much truth there is in that scenario, it is undeniable that other members of the Lange cabinet embraced the anti-nuclear policy and its consequences when they recognised its electoral popularity.

Partly because of the falling away from the bilateral defence connection with the United States, New Zealand through the 1980s and 1990s became more heavily committed to United Nations-sponsored peacekeeping operations. The country had been involved in such operations before, but only on a small scale and usually using police or territorials. The scale of involvement increased from the 1980s, in both the number of operations and the number of regular defence force personnel used – in the Middle East, Africa, Asia, the Balkans and the Pacific. Over these two decades New Zealanders earned a high reputation for being good at specific tasks, such as mine clearance and training locals to do this work, and for being skilled in interacting with civilians who had been traumatised by their proximity to armed conflict. The latter success owed something to the 'hands-on' approach, by which everyone from senior officers to lower ranks were involved in all duties, and was partly explained by what one commentator called the 'Maori–Pakeha mix and lack of formality'.

These successes culminated in a large commitment of troops to Bosnia between 1992 and 1996, after the break-up of the former Yugoslavia. Three army contingents were sent, each 250-strong – the first deployment of New Zealand troops to Europe since World War II. Troops were also committed to East Timor between 1999 and 2002, in what most New Zealanders were prepared to recognise as the country's neighbourhood. This operation involved 6000 personnel from all three New Zealand services. Five lost their lives: one in a militia ambush, three as a result of accidents, and one from suicide.

Despite the cooling of relations with the United States, New Zealand was generally well regarded in multilateral organisations through this period, as shown by its election to one of the UN Security Council rotating seats in the 1990s, and by the election of former Prime Minister Mike Moore to the director-generalship of the World Trade Organisation in 1999 and of former Deputy Prime Minister Don McKinnon as Commonwealth Secretary-General in 2000, the position his compatriot Alister McIntosh had narrowly missed out on 35 years earlier. (To those unprecedented achievements, two more could be added: by the early years of the twenty-first century two of England's most ancient and revered educational institutions, Eton College and Oxford University, were also headed by New Zealanders, John Lewis and John Hood respectively.)

The other international arena in which New Zealand continued to depart from traditional patterns was in seeking trading opportunities with countries outside the United Kingdom. Whereas the percentage of exports going to Britain had been 87.4 in 1940, by the close of the twentieth century that had fallen to a mere 6.2. There was a substantial rise in exports to Australia over the same period, accelerated by the Closer Economic Relations agreement, from 2.9 per cent to 21.4 and to the United States, European Community, Canada, Japan and other Asian markets such as China, Taiwan, Korea, Thailand, Indonesia and Malaysia.

The relative proportions of commodities sold had also altered considerably. Wool, which had made up nearly 50 per cent of the country's exports in 1880, constituted a mere 2.8 per cent by 1999. Meat was down from 27 per cent in 1940 to a smaller but still significant 13.2 per cent in 1999. And dairy products – butter, cheese and various milk derivatives – made up 23 per cent in 1999, a drop from its 1940 peak of 36 per cent but again still important. Forestry exports were up to 11.3 per cent from almost nothing 60 years before. Exports of other commodities such as seafood (5.5 per cent), wine and various pastoral products were also growing.

While most New Zealanders who lived overseas did so in English-speaking countries such as the United Kingdom, Australia, Canada and the United States, the ethnic mix of the population within New Zealand was changing, with significant increases in the Asian and Pacific Island populations. While the

Pakeha majority made up almost 73 per cent of the total population in 2001 (most with British ancestry) and those of Maori descent 18.4 per cent, some other ethnic groups which had not been significant before the mid-twentieth century were now growing: New Zealand Asians totalled 6 per cent and Pacific Islanders 4.6 per cent. Of those with a Pacific Island background, the largest groups were of Samoan and Cook Islands descent, followed by Tongans, Niueans and Tokelauans. Small Middle Eastern and African communities were growing as New Zealand took a low number of refugees from those regions.

Most interestingly, perhaps, the proportion of the New Zealand population born in New Zealand in 2001 was 80.5 per cent, as against 64.8 a century before. The largest portion of those born elsewhere, 6.3 per cent, still came from the United Kingdom, but that was well down from the 29 per cent of New Zealanders born there 100 years earlier. The next largest group in 2001 was the 4.7 per cent born in Asia, up from 0.7 per cent in 1896.

This far greater degree of ethnic diversity than the older British-Pakeha and Maori New Zealanders had known did create anxiety and insecurity in some quarters, and there were signs that the country's earlier racism towards Chinese immigrants was reviving. There were also occasional disturbances between particular minority groups. But it was Maori who were most affected by the social and political changes occurring in New Zealand at the end of the twentieth century. In this sector, the new policy directions initiated by the Lange–Palmer Labour Government and carried on after 1990 by the Bolger National Government were so extensive as to amount almost to a form of social engineering.

In this set of politically bipartisan policies, as many government services as possible, especially those associated with health and welfare and those previously the responsibility of the

Department of Maori Affairs, were to be devolved from the Public Service to iwi authorities. These authorities were to be well resourced either from state funding or from successful claims against the Crown for breaches of the Treaty of Waitangi. It was also accepted that the state had a responsibility under the Treaty of Waitangi actively to fund the promotion of Maori culture and language rather than simply allowing them to co-exist with mainstream Pakeha culture. As part of these policy shifts, the old Department of Maori Affairs was dismantled and replaced with a slimmed-down Te Puni Kokiri or Ministry of Maori Development.

A variety of measures contributed to these new directions. One of the most important, as noted earlier, was authorisation for the Waitangi Tribunal to consider claims going back to 1840. This new policy saw the number of claims registered with the tribunal swell from half a dozen in 1984 to almost 1000 by the end of the century. The largest settlements achieved in the first decade of the new policy were with Tainui and Ngai Tahu, for compensation packages of $170 million. Ngai Tahu began a programme of judicious investment and commercial activities which immediately began to increase the worth of their assets. Tainui, in part because of leadership disputes and personality clashes, got off to a near-disastrous start and lost large sums of money.

Another far-reaching policy change affecting Maori resulted from the restructuring of the state sector. The 1986 State Owned Enterprises Act had given the Waitangi Tribunal power to adjudicate on the status of land being transferred from government departments to SOEs. The following year, in a case arising out of this process, the Court of Appeal ruled that 'the principles of the treaty override everything else in the State Owned Enterprises Act, and these principles require the Pakeha and

Maori treaty partners to act towards each other reasonably and with the utmost good faith'.

This decision, and subsequent references to the Treaty of Waitangi grafted onto other bills and amendments to previous Acts, such as those governing health, education and conservation, gave the Treaty an explicit place in New Zealand jurisprudence for the first time. They also represented an acknowledgement by Parliament that the Treaty had not been simply a mechanism for transferring the sovereignty of the country from Maori to the Crown, but that it was now recognised as providing a framework for the present and future relationship of Maori and the Crown, the two Treaty partners.

While this wide interpretation of the significance of the Treaty was broadly accepted by the leadership of the country's two major political parties, it was not without controversy in other quarters. Some conservative politicians complained that the 'judicial activism' of the Court of Appeal had forced Parliament's hand, to which the president of the court, Sir Robin Cooke, replied that it was the responsibility of the courts to give 'sensible meaning' and effect to government legislation. Early in the twenty-first century the National Party showed some signs of wanting to retreat from the position it had taken on the issue almost two decades earlier.

In another major settlement, the National Government in 1993 offered Maori the so-called 'Sealords Deal', by which the Crown purchased 20 per cent of the nation's fish quota for allocation among Maori tribes. In return Maori were asked, and agreed through their tribal leadership, to drop Treaty-based claims to the country's fisheries resources. The actual distribution was to be carried out by a government-appointed Waitangi Fisheries Commission, which then became bogged down for more than a decade in trying to devise a formula that would accommodate all Maori claims and ensure that some of the multimillion-dollar resource also found its way to urban Maori, who lived outside recognised iwi boundaries and organisations.

By the turn of the twenty-first century, major and irreversible adjustments had been made to the relationships between Maori and Pakeha and between Maori and the Crown. Maori had become a far more visible component of every aspect of the country's life than they had been a generation earlier, though they were still under-represented in the professions and higher-income suburbs and over-represented in crime statistics. Maori elements were increasingly apparent in the arts, literature and rituals of the nation (and beyond: Keri Hulme's novel *The Bone People* had won the Booker Prize in London in 1985). Thanks to MMP, there were now 18 members of Parliament who identified as Maori rather than the smaller number who had held the specifically Maori seats. For the first time, all the country's institutions were bending slowly but decisively in the direction of Maori needs and aspirations. The momentum of these changes would be maintained – but not without controversy.

Posthistory

30

Configurations Old and New

The late twentieth century was the period in which New Zealanders dismantled many of the traditional certainties which had been their foundation for a coherent and national view of the world – in trade, defence, the use of primary resources, the operation of the parliamentary system, social welfare, the ethnic composition of the country's citizenry, the balance of the primary relationship between Maori and Pakeha. The combined effect of these changes would produce a period of uncertainty and adjustment in the early years of the twenty-first century, as New Zealanders waited for new patterns to coalesce and new understandings to percolate through society which might restore a measure of the cohesion that had been lost – or which, on the other hand, might not, if the price for greater plurality proved to be a degree of disjunction and social divergence.

Nowhere was the uncertainty about future configurations more clearly demonstrated than in the country's ambiguous relations with Asia. As trade with Britain necessarily diminished, New Zealand had sought to direct more of its products and produce towards the largest markets in the region, in the populous countries of South-east Asia. Prime Minister Bolger even began to talk of New Zealand finding at least part of its identity from its proximity to Asia. But even more of those exports went to a *combination* of 'Anglo-Saxon' countries – the United Kingdom, Australia, the United States and Canada. Moreover, the vast majority of New Zealanders resident abroad chose to live in the UK and the 'neo-Europes' in preference to Asia and the Pacific. And increased immigration to New Zealand from Asian countries in the 1990s – from Taiwan, Hong Kong, China and Korea – reactivated anti-Asian prejudice which had been so strong 100 years earlier, particularly in Auckland, which received most of those new immigrants. Statistics New Zealand estimated that there were 346,000 Asians living in the country in 2003, and expected that figure to rise to 604,000 or 13 per cent of the local population by 2021. This projection was taken as a warning by some political parties, especially New Zealand First, whose very name was an attempt to gain electoral traction from exploiting the feelings of insecurity which many Pakeha New Zealanders felt as the face of New Zealand became more ethnically diverse.

The most important political and social challenges of the new era would be those surrounding the sustainable use of the country's primary resources, finding sufficient stable markets abroad for its goods and services to sustain the degree of prosperity most New Zealanders had come to expect, constructing a welfare system that helped the genuinely needy but did not at the same time drain the enterprise of the potentially able, and negotiating a new social contract between Maori and Pakeha. History, as always, offered signposts to suggest ways in which these problematic territories might be negotiated.

In the case of the resource issues, there were the cautionary examples of the 'future-eating' activities of early Maori and the reckless extraction of the country's earliest industries, which had sacrificed long-term security in favour of spectacular short-term profit. There was also the spectacle of the conversion of much of the country into grasslands without a proper accounting of the benefits and deficits of such a strategy. The search for diverse and stable markets would always be conditioned by the twin spectres of the Great Depression and Britain's decision to join the European Community, both of which had revealed the vulnerability of countries that relied on too few markets for a limited range of products. And reform of the welfare system involved balancing the long-cherished concept of the welfare state against a realistic appraisal of the kinds of incentives that people require in order to contribute to the wealth of their own communities. As for the domain of Maori–Pakeha relationships, that more than any other would be shaped and reshaped by 200 years of shared experience.

'History,' wrote Arthur Schlesinger Jr, 'haunts even generations who refuse to [acknowledge it]. Rhythms, patterns, continuities, drift out of time long forgotten to mould the present and to colour the shape of things to come.' This observation is as profoundly true of New Zealand in the twenty-first century AD as it is of anywhere else in the world where humankind has managed to retain a foothold for any length of time.

Jean Pottier L'Horme of the French India Company, who came ashore with Jean de Surville in Doubtless Bay in December 1769, was the first European to describe a Maori powhiri. '[All] the people were scattered here and there on the hills and the shore, and were no doubt doing honour to the new arrivals by waving ... branches of grass ... to one side, as though to create a breeze ... [It] started right from when they first saw the boat, and went on until the captain set foot on land.' Pottier L'Horme was of the opinion that the Ngati Kahu people who performed this ceremony were 'barbarians' and of 'limited intelligence'. But he speculated that, exposed to the light of true religion and the gifts of European civilisation, they might be persuaded to alter their savage ways.

Were Jean Pottier L'Horme able to re-enter New Zealand more than three centuries after this glimpsed encounter, he would discover much that had changed in the landscape and in the behaviour of the indigenous people he had observed. And he would find it difficult to attach with any credibility the labels 'barbarian', 'savage' and 'heathen' to the appearance and behaviour of contemporary Maori. At the same time, if he returned to a Maori community, and returned with unfeigned interest and genial intentions, he would as likely be welcomed by a powhiri that involved his hosts waving greenery, 'as though to create a breeze', as he had been in 1769. As so often in history, elements of continuity in human affairs would be as noticeable and as interesting as elements of change.

There would be other elements of continuity: the strong degree of tribal competitiveness that delayed the distribution of fishing quota by the Waitangi Fisheries Commission; the tenacity with which Maori staked claims for recognition of their rights to the seabed and foreshore; the appetite for martial behaviour that animated urban Maori gangs and made the New Zealand Army a popular Maori career choice; the admiration of people who were cheeky and cunning in the mould of Maui-tikitiki-a-Taranga; the continued easy resort to song and story when there were messages of a communal kind to be trans-mitted; the continuing weight of unwritten tikanga or tradition; the I-am-we ethos of tribal culture in which the corporate self was more important than individual identity. All these elements were part of the 'rhythms, patterns and continuities' that emerged from time past to leave an imprint on the Maori present.

What was true of Maori culture was also true of that of the country as a whole. A myriad of echoes of old New Zealand still resonate within the contemporary culture. The notion that the country is special, and has features that the rest of the world could study with profit, lingers in the group memory of Seddon's characterisation of New Zealand as 'God's own'; the 'man alone' ideal, the hunting-shooting-fishing ethic and the solitary bachelor, survive from the frontier days when, because of a shortage of women, many men chose to live that way; the bach culture based on a strong desire to live simply on the margin between land and sea, or between tamed and untamed places; the determination to preserve access to rivers, lakes and beaches via Jock McKenzie's highly valued but insufficiently distributed bequest, the 'Queen's chain'; the highly practical do-it-yourself tradition of home maintenance that sets men to work on houses, boats and gardens; the fiercely egalitarian instinct which prefers to see resources spread widely and equitably throughout the community and not, as elsewhere, in massive disproportion between the very rich and the very poor; the reactions of dissenting individuals or groups in the face of authority; the largely informal social attitudes. All these phenomena have a history which can be linked to the attitudes and values formed in the nation's years of gestation.

The continuing popularity of attendance at Anzac Day services, the country's first example of non-Maori indigenous ceremonial, indicated a persistent and widespread belief that something of enormous significance to New Zealanders occurred on that distant peninsula in the Aegean Sea – not a 'baptism of blood', perhaps, but a degree of sacrifice for an ideal that gave New Zealanders a shared nationwide experience and was still a source of admiration when the ideal itself had evaporated. And with that belief went a growing admiration for all New Zealanders who had gone to fight wars in distant lands, an admiration that was only increased by the knowledge that such gestures on such a scale would never be made again. Some went so far as to suggest that the degree of unanimity generated by Anzac Day ought to be harnessed by making it the country's national day in preference to 6 February, Waitangi Day, which would always involve marking the score-card on race relations and a less than perfect verdict.

The criteria by which New Zealanders identified their own brand of heroes or persons of repute also had deep roots in shared memories and experience. To some extent, what New Zealanders admired could be deduced from what they disliked. Writing in 1951, the civil servant Reuel Lochore had attempted to define what it was about Continental immigrants that made Anglo-Saxon New Zealanders recoil. 'They lack discretion and tact. They revel in displays of emotionalism and self-pity, and fail to realise how we despise such lack of self-control. On social occasions ... they talk loudly and untiringly about their own affairs. Being bad listeners they cannot take a hint, nor sense an attitude, from what we leave unsaid.'

While these comments had about them the odour of old-fashioned New Zealand xenophobia, it could be noted that no one exhibited the converse of the attitudes and habits described more than Edmund Percival Hillary. Hillary, formerly a bee-keeper from Tuakau, had by the turn of the twenty-first century earned the uncontested title of 'greatest New Zealander'. His route to fame had been reaching the summit of Everest for the first time with Sherpa Tenzing Norgay in May 1953. Although that was the achievement for which he was knighted, he preferred to be known and to introduce himself by the very Kiwi name of 'Ed Hillary'. This was but one of many chords in his appearance and behaviour that had resonance for his compatriots.

For one thing, Hillary looked the part of an 'ordinary' New Zealand bloke, of the kind with which Wellingtonians were familiar from Neville Lodge cartoons: tall, gangling, raw-boned, with protruding ears and an unruly mop of hair, usually (when not climbing) standing in a decidedly 'at ease' posture. He had done several highly practical things New Zealanders admired, and had done them well. He had pitted himself against the natural world and won ('We knocked the bastard off', he said to his fellow countryman George Lowe as he and Tenzing descended Everest). He had led the first land crossing to the South Pole since those of Amundsen and Scott. He did not say a great deal, and what he did say was laconic and modest, and often eloquent in its stark simplicity. These things alone, combined with his climbing success, were sufficient to make him a hero at home for the rest of his life and beyond.

But Hillary did more than that. He used the almost accidental fame that Everest conferred on him to do a power of practical good in the world: to support humanitarian and conservation causes at home, both categories dear to the hearts of most New Zealanders; and to build schools and hospitals in Nepal. He did a stint as New Zealand High Commissioner in India. Through all this he remained reticent, strong, dependable, unboastful, good-humoured, a man who accepted with patience and grace the relationship his country had forged with him and the responsibilities and burdens that accompanied it.

A few other men approached Hillary's stature in the public mind but did not match or excel it. Colin Meads, All Black and farmer, shared some of Hillary's characteristics, including the inclination to do good by stealth, but not his palpable humanitarianism and spare eloquence. Charles Upham, farmer, soldier and twice winner of the Victoria Cross, was a man of immense courage and matching reticence. Howard Kippenberger ('Kip') was far and away the most liked and trusted of the New Zealand Division's senior officers in World War II, whose personal qualities reflected those of another civilian-into-soldier hero from World War I, William Malone, who had taken the peak of Chunuk Bair at Gallipoli in August 1915 but lost his life trying to hold it.

Yachtsman Peter Blake nudged Meads's stature in the sporting world and beyond after his round-the-world sailing exploits and winning the America's Cup for New Zealand in 1995. Blake's mana was enlarged by the circumstances of his murder in Brazil in 2001 when he was leading an environmental awareness expedition on the Amazon River. Peter Snell justifiably won a sportsman of the century award for his middle-distance running achievements, including winning medals at the Rome and Tokyo Olympics and setting world records, and was also much admired for his genial modesty. Wilson Whineray made the rare transition from captain of the All Blacks to captain of industry, working at the same time for community and charitable organisations. Jonah Lomu, the gargantuan New Zealand Tongan winger, gained heroic status among rugby followers at the height of his sporting career in the 1990s but did not seem to have any message of inspiration for his compatriots beyond that of sporting prowess and a good nature.

New Zealand had no Ned Kelly, and the smaller number of Irish and convict settlers in the nineteenth century ensured a narrower band of larrikinism in the population at large than that enjoyed by Australia (it is no surprise, therefore, that the nearest hero the country had to a Ned Kelly figure, fiery West Coast Red

Fed Patrick Hickey, chose to end his days in Australia rather than in the land of his birth, which had become rather too respectable for his liking). But when George Wilder, convicted of breaking and entering shops and car conversion, escaped from prison in 1962 and 1963, and evaded capture for 65 days on the first occasion and 170 on the second, newspaper readers followed his exploits with the excitement and admiration normally associated with sports spectatorship. In appearance Wilder was a 'short-arsed' version of Hillary with similarly 'ordinary bloke' features. He too was a man of few words, and perhaps the popularity of his efforts to evade the law said something about New Zealanders' attitudes towards those who pit themselves against both the elements *and* authority.

There were many others who acquired heroic or role-model status for particular groups of New Zealanders: those who typified the No. 8 fencing-wire ability to improvise successfully, such as would-be aviator Richard ('Mad') Pearse of Waitohi, who may have achieved airborne if not controlled flight months before the Wright brothers in North Carolina, and Christchurch motorcycle designer John Britten. There were those who enlarged New Zealand's sense of itself on the international stage – Peter Fraser at the United Nations, Rewi Alley in China, athletes Snell, Murray Halberg and John Walker at a succession of Olympics, Kiri Te Kanawa in the great opera houses of the world. Scientists and scholars acted as exemplars for those who followed similar paths rather than for the wider public: Nobel prize-winners Maurice Wilkins (DNA research) and Alan MacDiarmid (development of plastic conductors), the pioneer plastic surgeons Sir Harold Gillies and Sir Archibald McIndoe, the space scientist William Pickering, the Pacific and Cook scholar John Beaglehole, awarded the rare Order of Merit, the astrophysicist Beatrice Tinsley, who died just years short of the

Nobel Prize her closest colleagues were convinced she would earn. As prone to boosterism as ever, New Zealanders derived satisfaction from seeing their sons and daughters – but most often their sons – take on the best the world had to offer and perform creditably with what John Mulgan called 'the versatility of practical men'.

Other figures held heroic stature more specifically for women. Among them were Kate Sheppard, who had promoted women's suffrage from the ranks of the Women's Christian Temperance Union; Suzanne Aubert, who founded the only religious order to persist in New Zealand (the Daughters of Our Lady of Compassion) and, as Mother Mary Aubert, dispensed aid to the old, the poor, the sick and the illegitimate without concern for their religious affiliation; the aviator Jean Batten, of the 'girls can do anything' mould; and Janet Frame, whose self-rescue from psychiatric hospitals and eventual international recognition as a writer had resonance for people everywhere.

The Maori world too had its heroes and heroines, some – such as Te Puea Herangi and Whina Cooper ('the Mother of the Nation') – known and admired nationally. Others, such as Sir James Henare of Ngati Hine, John Rangihau of Tuhoe and Irihapeti Ramsden of Ngai Tahu, were far better known and better understood in Maori circles than non-Maori. There was also in this context a continuing admiration for the 'Maui' figure, the trickster or lovable rascal who bluffed and charmed his or her way through life and was perhaps best represented in the late twentieth century by the comedian Billy T. James, whose popularity was nationwide, as was the sense of loss at his early death in 1991.

That Maori and Pakeha, in addition to what they shared, should still have some separate heroes and heroines at the beginning of the twenty-first century was yet another indication that the habits, values and attitudes of both cultures retained sufficient force to be identified as separate traditions. And both continued to give New Zealand an ongoing bicultural character over and above the forces which, in other contexts, made the country multicultural. Multiculturalism was a reality too, for Maori culture was still predominantly tribal rather than nationally homogeneous, and Pakeha culture was made up of many strands, some of which – the Scottish, the Irish, the Jews, the Chinese – may wish to retain active links with their cultures of origin. In that sense, the quality of being a Maori, a Pacific Island, a Gujarati or a Jewish New Zealander may differ markedly in some contexts.

The dominant realities of New Zealand life, however, are still those of a mainstream Pakeha culture, in which almost every citizen has to participate in order to be educated, secure employment, play sport and engage in most other forms of recreation; and of a tangata whenua culture, in which the language, rituals of encounter and ways of farewelling the dead are still markedly different from those of the Pakeha majority and more visible and pervasive than those of other minority cultures. In addition, Maori is the foundation human culture of the land, the first repository of its namings and its histories and its songs; and it is the culture of the people who have, for as long as they want it, a special relationship with the government of New Zealand via the Treaty of Waitangi – a relationship which other peoples and cultures, including the Pakeha majority, lack. Whether other cultures need or want or deserve such a relationship is another matter. The fact is that the Treaty of Waitangi is still unmistakably there after more than 160 years, and its significance and relevance are ensured by both the Maori insistence that the document mediates a *living* relationship between Maori and the Crown, and by the majority Pakeha view that this constitutes an appropriate stance for the country to take. Should either of those views change, then the significance and the potential power of the Treaty too would change, because they depend for their force on the consent of those two constituent peoples.

Having passed through an era, up until the 1970s, in which the Treaty was not observed or honoured, however, and into one in which that deficit was being rectified, the country became aware of a strong Pakeha aspiration for the values and imperatives of *their* culture too to be recognised and taken as seriously by the government and the country as a whole as that of the tangata whenua. This impulse came from a growing conviction among Pakeha that their culture, like that of Maori, is no longer the same as the cultures of origin from which it sprang – that it has become, in fact, a second indigenous culture by the same processes by which East Polynesian people developed Maori culture: transplanting imported concepts and values from one place to another, observing them change over time in a new land and new circumstances, and eventually focusing attention away from the ancestral home and fully on the contemporary homeland.

That this increased valuing of their own heritage should lead Pakeha to become advocates for their culture was something of a surprise. The assumption most Pakeha grew up with was that their culture was strong enough and pervasive enough to persist through and despite any vicissitudes or challenges it might encounter. And perhaps it was. They imagined that the special measures undertaken as a Treaty obligation to protect and strengthen *Maori* language and culture were necessary because of their vulnerability, and that such measures would not in any way threaten the viability of Pakeha culture.

Then a series of events, none of them directly related,

appeared to suggest that the former imbalance was being corrected by the creation of another imbalance. In 1997 the Treaty Negotiations Minister, Doug Graham, was quoted as saying that Maori had spiritual feelings for mountains, lakes and rivers that Pakeha lacked – a statement strongly resented by the large number of non-Maori New Zealanders who habitually took their recreation in such places and regarded them with a respect and a reverence that at least equalled and in some instances exceeded that displayed by Maori. Then, in 1998, in the same month that the national museum, Te Papa Tongarewa, refused to remove from display in a visiting exhibition of contemporary British art the sculpture *Virgin in a Condom*, which was giving strong offence to some Christians, the Waikato Museum of Art and History withdrew a Dick Frizzell exhibition because moko on the face of a caricatured Four Square grocer offended Tainui kaumatua.

Four years later Transit New Zealand postponed work on State Highway 1 near Mercer on the ground that local Tainui people believed such work would disturb a taniwha or guardian spirit. At almost the same time the North Shore City Council announced that it would proceed with the widening of Esmonde Road in Takapuna, even though that would carve six metres off the front of Frank Sargeson's section, including the legendary 'hole in the hedge' and the area of former garden in which his ashes had been interred.

Both sets of events arose from different decisions by different officials in different institutions. But those in favour of Maori interests all grew out of Treaty-based obligations in legislation or mission statements to consult with Maori and to observe the principles of the Treaty of Waitangi. In the case of State Highway 1, the relevant factor was the obligation to respect wahi tapu or sacred places.

Most Pakeha had little difficulty accepting that. The problem they identified was that the country by this time had legislatively based procedures to protect the values and sensibilities of one culture and not the other. They did not want to see anything taken *away* from Maori, just to ensure that the measures of protection and respect extended from the one culture to embrace *both* cultures: to see wahi tapu of significance to Pakeha, such as Frank Sargeson's grave, given as much protection as wahi tapu of significance to Maori; and to have the history and experience of Pakeha New Zealanders valued by the country as a whole, and by its institutions, as much as those of Maori.

They were asking, in other words, for what might be called a 'mutuality of respect'. As another manifestation of that respect, just as Pakeha were now decades away from the stance which viewed Maori culture as 'primitive', 'backward' or 'barbaric', so Pakeha felt that they ought not to be viewed by Maori as tau iwi or aliens, representatives of a colonising power that merely stole material and cultural resources from Maori and gave nothing in return.

For the reality was that the two cultures were still in a relationship of mutual exchange that had begun as early as 1769. Contemporary Maori culture was so strong in its renaissant form in part because of the ability of its adherents to select successfully from the range of concepts and technologies that the Western world had to offer, and to incorporate those things into their culture on the basis of Maori needs and concepts of usefulness. One early and spectacular example was the Maori use of photography to take the place of ancestral representations in carvings in meeting houses and elsewhere, and consequently to strengthen the ability of the culture to remember and revere ancestors. The modern Maori concept of tino rangatiratanga, which we would now recognise as *corporate* tribal authority, developed because the Westminster parliamentary system of one person–one vote could not co-exist with the mid-nineteenth-century concept of *chiefly* authority, which was what Henry Williams had in mind when he formulated the term tino rangatira for the text of the Treaty of Waitangi. This, of course, means that the tino rangatiratanga that the Treaty promised to protect is not the tino rangatiratanga that contemporary Maori seek to have delivered. But there is nothing extraordinary in that: cultures, *all* cultures that are alive, change over time, and their words change their meaning. The Maori culture of the twenty-first century is not Maori culture frozen at 1769, nor at 1840. Nor should it be. It changed and grew dynamically according to changing needs and circumstances prior to the eighteenth century, and it continues to do so in the twenty-first century.

Similarly, Pakeha culture continues to borrow and to learn from Maori. That was one of the features that made it different from its European cultures of origin. It took words and concepts (mana, tapu, whanau, taonga, haka, turangawaewae), attitudes (the tradition of hospitality which, in the early nineteenth century, was so much more visible from the Maori side of the frontier than the Pakeha), ways of doing business (an increasing willingness to talk issues through to consensus in preference to dividing groups 'for' and 'against' a given motion), and rites of passage (a loosening up of formerly formal and highly structured funeral services).

There is, as yet, no sign that the cultures will bring an end to such exchanges, just as there is no sign that, despite the exchanges, the different character and flavour of each culture will be diluted or disappear in the immediate future. William Herries, a future Minister of Native Affairs, told the New Zealand Parliament in 1903 that he looked forward 'to the next hundred years or so, to the time when we shall have no Maoris at all but a white race with a dash of the finest coloured race in the world'. One hundred years on that vision is as far from fulfilment as at the time it was voiced. The bicultural reality remains a given, about which all New Zealanders need to be informed, and through which they will have to continue to negotiate – as national governments, as local governments, as community organisations and as individuals.

And most New Zealanders, whatever their cultural backgrounds, are good-hearted, practical, commonsensical and tolerant. Those qualities are part of the national cultural capital that has in the past saved the country from the worst excesses of chauvinism and racism seen in other parts of the world. They are as sound a basis as any for optimism about the country's future.

Further Reading and Acknowledgements

Three great headlands, twin-peaked Mount Belich and one Mount Oliver, dominate the terrain of New Zealand general history. James Belich's volumes are *Making Peoples* (1996) and *Paradise Reforged* (2001); W. H. Oliver's is *The Oxford History of New Zealand* (1981), which he edited with B. R. Williams. Geoffrey Rice has edited a second edition of the latter (1992). There is also the alpine range of five volumes of *The Dictionary of New Zealand Biography* (1990–2000), edited first by W. H. Oliver and subsequently by Claudia Orange. I am personally indebted to all these books. I commend to readers too *Environmental Histories of New Zealand*, edited by Tom Brooking and Eric Pawson (2002); *The Oxford Illustrated History of New Zealand* (1990), edited by Keith Sinclair; and the *Bateman New Zealand Historical Atlas* (1997), edited by Malcolm McKinnon. Ranginui Walker's *Ka Whawhai Tonu Matou* (1990) provides a specifically Maori perspective on the ground covered by all these books.

THE PENGUIN HISTORY OF NEW ZEALAND

For the prehistorical period, the outstanding book is *The Lost World of the Moa* by Trevor Worthy and Richard Holdaway (2002). The Alfred Crosby book from which I quote is *Ecological Imperialism* (1986). Kerry Howe has written authoritatively on the genesis of Maori and Polynesian cultures in *The Quest for Origins* (2003). Janet Davidson's *The Prehistory of New Zealand* (1984) is the standard book on pre-European Maori life. I have drawn on Sir George Grey's *Polynesian Mythology and Maori Legends* (1995) for traditional material; and the deconstruction of Stephenson Percy Smith's fabricated Maori legends can be found in David Simmons's *The Great New Zealand Myth* (1976). *How the Maoris Came to Aotearoa* (1947) gives a pleasingly literate account of that myth, and by a Maori writer, Harry Dansey. Michael King's *Moriori: A People Rediscovered* (1989) offers the full story of the indigenous settlers of the Chatham Islands.

Early Maori–European contacts have been most thoroughly and satisfyingly treated by Anne Salmond's *Two Worlds* (1991), *Between Worlds* (1997) and *The Trial of the Cannibal Dog* (2003). I have drawn from all three books and greatly admire their breadth and depth. In writing about sealers and whalers, Salmond builds on earlier research by Rhys Richards, to which I am also indebted. Trevor Bentley has devoted a whole book to *Pakeha Maori* (1999).

The most comprehensive books on the inter-tribal fighting which occurred immediately before 1840 are Angela Ballara's *Taua* (2003) and R. D. Crosby's *The Musket Wars* (1999). The topic is also well covered in *The Oxford Companion to New Zealand Military History* (2000), edited by Ian McGibbon, as are New Zealand's contributions to the South African, First and Second World Wars. James Belich's *The New Zealand Wars* (1986) is still the standard volume on that topic, and his biography of Titokowaru, *I Shall Not Die* (1989), adds valuable perspectives to the Taranaki dimension of the wars. Judith Binney's *Redemption Songs* (1995) is the definitive text on Te Kooti Arikirangi Te Turuki and Ringatu. Hazel Riseborough's *Days of Darkness* (2002) and Dick Scott's *Ask That Mountain* (1975) document splendidly the Parihaka story. I have relied heavily on Ian Pool's *Te Iwi Maori* (1991) for an understanding of Maori population figures in the nineteenth century.

The indispensable historical work for Treaty studies is Claudia Orange's *The Treaty of Waitangi* (1987). Philip Temple's *A Sort of Conscience – The Wakefields* (2002) will long be the authoritative account of this troubled family's contribution to the European colonisation of New Zealand. Among the books helpful for an understanding of Pakeha New Zealand in the second half of the nineteenth century are Miles Fairburn's *The Ideal Society and Its Enemies* (1989), R. C. J. Stone's *Makers of Fortune* (1973) and Raewyn Dalziel's *Julius Vogel* (1986). Judith Devaliant's *Kate Sheppard* (1992) provides background to the campaign by which women in New Zealand won the vote.

For the period in which the Liberal Government was in office I am especially indebted to David Hamer's *The New Zealand Liberals* (1988) and Tom Brooking's fine biography of John McKenzie, *Lands for the People* (1996). Derek Dow's *Safeguarding the Public Health* (1995) deals with health issues and the founding and subsequent history of the Department of Health. For the politics of the 1910s to the 1940s I have been grateful for Erik Olssen's *The Red Feds* (1988), and a cluster of good biographies: Olssen's *John A. Lee* (1977), Keith Sinclair's *Walter Nash* (1976), Michael Bassett's *Sir Joseph Ward* (1993) and *Coates of Kaipara* (1995), and Barry Gustafson's on Savage, *From the Cradle to the Grave* (1986). Tony Simpson's *The Sugarbag Years* (1974) is still by far the most evocative book on the effects of the Great Depression in New Zealand.

Ranginui Walker's biography of Apirana Ngata, *He Tipua* (2001), and my own on *Te Puea* (2003) explore some of the Maori dimensions of national politics. For the later period, I have made use of Gustafson's history of the National Party, *The First 50 Years* (1986), and his biography of Robert Muldoon, *His Way* (2000). Brian Easton's *The Nationbuilders* (2001) provides vivid portraits of twentieth-century New Zealanders who have earned that designation.

The Pawson/Brooking *Environmental Histories of New Zealand* (2002), already mentioned, is essential reading for understanding this element of New Zealand's past, and *Ecological Imperialism* (1986) by Alfred W. Crosby is helpful. Dorothy Campbell's description of the Napier earthquake comes from Louise Lawrence's (ed.) *The Penguin Book of New Zealand Letters* (2003). I found Colin James's *The Quiet Revolution* (1986) and *New Territory* (1992) and Michael Bassett's *The State in New Zealand 1840–1984* (1998) useful for an understanding of the revolution that transformed New Zealand in the 1980s and early 1990s. Malcolm McKinnon's *Independence and Foreign Policy* (1993) is a valuable survey of that topic.

Where relevant, of course, I have also drawn extensively from my own previous books on Maori, political, cultural and wider New Zealand history.

No subject is more collegial in its progress and processes than history. Over the years, the colleagues with whom I have had the most stimulating encounters, in conversation, literature, or listening to them lecture, include:

Ian Atkinson, Angela Ballara, Laurie Barber, Judith Binney, Edmund Bohan, Barbara Brookes, Tom Brooking, Christine Cole Catley, John Crawford, Raewyn Dalziel, Allan Davidson, Janet Davidson, Derek Dow, John Dunmore, Graeme Dunstall, Brian Easton, Miles Fairburn, Louise Furey, Ross Galbreath,

Phyllis Gant, Jim Gardner, Peter Gibbons, Jeanine Graham, David Grant, Anna Green, Roger Green, Ray Grover, Barry Gustafson, David Hamer, Glyn Harper, Philip Hart, Manuka Henare, Richard Hill, Kerry Howe, Colin James, Hugh Laracy, Peter Lineham, Dennis McEldowney, Robert Mahuta, Buddy Mikaere, Doug Munro, W. H. Oliver, Erik Olssen, Claudia Orange, John Owens, Dot Page, Ann Parsonson, Jock Phillips, Chris Pugsley, Irihapeti Ramsden, Marjorie Rau-Kupa, Geoffrey Rice, Ray Richards, Rhys Richards, Anne Salmond, Dick Scott, Peter Simpson, Tony Simpson, Keith Sinclair, Maui Solomon, Keith Sorrenson, Russell Stone, Jane Tolerton, Buster Walden, Ranginui Walker, Alan Ward, Ian Wards and Lydia Wevers.

Ian Atkinson, Wilf Davis, Brian Easton, Louise Furey, Peter Gibbons, Claudia Orange, Anne Salmond, Malcolm Templeton and Richard Woods all offered specific advice for parts of this book, for which I am immensely grateful; and Ellen Ellis and Kathryn Parsons helped me locate source material. As always in these circumstances, it is the author who is responsible for the use made of this assistance and for any inaccuracies or bad judgements.

Creative New Zealand made a grant to support the research and writing of the book; and Professor Bryan Gould and the University of Waikato made time available to me to complete it.

Finally I thank Maria Jungowska for patient logistic and moral support, Geoff Walker of Penguin Books New Zealand for commissioning the book, and Rebecca Lal for endless attention to the details of production. And I thank Andrew Mason for deft and sensitive editing of the text.

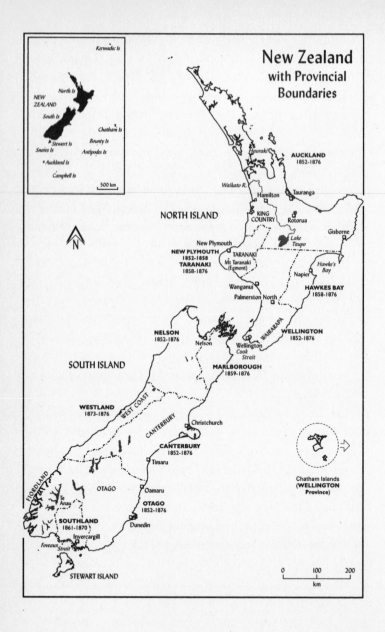

New Zealand
with Provincial
Boundaries

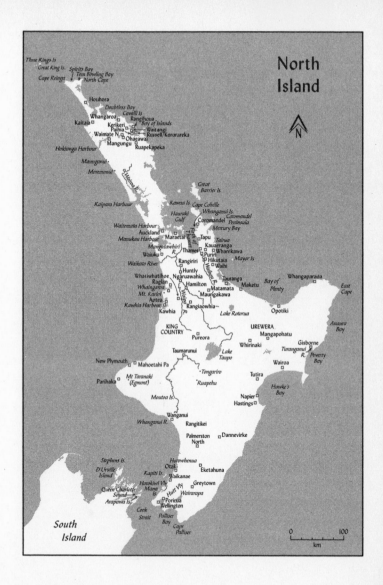

North
Island

N

Three Kings Is.
Great King Is. *Spirits Bay*
Tom Bowling Bay
Cape Reinga *North Cape*

Houhora

Doubtless Bay
Cavilli Is.
Whangaroa *Rangihoua*
Bay of Islands
Kaitaia Kerikeri
Paihia *Waitangi*
Waimate N. *Russell/Kororareka*
Ohaeawai
Mangungu Ruapekapeka

Hokianga Harbour

Maunganui
Moremonui

Great
Barrier Is.

Kaipara Harbour

Kawau Is. *Cape Colville*
Whanganui Is.
Hauraki *Coromandel*
Gulf *Peninsula*
Coromandel
Waitemata Harbour *Mercury Bay*
Auckland *Tairua*
Maraetai Tapu
Manukau Harbour *Kauaeranga*
Mangatawhiri *Wharekawa*
Thames Puriri
Waiuku *Hikutaia* *Mayor Is.*
Rangiriri Waihi
Waikato River Huntly
Ngaruawahia Tauranga Maketu
Whatiwhatihoe *Bay of*
Raglan Hamilton *Whangaparaoa*
Whaingaroa Matamata *Plenty* *East*
Mt. Karioi Maungakawa *Cape*
Aotea Opotiki
Kawhia Harbour Rangiaowhia~
Kawhia *Lake Rotorua* *Anaura*
UREWERA *Bay*
KING
COUNTRY Mangapohatu
Pureora
Whirinaki Gisborne
Turanganui *Poverty*
Taumarunui *Lake* *R.* *Bay*
Taupo
New Plymouth Mahoetahi Pa Wairoa
Tongariro
Parihaka *Mt Taranaki* *Ruapehu* Tutira
(Egmont)
Napier *Hawke's*
Moutoa Is. Hastings *Bay*
Wanganui
Whanganui R. Rangitikei
Palmerston Dannevirke
North
Stephens Is.
D'Urville *Horowhenua*
Island *Otaki*
Kapiti Is. Eketahuna
Waikanae
Queen Charlotte *Hawkhui Vly* Greytown
Sound *Mana* *Hutt Vly*
Arapawa Is. *Is.* *Wairarapa*
Porirua
Cook Wellington
Strait *Palliser*
South *Bay*
Island *Cape*
Palliser

0   100
km

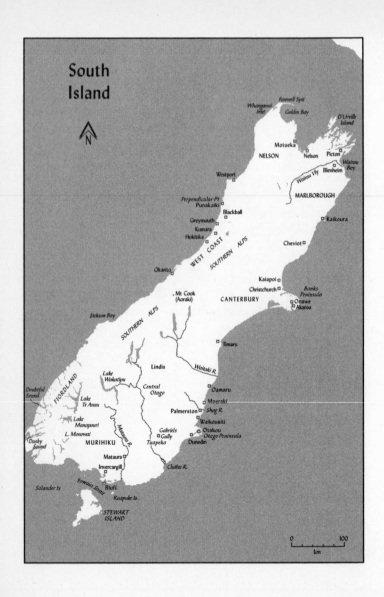

South Island

N

Whanganui Inlet
Farewell Spit
Golden Bay
D'Urville Island

Motueka
Nelson
Picton
NELSON
Wairau Bay
Westport
Wairau Vly
Blenheim
MARLBOROUGH

Perpendicular Pt
Punakaiki
Blackball
Kaikoura
Greymouth
Kumara
Hokitika
Cheviot
WEST COAST
SOUTHERN ALPS
Okarito
Kaiapoi
Christchurch
Bonks
Peninsula
Mt Cook
(Aoraki)
CANTERBURY
Onawe
Akaroa
Jackson Bay
SOUTHERN ALPS
Timaru
Lindis
Waitaki R.
Lake
Wakatipu
Oamaru
Doubtful
Sound
Central
Otago
Moeraki
FIORDLAND
Lake
Te Anau
Palmerston
Shag R.
Lake
Manapouri
Waikouaiti
Otakou
L. Monowai
Gabriels
Otago Peninsula
Dusky
Sound
MURIHIKU
Gully
Dunedin
Tuapeka
Mataura
Clutha R.
Invercargill
Solander Is
Bluff
Foveaux Strait
Ruapuke Is.
STEWART
ISLAND

0   100
Lm

526

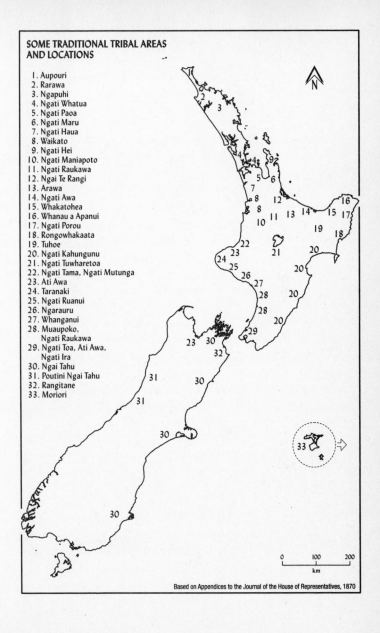

SOME TRADITIONAL TRIBAL AREAS
AND LOCATIONS

1. Aupouri
2. Rarawa
3. Ngapuhi
4. Ngati Whatua
5. Ngati Paoa
6. Ngati Maru
7. Ngati Haua
8. Waikato
9. Ngati Hei
10. Ngati Maniapoto
11. Ngati Raukawa
12. Ngai Te Rangi
13. Arawa
14. Ngati Awa
15. Whakatohea
16. Whanau a Apanui
17. Ngati Porou
18. Rongowhakaata
19. Tuhoe
20. Ngati Kahungunu
21. Ngati Tuwharetoa
22. Ngati Tama, Ngati Mutunga
23. Ati Awa
24. Taranaki
25. Ngati Ruanui
26. Ngarauru
27. Whanganui
28. Muaupoko,
    Ngati Raukawa
29. Ngati Toa, Ati Awa,
    Ngati Ira
30. Ngai Tahu
31. Poutini Ngai Tahu
32. Rangitane
33. Moriori

0   100   200
km

Based on Appendices to the Journal of the House of Representatives, 1870

527

Governments of New Zealand since the granting of responsible self-government

Bell–Sewell Ministry, 1856 (Premier Henry Sewell)

Fox Ministry, 1856 (Premier William Fox)

Stafford Ministry 1856–61 (Premier Edward Stafford)

Fox Ministry, 1861–62 (Premier William Fox)

Domett Ministry, 1862–63 (Premier Alfred Domett)

Whitaker–Fox Ministry, 1863–64 (Premier Frederick Whitaker)

Weld Ministry, 1864–65 (Premier Frederick Weld)

Stafford Ministry, 1865–69 (Premier Edward Stafford)

Fox Ministry, 1869–72 (Premier William Fox)

Stafford Ministry, 1872 (Premier Edward Stafford)

Waterhouse Ministry, 1872–73 (Premier George Waterhouse)

Fox Ministry, 1873 (Premier William Fox)

Vogel Ministry, 1873–75 (Premier Julius Vogel)

Pollen Ministry, 1875–76 (Premier Daniel Pollen)

Vogel Ministry, 1876 (Premier Sir Julius Vogel)

Atkinson Ministry, 1876 (Premier Harry Atkinson)

Atkinson Ministry, 1876–77 (Premier Harry Atkinson)

Grey Ministry, 1877–79 (Premier Sir George Grey)

Hall Ministry, 1879–1882 (Premier John Hall)

Whitaker Ministry, 1882–83 (Premier Frederick Whitaker)

Atkinson Ministry, 1883–84 (Premier Harry Atkinson)

Stout–Vogel Ministry, 1884 (Premier Robert Stout)

Atkinson Ministry, 1884 (Premier Harry Atkinson)

Stout–Vogel Ministry, 1884–87 (Premier Sir Robert Stout)

Atkinson Ministry, 1887–91 (Premier Sir Harry Atkinson)

Liberal Government, Ballance Ministry, 1891–93 (Premier John Ballance)

Liberal Government, Seddon Ministry, 1893–1906 (Premier and [from 1902] Prime Minister Richard Seddon)

Liberal Government, Hall–Jones Ministry, 1906 (Prime Minister William Hall–Jones)

Liberal Government, Ward Ministry, 1906–12 (Prime Minister Sir Joseph Ward)

Liberal Government, Mackenzie Ministry, 1912 (Prime Minister Thomas Mackenzie)

Reform Government, Massey Ministry, 1912–15 (Prime Minister William Massey)

National Ministry, 1915–19 (Prime Minister William Massey)

Reform Government, Massey Ministry, 1919–25 (Prime Minister William Massey)

Reform Government, Bell Ministry, 1925 (Prime Minister Sir Francis Dillon Bell)

Reform Government, Coates Ministry, 1925–28 (Prime Minister Gordon Coates)

United Government, Ward Ministry, 1928–30 (Prime Minister Sir Joseph Ward)

United Government, Forbes Ministry, 1930–31 (Prime Minister George Forbes)

Coalition Government, Forbes Ministry, 1931–35 (Prime Minister George Forbes)

Labour Government, Savage Ministry, 1935–40 (Prime Minister Michael Joseph Savage)

Labour Government, Fraser Ministry, 1940–49 (Prime Minister Peter Fraser)

National Government, Holland Ministry, 1949–57 (Prime Minister Sidney Holland)

National Government, Holyoake Ministry, 1957 (Prime Minister Keith Holyoake)

Labour Government, Nash Ministry, 1957–60 (Prime Minister Walter Nash)

National Government, Holyoake Ministry, 1960–72 (Prime Minister Keith Holyoake)

National Government, Marshall Ministry, 1972 (Prime Minister John Marshall)

Labour Government, Kirk Ministry, 1972–74 (Prime Minister Norman Kirk)

Labour Government, Rowling Ministry, 1974–75 (Prime Minister Wallace [Bill] Rowling)

National Government, Muldoon Ministry, 1975–84 (Prime Minister Robert Muldoon)

Labour Government, Lange Ministry, 1984–89 (Prime Minister David Lange)

Labour Government, Palmer Ministry, 1989–90 (Prime Minister Geoffrey Palmer)

Labour Government, Moore Ministry, 1990 (Prime Minister Mike Moore)

National Government, Bolger Ministry, 1990–97 (Prime Minister Jim Bolger)

National Government, Shipley Ministry, 1997–99 (Prime Minister Jenny Shipley)

Labour Government, Clark Ministry, 1999– (Prime Minister Helen Clark)

Index